M000314274

THE STATE OF THE PARTIES

THE STATE OF THE PARTIES, 2018

The Changing Role of Contemporary American Political Parties

Edited by
John C. Green,
Daniel J. Coffey,
and
David B. Cohen

ROWMAN & LITTLEFIELD
Lanham • Boulder • New York • London

Published by Rowman & Littlefield
An imprint of The Rowman & Littlefield Publishing Group, Inc.
4501 Forbes Boulevard, Suite 200, Lanham, Maryland 20706
www.rowman.com

Unit A, Whitacre Mews, 26–34 Stannary Street, London SE11 4AB

Copyright © 2018 by The Rowman & Littlefield Publishing Group, Inc.

All rights reserved. No part of this book may be reproduced in any form or by any electronic or mechanical means, including information storage and retrieval systems, without written permission from the publisher, except by a reviewer who may quote passages in a review.

British Library Cataloguing in Publication Information Available

Library of Congress Cataloging-in-Publication Data

Names: Green, John Clifford, 1953- editor. | Coffey, Daniel J., 1975- editor. | Cohen, David B., 1967- editor.
Title: The state of the parties, 2018 : the changing role of contemporary American political parties / edited by John C. Green, Daniel J. Coffey, and David B. Cohen.
Description: Lanham, Maryland : Rowman & Littlefield, [2018] | Seventh edition: 2014. | Includes bibliographical references and index.
Identifiers: LCCN 2018024332 (print) | LCCN 2018026517 (ebook) | ISBN 9781538117675 (Electronic) | ISBN 9781538117668 (Paper) | ISBN 9781538117651(Cloth : alk. paper)
Subjects: LCSH: Political parties—United States.
Classification: LCC JK2261 (ebook) | LCC JK2261 .S824 2018 (print) | DDC 324.273—dc23
LC record available at https://lccn.loc.gov/2018024332

∞ ™ The paper used in this publication meets the minimum requirements of American National Standard for Information Sciences—Permanence of Paper for Printed Library Materials, ANSI/NISO Z39.48–1992.

Printed in the United States of America

Contents

List of Tables

List of Figures

Acknowledgments

THE RESEARCH EFFORT that produced this book is the product of more than two decades of scholarship. The first edition originated from research coordinated in 1993 at the Ray C. Bliss Institute of Applied Politics on the changing role of political parties in American politics. The second edition reflected the impact of the 1994 elections, while the third through seventh editions reported further changes after the 1996, 2000, 2004, 2008, and 2012 elections, respectively. The present eighth edition considers the impact of the 2016 election and subsequent events.

From the beginning of this effort, our goal has been to bring together party scholars from around the nation to discuss the state of American party politics and new avenues of research. On each occasion, we have been privileged to field a "dream team" of contributors, and although the roster has differed each time, the team for this edition is just as strong, including a mix of veteran and emerging scholars. We are deeply grateful for their participation. Taken together, the essays in this volume offer insight into the "state of the parties" now that the twenty-first century is a decade old.

The development of this volume was greatly aided by the staff of the Bliss Institute. Janet Lykes Bolois was not only instrumental in compiling the chapters and managing the layout but has also honed the unique skill of putting up with the editors—no simple task, to be sure. In addition, we would like to thank Janet, Jenni Fitzgerald, our other colleagues, and our student assistants for their help with the 2017 State of the Parties conference, where these papers were first presented. As in the past, we owe a debt of thanks to Jon Sisk, Kate Powers, Elaine McGarraugh and their associates at Rowman & Littlefield. Finally, we would be remiss if we did not acknowledge our families, principally Mary Coffey, Dawn Cohen, and Lynn Green. Without their unwavering support and encouragement, *The State of the Parties* would not have been possible.

1

The State of the Parties

Change and Continuity in 2016

Daniel J. Coffey, John C. Green, and David B. Cohen

O N NOVEMBER 7TH 2016, Donald Trump won the election as president, after two terms served by Democratic president Barack Obama. Few had predicted that Trump, a political novice who had never held elective office, would win the Republican nomination, much less the general election. While 2016 was historic and left Republicans in the party's strongest electoral position since the 1920s, the era of intensely competitive balance between the two political parties held firm as the election came down to shifts in voting patterns in a small number of battleground states.

In the last edition, the contributors to this volume argued that political parties are as central to the operation of American government as they have ever been. This conclusion is still largely the judgement of the contributors in this volume. Republicans and Democrats are the center of gravity of the American political system. Parties have continued to adapt despite social and economic upheaval. This pattern arises in part because American political parties are made up of networks of activists, donors, and the general public. The parties, centuries-old institutions, are structured in such a way that new candidates, new movements, and new ideas are allowed to find a place, re-invigorating the parties themselves. Combined with ideological polarization, the parties are able to assemble armies of supporters every two years with the outcome of national elections often depending on which party is better able to mobilize its supporters.

Yet 2016 provides reason for pause in this assessment. It also must be noted that such challenges to dominant party systems are occurring else-where in established democracies, notably France and Italy, in which newly established parties have managed to capture political power, while major parties in the United Kingdom and Germany have been forced into coalitions with new parties to form governments. Such examples point to larger systemic-level disruptions of electoral politics internationally, due in part by globalization and technological change (Akkerman, de Lange, and Rooduijn 2016). Whether parties will retain their central position in western democra-cies is a question with considerable urgency.

This collection of essays is the eighth in the series that assesses the state of the parties after an American presidential election (Shea and Green 1994; Green and Shea 1996, 1999; Green and Farmer 2003; Green and Coffey 2007, 2011; Green, Coffey, and Cohen 2014). In this volume, a group of prominent and emerging scholars examines the "state of the parties" from a variety of perspectives. These essays reveal American political parties to be vibrant and dynamic institutions, central to all these aspects of politics in a functioning democracy, and worthy of special study in their own right. But before turn-ing to these essays, a brief review of years leading up the 2016 election is in order.

The 2016 Presidential Campaign

The 2016 presidential election was a tumultuous, and at times, unpredictable election year. Importantly, to reiterate a point made in the previous edition, while 2016 was a tumultuous and often-unpredictable election, structural forces matter a great deal in constraining electoral outcomes. These forces include the economy, but also the partisan balance in the electorate and how many terms the incumbent party has been in office (Campbell 2016a). Indeed, 2016 is similar to 1960, 1988, 2000, and 2008. In three of these four cases, the incumbent party was unable to win a third term, a factor, which our contributor Alan Abramowitz includes in his "time for change" forecast model of presidential elections (Abramowitz and Webster 2016).

The environment should have favored the Democrats. The economy, a central factor in explaining electoral outcomes, was growing. Over the previ-ous four years, unemployment had dipped below 5 percent for the first time since before the Great Recession (Bureau of Labor Statistics). Nevertheless, as is explained in some of the chapters below, the pattern of retrospective voting, in which incumbent parties are rewarded for strong economic per-formance (and punished for poor performance), has been inhibited in the American context by polarized and entrenched mass partisan attitudes

(Evans and Pickup 2010) and may matter less in open-seat elections (Campbell, Dettrey, and Yin 2010). Obama's approval rating, for example, was about 54 percent in October 2016, up from the 40-percent mark of early 2014.

Over the previous four years, the political balance of power between the parties had shifted slightly in the Republicans' favor. In what would become a dominant theme in post-election analysis, growth was highly uneven throughout the United States. In large metro areas, economic growth had surged while in rural areas and small cities, the Great Recession had not really ended. As Brookings analysts Mark Muro and Jacob Whiton pointed out, "over and over, the stark unevenness of the nation's city and regional economic map reads like a Rosetta stone of the nation's frustration" (2017). The impact of the Great Recession was still being felt in much of the country, particularly in areas dependent on manufacturing and resource extraction. This situation was made particularly acute by a raging opioid-crisis that disproportionally affected areas that used to have strong manufacturing bases. In fact, Trump won four of the five states with the highest rates of opioid-caused deaths in 2016 (West Virginia, Ohio, Pennsylvania, and Kentucky) (Hedegaard, Warner, and Miniño 2017).

Politically, the overall pre-election environment left the GOP in a strong position headed into 2016. Republicans had performed quite well in the 2014 midterm elections. In these elections, Republicans gained 13 House seats, and a remarkable nine Senate seats, giving the GOP full control of Congress. Republican gains were widespread; the party won 350 state legislative seats across every region of the country to control their highest proportion of state legislative seats since 1920. The GOP won unified control of 23 state governments compared to just 7 for Democrats. In addition, the GOP won 24 out of 36 gubernatorial elections. The 31 state governors represented the highest total for the party since 1928.[1] Indeed, many Democrats felt Obama's support was largely personal and Obama had not done enough to translate this to help the party (Draper 2017).

Obama's second term was somewhat characteristic of a second-term president. With a Republican Congress, there was little incentive to pursue major legislative initiatives. Some of the most consequential policy changes came from the Supreme Court, which struck down the Defense of Marriage Act in 2013 and upheld a constitutional right to gay marriage in the *Obergefell v. Hodges* ruling in 2015. While public opinion had shifted rapidly on what used to be a lightning rod social issue, a new set of challenges arose through proposals by conservatives to freedom of religion statutes in many states.

In terms of foreign policy, the United States remained entrenched in the War in Afghanistan for a second decade despite drawdowns in the number of troops. The civil war in Syria raged on and the United States was often criticized for its strategy while Russia entered the war in earnest in 2015. An important nuclear deal between western powers was signed with Iran in 2015 that appeared to be a major policy achievement for the Obama administration, but was roundly criticized by Republicans, especially Trump. Meanwhile, in the summer of 2015, large numbers of immigrants came into the country from Central America, a story that by some measures, increased the salience of immigration for Republican voters, an issue Trump made central to his campaign.

The 2016 Presidential Primary Season

After Obama's two terms, as is the pattern in open-seat elections, a large number of candidates entered the race for president. The election was a bit of a free-for-all; 17 candidates vied for the Republican nomination and five candidates competed for the Democratic nomination.

The Democratic nomination seemed to be a forgone conclusion. Clinton, denied the nomination in 2008, was the front-runner. Her opponents, former Virginia Senator Jim Webb, former governor of Maryland Martin O'Malley, former governor of Rhode Island Lincoln Chafee, and Harvard law professor Lawrence Lessig were not well known nationwide and Vermont senator Bernie Sanders was technically not even a Democrat. The opposition appeared to be token in nature.

Signs emerged early on, however, that Clinton's path would be difficult. Vice-President Joseph Biden considered entering the race, but decided against it, a decision that would magnify in importance over time. Considerable efforts were made to draft Senator Elizabeth Warren, the popular liberal firebrand from Massachusetts. She also declined to run but the point was clear that Democrats were not ready to anoint Clinton the nomination without a contest.

By the Iowa caucuses, nearly all of the other candidates had backed out. Sanders, however, performed well among a Democratic base skeptical of Clinton's commitment to the party's policy goals. He nearly won the Iowa caucus in a razor-thin finish and decisively won the New Hampshire primary. Clinton's weaknesses seemed to magnify as the nomination wore on. While she nearly always won the major states on Super Tuesday contests, Sanders tended to do better in smaller states and those with caucuses, and the narrative emerged that Sanders had stronger appeal to younger activists within the party. This was in part because Sanders also tended to sound more populist in many of his attacks against Clinton. The party had changed since the early 2000s when she first began running, and even more so than when her husband had run in the 1990s. As in 2008, Clinton had the backing of party elites, Superdelegates, and largely offered a centrist, inclusive message. Clinton won the nomination by early June, but in part because of her efforts in 2008 to keep that race going until every contest was completed, she did not call on Sanders to withdraw. Sanders did not officially endorse Clinton until early July.

On the other side, the GOP nomination was also a surprise, but in this case, the insurgent candidate won. Donald Trump, who had been behind the "birther" movement questioning President Obama's citizenship, emerged as a legitimate candidate after a long series of debates beginning in the summer of 2015. The large number of candidates indicated two things: the general election seemed winnable for a Republican, and there was no clear front-runner. As a result, many of the candidates were high-profile candidates, such as former presidential candidates Mike Huckabee, Ben Carson, Rick Santorum, and Rick Perry. In addition, also running were Texas senator Ted Cruz, Ohio governor John Kasich, Florida senator Marco Rubio and former Florida governor Jeb Bush, son of former president George H. W. Bush and brother of former president George W. Bush.

The candidates went through a grueling debate schedule. Trump attracted the most attention by often ridiculing the other candidates, and making bombastic statements. The other candidates had difficulty distinguishing themselves in the crowded field. The crowded field in part explains why the dynamic on the Democratic side—an established front-runner versus a more ideological alternative, never emerged. By Iowa, many candidates dropped out, while Cruz managed to hold off Trump, who then won New Hampshire. Shockingly, by South Carolina, a state that had delivered key victories to his brother and father, Jeb Bush was forced to withdraw.

From this point, Trump gained steam. While Rubio emerged as the establishment candidate and Cruz was the ideologue, Kasich managed to gain a footing as a centrist alternative. A persistent narrative emerged that the party would eventually settle on some alternative to Trump, but none of the other three candidates could secure this. When Rubio dropped out in March, serious discussions took place as to how the party rules could be used to deny Trump the nomination. By May, however, the RNC stated it would back Trump and Trump won the necessary delegates to win a convention roll-call vote. Significantly for Trump, turnout in the Republican primaries had surged to a near-record for vote totals for a Republican nominee (Bump 2016b).

The General Election

The 2016 election seemed to be Clinton's to lose. Importantly, however, despite the strengthening economy, the global political environment was unsettled. A shocking event occurred in late June when Britain voted in a popular referendum to leave the European Union, despite most polls indicating Britain would vote to stay. Prime Minister David Cameron unexpectedly resigned. Populist anger in Europe was triggered in part by a refugee crisis from Syria and North Africa as migrants poured into Europe. While most governments were sympathetic to the migrants, including the powerful German Chancellor Angela Merkel, a number of right-wing parties emerged across Europe. The UKIP in Britain had backed the withdrawal. Marine Le Pen, head of the right-wing Le Pen, based much of her campaign for the French presidency on an anti-migrant nationalism in the lead up to the 2017 French presidential election. The *Alternative für Deutschlan* (AfD) had performed well in regional elections in Germany largely attacking Merkel's refugee policy, and Geert Wilders's party, the *Partij voor de Vrijheid* (PPV) which espoused unabashed right-wing populism, had emerged as a serious force in the Netherlands and caused all of the other Dutch parties to pledge not to work with the PPV to form a coalition government (Aisch, Pearce, and Rousseau 2017).

As the U.S. election went on, polling indicated Clinton had a sizable and largely stable lead. Clinton's lead in national polls often extended for weeks at a time without a single poll showing Trump leading. In fact, according to realclearpolitcs.com, of 182 national polls measuring Clinton versus Trump head to head from June 1 to Election Day, Clinton lead in 155 polls, while Trump lead in just 19 and nearly all were polls conducted by Rasmussen and the *LA Times*. As will be discussed later, Clinton's leads were often small—less than 5 points, but occasionally peaking at 10 points—but the stability of her lead in so many national polls led many to conclude there was little chance Trump could defeat her.[2]

The Republican convention was less dramatic than had been expected. In July, just before the convention, the RNC voted down efforts to allow delegates to vote for whichever candidate they wanted, thereby removing the suspense of the convention turning to an alternative. Trump had also nominated traditional conservative Mike Pence, former congressman and Indiana governor. The convention in Cleveland aroused public protests, but they were generally peaceful. Trump, for his part, gave an unusual speech, largely negative in tone and uncharacteristic for a nomination acceptance speech. Somewhat surprisingly, given that many establishment Republicans avoided the convention and given the tone of Trump's speech, was the fact that Trump took the lead in a few national polls and had closed the gap in many others.

The Democratic convention by and large went well for Clinton. She had selected Virginia senator Tim Kaine as her running mate, a safe choice largely meant to secure support among more traditional Democratic voters and to help Clinton win Virginia, a newly emerging swing state. Clinton had had to battle a scandal involving Wikileaks in which thousands of emails showed the DNC staffers discussing how to harm the Sanders campaign. The scandal resulted in the resignation of DNC chair Debbie Wasserman Schultz just before the convention. At the convention, Clinton's nomination as the first female presidential nominee was briefly distracted by vocal protests by Sanders supporters. While it wasn't quite 1968, the images of young Sanders supporters protesting and booing Clinton indicated that the Democratic Party was left with important divisions. Clinton did get a brief bounce, as her lead expanded in some polls to double-digits, but by mid-August it was back to where it had been in June, about six to eight points.

Clinton entered the general election season with a perceived advantage. The race was somewhat closer than expected; Clinton led by single digits through most of September and a great deal of media coverage was devoted to a fainting spell Clinton suffered at a 9/11 ceremony. The first debate on September 26 generated massive interest with over 84 million viewers, more than the 80 million that watched the 1980 presidential debate. Clinton was largely viewed to have won the debate and seemed to be poised to break away from Trump and subsequent polls showed a modest bounce for Clinton. A vice-presidential debate, however, was seen as a win for Pence over Kaine, but overall had little impact on the race.

Things seemed to fall apart for the Trump campaign in early October when a tape was released from 2005 with Trump and media personality Billy Bush making disparaging remarks about women. Clinton's poll lead surged and talk again resumed about the RNC stepping in to replace Trump. Most polls suggested Clinton won the second debate, but there were some indications that audiences felt Trump, who was unapologetic, had performed better than expected (Agiesta 2016). The campaign settled down somewhat by the end of October, as talk of Trump being removed faded. A third debate did little to impact the race.

The results on Election Day were shocking. Trump, despite losing the popular vote, 48.2 percent to 46.1 percent, managed to win over 300 votes in the Electoral College. A key to this victory was the fracturing of a "blue wall," in which Clinton lost several states that had not voted for a Republican in decades, including Pennsylvania, Wisconsin, and Michigan. Trump also won several other swing states nationally that Obama had won, including Florida, Ohio, North Carolina, New Hampshire, and even an electoral vote in Maine. This represented a large shift from 2012, in which Obama won 332 electoral votes. There was little change in Congress; Democrats gained two seats in the Senate, which they already controlled, and the Democratic gain of six seats in the House left them well short of a majority.

One of the most fascinating stories of the election was the pre-election polling. In 2008 and 2012, election analysts such as Nate Silver at FiveThirty-Eight.com, had successfully predicted not only the results of the national election, but also often correctly predicted most state results, even intensely competitive states. As a result, polling achieved a degree of both attention and authority. Polling indicated a race that Clinton was running away with the race and many websites, considered authoritative, predicted Clinton would win well-over 300 and possibly even 400 electoral votes. If the *LA Times/USC* tracking polls were excluded, Clinton led every single national poll from October to Election Day, with some margins exceeding double-digits. In contested battleground states, such as Pennsylvania, Wisconsin, and Michigan, Clinton led in nearly every poll taken in the two weeks before Election Day, sometimes with margins in the double-digits.

The main question motivating much of the discussion of this book and post-election analysis was what went wrong, particularly with polling. A number of polling organizations had posted winning probabilities, often updated daily during the race. These probabilities varied from day to day, but most had Clinton with a nearly 3 to 1 chance of winning the election; FiveThirtyEight.com placed the winning percentage at 71 percent, while the Princeton Election Consortium placed Clinton's probability of winning at 99 percent. Most models predicted Clinton would win over 300 electoral votes; the *New York Times Upshot* models, for example, found that, based on their statistical models of different state outcomes, of the 1,024 plausible iterations of state outcomes, Clinton had 693 plausible paths to an Electoral College win, while Trump had only 315 (see Katz 2016).

The problem is in part that the forecasts were largely based on polls, and the public tended to misinterpret the certainty that models provided. In fact, while Trump did do better than predicted, overall, national polls were actually closer than they were in 2012 (Silver 2017a). Silver chastised the media for misunderstanding probability; many swing states were quite close and small shifts could easily flip a state from red to blue (Silver 2017b). In fact, a narrowing of the race, as undecided voters tended to break toward one candidate disproportionally, was largely ignored. Forty-six states voted the same way that they had in 2012 and the number of vote shifts in the remaining four were tiny by historic standards.

A number of factors played into the polling error. The 2016 election is for polling in some ways a modern version of the *Literary Digest* debacle of 1936. In this case, polls suffered from sampling error, missing many Trump voters, often rural whites who in a normal election can be difficult to sample. Since polls undersampled Trump voters, the statistical margin of error does not capture what the public tends to think it does; the margin only captures that estimated parameter that would be obtained using the same sampling technique. If the measure contains a sampling error, as it had in 1936, the measure only captures the views of voters similar to those in the sample. In fact, many pollsters have found evidence that swings in polling are often traceable to differences in the proportion of Democrats and Republicans included in a sample rather than a true change in public opinion. Importantly, these Trump voters were more decisive in exactly the states that the polls and forecast models mispredicted, such as Wisconsin, Pennsylvania, and Michigan (Silver 2016).

One reason for this is the dissonant nature of the campaign. In 2012, the major campaigns ran candidates who were in large ways archetypes of the Roosevelt-Reagan dynamic. Clinton, for her part, tended to downplay overt class appeals, while Trump often offered protectionist messages that appealed to traditional blue-collar, Democratic Midwestern voters. One major study found Clinton's ads in the Midwest were virtually devoid of specific policy content (Fowler, Franz, and Ridout 2016). Additionally, third-party candidates Jill Stein of the Green Party and Gary Johnson of the Libertarian Party, accumulated enough votes to cost Clinton in key swing states. Finally, Democratic voter turnout declined in many major cities, especially urban areas in swing states that Trump and Obama won (Soffen et al. 2016a).

The surprise of the result had produced in a number of explanations, some of which continue to reverberate across the political spectrum. Clinton's campaign and the DNC were, somewhat deservedly, blamed for a number of strategic missteps. The Wesleyan Media Project found that in two of three of Clinton's surprise losses, Michigan and Wisconsin, Clinton did not begin advertising until the last week, while nationwide, her campaign had a small local advertising advantage (Fowler, Ridout, and Franz 2017). The campaign seemed to have waited too long to deploy key resources, especially as an unusually large number of undecided voters were making their decisions (Silver 2017a, 2017b). Clinton probably wasted time in states she had little chance to win (Ohio and Arizona) and were not "tipping point" states by most empirical models (Silver 2017a, 2017b). Trump, in contrast, campaigned more broadly and the RNC provided a much needed behind-the-scenes field effort.

The ground games of both campaigns seemed to be less effective than in 2012. Clinton had fewer field offices than the Obama campaign and Trump staffed few field offices, far less than Romney or Bush. Clinton had more field offices (nearly 500) than Trump, by nearly 300 by some counts, but she had far fewer than Obama did (nearly 800) and in nearly every battleground state she had fewer offices than Obama had (Milligan 2016).

The large number of undecided voters at the end of the campaign were probably also swayed by ephemeral factors, such as the release of the Comey letter. In this case, FBI director James Comey released a letter on October 28 that stated that emails had been discovered that could be related to the ongoing FBI investigation of Clinton's use of a private email server when she had been secretary of state. While political science generally has found campaign effects are limited and that poll variations are largely artifacts of measurement, in the closeness of the 2016 race, the larger-than-usual percentage of undecided voters and particularly the closeness in key battleground states, it certainly seems to have played a major role in tipping the Electoral College vote to Trump.

Finally, there is the issue of Russian interference. After the election, it was announced that U.S. intelligence had confirmed that the Russian government had ordered cyber attacks on the DNC and had orchestrated the release of numerous emails, including those of Clinton campaign manager John Podesta. Later, it was revealed that several Trump associates, including son-in-law Jared Kushner and Trump's first national security advisor Michael Flynn, had met with Russian operatives to discuss potential damaging information about Clinton. A report filed by former British intelligence officer Christopher Steele indicated that the Russians possessed compromising material on Trump. The Russian government had been involved in a number of Western elections and its primary goal, disrupting and undermining Western democracies, seemed to be at work in the 2016 election, which appeared to have benefited Trump.

Given the closeness of the election and the massive number of factors at play in a presidential election, it is a fool's errand to try to specify which factor was the tipping point. All told, all of the factors mentioned above played a role in Trump's victory.

President Trump's first year in office was a whirlwind of controversy. The president, fond of using Twitter, made a series of ill-advised public statements, including disparaging remarks about key allies such as Britain and Canada. Trump proposed a travel ban on seven countries that was repeatedly struck down by federal courts as an invalid religious test. The president's advisors, such as Kellyanne Conway and Sean Spicer, were often ridiculed for presenting demonstrably false information as real, such as exaggerated claims about the size of his inauguration crowd compared to President Obama's. The president pulled the United States out of the Paris Accords to reduce global carbon emissions, which President Obama had been instrumental in helping to negotiate. The massive Women's March was held in January with marches across the country and a similar March for Science was held in May.

The White House became a revolving door of staff as one advisor after another left or was fired, including Spicer, Secretary of State Rex Tillerson, two national security advisors, and communications director Hope Hicks, among others. The president's daughter Ivanka and son-in-law Jared Kushner were given extensive roles in the White House early on, but Kushner seemed to be in over his head. His personal business dealings became an issue as it was revealed foreign governments stated that Kusnher's business debt made him susceptible to influence. Chief of Staff John Kelly repeatedly clashed with Ivanka Trump and Kushner and Kelly had Kushner's security clearance reduced.

At times, the presidency seemed to stabilize. Airstrikes against the Syrian government were widely applauded across the political spectrum. A conservative justice, Neil Gorsuch, was nominated and confirmed for the Supreme Court. While efforts to repeal Obamacare largely failed, a massive tax overhaul was passed into law, the first such overhaul to the tax code since 1986. While the president's approval rating was stuck at historic lows for a first-year president, his approval rating remained high among Republicans, in part due to these successes.

Yet concerns about Russian involvement dominated Trump's first year in office. In January, just weeks after his inauguration, National Security Advisor Michael Flynn was forced to step down and was later charged with lying to the FBI. Attorney General Jeff Sessions, it was revealed, withheld information about his meetings with Russian operatives during the campaign. In May, FBI director James Comey was fired by President Trump after Trump demanded loyalty from Comey, who testified to Congress about the pressure Trump appeared to place on him to drop the Russia investigation. Following that, a special prosecutor was announced, former FBI director Robert S. Mueller.

The rest of this book examines the impact of 2016 on the "state of the parties," noting both change and continuity. This examination proceeds in five parts: an overview on the state of the two-party system; the role of party activists; the presidential nomination process; the electorate; polarization and political elites; and Super PACs and partisan resources. A brief review of each section follows.

The State of the Party System

In part I, the essays discuss the state of the party system in light of the results of the 2016 presidential contests, including the adaptability and contents of the major parties as well as the impact of elections themselves.

In chapter 2, *Mildred A. Schwartz* argues that parties are adaptive institutions. She points out that parties face a number of external challenges, and their success in navigating these challenges is due to four main factors. Decentralized parties allow for new types of support and more agility, but also present potential instability in the parties' coalitions. Adaptive parties also have strong cultures, are goal directed, and have a power structure that allows the internal network to successfully acquire resources to further its pursuit of electoral success and political power. Schwartz argues that these are dimensions of adaptability and each party displayed shortcomings in response to adapting to the environment in the 2016 presidential elections.

In chapter 3, *Daniel Schlozman* and *Sam Rosenfeld* continue the discussion of how parties have responded to a changing political and social environment. They are less optimistic about how parties have adapted. Despite massive financial resources and public polarization, they instead claim parties are "hollow." Schlozman and Rosenfeld challenge the dominant paradigms of parties as groups of ambitious politicians or policy-demanders. Instead, judged in the historical sense, parties lack the ability to structure conflict and the network that other scholars see is, in their view, a "blob" of actors with little in common. Hollow parties are, in their view, unable to help parties provide society with a meaningful understanding of societal conflicts or a programmatic vision to bring order to political chaos.

In chapter 4, *Daniel M. Shea* continues the discussion of the place of parties in contemporary society by raising the question of whether American democracy is suffering from an overload of elections. Shea argues that rather than providing certainty, elections confuse and disappoint. Citizens and politicians are incentivized to wait for the next election, inhibiting parties' ability to govern society's ability to move on from elections to find a collective good. Similar to Schlozman and Rosenfeld, Shea finds a solution on the revitalization of local parties as well as the fact that democracy requires multiple pathways for action, rather than just elections.

Party Activists

In part II, the chapters turn to assess the state of party activists. The network of party actors is, in most models, dominated by party activists. How these actors define party agendas and shape party goals is illustrated by the chapters in this section.

In chapter 5, *Jeffrey M. Stonecash* asks what conditions allowed Trump to be able to successfully win the Republican nomination and then the general election. Rather than focusing on the characteristics of voters who supported Trump, Stonecash identifies Trump's successful use of narrative in articulating what voters perceived as the reality of American society. In contrast to many claims that Trump was different, Stonecash argues that Trump made use of Republican orthodoxy in successfully appealing to GOP voters, but emphasizing declining economic fortunes and threats to the cultural fabric.

In chapter 6, *Julia R. Azari* and *Seth Masket* look at the insurgent campaign of Bernie Sanders. They see parallels between him and his supporters call for more openness in the Democratic Party with previous calls for more democracy within the parties. Azari and Masket offer a cautionary view of the linkage between democracy within the parties and their legitimacy as representative institutions. Instead, since at least the Populist Movement of the late nineteenth century, the Democratic Party has become more open and democratic, but not always better able to unify and win elections. They argue Democratic legitimacy, while an important goal, comes with costs.

In chapter 7, *Daniel J. Coffey* assesses the changes within the state parties. Coffey finds that while the national parties faced internal ideological struggles, there is little evidence of change in the agendas of state parties since 2012. Using quantitative text analysis methods, Coffey analyzes differences in platforms in states won by Sanders and Clinton and Trump and establishment Republican candidates. The analysis of state party platform ideology, emotional sentiment, and issue topics demonstrate the primary source of conflict in between and not within the parties. Coffey finishes his analysis by questioning how the traditional party vehicles of representation, such as the platform, will survive as policy demanders have more direct methods of pushing their agendas into the public sphere.

In chapter 8, *Eric C. Vorst* looks at how Twitter networks reveal how elite polarization translates into mass polarization, a question that has long concerned scholars of public opinion. By focusing on the use of social media, Vorst is able to provide new insights into the mechanism by which elite attitudes and cues become internalized by mass audiences and converted into their own opinions. Vorst finds that while traditional forms of media such as televised campaign speeches have a stronger influence on social media discussion networks, transmission of affective language through the network is robust. Importantly, Vorst finds that affect, or emotional language, encourages more discussion both within and outside of a social media network, which has normative implications for understanding the role of affect and polarization.

Party Nominations

In part III, the authors assess how party nominations have changed in the previous four years. Parties continually tweak these rules, but the results do not always seem to produce the intended consequences.

In chapter 9, *Drew Kurlowski* explores changes in party nomination rules between 2012 and 2016. Even though a presidential election is a national one, the nomination process is largely governed by state laws. While the national party committees have some control over this process, both the goals and the end of rules changes are uncertain. Party committees, for example, might move to an open-primary system to produce a more moderate electorate, but it is unclear if open (as opposed to closed) primaries do in fact produce more moderate electorates, never mind more electable candidates. Since parties and the factions that make them up have different goals, reforms to nomination processes tend to produce results that are confusing, and contradictory.

In chapter 10, *Caitlin E. Jewitt* also notes that party factions are deeply divided over the nomination process, but turns to look at how the public perceives the process. Jewitt finds high levels of distrust and dissatisfaction among voters, even rank-and-file party supporters. Importantly, strong partisans are not more supportive of caucuses and rank-and-file party members and most voters, she finds, do not support the use of Superdelegates. In addition, rank-and-file party members saw the insurgent candidacies of Trump and Sanders positively. Jewitt concludes that parties, which engage in a nearly quadrennial reform process, would do well to understand how voters perceive the nomination process when making reforms.

In chapter 11, *Wayne Steger* takes on a popular theory of political science in recent years, that the "party decides." The thesis, developed by scholars associated with the "UCLA" view (discussed in chapter 3) of parties as networks of policy-demanders, posited that party nominations are like auditions for a part. Rather than parties following the most popular candidates, candidates are really focused on winning the most endorsements from party elites. Steger finds 2016 as the rise of Populist candidates undermined the ability of the party networks to coordinate the selection of a single candidate, although this was more of the case on the Republican side than the Democratic side. This was because neither party had a clear frontrunner and the ability of the network to coordinate is contingent on an ideological orthodoxy to unite the network in the coordination effort. Populism, Steger argues, threatens to undermine parties and their ability to unify around a single candidate.

Party in Electorate

In part IV, the authors assess the sources of partisan polarization and the role of emotional or affective partisanship. Growing polarization, the authors find, is a destabilizing force in American politics.

In chapter 12, *David C. Kimball*, *Joseph Anthony*, and *Tyler Chance* explore the role of psychological dimensions of party polarization, an area that has generated more interest among political science researchers of public opinion in recent years. In somewhat of a return to the past, Kimball, Anthony, and Chance find that affective polarization is largely driven by group attachment rather than ideological or policy evaluations. This is in part, they argue, because candidates like Trump used group-based language in their appeals to prime perceptions of threats among supporters and to motivate political participation. They find that since affective polarization is not rooted in policy support, it makes governing difficult as supporters refuse to work with an opposition defined as a threat to the political system.

In chapter 13, *Alan I. Abramowitz* and *Steven W. Webster* focus on a similar theory, what they call "negative partisanship." Partisan loyalty, in terms of attachment and voting, is at historically high levels. Yet, this support is largely based on antipathy toward the opposition party rather than enthusiasm for one's own party. Anger, they find, is a particularly powerful motivator, overcoming doubts party voters have about their own candidates. Abramowitz and Webster raise similar concerns that triggering emotional buttons for support threatens the ability of the parties to govern once in office. The hallmark of the Van Buren party system, accepting the legitimacy of the opposition party, may no longer be a political norm and could lead parties and elected officials to take steps to undermine free and fair elections.

In chapter 14, *Edward G. Carmines*, *Michael J. Ensley*, and *Michael W. Wagner* take another look at populism, similar to their chapter in the previous edition of this book. Their analysis of voters has, in the last four years, become quite relevant. They show that while politics in the United States tends to be unidimensional, many voters are "ideologically heterodox," so that attitudes can be placed along a two-dimensional spectrum that encompasses five groups of identifiable clusters of opinion. In particular, white voters with lower education levels had populist views, mixing economic liberalism and cultural conservatism. These voters were key to Trump's victory, but Carmines, Ensley, and Wagner also find that many other voters, including libertarians and moderates, also supported Trump.

Party Resources

Finally, in part V on party resources, the authors find that money continues to dominate politics, but the role between large Super PACs, candidates, and parties is not as clear-cut as often assumed.

In chapter 15, *Robin Kolodny* asks the question of how much money really matters in elections, given that Trump won the election despite being outspent by a number of different measures. Kolodny argues that a myopic view of money ignores the way in which wealth and power influence politics. Even large contributions pale in comparison to the amount interest groups spend on lobbying. Trump's election undermines much of the conventional wisdom about the role of money in politics and the need for candidates to raise funds through traditional means. Trump's election may, Kolodny argues, point toward a new paradigm for acquiring the necessary resources to win a nomination.

In chapter 16, *Diana Dwyre* examines whether interest groups and Super PACs have supplanted parties as the primary sources of funds for candidates. Rules for financing campaigns are in constant flux and parties have had to repeatedly adapt to these changes. Various studies using network analysis reveal a symbiotic relationship between independent donors and parties in financing federal candidates. Understanding the overall patterns is difficult; while the role of the formal party institutions in providing resources directly seems to have declined, it is also the case that parties may retain the ability to orchestrate the direction of campaign resources to help achieve party goals. Allowing parties, as opposed to independent groups, to have access to more resources could produce the benefit of increasing the number of competitive federal races.

In chapter 17, *Paul S. Herrnson, Jennifer A. Heerwig,* and *Douglas M. Spencer* find that Super PAC organizational characteristics influence their fundraising patterns. Super PACs, their study finds, have been adept at identifying strategies to make their donations efficacious. Their analysis finds that groups that make independent expenditures or fund presidential candidates raise more money. Super PACs that raise at least some funds from organizations that do not disclose their donor raise more funds and groups that have been involved in several election cycles also tend to raise more money. In sum, not all Super PACs have the same ability to raise funds. Overall, the implication is that this serves to make elections less competitive.

In chapter 18, "What Happened to the Ground Game in 2016?," *Paul A. Beck, Richard Gunther,* and *Erik Nisbet* explore a topic that became the focus of explanations for why Clinton lost the general election. Since the closely contested 2000 presidential election, both parties and their presidential candidates had greatly expanded their field operations. Numerous indicators of campaign contact confirm that the "ground game" had taken on a central role in campaign efforts and to a large extent, could make the difference between winning and losing. In 2016, however, the ground game for both parties seemed to recede. Beck, Gunter, and Nisbet find, using data from the Comparative National Election Project (CNEP) in 2016 and comparing this to data from 2012, that party contact fell from 2012, especially in the crucial battleground states that Clinton wound up losing. Surprisingly, Republicans reached parity with Democrats in terms of voter contact, and in several crucial battleground states, Republican voter contacts outpaced Democratic contacts. The authors conclude that 2016 demonstrates the importance of party and personal contact for voter turnout and understanding the surprise outcome of the 2016 election.

Unanswered Questions

These essays provide a detailed review of the "state of the parties" after 2016. But they also raise a number of unanswered questions about the state of the parties in the future. Among the most important are:

- What will be the legacy of the Trump administration? Will he be able to maintain support of his unorthodox coalition? Will Trump fracture the Republican Party as it seeks a nominee for 2020? Can libertarian and social conservatives coexist in the Republican Party?
- Will the Republican Party establishment reassert control over the party?
- Is the Democratic Party moving further to the left, jettisoning the Clinton centrism that some believe has dominated the party since the 1990s? And what is the true legacy of the Obama years: a continuation of the Clinton era or the beginning of the Populist movement in the party?
- How will both parties adapt to an ever-changing social and technological environment?
- Will the trends in campaign finance evident in 2016 continue to break new records in every election cycle? Will the individual donor pool remain larger and continue to expand? Or will new innovations in campaign finance—including new rules and laws—once again change the source of party resources?
- Will the high level of partisan polarization persist in the presidency and the Congress? Or will polarization decline, reducing political tensions but also limiting the responsiveness of American government?

Chapter 1

Notes

1. http://www.ncsl.org/research/elections-and-campaigns/statevote-2014-post -election-analysis635508614.aspx.

2. Polling data is from realclearpolitics.com; generally, polls averages reflect polls of Trump versus Clinton in a head-to-head matchup and for consistency, I did not use polls measuring third-party candidate support. See: https://www.realclearpolitics .com/epolls/2016/president/us/general_election_trump_vs_clinton-5491.html.

Part I

State of the Parties

2

Failing Party Organizations

Lessons from the 2016 Election

Mildred A. Schwartz

E XPLANATIONS FOR THE OUTCOME of the 2016 presidential election are expanded by examining the organizational underpinnings of both parties. That outcome was foreshadowed by the failures of both the Democratic and Republican parties to adapt to the electoral environment, including changes in technology, methods of campaigning, and national and global economic forces. A good place to begin is by reviewing key features of party organizations relevant to such adaptation.

The Adaptive Party

This analysis is premised on conceptualizing party organization as a network of relations among both official and unofficial components linked through a single label. It begins with a model of a working party, emphasizing its organizational capacity, not whether it is ideal or unusually strong. I term this an "adaptive" party—one that displays the ability to alter itself in response to a continually changing environment (Schwartz 1990, 17). Building on previous research on parties and theoretical insights from the organizational literature, four characteristics are identified that capture the tensions parties face as they go about their normal activities. Although the ideal amount of those attributes cannot be precisely defined, we can still evaluate what represents greater or lesser optimality.

Loose Coupling

An adaptive party is loosely coupled (Orton and Weik 1990) in order to hold together the disparate components of the party network and allow enough flexibility for each to respond to challenges encountered in its own environment. Problems found in one arena, like specific congressional districts, may be dealt with independently without affecting other arenas. Looseness allows new political actors to enter the party and become incorporated into the network. In the face of an uncertain environment, looseness is a sign that the party is open to changing influences and sources of support.

Loosely coupled structures are often unstable. The failure to achieve electoral victory may, for example, spur a push for tighter coupling that may be temporarily effective by turning aside the influence of newcomers with their own agendas. But, in the long-run, the tighter the coupling, the less adaptable the party is likely to become. Coupling may also be too loose, signaled whenever the network cannot protect party boundaries from penetration by disruptive incursions.

Meaning System

An adaptive party is a cultural system that offers its own ways of interpreting the political world. Culture provides the core of a party, "the soul that keeps its boundaries from being eroded" (Schwartz 1990, 282). It can be symbolized by a president or by presidential contenders (Alexander 2010); it is found in party platforms and in an ideology. Given the diverse actors within a party's network, diverse ideological emphases may emerge, along with variations in commitment to any one of them.

A party without such a soul is one that exists without an identifiable brand that sets it apart. Such a situation may arise from complacency generated by a lengthy period of electoral victories. After defeat, party actors may compete to establish a coherent identity, with different voices vying for dominance. Over-commitment to any single ideology leads to unwillingness to compromise, making for inflexible and conflict-ridden relations.

Goal-Directed

An adaptive party is a rational, goal-directed body, in search of ways to enhance its electoral advantage. When organizational theorists speak of rationality, they refer to the efficiencies that come from dividing work into coherent tasks, assigning personnel based on training and competence, and linking elements through free information flows. In parties, such rationality is demonstrated when new techniques of organizing and campaigning are employed and by a search for winning candidates.

Too much emphasis on efficiency can lead to excessive attachment to established routines and party actors. The latter may be manifested by underestimating the potential contributions of political entrepreneurs who come from outside the usual pool of candidates or contributors (Schwartz 1990, 281). Too little emphasis can lead to misjudging trends among population groups and planning for the future.

An example of how candidate selection can affect a party's goal-directed behavior occurs when an individual who has gained fame in another arena runs for office. The challenge comes from celebrity candidates who bring with them their own resources and direct the party in new directions.

Power System

An adaptive party is a system of power, able to exert its authority internally to keep the network focused on winning elections and, externally, to gather resources with which to control the uncertainty intrinsic to its environment (Schwartz 1990, 291). But the range of actors within the network raises the potential for an internecine struggle over resources. An adaptive party will be one that recognizes that searches for the best routes to acquire resources without unduly constricting particular network members from independent searches.

Weaknesses in power limit how effectively a party is able to mobilize resources of money, influence, and support. An adaptive party forges long-term connections with supportive interest groups and financial contributors without becoming subordinate to them.

The Electoral Environment in 2016

Parties operate in multiple environments that present constraints on and opportunities for gaining resources. The electoral environment typifies this resource dependence (Pfeffer and Salancik 1978). Over time, voters in particular states and regions, of different racial and ethnic origins, religions, genders, and class positions may demonstrate loyal support for one of the two major parties but those loyalties can also be shaken. In efforts to gain more votes, adaptive parties need to assess both the relative stability of past loyalties and the current vulnerability of their voters.

If the Republicans had done such an assessment in 2016, they would have felt secure in expecting success in all their usual strongholds. In addition, five states that had voted Democratic in the past—Iowa, Ohio, Michigan, Wisconsin, and Pennsylvania—now showed signs of weakened attachment to that party.

Disgruntled voters signaled opportunities for the Republicans in a number of economic and racial/ethnic indicators. Based on an analysis of census data, the ten most economically distressed cities included four already in the Republican fold plus three others—Youngstown in Ohio and Flint and Detroit in Michigan—that would swing to that party (Florida and Bendix 2016). Those measures of distress were reflected in evolving realignments in class voting. Blue-collar workers had been switching to the Republicans since the 1970s (Hout and Laurison 2014, 1040). Another sign of that changing alignment was a widened educational divide, with those with a college degree overwhelmingly favoring Hillary Clinton (Suls 2016).

In contrast, there was clear cause for the Democrats to be alarmed. Its once loyal white working-class supporters were angry at an establishment that they felt did not serve them but favored the less deserving (Hahl et al. 2018; DiTomaso 2017). The absence of a galvanizing presidential candidate introduced uncertainty about African-American participation, later confirmed by that group's lower turnout (Mellnik et al. 2017).

Religious minorities tend to be Democratic as do those without any formal religion. White Protestant Evangelicals are mainly Republican and mainline Protestants and Catholics are divided more or less equally between the two parties (Lipka 2016). This distribution of partisanship occurs at the same time as white Christians have become a religious minority (Shepard 2017). Religion, like race/ethnicity, reflects the changing character of the United States, where the ascendancy of what were once the dominant groups in the society is threatened and the Republican Party appears as a savior.

Gender and age also divide the parties, with Republicans generally doing more poorly among women and younger voters. Since 1980, a majority of women have voted for the Democrats and have higher rates of turnout than men (Chaturvedi 2016; Center for American Women and Politics 2017). For younger voters, however, while a leaning toward Democrats is clear (Fischer and Hout 2006, 235–36), it has been offset by their lower turnout (Schlozman et al. 2012, 199–231).

Meeting Environmental Challenges in 2016

Loose Coupling

Going into the 2016 election, most looseness was demonstrated by the Republicans. One measure is the large number of candidates—17 in all—that presented themselves during the primaries. Of these, five were current or former U.S. senators and nine were former or current state governors. The remaining three came from business or the professions. Party insiders—those network actors who make up the party apparatus, hold key legislative positions, or constitute the informal core of the network—had already picked a former governor, Jeb Bush, as their choice for president. His lack of broader support from the larger network invited challenge from both those with political experience and those outside the party.

The looseness of Republican network ties was even more evident from the variety of interests that had already penetrated the party. Among them are evangelical Christians, the Tea Party (Almeida and Van Dyke 2014; Skocpol and Williamson 2013), pro-life activists, libertarians, federalists, big business interests, and sympathetic media outlets. These were augmented during the 2016 campaign by the so-called alt-right that was advancing the cause of white nationalism (Schwartz 2016; Marantz 2016). They steer the Republican Party in their direction even as they come in conflict with each other and with more pragmatic congressional leaders.

Like Republican insiders, Democratic ones were also attracted to the potential of a dynastic standard bearer but more successful in elevating their choice to be the presidential candidate. Of the others, Bernie Sanders, who ran as an Independent in home-town races for mayor and then for Congress, caucused with the Democrats and was rewarded with committee appointments. In entering the primary race for president, he did so as a Democrat only loosely attached to the party. His candidacy revealed the limited extent of loose coupling in the Democratic organization.

Democratic Party boundaries were also stronger than Republican ones in keeping out disruptive competing interests. Although many groups had a long history of attachment to the Democrats, with an established place for their agendas in the party's platform, the Democrats represented a more tightly coupled organization. But that was also a sign of their weakness, a weakness, exploited by Sanders, able to tap into otherwise under-represented progressive interests, hungry for change.

Meaning System

The Republican Party offers a consistent conservative ideology, legitimated during the 1964 election by Barry Goldwater (Wildavsky 1965), reinforced under the guidance of Newt Gingrich in 1982 (Petrocik and Steeper 2010), and strengthened through the actions of the Tea Party movement (Williamson et al. 2011). Although some conservatives were disparaging of Donald Trump's attachment to their core values, a study of Tea Party members found that their eventual willingness to support Trump was linked to shared perspectives on immigration, taxes, and national security (Yates 2017). In addition, Trump's slogan of "Let's make America great again," both echoed a similar message from Ronald Reagan's campaign and tapped into voters' strong identification with nationalism (Bonikowski and DiMaggio 2016).

The Vietnam War and the cultural revolution of the 1960s and 1970s had driven away support for the Democratic Party from working class and Catholic voters while the effects of the civil rights movement alienated whites in the South (Manza and Brooks 1999). Yet the seriousness of these defections did little to inspire a new message. Hillary Clinton's early speechwriters were said to conclude that the campaign suffered from "tangled lines of authority, petty jealousies, distorted priorities, and no sense of greater purpose. No one was in charge, and no one had figured out how to make the campaign about something bigger than Hillary" (Allen and Parnes 2017, 13). The message conveyed was limited to the benefits of Clinton's prior experience and the value of electing a woman as president. Sanders, in contrast, had no difficulty in formulating a populist appeal centered on income inequality and the need for campaign finance reform.

The Republican Party displayed its weakness in having too much polarizing ideology (Iyengar and Westwood 2015). Even before Donald Trump entered the political arena, questions were raised about how long the Republican message about immigrants, non-whites, and the economically disadvantaged could continue without negative electoral consequences (e.g., Skocpol 2012). The recent addition of the alt-right's perspective to the Republican message has made questions about the party's future even more pertinent (Green 2017).

Goal-Directed Rationality

For party insiders, organizational rationality lies in locating the candidate most likely to win while not alienating others whose eventual support will be needed. To influential Democrats, the choice of Hillary Clinton was a relatively easy one, given her political experience and connections to the Democratic network, including major donors and fundraisers (Confessore et al. 2015). Although she also had negative attributes, these were apparently dismissed though they would become important during the campaign (Cohen 2015).

Bernie Sanders entered the race because he was unhappy with how the party establishment was defining the issues by anointing Hillary Clinton as its favorite. As an outsider, he operated without concern about how his policies might create conflict. But his ability to attract media attention, support, and money soon meant that the party establishment had to take him seriously. He became a more central-network actor because of his access to these multiple resources but also a source of concern over the issues he advocated for and whether he would support the party's winning candidate. In other words, his candidacy challenged the boundaries of organizational rationality.

Republican insiders saw Jeb Bush as the best candidate because of his experience as governor, strong name recognition, access to major funding, general likability, and identification with less strident forms of conservatism. Other experienced politicians running in the primaries had drawbacks in one or more of these respects. Network openness to entrepreneurial outsiders can then be a sign of rational responsiveness to a changing electoral environment if it produces a winner. But Donald Trump, coming from beyond the usual path to candidacy, did not appear to have that potential. In fact, Trump was highly disruptive of normal party procedures and relationships (Wagner-Pacifici and Tavory 2017).

In addition to candidate choice, organizational rationality affects how election campaigns are run. At one level, there is little difference between the two parties in becoming essential service providers for candidates (Galvin 2012), affected by the enlarged sources of funding that go directly to candidates and reduce the parties' organizational impact, relying on professional advisors and campaign managers (Laurison 2017a; Schwartz 2011, 44), and responding to the opportunities opened by electronic media. But beyond those similarities, organizational rationality was altered through the agency of specific candidates and their campaigns. Clinton's campaign appears to have been an over-professionalized organization, with too many advisors, leading both to infighting and to strong pressure for consensus. With a candidate reluctant to move beyond her comfort zone and commitment to a model that downgraded campaigning on the ground (Allen and Parnes 2017, 597–98), local Democrats were dismayed. For example, according to Virgie Rollins, DNC member and chair emerita of the Michigan Democratic Women's Caucus, "When you don't reach out to community folk and reach out to precinct campaigns and district organizations that know where the votes are, then you are going to have problems" (Dovere 2016).

Not as much is known about the Trump campaign. The candidate entered the race as a virtual outsider to the Republican Party, whom party insiders were initially reluctant to endorse. He was a media celebrity inexperienced in electoral politics who introduced an unprecedented level of coarseness and animosity into national politics. In giving Steve Bannon leadership of his campaign, Trump allowed Bannon to introduce a version of ethnic nationalism and deliberately disrupt political expectations (Green 2017). Yet, at the same time, it appeared to some Republican advisors that the Trump campaign was relatively traditional in its approach to campaign basics (Laurison 2017b).

In following the path of organizational rationality, the Democrats were inclined to over-rationalize, limiting opportunities for new candidates to energize the party and sticking too closely to a formal model of how campaigns should be run (Allen and Parnes 2017, 397–98). The Republicans, in contrast, were under-rationalizers, making it too easy for outside candidates to disrupt the party and impose new approaches to campaigning.

Power System

An adaptive party has the capacity to use its power to reduce the uncertainty that accompanies every election by mobilizing resources of support and money. Today, a party's ability to raise significant sums has been seriously undercut by the rise of Super PACs with their own agendas that support specific candidates. In the last election, Super PACs raised $615 million; candidates, $1,463 billion (Center for Responsive Politics 2017c). Money as a usable resource has now shifted from parties' central, senatorial, and congressional committees to a locus in the unofficial component of the party network.

In the past election, Clinton raised almost twice as much as Trump, who, in contrast, aided his campaign by sizable contributions of his own money and other personal resources (Allison et al. 2016). Trump's television career created his celebrity status that then became convertible into an unanticipated political resource (Nussbaum 2017). Every unconventional activity gave him "earned media" in the form of unpaid coverage, estimated to have been worth $2 billion by the middle of the primary season (Confessore and Yourish 2016).

With money no longer a major resource usable by the official parties, they could still offer the resource of a loyal electorate. Before the 2016 election, the Democratic Party was home to racial/ethnic minorities, professionals, students, declining numbers of trade unionists, and regional strongholds in the Northeast, the west coast, and big cities. But this combination went along with continuing loss of support from the white working class (Teixeira and Rogers 2000). According to DiTomaso (2017),

> The problem in the Democratic Party has not been that they have forgotten the white working class, but rather that they have not been able to resolve the internal conflict within the Party to create a policy agenda that is mutually

beneficial to both the white working class and race and ethnic minorities, who perceive themselves as competing with each other over access to good jobs.

The party's offer of electoral support was therefore shaky, compounded by competition from Bernie Sanders among the young and those attuned to a progressive agenda (Cohen 2015). Although Debbie Wasserman Schultz, chair of the DNC, responded by trying to undermine Sanders's appeal, revelations of her actions generated an internal party crisis. It also brought into question whether Sanders and his youthful followers would go on to support Clinton (Allen and Parnes 2017, 263). In addition, the failure to mobilize turnout by Blacks and Hispanics, especially in key states, contributed to Clinton's campaign failures (Mellnik et al. 2017).

The Republican Party could, in contrast, offer its candidate a more stable level of support in the South, Southwest, and the Midwest from conservative Christians, whites, the more prosperous, and those who lived in small towns and rural areas. It brought along those self-identified Republicans who had become more likely to oppose government action in the economy (Baldassarri and Park 2016). The party operated in a climate where anti-immigrant sentiment was high and accompanied racist resentment (Tesler 2016), exploiting nationalist and populist sentiments but without transforming the party into one that primarily represented the economically depressed (Atkins 2016; Manza and Crowley 2017; Mellnik et al. 2017).

Adaptive Failures

Although loose coupling is a characteristic of U.S. political parties, the Democratic network was judged to be too tightly coupled by making the nomination of Hillary Clinton a foregone conclusion. Instead of allowing a range of candidates to emerge who could bring new messages and new support or energize old ones, she faced serious opposition only from Bernie Sanders, coming from the party's periphery.

In contrast, the Republican network was too loosely coupled, permitting entry from a broad range of contenders and quickly forestalling opportunities for the formal party to make its choice dominant. That loose coupling became the avenue for Donald Trump, unmoored from the party network and from political experience, to become the successful contender.

A similar assessment can be made about each party's ability to present a comprehensive and unifying theme, spelling out its brand. On one side, the Democrats have been unable to generate such an appealing message at least since the 1960s, although this has not always prevented it from winning the presidency. Sanders had a clear message but was only modestly successful in persuading party officials to adopt portions of it into the party platform. More critically, Clinton was never able to find an appealing message that made a mark during the campaign.

The Republican case was the extreme opposite. Although there has been a history of a core conservative ideology, it has been elaborated by the addition of many more themes: nationalist, small government, anti-regulatory, states' rights, moralistic Christian, and anti-immigrant. Any Republican candidate then had an array of ready-made messages on which to build a campaign and Trump's campaign incorporated some of the more extreme themes to his advantage. Although an excess of ideology could be anticipated to divide party supporters, its presence in 2016 was used effectively to mobilize support from, for example, Evangelicals, Tea Party supporters, and disgruntled working class voters who might otherwise find Trump an unattractive candidate. Rather than being foreign to the mainstream of Republican values, Trump's message was a reflection of what already existed (Mast 2017).

The adaptive capacity of a rationally organized, goal-directed party is premised on its capacity to find the most efficient means to mobilize voters and select winning candidates. By these criteria, both parties displayed weaknesses. The Democrats' inner circle over-rationalized its efforts by picking Hillary Clinton as its candidate too early in the electoral cycle. The Republicans did the same in their choice of Jeb Bush and quickly lost control over candidate selection, ending up with one who had only modest ties to the official party. Clinton's own organization's rigidity continued, becoming the Democrats.' Clinton won substantially more popular voters than did her opponent, but her campaign's assessment of where to put resources failed to anticipate how much the final outcome would depend on the Electoral College—a failure in organizational rationality. In contrast, even with an uncontrollable candidate, the Trump organization found the key to victory.

Finally, an adaptive party is one able to obtain and deploy resources in ways most beneficial to it. I tend to be dismissive of how powerful a role money now plays in the activities of the party apparatus, given the diffusion of fundraising capacity to other party units and the growing influence of the largely free new social media. Money may even have lost some of its power in the campaign process. For Trump, it was both the social media and his celebrity status that gave him "earned credit" from the old media without requiring payment. Together, that gave him a substantial, if not overwhelming, advantage.

More critical even than money is the existence of a loyal social base that can be mobilized to vote for the party candidate, regardless of who has that position. The Democratic base has been eroding and the Clinton campaign was not effective in mobilizing its known support while facing uncertainty in winning over Sanders's base. The Republican base has become firmer and passed on this advantage to the Trump campaign.

Of the many factors contributing to Donald Trump's victory and Hillary Clinton's defeat, proper weight must be given to the contribution made by each party's organizational network. Both parties demonstrated failures to adapt to a changing electoral environment, but overall, it was the Democratic Party that displayed the most shortcomings.

3

Party Blobs and Partisan Visions

Making Sense of Our Hollow Parties

Daniel Schlozman and Sam Rosenfeld

CONTEMPORARY AMERICAN PARTIES are hollow parties. This chapter steps back from the events of 2016 to offer a conceptual framework that attends to party dynamics across multiple, interacting fields of action. American parties, we argue, should not be understood as either classically "strong" or "weak" (Azari 2016a). Instead, they are hollow—top-heavy organizations that are under-legitimized as shapers of political conflict. By historical standards, centralized party leadership in Congress is alive and well. At the mass level, party identification steers public opinion and voting. In the spaces in between, however, parties are neither organizationally robust beyond their task to raise money—and increasingly losing out even there to candidates and para-party groups drawing plutocrats' dollars—nor meaningfully felt as a real, tangible presence in the lives of voters or in the work of engaged activists. Parties cannot inspire positive loyalties, mobilize would-be supporters, effectively coordinate their influencers, or police their boundaries.

This hollowness has had dire consequences. The parties have failed to meet the combined challenges of polarization and fracture. As Thomas Edsall summarizes, "Over the past 50 years, overarching and underlying conflicts about morality, family, autonomy, religious conviction, fairness and even patriotism have been forced into two relatively weak vessels, the Democratic Party and the Republican Party" (Edsall 2017a). The parties' divergent visions for state and society define American politics, yet the parties themselves are bystanders to fights waged in their own name.

This chapter first identifies general traits in a system defined by hollowness

—its formless blob, its negativity, and its distance from Americans' lived experience. Because such hollowness serves to obscure party purposes, we then turn to a genealogy of contemporary partisan visions. We construct portraits of six ideal-types of partisan actors, rendering explicit the views about party they typically express either in fragments or sub rosa. We examine insiders and outside insurgents in both major parties, and also, from the center, "New Realists," who look back fondly on dealmaking parties of yore, and anti-party centrists lusting after a solutions-oriented technocracy. The through-line across these partisan visions is the inability of anybody, whether the formal parties themselves or informal actors in the circles around them, to bring elites and the mass public together in common purpose and mobilize loyalties in a purposeful direction. And though hollowness has manifested itself in ways particular to American conditions, the themes here link with broader maladies across the West (Mair 2013; Katz and Mair 2018).

Our approach is historical and institutional: historical in emphasizing the deep roots of contemporary party hollowness, and institutional in emphasizing formal parties as distinct from various para-party groups. We treat parties as autonomous and thick collective actors. Parties emerge from complex, iterative interactions among diverse actors and exist in dense networks. Ideas, institutions, and rules all matter—and they do not emerge simply from congealed preferences. Parties should not be understood solely as the solution to the coordination problems of other, prior players on the political stage.

The most prominent explanations in contemporary scholarship, by contrast, posit parties as the vehicles respectively of ambitious politicians or of groups eager to extract benefits from the state (Aldrich 2011; Bawn et al. 2012). Make analytical sense of the underlying forces and the incentives they face at any given period in American history and the resultant parties fall into place. Parties, one might say, are the things that emerge from prior actors' coordination. Party positioning comes as the groups that collectively comprise a "party" label jostle against one another. When the environment shifts, whether because the same actors face new pressures or change their preferences or because new actors enter the scene, the parties change in turn (Karol 2009; Noel 2013; Baylor 2017).

Yet in these approaches, the road from politicians' or groups' desires for power to parties' wielding of it remains underdetermined. When the whole game is explaining coordination, preferences are exogenous by design. We reverse figure and ground. Rather than asking what parties do for their claimants and then seeing what conclusions follow for parties, we put parties first. We seek to understand both parties' internal workings as they seek to win elections and their external goals to wield state power and remake the polity.

That parties want to win elections and wield power is an essential truth separating them from all other actors in the political game—but only a paper-thin one. As a matter of definition, we follow E. E. Schattschneider (1942, ix): "a political party is an organized attempt to get control of the government." Nevertheless, what else partisan actors have wanted has varied across American history and today. Some want spoils; others want policy; still others want reform. Some empower the loyal partisan activists while others happily let the boss rule. Still others look to a transformative leader. Answers along one set goals feed back to and impinge on others. They change the incentives facing group claimants—which have their own internal structures and dynamics. A synthetic view of parties sees these as a series of nested problems—and parties as more than the sum of their roles or tasks.

Such a view also emphasizes how parties conceive of themselves when they exercise power. Parties have held very different ideas about whom to reward and about how to entrench themselves across the sprawling American state (Shefter 1994) and those ideas have not served as mere dross or superstructure. Doctrine matters, both on the place of party in American political life and on the party's vision for the republic (J. Cooper 2017; Rosenblum 2008). Even in an era of hollow parties, those visions have consequences.

Making Sense of Hollowness

In parties, as in American life more generally, ours is an "Age of Fracture" (Rodgers 2011). The hollow parties tell their own version of the story, bearing the imprints of and tensions among distinct partisan lineages spanning two centuries (Schlozman and Rosenfeld 2018). We still live with the legacies of the locally oriented, federated parties of the nineteenth century as well as the reforms of the Progressive Era, when suspicion of parties' machinations dented but did not destroy such parties. The reworking of parties in the era of the Democrats' McGovern-Fraser Commission took up the Progressive suspicion of backroom deals more than it affirmed a positive vision. As the reentry of the South into two-party politics sorted Democrats and Republicans geographically and ideologically, the parties could not contain the conflictual politics that ensued. The fruits of these intersecting developments are evident in party hollowness: the amorphous, mercenary, money-driven, candidate-led, nationalized game of contemporary party politics.

The party-as-organization has held on in the money chase (Herrnson 2009; Dwyre and Kolodny 2014a), but without distinguishing itself as much of an innovator or even an ongoing day-to-day presence felt by the politically engaged, at a time when increased loyalty to the party team might have made it so. Local parties soldier on, however tenuously linked to the para-organizations and movements that have roiled American politics, even as federated membership groups wither (Roscoe and Jenkins 2016; Skocpol 2003). State parties have sustained their organizations and even bolstered their technological capacities while losing relative influence (Bibby 2002; Hatch 2016; La Raja and Rauch 2016). Recent work-around schemes have emasculated state parties, rendering them as mere conduits in directing large-dollar donations to presidential candidates' coffers (Kolodny and Dulio 2003; Greenblatt 2015; Brazile 2017). The national committees, while comparatively robust, have found themselves eclipsed by para-organizations that reflect the influence of the ascendant super-rich. Vast spending on campaigns goes mostly to television, despite its dubious effectiveness. And even the modern revival of person-to-person canvassing comes from the top down. Staffers parachuted in from outside coordinate lists concocted by uncertain and unseen algorithms. Para-organizations and campaigns alike close their storefronts the morning after Election Day, not to reopen again until the next cycle (Schlozman 2016).

The unfolding story of Trump-era "resistance" highlights the long-term costs of a top-heavy, hollowed-out party system. Citizens across the country seek to fill voids in Democratic organizations. Yet, despite some bright spots, formal party actors at the national and, in many instances, state and local levels have typically offered little help, and have little help to offer (Putnam and Skocpol 2018).

The parties still organize the quadrennial presidential nominating conventions. But the rules for delegate selection seem opaque and the process confusing. The primaries and caucuses that select the delegates provide months-long fodder for grievances by rival candidates and their supporters. To state the obvious reality from 2016, Republican Party leaders, with no single favored alternative, failed to unite to stop a nominee whom few of them would have chosen. Thus, the process of nominating a president, the preeminent though far from singular task of American political parties, serves not as a celebration of party but as an extended opportunity to bash it, without the parties themselves, or anybody on their behalf, offering principled responses. Regardless of whether "the party decides" the nominee (Cohen et al. 2008, 2016), it wins few friends in the deciding.

To repeat a central premise, our theme is not weakness but hollowness. Polarization is the preeminent fact of contemporary politics, but it is a form of polarization with particular and corrosive dynamics. At the top, with the parties evenly matched and the stakes high, minorities in Congress have incentives to fight rather than to compromise (Lee 2016). Repeatedly, presidents promise to cut through the gridlock and bring Americans together, yet the reach of the rhetorical presidency exceeds the grasp of an ever-more-partisan administrative presidency (Tulis 1987; Skinner 2006; Milkis and York 2017; Rudalevige 2016). To these dynamics, add negative partisanship in the mass public (Abramowitz and Webster 2016), whose suspicion of disloyalty and distaste for process looks nothing like the older, positive partisanship of the torchlight parade. Nor does it resemble the issue- and rules-oriented partisan citizenship that liberal reformers long hoped to inculcate.

Inhabiting the space where parties once dwelled is a disorderly assortment of actors that we term, collectively, the Party Blob. Today's parties are distinctive for the presence of so many figures entwined with but not organizationally part of their formal structure. The list goes on and on: issue groups, many of them with paper members or no members at all; media from talk-show hosts to Twitter personalities, guided by profit and celebrity at least as much as by ideological or electoral goals; policy experts in think tanks generating party programs by proxy; engaged activists giving time or a few dollars to prominent and often extreme candidates; ideological warriors at CPAC and Netroots Nation; the mass affluent munching on canapés at fundraisers; high rollers with real access and, often, very specific agendas of their own; PACs; nominally uncoordinated "Super PACs"; leadership PACs from politicians looking to build their own brands and get chits out to colleagues; and consultancies and staffers hoping for a share of all the money sloshing through the system.

See this Blob as a whole, grasp, if you will, its shapeless shape, its formless form, its headless body and the picture starts to fall into place. Its constituent pieces—"members" is too strong a term—all have internal incentives of their own, many of which militate for them to work against rather than with other parts. The drivers of the behavior—the principals—and the underlying goals being pursued are difficult to identify. The figures in the Blob cannot be reduced to a single analytic category without losing the internal variation that is precisely its defining feature. This jumble of principals and incentives is how the Blob contributes to hollowness. A disorganized multiplicity of actors with doubtful loyalty to the long-term interest of their allied party ultimately weakens it.

The Blob is porous, amorphous, and frequently directionless. Its actors include but are not limited to "policy demanders" who want goodies from the state (Bawn et al. 2012). Nor are they just candidates, their supporters, or members of the candidate-money-consultant nexus. Nor are they just "groups," with the internal structure that that label implies. Parts of the Blob tend to polarize the system, others to bring it toward the center (Karol 2015). Activity in the Blob is variously motivated by material incentives (typically not the patronage of yore but rather the rewards of, say, a tax break or a share of the lobbying dollars), solidary incentives (even the solitary solidary incentives of online activism); and purposive incentives (though, again, not always in a straight or clear line) (Wilson [1974] 1995).

The Blob looks different in the Democratic and Republican Parties. Whether or not, as Matthew Grossmann and David Hopkins (2016) argue, "ideology" is the distinctive characteristic, still less the glue, of the Republican Party, the GOP has adopted a take-no-prisoners, don't-sweat-the-details zeal on both procedure and substance with no parallel on the other side, as our discussion of left-populism, with its heavy dose of Progressive reformism, well shows.

Proof of the Blob's asymmetries is found in the exercise of electoral and political power. The signal political victory in our 50–50 era of party competition has been Republicans' success in the states. Via gerrymanders in congressional districts and aggressive state lawsuits against the Obama administration, they have imprinted that victory on national politics. Rather than stemming from strong state parties, their state-level success has emerged from linked actors outside, but entwined with, formal parties. The critical non-party actors, including the Koch network and the American Legislative Exchange Council, seized the opportunities that the midterm gains of 2010 offered, consolidated power, and changed the playing field by starving out their opponents, foremost in public-sector unions. The structural power of business, the alliance between conservatism and right populism, and, critically, a set of powerful actors that knew what it wanted, all came together (Mayer 2016; Skocpol and Hertel-Fernandez 2016). (Such achievements, to be sure, do not characterize the entire Republican story, as the shambles of the 2016 nomination contest and first year of unified national GOP control indicate.)

They have no equivalent on the other side. Liberal efforts to engage in states have repeatedly failed. The Democracy Alliance, a collection of liberal interest groups and rich donors established explicitly to resist short-termism and fragmentation, quickly replicated those very maladies, and made no discernable impact on the structure of American politics (Sclar et al. 2016). Rather than building institutions that would push a clear partisan or ideological vision, the Democracy Alliance straddled the Democrats' internecine battles and spread its cash thinly and widely, in the end accomplishing little more than to pump money into the Blob.

Other scholars have termed the same underlying reality the "networked" party (Koger, Masket, and Noel 2016; Schwartz 1990). Such an approach has both great virtues and significant limits. In specifically political networks, the internal structures and motivations of participants are as important as their external patterns of cooperation and non-cooperation. We emphasize less the particular points of cooperation and coordination than the overall structure (or non-structure) of the party network, and the weaknesses of the connections that might bring its pieces together. The limits of coordination in contemporary parties go beyond signaling games, in nomination or elsewhere. The vast failure to build the collective goods through which parties helpfully channel citizens' passions and organize political conflict is the central non-event in the hollow parties. The Blob is more than just its nodes and ties, even though the looseness of contemporary parties makes network analysis a particularly appealing strategy. We see the Blob as a void to be filled, and merely focusing on how it is filled risks missing the point.

Visions of Party in an Age of Hollowness

Because we understand parties as autonomous and complex institutions, we take seriously partisan actors' normative, programmatic, and instrumental goals. Table 3.1 offers an account of the visions of party that animate six important collective actors in contemporary American politics. These six actors are ideal types, useful in making sense of a complicated landscape. They reflect our distillation of the politically savvy and sophisticated actors in each category. Precisely because contemporary American politics has both undermined parties' legitimacy and rendered their work opaque, we have had to serve, as best we can, as interpolators of actors' oft-inchoate sentiments rather than as stenographers of their coherent and comprehensive views.

We consider, moving row by row, the Democratic and Republican parties and then the center, with the more pro-party actors in the left-hand column of the table and the anti-party actors on the right. The Democratic Institutionalists and Republican Establishment see themselves as central to the Blob—and as our discussion should show, calling these congeries "pro-party" is, in absolute terms, a stretch. One would be hard-pressed to find nowadays a politician who consistently upholds in word, still less in deed, the nineteenth-century maxim to put party before self. But compared with their internal antagonists, the Left and Right Populists, each defends its prerogative and believes that nominations and campaigns do not mimetically reflect the popular will. In contrast, the Left and Right Populists reject such a worldview, instead seeking parties that speak authentically for the people, albeit for different purposes.

Finally, we consider two kinds of centrists aiming to combat polarization and return American politics to the sensible middle, respective heirs to the

TABLE 3.1
Contemporary Party Visions

Party facets	Contemporary Actors	
	Democratic Institutionalists	*Left Populists*
Privileged partisan actors	DC cross-institutional; groups	Grassroots activists
Method of choosing nominees	Mixed	Pure primary
Orientation to inter-party compromise	Rare but not unacceptable	Unacceptable
Goals in wielding state power	Mixed	Ideological patronage
Funders of party	Mixed; high- and low-dollar	Low-dollar checkbook activists
Great or small parties	Small	Great but under-theorized
	Establishment Republicans	*Right Populists*
Privileged partisan actors	DC cross-institutional; donors	Strong leader
Method of choosing nominees	Mixed	Pure primary
Orientation to inter-party compromise	Unacceptable	Unacceptable
Goals in wielding state power	Ideological patronage	Ideological patronage via status
Funders of party	High-dollar donors	Anyone they can find
Great or small parties	Small but radical	Leader's party
	New Realists	*Technocratic Centrists*
Privileged partisan actors	Election-seeking pols and donors	None (solution-oriented individualists)
Method of choosing nominees	Ideally, convention	Agnostic
Orientation to inter-party compromise	Acceptable	Desirable
Goals in wielding state power	Perquisites of office only	Efficient governance
Funders of party	Interest-seeking donors	High-dollar donors
Great or small parties	Small	Irrelevant parties

venerable traditions of machine and reform. The New Realists look back fondly to transactional parties of yore and want to strengthen actors more interested in holding office than in remaking state or society. Technocratic Centrists, who take after elite strands in Progressivism, instead seek to subordinate parties and partisanship in the name of public-spirited efficiency. These centrists' policy prescriptions may not differ much, but their views of party diverge radically.

The six facets of party delineated in the table cover critical dimensions of the complex American political system, with its comparatively decentralized but also highly regulated parties (Epstein 1986). Parties, both rhetorically and practically, privilege certain actors, making them the repositories for the party's *raison d'être*. In parties, beset with principal-agent problems, exactly who takes orders (or even cues) from whom depends on both doctrine and circumstance. Who, in the views of our actors, speaks for "the party?" We then ask about views on the core task of nomination, and particularly presidential nomination. These views reflect beliefs not only about who should nominate, but about who should rule and in whose interest. Next, we ask about orientation to compromise. Should parties seek agreement across their divides, or stand apart on principle? What kinds of compromises should parties accept? And by what principle?

These first three facets of party cover much of the traditional remit of party scholarship, but they do not exhaust our inquiry. Because parties organize conflict and mark out the organizable alternatives in national politics (Schlozman 2015), we want to know how they seek to reshape society. Those are the real stakes in party politics (Hacker and Pierson 2014). Some parties may content themselves with the rewards of office or with presiding over an efficient government, while others seek to remake America. A direct line connects privileged partisan actors and their goals in wielding power. Parties' search for funding, and donors' concomitant motivations to give, condition their goals, and so we ask both about who funds each prophet of party, and how those funders relate to other facets of party. Finally, we apply Tocqueville's venerable distinction between great parties "more attached to principles than to consequences" and "to ideas rather than to causes" (1966, 175), and small parties, for whom private interests and pragmatic power-seeking define and delimit their vision. If the labels of "great" or "small" party seem, to the contemporary eye, fusty or else overly subjective, they usefully fuse what parties *are* and what parties *do*, and so capture the possibilities for the political regime to accommodate partisan actors' visions of democracy.

Democratic Institutionalists

The Democrats at their party's core suffer from the ailments of a hollow age, constantly engaging in the art of the deal within their own party. Even more than their counterparts in the Republican establishment, Democratic Institutionalists lack recourse to a shared, affirmative language of *party* tradition and lineage beyond celebrations of particular politicians' leadership and denunciations of intransigent opponents. McGovern-Fraser's children have grown up to become the party establishment (Miroff 2007), but, squeezed between the regular and reform traditions, the role of Democratic Institutionalist has not been an easy one. On the one side comes accommodation to the party's many stakeholders, itself a reflection not only of the party's coalitional diversity but of the less reformist strands in its heritage. On the other side lies the commitment to continual reform in search of a common good.

In program and organization alike, Democrats stand out in the modern era by their association with the politics of straddling. The *groupedness* of the Democratic coalition of interests is more visible and pronounced than in the GOP case—comparatively speaking, the seams show (Grossmann and Hopkins 2016). The party's twentieth-century transformation on civil rights has hardly solved for the party of "out-groups" the thorny electoral and coalitional politics of race and what detractors term "identity politics" in the twenty-first century. So, too, the Democrats remain cross-cut and compromised programmatically on questions of political economy. Their historic New Deal commitments, reinforced as sorting removes the moderates and conservatives who long frustrated liberals' ambitions (e.g., Abramowitz 2010), stand often in tension with increased support from the upper-middle class (Geismer 2014; Gross 2000). The rising costs of campaigns and the long decline of organized labor have helped to ensure that the Party of the People relies for financial support on business and super-rich donors (Hacker and Pierson 2010; Ferguson, Jorgensen, and Chen 2013).

Some Democratic Institutionalists, at their most candid, echo the new political realists (their scholarly champions) in emphasizing the unromantic exigencies of elections and the political inevitability of mammon. Hillary Clinton, in her own moments of frankness during her nomination battles with Barack Obama in 2008 and Bernie Sanders in 2016, sounded just such notes—to her political detriment (Klein 2016). Far more often, with the language of participation the coin of the realm, the institutionalists dare to voice old defenses of party regularity and pluralism only sotto voce.

If pragmatic Democratic Institutionalists shy away from open statements of party principle, so, too, do exponents of a somewhat different strand in this tradition, one that seeks good government and looks to the common good. Though these Democrats aim to reap the rewards of good policy, they feel no need to make the connections to the grubby world of party politics (Galvin and Thurston 2017). Favoring gentle deliberation over open conflict, they see their moderate-liberal views as the fruits of "simply being reasonable and rational" (Muirhead 2014, 14)—unlike the intransigent and maybe even crazy folks on the other side. Jon Stewart is the patron saint of this view. More consequentially, though Barack Obama also played the Democratic Institutionalist straddle, he never lost "his conviction that reconciling differences contributes more to contemporary democratic culture than exacerbating conflicts" (Kloppenberg 2014, 284).

Whether hard-nosed or high-minded, Democratic Institutionalists prove unable to make positive claims of party legitimacy. In February 2016, Democratic National Committee chair Debbie Wasserman Schultz spoke up for those beleaguered embodiments of institutional party authority, the unpledged "Superdelegates" to the national convention. But she did not offer the straightforward defense that leading, loyal Democrats should have a voice in picking their party's nominee. Instead, she risibly argued that their purpose was to allow grassroots activists a chance to attend the convention without having to run against elected officials to earn a slot (Borchers 2016). Little so perfectly captures the disappearance of a public rationale for party than the Democrats' chair cloaking her own party's hard-fought procedures in a bogus, people-versus-the-establishment cover story. Many of the sincerest partisan soldiers in American politics, are, ironically, also the most cowed and surreptitious in their defense of party itself.

Left Populists

The left dissidents in and around the contemporary Democratic Party chafe against the blatantly transactional politics of a decidedly small party. (The term "populists," which we use out of deference to an ongoing discussion, fits better in a specifically American lineage than in the contemporary global context—see Harris 1973; Kazin 1998.) Such politics, in their view, explain the Democrats' present electoral woes (e.g., Action for a Progressive Future 2017). Bernie Sanders in 2016 came close to winning the nomination of a party that he steadfastly refuses to join, despite loyal parliamentary support across a quarter-century in Congress. His candidacy coalesced a broader critique than his candidacy, one that raised but did not answer central questions of party.

Today's left populists embrace radical democracy, but—reflecting the influence of intellectuals like Chantal Mouffe (e.g., 2005)—have less sense of what form the political party ought to take as a means to realize that vision. Cause and justice come before party. Thus, the disconnects between the scale of organizing and the critique of party, and between substance and procedure. Sanders, an ardent admirer of Eugene Debs, ran to recreate and then to transcend the limits of the New Deal order. His internal critics look also to feminism and the black freedom struggle. Yet Sanders's call for a "political revolution" hardly embraced the radical possibilities in mass politics that such a lineage might suggest, instead leaning hard on the tradition of procedural reform.

Like the framers of McGovern-Fraser, and before them the Progressives, left populists elevate openness, decry grubby deals, and show impatience with any special role, in nominations or elsewhere, for long-serving party functionaries or elected officials. Yet where reformers in the 1970s put procedure on a pedestal, left populists, impatient with manipulable rules and anxious for substantive change, show little serious interest in it. "Superdelegates" come in for special opprobrium, as part of an abiding, perhaps even conspiratorial interest in the activities of the Democratic National Committee, imputed with powers far beyond its actual remit. Nor do the left dissidents embrace party democracy even as aspiration. Their justifications, instead, are instrumental. Calls for openness in opposition to closed primaries soon become defenses of engaged participation in support of delegate-selection caucuses. And after Sanders, in a concession not uncommon from winning candidates, extracted a 2016 platform much to his liking, the erstwhile opponents of overweening parties became positive apostles of party responsibility, urging candidates from Hillary Clinton on down to fall in line behind the stated positions of the Democratic Party. Throughout the caterwauling and factional struggle, a left vision of party remained tantalizingly just out of reach.

Establishment Republicans

Mainstream conservative Republicans in the twenty-first century, doctrinaire heirs to the tradition of Ronald Reagan, embody some of the very deepest paradoxes of party hollowness, joining tenacity with weakness and militancy with lassitude. Another juxtaposition helps to set the puzzle of modern Republicanism in relief. In the drama of Donald Trump's capture of the party's presidential nomination, coverage and commentary often depicted a team of sober-minded "grown-ups" scrambling belatedly but earnestly to resist a political force they associated with reckless extremism—and, more to the point, electoral weakness. In the years leading up to 2016, however, that very same staid establishment had become the subject of increasingly alarmed diagnoses depicting the modern GOP as an extremist "insurgent outlier" in American politics (Mann and Ornstein 2016, xxiv) driving forth "a slow-moving constitutional crisis" (Hacker and Pierson 2015, 60). To distinguish Trumpist populism from the GOP mainstream is correct—Trump's takeover truly was a hostile one. But the longstanding interpenetration of ethno-cultural and nationalist elements speaks to the distinct incapacities of the party to claim internal authority and police boundaries.

Establishment Republicans, more so than their Democratic counterparts, do have a shared story they tell themselves and their cadres to cement loyalties to a party lineage: that of the modern conservative movement. The postwar remnant, the Goldwater insurgency, and the apotheosis of the Reagan presidency all provide the narrative backdrop for a party catechism—a language of common purpose and commitment—recited by virtually every leading GOP figure (Edwards 1999; Phillips-Fein 2011; Tanenhaus 2017). Behind that lingua franca, however, is a decidedly more pragmatic coalitional and electoral bargain. GOP electoral success over the last half century has ridden the realignment of the South and the potency of racial resentments and cultural grievances felt by white voters, North and South. Appeals that speak to identity and culture have won the party majorities—which in turn have facilitated a policy agenda advancing regressive economic and fiscal policies far dearer to the party's donors than its voters (Edsall and Edsall 1991; Francia et al. 2005; McElwee, Schaffner, and Rhodes 2016).

Trump instinctively identified and exploited that gap in his nomination campaign, doubling down on the virulent politics of in-group identity while jettisoning rhetorical or substantive fealty to the economic side of the conservative catechism. Remarkably, Republican elites' "what-would-Reagan-say" charges of ideological apostasy fell largely on deaf ears, undercutting establishment Republicans' key claim to party stewardship. Once Trump's unlikely candidacy led to Trump's unlikely election, however, the GOP establishment proved characteristically disciplined in coalescing support for their new president and sustaining—however unsteadily—the basic GOP bargain in governance.

The tests that Trump's presidency poses for the American political system are thus *fundamentally party tests for the Republican Party.* Animated by cycles of insurgency and the language of ideological purity, the GOP has shown itself disinclined to police boundaries and set lines (the "cordon sanitaire") that cannot be crossed. Here the historical experiences of conservative parties that proved weakly resistant to radical infiltration—that lacked, in Daniel Ziblatt's words, "the capacity to stimulate but subordinate outside groups" so as to balance party activism and temperate forbearance (2017, 49)—become illuminating, and worrisome. Facing a substantively disaffected rank and file, an array of conservative institutions structured to stoke permanent outrage at GOP capitulation, and a decreasingly resonant rallying cry for the party itself, establishment Republicans proceed full tilt down a political highway devoid of guardrails.

Right Populists

With the election of Donald Trump, the United States found its own version of a revanchist right populism that has manifested itself, in various guises, across the globe. "People who work hard but no longer have a voice," he told the Republican convention in language that uncannily matched scholars' definitions of transnational populism, "I am your voice!" (Mudde and Kaltwasser 2013; Müller 2016; Finchelstein 2017).

Right populism is, in a curious sense, the tendency in contemporary American party politics least riddled with inconsistencies: it is fundamentally anti-party. And it has a dispositive resolution to any tensions inside its worldview: the privileged partisan actor under right populism is unquestionably the leader and the leader knows best. That leader's legitimacy is rooted in an essential connection with supporters among the people, whom the leader conjures up, and for whom the leader alone may speak.

Right populism ceaselessly exploits divisions between the people and the forces out to thwart them, while denying political parties their place as mediating institutions and their role in restraining the baser passions. While parties themselves would not wither away, what Schattschneider long ago described as "[t]he zone between the sovereign people and the government, which is the domain of the parties" (1942, 15) empties out. The usual meso-level players inside parties, group or politician, Blob or otherwise, may serve an instrumental but not a legitimizing function. Ironically, for an ideology that celebrates the traditional ties of church, family, neighborhood, and, at times and more ominously, race, the political party, maybe *the* defining intermediary institution in civil society, has no meaningful role to play (Mitchell 2017; Mus [Anton] 2016).

New Realists

Cutting deliberately against the grain of pan-ideological sentiments concerning the benefits of transparency and appeal to political principle, scholars and journalists loosely grouped under the moniker "new political realism" offer hardnosed counsel tinged with nostalgia (Cain 2014; Pildes 2014; La Raja and Schaffner 2015; Rauch 2015; Persily 2015). Their prescriptions aim to channel power and resources away from ideologues and toward formal parties. Because parties are the only institutions in the system tasked chiefly with winning elections, they have incentives toward moderation and bargaining. Stronger formal parties, the new realists suggest, can rescue us from polarization.

The New Realists' comprehensive critique of the "romantic" reform tradition indicts its misbegotten efforts to keep money out of campaigns, bring the grassroots into party decision making, and let the sunshine of transparency disinfect political and legislative relations. All of these, they contend, have rendered the political system prisoner to extremists and purists who prevent the "everyday give-and-take of dickering and compromise" that American political institutions require to function (Rauch 2015, 2).

The nostalgia that suffuses their provocations is for the pragmatic transactionalism that distinguished American parties from their nineteenth-century heyday into the later twentieth century, celebrated in a lineage that runs from George Washington Plunkitt (Riordan 1963) to James Q. Wilson's *The Amateur Democrat* (1962). The new realists notably echo the institutional arguments offered by the anti-McGovern-Fraser Democrats who organized the Coalition for a Democratic Majority in the early 1970s (Kemble and Muravchik 1972). Though dutiful in acknowledging the infeasibility and undesirability of replicating old-style machine politics under modern conditions, the New Realists emphatically embrace mercenary motivations over ideological zeal. Nathaniel Persily, a leading new realist, has defined his view as a "'pro-party' 'bad-government' approach" to analysis and reform (2015, 126). The realists envision parties controlled by professionals, funded by pragmatic benefit-seekers, skilled in the art of the bargain, and in the Tocquevillian sense, proudly—productively!—small.

Technocratic Centrists

If the New Realists and their anti-reform reform agenda occupy a cohesive public niche, a far more diffuse but broadly disseminated reform disposition shares with them a common enemy—the politics of ideological extremism—while challenging it from the opposite procedural direction. The Technocratic Centrists see political parties not as the solution to purism but as its handmaiden. For these centrists, policy emerges not from conflicts over values and power but from the rational pursuit of "solutions." The soundness of real solutions arrived at through deliberation and compromise—like the objective "public interest" such solutions serve—is self-evident (Berman 2017).

The assumption of an underlying and unitary common good, distorted by the mischiefs of faction, traces a line from republican thought in the Founding period through the Mugwumps who despaired at parties in the Gilded Age to the technocratic strain in Progressivism. Whether calling for bipartisanship, a third party, or, as the Centrist Project advocates, "America's first Unparty," the centrists seek end-runs around the barriers to solutionism. This tendency, manifested in the output of elite commentators (Friedman 2010; Fournier 2013; VandeHei 2016) as well as splashy efforts like Unity '08,

Americans Elect, and No Labels, serves as a perennial punching bag for political scientists. The centrists' blitheness to the collective logic of party formation is one reason, as is their cluelessness that the substantive commitments they assume an antiparty reform project would advance—business-friendly deficit hawkery, and social liberalism—are staunchly unpopular with the American electorate. By contrast, their outlook on democracy and conflict resonates with enduring popular assumptions (Hibbing and Theiss-Morse 2002).

The language of personal courage and honesty suffuses the Technocratic Centrists' admonishments to public officials. Fittingly for an outlook that tends toward savior scenarios during presidential election years, their institutional prescriptions betray a presidentialist streak—fast-track legislative authority, line-item veto power, quick up-or-down votes on appointments (e.g., No Labels 2011)—running alongside measures to induce deliberation and compromise in Congress (e.g., No Labels 2012). Though they hardly seem to realize the paradox, their discourse on markets, innovation, and disruption sits uneasily with classic Progressive reliance on independent expertise and nonpartisan regulation through multimember commissions (Gehl and Porter 2017). Underlying both tendencies is the desired evasion of organized, enduring conflict in politics—and thus the escape from party politics entirely.

Filling the Void

The hollow parties have proven incapable of bringing order to a politically divided society. For all the important and distinctive understandings of party that cleave left, right, and center, none of them squarely confronts the problem of hollowness—and each in its own way can contribute to the Blob. The promise and peril of parties lie in whether they turn group conflict into principled disagreement or tribal hatred (Berelson, Lazarsfeld, and McPhee 1954, 305–23).

If the diagnosis is hollowness, strengthening parties offers a solution in a polity divided but also disordered. Parties, at their best, offer clear and compelling choices. We have deliberately focused on parties, and not on partisans, on cue-givers and not cue-takers. We take as a starting point voters' lack of sophistication around issues (Achen and Bartels 2016), which leaves the parties' role in shaping the polity all the more important. Party politics, in this view, reflects a clash of interests, with the prize being control over state power and the ability to articulate and enact the party's (partial) democratic vision.

We have no real idea how to heal the partisan divide—nor as a normative matter do we want to. Instead, we seek robust parties with complementary commitments to mobilize voters, define priorities, and organize conflict. We enlist ourselves in the venerable cause of party renewal and embed party renewal in a civic renewal to make parties positive lived presences in citizens' lives. Like the New Realists, we seek to strengthen party, but we emphasize parties not as brakes on polarizing groups and candidates but solvers of collective problems. Like the reform Democrats of the mid-twentieth century, we celebrate parties offering clear and compelling choices rooted in principle (Wilson 1962; Rosenfeld 2018). We seek parties that do active things—starting, critically, with the local parties that do the work at the grassroots.

Given the evolution of norms about intra-party democracy, we call on parties to face the legitimacy problem foursquare. That means party actors will have to go beyond *sub rosa* workaround solutions, and openly and clearly make the case for strong parties. As a scholarly Committee on Party Renewal affirmed four decades ago, "Without parties, there can be no organized and coherent politics. When politics lacks coherence, there can be no accountable democracy" (1977, 494).

4

Saving Democracy from Elections?[1]

Daniel M. Shea

IN LATE AUGUST 1968, Americans watched Chicago police beat and gas young Americans who had gathered to protest the nomination of Hubert Humphrey as the Democratic Party's presidential nominee. It was a disturbing, gut-wrenching spectacle that became known as the Battle of Michigan Avenue. The event was cast across the black-and-white television screens of the nation as if some surreal punctuation to a turbulent decade that saw widespread demonstrations and small acts of defiance. A drive for civil rights had shaken the establishment and mass protests had challenged the legitimacy of a war. Cities erupted in flames and the nation mourned the murder of civil rights leaders, a president, and his younger brother. The country, it seemed, was coming apart at the seams.

And yet, even during the unbridled, transformative period of the 1960s, vast majorities of Americans had faith in their government. Most believed change would come from *within* the system.

Today, one would be hard pressed to find anyone who feels good about the conduct of our politics or the effectiveness of our government. Pessimism has turned to despair and frustration has morphed to anger. Only one in five Americans believe elections make officials responsive and fewer yet trust government to do the right thing (ANES 2016). Many openly ponder if the grand democratic experiment, charted 240 years ago, has run its course. How have things gotten so bad and what happens when the very instrument we rely upon to fix things becomes the root of the problem? Can our nation redeem its democratic character?

This chapter will offer a novel argument—particularly for someone who has spent his career writing about parties and elections. Since the mid-1800s, the United States has defined its democratic character through elections. We have been, in many ways, an election-crazed nation, putting most of our civic marbles in periodic events that choose the personnel of government. But momentous shifts—some building slowly over the decades and others emerging rapidly—have distorted how these contests are conducted and the impact they have on public policy. Elections for federal office candidates, in particular, no longer yield a common good and too often produce results incompatible with our structure of government. Clinging only to elections will only harden cynicism.

But all is not lost. The chapter will conclude with a call for the revitalization of associational life, the channeling of political mobilization through local party organizations, and for the consideration of the various pathways of action. The renewal of America's democratic spirit can only happen through diverse avenues and at the local level.

Breaking Rules, Norms . . . and the System?

The hours and days after an election are always filled with divergent emotions, ranging from relief to regret, joy to despair. The aftermath of the 2016 race was different. Since the advent of sophisticated polling, colossal surprises had been rare. Races can be tight, sometimes too close to call, but true shockers are few and far between. Even seasoned GOP operatives were astonished by Trump's easy win (Ward 2016). His core supporters were euphoric; they had snatched the presidency away from "The Clintons" and "The Establishment" and their outspoken, unconventional hero would renew America. Clinton and her supporters were thunderstruck, despondent beyond measure. Clinton herself was badly shaken, unable to utter a concession speech until the next day.

So, for many Americans, the outcome of the 2016 presidential election was certainly *not* disastrous. While his unfavorable ratings might have been record high, Trump's victory was interpreted by many as a vivid, direct response to a growing list of unwelcome changes in the economy and society. Trump, a truly different sort of candidate, would usher in a new policy agenda. The great, slumbering mass of discouraged and dislocated working-class Americans had risen and pounded its chest. For them, Election Day delivered a long-awaited fundamental change. In states and communities across the country, conservatives were emboldened by the election.

But for other Americans, especially those on the ideological left, Trump's victory was catastrophic. Not only had they lost the presidency in what many thought was a slam dunk, but both houses of Congress were captured by the

GOP. Two-thirds of state legislatures would also be controlled by Republicans and a majority of governorships as well. All this had transpired during a time when more Americans considered themselves Democrats than Republicans. In fact, when it comes to self-identified partisanship, Democrats had been the majority party for decades (ANES 2016).

Still, others started to question the viability of the entire election process. Has the election/democracy nexus in the United States been strained, if not broken? All manners of critiques were offered in the weeks and months following the election, from full-length volumes to opinion pieces (see, for instance, Page and Gilens 2017; M. Cooper 2017; Eichenwald 2016; McGeough 2016; Shea 2017). Did the election punctuate the decline of American democracy?

All this begs the question of what should we expect from elections in the American setting? Pared down, there are four core functions—what we might call the cornerstones of an election-centered democracy.

1. *Create a Dependence on the People*—By choosing the personnel of government, these events should afford citizens the regular opportunity to influence what government does and does not do. "Frequent elections," noted James Madison, "create a dependence on the people."

2. *Reflect the Common Good*—Open, competitive elections should produce outcomes that reflect a broad consensus. The necessity of candidates and parties to mobilize moderate forces to win office should mitigate the weight of radical, fringe elements. Elected officials, the winners, will promote policies pro public bono (in the public interest) because they want to stay in office. Put a bit differently, elections check the weight of those at the ideological extremes.

3. *Produce Stability and Legitimacy*—Elections channel popular dissent, thereby creating stability and legitimacy. Elections should ease mounting social/economic pressures by creating a safety valve—a viable route for addressing big issues. Done properly, competitive elections grant those exercising power the comfort of a social mandate—a widely held view that they have the right to chart the course of public policy. We might not like their choices, but they have the right to be in power, at least for the time being.

4. *Make Better Citizens*—Beyond systemic benefits, elections should turn private citizens into public citizens and make them feel better about their role in government. They should build trust and foster a sense of efficacy. Periodic elections should afford a crash course on the issues of the day and help link like-minded into civic associations.

Chapter 4

A Dependence on the People

Elections should serve as an expression of popular will. "The people are a sovereign whose vocabulary is limed to two words, 'yes' and 'no'" wrote E. E. Schattschneider (1942, 52). We select leaders based on their experience, character, and intelligence, but also their policy positions. This process centers on that rationality—both the voter's and the elected official's.

But do voters pay enough attention to public policy questions to redirect the course of government? Maybe it is not policy issues that drive vote choice, but rather vague, nebulous views of candidate traits and other idiosyncratic factors. There is a long literature on voter information-processing, much of it unflattering (Converse 1964; Niemi and Weisberg 1993; Caplan 2007; Niemi et al. 2010, part II; Nardulli 2005, chapter 2). It is not at all clear that voters have ever absorbed a broad range of information or shifted though competing evidence. It is likely elites have always been able to manipulate mass opinion, to some degree. Heuristics, especially party identification, are used to sort and filter (Berelson, Lazarsfeld, and McPhee 1954; Popkin 1994; Lupia and McCubbins 1998).

But a new volume penned by Achen and Bartels has shaken our understanding of voter motivations. Their book, *Democracy for Realists: Why Elections Do Not Produce Responsive Government* (2016), is aimed at understanding the rationale behind vote choice and party identification. With bushels of data to support their claim, these two authors find that "issue congruence [between voters and parties], in so far as it exists, is mostly a byproduct of other connections, most of them lacking policy content" (301). They argue voters align themselves with racial, ethnic, religious, occupational, and other groups. It is their group identity that determines vote choice, not a particular policy concern or array of policy preferences. People do not seem to like or even understand the policy choices they make.

Achen and Bartels further argue that in most elections the balance between Democrats and Republicans is close, so the outcome often hinges on "pure Independents." This group is also not especially issue-oriented, basing their vote choice on familiarity, charisma, a "fresh face," or other non-policy cues. In this case, the election outcome is nothing more than "random choices among the available parties—musical chairs" (312).

This may help explain the odd coalition that brought Donald Trump to power in 2016. On the one hand, many of the policies espoused by Trump such as tax cuts for the wealthy, the easing of banking regulations, opposition to raising the minimum wage, and scaled-back health insurance guarantees would seem at odds with the concerns of blue-collar workers. But on the other hand, the group identity of his supporters was rather well defined. The heart of the Trump winning coalition was working-class and middle-class white men. Jim Tankersley of the *Washington Post* put it this way: "Whites without a college degree—men and women—made up a third of the 2016 electorate. Trump won them by 39 percentage points . . . far surpassing 2012 Republican nominee Mitt Romney's 25 percent margin. They were the foundation of his victories across the Rust Belt" (2016).

On top of all this is the potentially game-changing development that emerged during the 2016 campaign and in the early months of the Trump administration: "alternative facts" and "fake news." The barrier for evidence has evaporated and emotion-rich information is used to draw more viewers, readers, and listeners. If we add the continual drive for fresh "news," the costs of traditional journalism, and the prospects of meddling by hostile foreign nations, we are left with no consensus or authority. *New York Times* blogger Farhad Manjoo noted, "We are roiled by preconceptions and biases, and we usually do what feels easiest—we gorge on information that confirms our ideas, and we shun what does not" (2016).

Again, citizens as voters are called upon to judge those in power. If officials have done a good job, they are returned to office; if not, they are sent packing. Elections make the governors accountable to the governed. There *must* be an objective standard for the assessment—which is why the constitutional framers put so much stock in a free press. But with fake news and alternative facts, "your side" has *always* done a good job and the "other" party has *always* failed (Shea 2017).

Reflecting the Common Good

Social scientists have long-understood how self-interest in politics could yield a collective good. Anthony Downs in *Economic Theory of Democracy* (1957), for example, argued that rational, vote-seeking candidates and parties will find the center of the distribution of voters. The outcome of government would fit the preferences of the median voter and is the most democratic. The selfish interest of the candidate would yield a common good for the system.

Things have changed since Down's era. First, there is geopolitical sorting, where citizens cluster in ideologically like-minded communities (Bishop 2009). In 1976, about 25 percent of the counties in the United States produced a landslide presidential outcome—meaning the winner received more than 60 percent of the vote. By 2016, the figure had jumped to an astonishing 71 percent. Even though the *overall* Clinton/Trump contest was close, there was a blowout in nearly three-quarters of the roughly 3,200 counties. Clinton won 199 counties by 60 percent or more, and Trump won a staggering 2,035 by that margin. A whopping 40 percent of counties yielded a winner who received over 70 percent of the vote.

But what does sorting have to do with reflecting the common good? Through balances and shared powers, the framer hoped the system would force moderation and incremental change. It would be a stable, safe system, albeit a slow moving one. Compromise was possible because there was a vibrant center in most states and in *enough* congressional districts. Today, few elected officials value moderation. They don't worry about the next general election, but fret mightily about offending their base and the ever-looming primary contest (where only a handful of voters turn out). To their base, any whiff of compromise becomes sedition (although the type of primary system could mitigate this dynamic; see Boatright 2013).

The nature of partisanship has dramatically changed, too. Whereas in the past our attachment to a party was centered on policy disputes or cues from groups and associations, today's version is grounded in the fear and loathing of the other side. Each sees the other party as crazy and even dangerous. Recent polls by the Pew Research Center (2016) finds that the percentage of Republicans who have a very negative view of Democrats went from 21 percent in 1994, to a staggering 58 percent in 2016. The percentage of Democrats who have a very unfavorable view of Republicans went from 17 to 55 percent during that same time period. Why work with the other side when they (or at least their positions) threaten the nation?

Produce Stability and Legitimacy

It is a widely held belief that as public policy veers away from the concerns of citizens, new leaders are elected to correct the course. Elections become a safety valve, expressing majority sentiment. They can even be, according to Burnham, the "chief tension-management device," bringing an "underdeveloped political system" in alignment with "the changing socioeconomic conditions" (1970, 181). Nevertheless, there is powerful new evidence to suggest the actual interests of voters have little impact on the acts of elites after elections. Using a stunningly large dataset—some 1,779 instances between 1981 and 2002 in which a national survey of the general public asked a favor/oppose question about a proposed policy change—Gilens and Page (2014) cast doubt on the "majoritarian theory." They write, "Our analysis suggests that majorities of the American public actually have little influence over the policies our government adopts. . . . America's claims to being a democratic society are seriously threatened." In fact, there are a growing number of scholarly works on the strained, if not broken, link between voter preferences and policy outputs (see, for instance, Bartels 2016).

In a thought-provoking article published in the midst of the 2016 election, scholar Roslyn Fuller (2016) offered another perspective on the elections/policy nexus in the United States. "Americans," she writes, "made one fatal mistake in attributing the fruits of their labor solely to their own hard work, and another in believing that just because they were doing well economically, occasionally voting actually put them in control of the government." Much of the success of our "grand experiment" did not spring from Madison's novel scheme or participatory democracy, she argues, but instead the exploitation of groups (slaves, immigrants) and seemly inexhaustible natural resources. That is to say, elections were an effective placebo so long as each generation had a higher standard of living. But that's gone. The masses are as "superfluous to the economy as they always were to the political system, required to act merely in a superficial capacity as consumers or as voters—roles that have increasingly come to coincide."

Thus an irony: The framers of the Constitution forged a system of checks and shared powers because they assumed social-conflict would define the American condition. Indeed, Madison's "republican remedy" in Federalist No. 10 is aimed at class-based and to a lesser extent, faith-based factions. Recall that Shays' Rebellion, the focusing event that led to the Constitutional Convention, surfaced from economic pressures. But perhaps it was the lack of significant class-based conflict that allowed elections to define our politics. The framers paid scant attention to elections because they assumed a different dynamic—the clash of interest groups—would shape our politics. Economic interests were muted because there were abundant resources and a growing pool of labor (Shea 2017).

Today, no reconfiguration of policies can resurrect the fading American dream. As Nicholas Eberstadt points out in a recent essay, "For whatever reasons, the Great American Escalator, which had lifted successive generations of Americans to ever higher standards of living and levels of social well-being, broke down around then—and broke down very badly" (2017). While some elites may hold the economy remains sound, "this is patent nonsense." It is no wonder that there is growing distrust of nearly every major social or political institution. The American dream is dying.

Making Better Citizens

Finally, one might expect that elections will draw citizens into the political process in sustained, meaningful ways. They help turn private citizens into public citizens, albeit for a brief period. Much of this expectation springs from a belief that elections matter and that their input can make a difference.

The percentage of Americans who believe that elections can make officials pay attention to voters' concerns has dropped from about 65 percent in the mid-1960s to around 25 percent in recent years (ANES 2016). Legitimacy is critical in any system, but it is foundational in a democracy. In a 2017 poll by the *Washington Post* and the University of Maryland suggests waning faith in the process (Wagner and Clement 2017). While the poll finds low levels of trust toward the federal government, which is certainty no surprise, it also finds that pride in U.S. democracy is eroding. "The share of Americans who are not proud of the way the country's democracy is working has doubled since three years ago—from 18 percent to 36 percent." Doubts about democracy are not limited to strong Trump critics. The poll finds that even 25 percent of his supporters are not proud of the way democracy is working. That's a higher figure than for the general public since at least the 1990s.

Rediscovering our Democratic Roots

American history has shown that significant change can occur when average citizens mobilize, lobby elites, take matters to the courts, or seek changes in political culture. Writing of the civil rights movement during the 1960s, the late Howard Reiter noted, "From organizing voter-registration campaigns under threats of violence in the South to massive rallies in the North, the civil rights movement resorted to almost every form of political participation besides voting in order to overthrow the old system in the South" (1993, 4). A more contemporary example might be the drive for LGBT rights. Incredible changes have been ushered in over the last decade, and very few of them by elected officials. By putting our eggs in only the elections basket, so to speak, the will of the people may actually be stifled.

Democracy, in its purest form, is a process that brings citizens together to resolve issues and disputes. This implies face-to-face deliberation—airing your views and listening to the concerns of others. Through discussion and extended deliberation citizens become better informed not only about their own view on a particular matter, but also more sensitive to the opinions of others in the community. As noted by the philosopher John Stuart Mill, "He is called upon, when so engaged, to weigh interest not his own; to be guided in causes of conflicting claims, by another rule than his private partialities" (1861).

Yet participation in contemporary American elections is usually an isolated, individualized act. We discuss candidates and platforms prior to the election with friends and family, but when it comes to our behavior (casting our vote), it is a private matter, done in the concealment of the polling booth. By turning elections into an individual act, private interests are more likely to displace the public spirit. In other words, is it possible that the current model discourages thinking about the collective? The long-term stability of a system is predicated on citizens looking beyond their own short-term interest to the general welfare. The privatization of politics makes that less likely.

If elections no longer fuel the democratic process in the United States, are there other viable pathways of participation? Fuller suggests the prospects are grim: "Under the present constitutional system, there simply isn't much that those masses can threaten [public officials] with. They are as superfluous to the economy as they always were to the political system, required to act merely in a superficial capacity as consumers or as voters—roles that have increasingly come to coincide" (2016).

But is the patient terminally ill? For instance, could social media-based involvement spur meaningful engagement, as many have conjectured? Social media engagement has mockingly been dubbed slacktivism and arm-chair activism. Several years ago, Gladwell offered a swat at any relationship between social networking sites and broad democratic engagement. Contrary to the hopes of the "evangelists of social media," he argues new modes of communication have not drawn young citizens into the political fray. "Social networks are ineffective at increasing participation—by lessening the level of motivation that participation requires" (2010). Empirical findings connecting acts of support online and subsequent cost-intensive behaviors have been muddled—at best. Boulianne recently conducted a meta-analysis on the relationship between social network engagement and broader political involvement. Her findings suggest a small positive relationship but notes studies relying on panel data are less likely to report positive and statistically significant coefficients, compared to cross-sectional surveys (2014).

One of the defining characteristics of contemporary politics is the breadth of political engagement. While levels of turnout have remained more or less constant, other indicators of engagement have shown remarkable growth. For example, the percentage of Americans who attended a political meeting has more than doubled since the late 1990s (ANES 2016). A 2014 study found that 40 percent of liberals and conservatives remain mobilized during non-election periods (Pew Research Center 2014a). Americans of all stripes stand ready to engage.

We might consider the Tea Party movement. It is hard to dispute the influence that the Tea Party had during Barak Obama's administration. Who could have anticipated rancor over raising the debt ceiling? And what about the steady drumbeat for the repeal of Obamacare? How many Americans had ever heard of sequestration prior to the Tea Party? Who could have imagined that John Boehner's troubles would come from the right? The movement was certainly not as organic as initially thought, but it is only honest to admit that much of the smart money in politics during the last two decades has been spent on group mobilization after the polls were closed.

There is evidence that the political left has gotten the memo. Beginning with huge demonstrations the day after Donald Trump's inauguration and continuing at numerous venues, particularly the town hall meetings of federal legislators, progressive groups have sprung to life. As with the Tea Party, it's likely that this mobilization comes from both professional groups and the anxieties of average folks. In April of 2017, Massachusetts Senator Elizabeth Warren (2016) echoed the call for a new form of activism:

> This is not about what happens every four years, or what happens four years from now. We have to be in this fight right this minute. This is what has changed in democracy in America. It's not the case that we can simply put this off and every four years we'll all kind of get interested in one big race—or maybe every two years for congressional races or Senate races. . . . We have to be engaged, and we have to be engaged right now. I mean, between now and the end of the day. (NRP Interview, June 27, 2016)

But local interest mobilization is not a new tool. How might this approach be refined for the twenty-first century? There is no "silver bullet" reform, but the renewal of *local associational life* offers much hope. From food and employment, to housing, recreation and culture, Americans are discovering the power and potential of "local." In some ways, the argument will parallel Levin's conclusion in *The Fractured Republic* (2016) regarding the revival of the middle layers of society—families and communities, schools and congregations, charities and associations, local governments and markets. Junger's latest work (2016) strikes a similar note: "We have a strong instinct to belong to small groups defined by clear purpose and understanding—tribes." He suggests local connections will be the key to our psychological well-being, and the same can be said about our politics.

What is more, there is a growing understanding that deep cultural differences will continue to make inclusive, national policy solutions difficult. As Levin notes, "We are now a highly diverse and multifarious society defined by its profusion more than its solidity" (2016, 186). For decades, conservatives clamored for local control, but today many on both sides of the ideological divide understand that reaching a collective good is less likely for issues linked to rights and equality, especially given the ideological homogenization of communities. For conservatives and liberals, "new federalism" is an increasingly accepted response to the strains of the federal policy morass.

All this underscores a key change in the American party landscape. Since the 1970s, the national and state party organizations have become revitalized and once again relevant, due in no small measure to mounting resources, an expanding network of allied organizations and campaign expertise. But local party committees, once considered the key cogs in the electoral system, have withered. There is some evidence that these structures are hanging on and in some way adapting to the social media age (Roscoe and Jenkins 2016), but they have little resonance for younger citizens (Shea and Green 2006) and few candidates pay them even scant attention. But throughout American history, local party units have been the entry point for generations of citizens coming of age. They encouraged some citizens to run for office (while filtering out others) and performed a host of social functions. For nearly 200 years, local party committees were the intermediary between private citizens and their government. One might hope that along with the growing movement to resurrect the "local" that party structures might find new life and new meaning. We might also aspire that these revitalized organizations expand their efforts beyond elections to also include effective approaches to better shift public policy to reflect the interests of their local partisans.

Elections have consequences. It matters that Donald Trump was in the White House and that the GOP controlled both chambers of Congress after the 2016 election. We will all continue to pay close attention to this dimension of politics if for no other reason than that they are narrative-driving spectacles, guaranteed to rack up viewers, ratings, and hits. But elections matter less than we think and less than at other points in our history. They have become the show horse, when what we need is a work horse. It is a mistake to imagine that elections will, by themselves, compel the governors to heed the wishes of the governed; they are foundational, but clearly not transformative events.

Even the supporters of the victorious candidate will get frustrated by the slow pace of meaningful change and it's fair to say that the scope of policy adjustments after "big" elections can be narrow. There is more than an ounce of validity to George Wallace's adage that there's not a "dime's worth of difference between the two parties." It is also certainly true that Congress seems mired in gridlock and we have less confidence that elections are fair— and that the "best" candidate wins. The role of big money can be upsetting, to be sure. And yet, those who sit in positions of power are better able to bend government outputs to their interests than those who do not. Barack Obama might not have been able to usher in all or even most of his "change" agenda, just as Donald Trump will probably not transform the economy. But they took up residence in the White House and their opponents did not.

One of the grand canards of our politics is that voting defines democratic engagement. We will sometimes hear that if you don't vote, you should keep quiet. Non-voters lose the "privilege" to air concerns. Whether this silly notion grew naturally like a weed in the garden or was planted as yet another hegemonic tool can be debated another day. But we do know that political activism in a democracy can move along many different pathways. Many of the most portentous changes in our government and society occurred despite repeated expressions of the majority's will. The solution to our troubles, as it is in any vibrant democracy, is not one mode of activism or another—but *all of the above.*

Note

1. Portions of this paper were published in Shea, Daniel M. 2017. "Our Addiction to Elections Is Killing Us," *The Nation.*

Part II

Party Activists

5

The Power of a Narrative

Donald Trump and the Republicans

Jeffrey M. Stonecash

THE ELECTION OF DONALD TRUMP presents an interpretative challenge. Throughout the 2016 elections, he was seen as having questionable character and as lacking the temperament to be president. He had a long string of bankruptcies, raising questions about his business acumen. He would not release his tax returns. He taunted others and lied regularly. He was a powerful divisive force, inflaming passions against minorities. He relentlessly presented a portrait of a nation in decline. His slogan, "Make America Great Again," summarized his theme: America had once been great, but no longer was.

Equally important was his explanation for how this happened. This was brought about by "stupid and corrupt" elites. He made that remarkably clear in his inaugural address:

> For too long, a small group in our nation's capital has reaped the rewards of government while the people have borne the cost. Washington flourished—but the people did not share in its wealth. Politicians prospered—but the jobs left, and the factories closed. The establishment protected itself, but not the citizens of our country. Their victories have not been your victories; their triumphs have not been your triumphs; and while they celebrated in our nation's capital, there was little to celebrate for struggling families all across our land."

Trump's solution was to "drain the swamp," a phrase that suggested that American government was dominated by people who were destroying America for their own personal gain.

The concern here is why Donald Trump's presentation connected with enough voters to win. What was it within the electorate, and particularly the Republican electorate, that resulted in the election of someone of questionable character who painted such a negative view of American society? What has changed in recent decades that made such a negative presentation appealing, or at least acceptable? Who did his ideas attract? By multiple accounts, much of his electoral base was the white working class. If that is accurate, why did those voters support a man with a long history of stiffing blue collar workers?

There are two somewhat complementary approaches to trying to explain any election outcome. One explanation focuses on coalitional politics: what themes are expressed and what types of people support a candidate. The other focuses on narratives each party presents as to how it will respond to social and economic problems. Both approaches are at work at the same time, but the emphases in conducting analyses differ.

The first approach focuses on how many voters have certain dispositions or opinions and how successful a candidate is in communicating stances, attracting those favorably inclined, and mobilizing them to vote. What partisan and policy appeals did Trump make, how many held opinions similar to his, and how well did he do in attracting their support? Was he skilled at animating and attracting those driven by racial resentment, authoritarianism, cultural resentment, anger about illegal immigrants, or anti-intellectualism? Or, was he appealing to those experiencing economic stress? The essence of this approach is that issues and stances are used to connect with groups of voters. Voters may not be ideological, but they possess party identifications, general policy concerns, or social identities and these factors drive voting. Campaigns consist primarily of trying to connect with specific groups and attract their support.

Although the focus on individual attributes has considerable merit, it neglects something very important. The narrative approach focuses more on contextual conditions and how the candidates exploit them with arguments about how to respond to current conditions. Franklin Roosevelt responded to the Great Depression by presenting government as a mechanism to problem solve and help those suffering. Lyndon Johnson capitalized on a time of liberal ascendancy by proposing programs to enhance equality of opportunity. Ronald Reagan responded to an economy in disarray by arguing government was interfering too much, and tax cuts and regulation would revive the economy.

The argument to be presented here is that Donald Trump presented his own narrative. He argued that the society and economy of America are in decline. He would reverse the trends in America and "make it great" again. He presented vague policy proposals, but he did present a clear sense that "stupid politicians" were the source of the problems. Perhaps most importantly, despite all of the claims that Trump was different, he embraced the essential argument the Republican Party has presented in recent decades.

This analysis proceeds as follows. First, the conclusions of the coalitional politics approach will be briefly summarized. This approach has considerable merit, but the reasons to be cautious in treating them as a full explanation will be presented. Then the narrative approach will be presented and its implications for assessing coalition approach examined.

Coalitional Analyses of 2016 Results

A central theme of many analyses of the 2016 election is that Trump successfully appealed to two groups of individuals. First, with high levels of partisan polarization within the electorate, Republicans gradually came to the conclusion that Trump was better than Clinton and they "came home" to vote for their party candidate. Second, he was also able to appeal to those seen as aggrieved about various matters or intolerant of those different. He received strong support among those resentful of blacks (Klinkner 2016) and immigrants (Wood 2017). In this regard, his language and criticism attracted voters focused on white identity (Tesler and Sides 2016). His emphasis on law and order attracted strong support among those anxious about disorder (Taub 2016). In general, it was widely stated that he drew upon a less tolerant non-college-educated electorate. These analyses are reflective of a broader argument that Republicans spent the past half-century incorporating socially conservative, non-college-educated whites into their ranks (Frank 2004), to the point that these voters became the dominant faction within the party (Drutman 2016). Trump combined the Republican base prior candidates had attracted plus the aggrieved, but with perhaps greater support among the aggrieved than prior GOP candidates.

These analyses have considerable validity, and there are, to be sure, Americans who are racists and believe non-whites are inherently inferior. There are also those intolerant toward immigrants, diverse values, and homosexuals and who dislike the cultural changes that began in the 1960s. But the issue is whether these indexes are just about racial resentment. There are reasons to be cautious about these indexes. First, analyses using various resentment/intolerant scales are cross-sectional within 2016. Clearly, those higher on these scales voted strongly for Trump, but is this different from prior years? First, the overall level of resentment was not higher in 2016 than in prior years. Trump appears to have mobilized those high on this scale a bit more, but that only continues a trend that has been developing for decades (Enders and Scott 2018). Even if he did increase his appeal among the resentful relative to prior Republicans, his positions may have also alienated those less resentful such that his net support was no greater.

Second, the overall level of resentment was expressed by their intolerance when voting for Trump. But another interpretation is possible: resentment may reflect perceptions of fairness, whether one has to play by the rules and whether the "system" has become rigged against those who have lived by playing by what they thought were the rules (Edsall 2017d). Bill Clinton once said, "The American Dream is that if you work hard and play by the rules you can go as far as your God-given talent can take you" (Hochschild 1996, 18). What if the supposed resentment is really a reflection of a sense that playing by "the rules" is not working, with some people getting an advantage because of social sympathy for past treatment (Williams 2017; Edsall 2017c)? The issue is one of validity. Do these indexes measure intolerance or a sense that "the rules" for success should apply but don't? What is the resentment about? Despite all the discussion of Trump's support from white working voters, some caution is warranted in assessing their relative importance. Whites without a college degree have been voting Republican for decades. Those without a college degree or with a high school or less degree have voted Democratic in only four of the last seventeen presidential elections. It is not new that whites are voting Republican. What is different is that in 2012–2016, those worse off economically voted against the exiting administration's party to a greater degree than in prior years (Stonecash 2017).

Economic Conditions and Seeking Answers: The Power of Narratives

The background to such narratives involves economic context—trends in the American economy in recent decades. The central economic fact of our recent decades is economic stagnation for some and significant gains for others (Urban Institute 2017). Median family incomes have not grown for years (Leonhardt 2014; Chen 2016). Workers with less education are experiencing economic decline (Shapiro 2018). The differences in how people have fared by education levels go far beyond current wage rates. Inequality in net worth levels of households have increased, with those with less education suffering declines and those with more education experiencing increases (Fry and Kochhar 2014). People with less education are less likely to be married, which means fewer units with two individuals earning income (Parker and Stepler 2017). People with less education are less likely to have jobs that provide health insurance (Barnett and Vornovitsky 2016). They are more likely to experience social isolation (Chen 2016), health problems (Ehrenreich 2016), and higher suicide rates (Case and Deaton 2015). In short, a multitude of problems come with less education and lower incomes, and these problems have been getting gradually worse since the 1970s. A 2017 report found that 40 percent of workers struggle at some time to pay for necessities (Consumer Finance Protection Bureau 2017).

There are two main narratives of what is shaping job and economic prospects in America. Conservatives argue for the virtues of free markets and the detrimental effects of government. They argue that economic growth is being held back by government policies. In contrast, liberals argue for the importance of government policies in limiting and mitigation the excesses of capitalism. Only a "mixed economy" will thrive, protect citizens, and distribute benefits widely. Globalization is of increasing importance in both narratives, but plays out very differently in the two.

These narratives are crucial to voters who are trying to understand the conditions of their lives. The former is simple, intuitive, and has become dominant; and it was central to the success of Donald Trump. He was able to exploit an enduring Republican narrative to win traditional Republicans and those seeking policies to improve their fortunes—including many resentful of their situation.

Embracing the Conservative Narrative

Conservatives have devoted considerable attention to developing the argument that free markets work better than government managed capitalism (Mayer 2016). They argue that free markets are not only more efficient and productive, but maximize the prized value of freedom (Friedman 1962). Conservative think tanks argue that the economy and incomes are not growing because government makes it difficult for businesses to grow (Brooks 2010). The corporate tax rate in the United States is among the highest in the western world. To the extent that government takes the profits of business, there is less money to invest in new equipment and products and less money for hiring new workers.

The ability of business to grow is further hindered by excessive regulations. There are costly labor regulations and too many expensive environmental regulations. "Our current regulatory burden is not only a strain on job growth, it is preventing many would-be entrepreneurs from starting their own business" (Mandelbaum 2017). Government adds burdens to business through rigid rules and laws which create high wages and benefits for union workers. All these regulations make it difficult for business to grow and compete. They limit the freedom of job creators to use their capital and private property to create business and jobs. Businessmen are the "job creators" of the economy. "Takers" receive benefits supported by taxes paid by job "Creators," who are penalized for achieving (Eberstadt 2012).

The answer is to reduce taxes and regulations, which will allow businesses to expand. It will encourage entrepreneurs to invest and take risks that may generate more profits, and more jobs, which will, in turn, create more sales and higher incomes. Tax cuts and deregulation will expand economic activity and ultimately generate more tax revenue for governments, so there will not be larger deficits (Norquist and Lott, Jr. 2012).

This narrative is part of a larger story that conservatives have built over the last 50 years that government actions and programs have a detrimental impact on American society (Ornstein and Mann 2016). Children are not receiving a good education because government allows unions to resist accountability and protect bad teachers (U.S. Department of Education 1983). Government programs to help the poor create dependency and discourage the development of the personal responsibility that leads to economic success. (For an overview of this debate, see Brewer and Stonecash 2015.) The ultimate effect of a too-generous safety net is that too many people become dependent on government and withdraw from the labor force. If there is a problem of many people not faring well in the American economy, it may be cultural in that many have lost the right work habits because of the safety net and cultural decline (Sykes 2011; Murray 2012). If businesses and work efforts were encouraged more, the economy would flourish.

Despite all the discussion that Donald Trump was a wild card populist who did not fit with either party, he embraced the essential Republican logic, adopted one seemingly heretical stance, and then added other specific culprits causing the economic "carnage," creating a politically appealing narrative for those not faring well. He argued "We are the highest taxed nation in the world" and that there were far too many regulations. He embraced the essential supply-side logic that business would increase investment and jobs if only their profits were not taken by government. The issue of whether consumers have the income to consume products was not seen as something government might affect. The capacity to consume would rise as business rose and paid workers more.

Trump also embraced non-economic elements of conservatism that are sometimes linked to the conservative narrative on the economy (Cox, Lienesch, and Jones 2017). He made strong appeals on national sovereignty and national security, adding a foreign policy dimension to his claim that "we don't win anymore." Here his mantra was "America first" in international relations. Trump also courted religious conservatives by promising to pursue policies to restore traditional mores. At one point he suggested that women having an abortion should be punished—somehow. He promised to change the tax laws to make it easier for congregations and religious organizations to engage in politics. Finally, Trump stressed law and order, praising the police and first respondents—and strongly supporting the right to keep and bear arms. Indeed, he accused Hillary Clinton of planning to undermine the Second Amendment. Many of these themes were covered by his promise to appoint a judicial conservative to the vacant Supreme Court seat.

The Trump Embellishment

At the same time, Trump offered a heretical embellishment of the conservative narrative. He claimed that trade was hurting workers because United States officials had negotiated bad trade agreements. Global elites and globalization were moving well-paying jobs out of the country. Political elites were corrupt and were facilitating these changes. They were accepting trade agreements, such as NAFTA, that moved manufacturing jobs to Mexico and elsewhere.

His other crucial addition to the conservative narrative was to name specific culprits who were taking jobs from American workers from within the American borders: immigrants, especially but not exclusively those who had entered the country illegally. In addition to taking jobs from American workers, immigrants were bringing drugs and crime, exploiting welfare programs, and living off taxpayers. They were threatening American culture. Elites were accepting the entry of millions of illegal immigrants who were willing to work for less than American workers, taking their jobs and driving wages down (Merry 2017).

His promise was to renegotiate bad trade agreements and prevent—and even remove—illegal immigrants. "Stupid" political elites were allowing the destruction of American manufacturing and he would reverse the trends. These actions would return well-paying manufacturing jobs, which would be filled with American workers. Much like FDR had his "economic royalists," Trump had his elites who were harming America. Trump's bad elites were politicians and "The Establishment." He presented himself as a businessman who could implement the logic of this narrative. He was able to capitalize on a negative sense of the direction of America within the electorate.

His positions provided an answer to the tension within the Republican coalition. The party had spent the last few decades assembling a coalition that was libertarian economically and conservative in social policy (Dionne, Jr. 1996). That created a continual tension within their party in that the churning of the economy, led by business decisions, could be destructive to communities (Moretti 2013). Factories and jobs were moved where costs were cheaper, often making life very difficult for workers. Trump recognized that many workers and families were losing as economic change unfolded. His uniqueness was in his answer to the tension created by continual economic change. The tension was that it was business decisions that were harming American workers. His creative answer was to not blame business but to take a populist stance and present himself as speaking for the people and against political elites. Political elites were out-of-touch "experts" who were benefiting and were corrupt. As he stated in a *Wall Street Journal* op-ed,

> The only antidote for decades of ruinous rule by a small handful of elites is a bold infusion of popular will. On every major issue affecting this country, the people are right and the governing elite are wrong. The elites are wrong on taxes, on the size of government, on trade, on immigration, on foreign policy. (Oliver and Rahn 2016, 189)

The answer was to cast aside political experts and rely on a businessman who was not part of the corrupt elites. As he stated in his convention acceptance speech, he would be "their voice" and "only I" can solve these problems. He would fund his own campaign. Republicans did not want to discuss the effects of the "creative destruction" that business creates as new businesses form and old ones die. He avoided the problem of the cumulative impact of business decisions by blaming political elites for problems.

Just as important as his narrative, he was also the only one to be trusted to explain this to his supporters. He relentlessly criticized mainstream news outlets as corrupt, hiding the reality of what government was doing, and as producing "fake news." That meant that criticisms of his arguments were driven by malice of the sources and were not to be trusted. He was a disrupter who would change a corrupt system, free businesses to grow, and provide good jobs for "the people."

These doubts about government have been relentlessly reinforced by a growing conservative media that presents an image of America in decline (Perlstein 2012) and sees government as both ineffective and detrimental to economic growth (Hemmer 2016). Conservatives rely on conservative news outlets such as FOX, which consistently presents the narrative that free-markets work best and that government policies and regulations restrain growth (Pew Research Center 2014c). This anti-government narrative is appealing to conservatives. It fits with their instinctive reactions and it seems logical and simple and has won considerable acceptance among Republicans.

Trump's Style

A persistent criticism of Trump involves his style. He projected a blunt and crude (demagogic and bombastic to his critics) style that connected well with alienated voters. Conservative voters saw elites that were not preserving the economy or values. That perception creates a state of mind about politicians. David Frum expresses it well:

> White Middle Americans express heavy mistrust of every institution in American society: not only government, but corporations, unions, even the political party they typically vote for—the Republican Party of Romney, Ryan, and McConnell, which they despise as a sad crew of weaklings and sellouts. They are *pissed off*. And when Donald Trump came along, they were the people who told the pollsters, "That's my guy." (2016)

As another student of the Republican electorate put it,

> Scratch a Trump supporter, and you're likely to find someone deeply pessimistic about America and its future. Few believe that he will be able to bring back the good times (however they define them) because they're convinced that the system is rigged: The "deep state" is too entrenched, the demographic tide too advanced and the global elite too powerful to allow real change. Still, they appreciate President Trump for fighting the fight, especially when it involves going against the wishes of his own party and the customary norms of presidential behavior. (Kabaservice 2017)

Trump's supporters found someone who expressed their dislike of elites (Pew Research Center 2012). He was "the Abbie Hoffman of the right," mocking propriety and conventional norms (Brooks 2017). His behavior was an asset to some, not a detriment. To ideological conservatives, his behavior was to be tolerated if he would deliver on deregulation, tax cuts, and imposing socially conservative norms. To those resentful about changes in America, his style was a positive because it spoke to their frustrations. Indeed, a substantial percentage of the electorate says they do not trust government data, such as the unemployment rate (Rampell 2016). They don't believe "their side" is getting fair treatment in political debates (Fingerhut 2015).

The Liberal Narrative

Liberals present another narrative about what is affecting workers in America. It is more complex and less amenable to present during a campaign. Their interpretation begins with recognition that economic change is relentless and driven by technological innovation, transportation, and labor costs. At one time, production and consumption were confined to local communities because of the costs of moving goods. Then transportation costs declined and trading goods increased. That was followed by a greater ability to move the technology of production elsewhere to exploit lower labor costs. Apple could move production of iPhones to China and then sell that product to U.S. customers (Baldwin 2016). This created a continual movement of manufacturing from high-wage countries to low-wage countries, while taking advantage of lower transportation costs to bring goods back to industrialized nations. Further diminishing rewards to labor is that manufacturing has become much more efficient, with far fewer workers needed to produce more output (DeSilver 2017). These changes are detrimental for U.S. workers, but it yields products available at much lower costs, making higher standards of living available.

Globalization has accelerated in recent decades and has been accompanied by steadily growing inequality in the distribution of income and wealth. To some, this is simply a natural reflection of the growing returns to education. Those operating in an information and technology driven economy fare better and others do not fare as well. It may create difficult situations for some as jobs disappear or shift to metropolitan areas, but change is inevitable.

The liberal narrative also identifies economic inequality as a major problem. The issue is whether inequality is inevitable in a changing economy. In recent decades, the bulk of increased income has gone to the top 1 percent (Piketty 2017). Liberal critics of growing inequality argue that this increase is not just a natural development of capitalism. Inequality has been increased by policies that diminish income gains for middle-income workers and increase them for the most affluent (Hacker and Pierson 2016). Thus, the liberal narrative sees inequality as a pursued policy, not something inevitable. Unions provide a means of leverage for workers to obtain higher wages. Conservatives have enacted right-to-work laws that make forming unions harder. Employers have moved pension plans from defined benefit to defined contribution commitments. More employers are making workers sign noncompete clauses, which prohibit workers from seeking offers of higher pay from competing companies. Workers are increasingly being required to sign contracts mandating that they take employment discrimination cases to arbitration where they do not fare as well as when they ban together in classaction lawsuits. Companies are allowed to classify any worker making more than $23,600 as management, so they can be required to work extra hours without overtime pay. These policies limit pay increases for workers and have created a steady divergence between productivity and the median family income since the 1980s. Productivity has continued to rise, but the income going to workers has increased very little in the decades since 1980.

The affluent directly benefit from other policies. Over time, those in the top one percent have steadily accumulated more capital assets. The returns from capital are taxed at lower rates, allowing even greater accumulations of income among those wealthy. The tax laws further increase inequality by allowing large-income deductions for retirement accounts and second home mortgages. Trust funds can be used to pass wealth onto children. Tax laws allow the affluent to claim tax deductions for contributions to think tanks that promote their agenda. Hedge-fund managers, who manage other people's money, are allowed to treat their fees as capital gains, and pay a much lower rate on the income they earn. The wealthy can fund lawsuits such as that which resulted in *Citizens United*, which allows the wealthy to spend even more to present their arguments during campaigns. CEOs of companies are awarding themselves greater and greater compensation, much of it in the form of stock options. In recent years, corporations have used much of their profits to repurchase company stock with corporate profits, boosting the values of stocks and the compensation that executives receive in stock options. CEO compensation, compared to average workers' pay, has steadily risen.

Given all these changes, liberals argue that there is a need to provide a public safety net for those who are harmed plus job training and education to improve their employment prospects. Wise fiscal and monetary policy plus a host of public investments, business regulations will to improve domestic market performance, while expanded trade, immigration, and international cooperation will help on the international front. Higher taxes on the rich and businesses will pay for these efforts, while helping to reduce economic inequality.

To many Republican voters, the liberal narrative was unpersuasive because it increased the role of government and decreased the role of the private sector. Here Trump's embrace of the conservative narrative was effective politics. Trump's embellishment of the conservative narrative spoke to many voters harmed by economic change, who under other circumstances might have found the liberal narrative persuasive. He promised to restore jobs and income to these voters by direct and aggressive action against well-defined targets. These targets included some targets of liberal policies—corporations and the wealthy—but also many government policies and the experts that managed them. Trump would push back against economic change and confront those who betrayed America, in the name of the self-determination, personal security, traditional values, and national identity. (See the closing ad for the Trump campaign, "Argument for America, accessed October 20, 2017.)

The Trump Coalition Revisited

Voters react to narratives based on their predispositions, their information sources, and the logic of arguments presented to them. In 2016, the combination of these factors made a substantial proportion of the electorate receptive to Donald Trump. It is no surprise that there were endless essays about Trump's "populism." His language suggested that he was a populist (Molyneux 2017), but the reality was much different and far more complex.

Republicans embraced Trump's argument that America is declining economically and faces eroding cultural values. Republicans have accepted this pessimism about the country's future. They see immigrants as taking jobs and changing the culture. Their trust in government has declined steadily since the 1970s. They don't believe "their side" is getting fair treatment in political debates. Trump's argument fit well with this Republican electorate. He presented himself as representing a movement to unseat a corrupt political establishment that was selling out American workers. He would fix things by "draining the swamp," which he meant as diminishing the influence of government elites. He was a populist, but with a twist. Populism often means an attack on corporate elites and wealth, but his attack was upon government elites, saying they were faring well, while harming workers. He was a wealthy businessman and knew how to create economic growth. Trump would cut taxes and regulations and the economy would flourish, providing more good paying jobs. He embraced the religious right and reassured the culturally conservative that he would pursue policies to restore traditional mores. These Republican doubts about government have been relentlessly reinforced by a growing conservative media such as FOX that presents an image of America in decline and sees government as both ineffective and detrimental to economic growth.

Donald Trump's electoral coalition was a mix of economic and social conservatives (Carnes and Lupu 2016). Traditional conservatives were willing to accept his flaws as long as he stood for limited government, lower taxes, and deregulation. Likewise, social conservatives put up with Trump's background and lifestyle in hope of conservative social policy, and especially a good Supreme Court nominee. Their acceptance of Trump was made easier by the rising tribalism and dislike of the other party (Abramowitz and Webster 2016).

Trump added to the Republican base rural residents who felt left behind and thought government supports the undeserving (Hochschild 2016), and working class voters struggling economically. Many had voted for Obama but found no improvement in their lives and decided to give Trump a chance (Sides and Tesler 2016). Others were alienated from a Democratic Party that they saw as dominated by urban elites out of touch with mainstream values (Edsall 2017b). It is not an ideologically unified coalition. To label it as comprising a single type misses its complexity.

6

"The Mandate of the People"

The 2016 Sanders Campaign in Context

Julia R. Azari and Seth Masket

T HIS CHAPTER SITUATES the 2016 Democratic presidential campaign of Bernie Sanders within the long history of democratic claims in intra-party conflicts. We examine the Populist arguments for political reform in the 1890s and how those became incorporated into the Democratic coalition, as well as the failed presidential nomination bid of William McAdoo in 1924. These findings suggest that modern-day arguments for openness, transparency, and democracy within the Democratic Party saw their genesis far earlier than is generally understood, and that populist appeals to democracy can have destabilizing consequences further down the road.

Intra-party Democracy: Complexity and Counterclaims

Modern presidential nominating conventions are known for their predictability and camera-ready displays of support for the nominee, usually someone chosen months earlier. The 2016 Democratic National Convention broke with this norm. Although the four-day event in Philadelphia showcased the party's nominee, former senator and secretary of state Hillary Clinton, supporters of her primary rival, Senator Bernie Sanders (I-VT), disrupted the image of unity. While Sanders and Clinton had a few notable policy differences, the main objections raised by Sanders's supporters at the convention were over process—they claimed the contest had been "rigged" and that their voices had been silenced. Internal party democracy had become the core rationale for his candidacy.

What is democracy and how does it apply to political parties? These questions defy simple answers. Political scientists—primarily writing about comparative democratization and democratic theory—have clashed over the core properties of democracy, whether it is a continuous or dichotomous concept, and even why it is important.

Democracy is a multi-faceted concept. Some theorists have defended a procedural definition, arguing, as Adam Przeworski (1999) does, that "voting generates winners and losers, and it authorizes the winners to impose their will, even within constraints, on the losers. . . . It is the voting that authorizes coercion, not the reasons behind it." Other perspectives emphasize the importance of deliberation and substantive representation. Amy Gutmann and Dennis Thompson (2002) argue in favor of deliberative democracy, in which expressing reasons and continuing a dialogue beyond the point of decision making are critical to the process. Democratic theorist Iris Marion Young also highlighted the importance of inclusion for democracy, arguing that "the normative legitimacy of a democratic decision depends on the degree to which those affected by it have been included in the decision-making process and have had the opportunity to influence the outcomes" (Young 2000, 6).

Procedural and substantive definitions of democracy both play a role in our account of early democratic struggles within the Democratic Party. We address the development of direct primaries, a plebiscitary turn, and the larger implications of the principles that emerged in that debate for Sanders's 2016 candidacy. However, the intra-party debates that brought about these changes also featured arguments about which voices were elevated and which groups within the party were afforded dignity and a seat at the table. Meeting standards like inclusion, as Young prescribes, present thorny questions for parties: it is difficult to assess who constitutes the critical constituencies within a party and who must be consulted in order to make decisions legitimate.

Despite these kinds of ambiguities, two developments inform the 2016 Sanders case. First, the adoption of more open, plebiscitary forms of decision making has been associated with more liberal candidates and perspectives in the Democratic Party (Miroff 2007), while reassertions of party control, such as the adoption of Superdelegates, have been the result of drives to move the party back to the center (Norrander 1992). The second factor is the emergence of a norm within the party that decision making, especially about presidential nominees, should be democratic. This norm has generally been characterized by a broad focus on voter input, castigating efforts at party control as "backroom deals" (Schor and Glaister 2008).

Untangling the normative questions about how intra-party democracy should be assessed is beyond the scope of this chapter. However, we attempt to understand how party actors have used the concept and sought to employ it for political gain in the context of intra-party conflicts. As we note in the introduction, contemporary politics places a high value on the rhetoric of democracy, without a clear definition of what democracy means for internal party dynamics.

We begin with two basic, and somewhat paradoxical, hypotheses. First, U.S. political parties have endeavored to become at least nominally more democratic over time. They have opened up participation in nomination decisions, mainly in the form of binding primary contests to choose delegates. The Democratic Party has adopted a number of rules in an effort to foster representation among women, minorities, and the LGBT community (Schickler 2016).

Second, unlike states or other types of organizations, parties undergo democratization—or debate about it—while also trying to win elections. We find that democracy claims are often mixed with claims about popular appeal and electoral viability, sometimes including the suggestion that the nominees of undemocratic party processes lack legitimacy and do not deserve to win. Witness, for example, arguments by some supporters of Hillary Clinton's 2008 presidential bid that she was unjustly deprived of the Democratic nomination (while having amassed, by some counts, the most votes) and that her supporters should cross parties to support John McCain (Fairbanks 2008).

The allure of democratic claims within a party is fairly obvious. In any given contest over a nomination or the direction of a party, there tends to be one winner and several losers, and democracy, to put it bluntly, is the argument of the loser. In the framework of Schattschneider (1960), democracy is a way of expanding or "socializing" the conflict so that the weaker faction gains allies. A group or individual who appears to be losing ground in an internal fight may make democratic appeals to a broader base of individuals. This certainly doesn't guarantee a victory, but it makes a loss somewhat less certain.

"Conflicts," Schattschneider notes, "are frequently won or lost by the success that the contestants have in getting the audience involved in the fight or in excluding it" (1960, 4). What's more, the "latent force" (1960, 5) of the crowd presents a tempting target for an actor involved in a political excuse. Why not seek to engage the masses when a conflict is otherwise not going your way? Meanwhile, the actor who was already prevailing in the conflict will likely try to keep new voices out of it, "privatizing" the struggle.

This framework is often invoked in contests between political parties, but it works nearly as well within them. As Ostrogorski and Clarke (1902) and

Michels (1915) noted, parties tend to be run as strong hierarchies, even oligarchies, with a small cadre of elites making the key decisions about whom to nominate, which organizations to include in the coalition, and what public stances to take. But in any given internal party conflict, particularly involving nominations, someone will perceive him or herself to be losing. If it's a close contest (e.g. the factions involved are near parity in size and/or strength), there is a strategic logic in the losing faction socializing the conflict, appealing to a broader group of allies in the hopes of changing the outcome.

At least since the rapid expansion of the direct primary in the early 1900s (and possibly before), parties have had a large group of potential allies within their tents—voters. Voters can, of course, be mercurial in their preferences, and parties are not inherently obligated to follow those preferences. But it is difficult for party elites to make decisions that go against the expressed clear preferences of party voters, if for no other reason than it threatens the ongoing leadership of those elites. Thus, when a losing faction seeks to rally voters to its side, it is seeking to force elites to change their views rather than anger a potentially dangerous opponent.

Historical Legacy

The Populist Party (also known as the People's Party) made use of some of these rhetorical appeals and strategic goals during its heyday in the 1890s. Largely an agrarian protest movement in Western and Southern states, it advocated for farmers, wage workers, and others concerned about massive technological changes and the concentration of wealth and corporate power (Postel 2007). Its 1892 platform urged a host of reforms designed to ease the plight of impoverished farmers, including silver coinage, progressive taxation, shorter work hours, and an end to government subsidies for major corporations. But it also included a number of political reforms designed to make politics more open and accessible, reforms that would be recognized by self-described progressives today as seeking to minimize corruption and open politics to outsiders. Examples include an Australian secret ballot, term limits for presidents, initiatives and referenda, and the direct election of U.S. senators (Populist Party 1892). The surprising strength of the party in 1892—taking 8.5 percent of the popular presidential vote along with 22 Electoral College votes—suggested to the major parties that there was significant potential payoff to wooing its supporters.

Over the course of the next few years, the Democratic Party would come to embrace many of the Populists' economic planks, if not always the ones based on political reform. As Gerring (1998) argues, the Bryan campaign and the experience with Populism fundamentally changed the Democratic coalition and its approach to governing, defining its ideological outlook for the next half century. The Democratic Party "reframed its understanding of democracy from minority rights to majority rule" (193). Its nominees would castigate wealthy corporations that sought to influence political processes, using class-based appeals to rouse suspicion of and opposition to concentrations of money and power. They would view governance in moralistic terms, seeing the state as something to be used to uplift the downtrodden and to erase massive differentiations in power and wealth. Thus the Democratic Party's experience with Populism would shape its later embrace of Progressivism and its policymaking during the New Deal.

According to Gerring (1998), we cannot really understand Franklin Roosevelt's presidency without understanding Woodrow Wilson's embrace of Progressivism two decades earlier, and we cannot understand that without understanding the Populist takeover in the 1890s. Gerring endorses Herbert Hoover's claim that the New Deal was "Bryanism under new words and methods," as well as Sarasohn's (1989) description of Wilson's agenda as "Bryanism with a Princeton accent." It is thus unsurprising to find Democratic rhetoric since that time based upon the ideal that concentration of power is inherently corrupt and that the only way to remedy it is to grant people more political tools for empowerment.

This Populist legacy would echo in the Democratic presidential contest of 1924. A famously messy nomination contest, it saw a large field of candidates, each with notable virtues and vices, and a national convention that took 15 days and 103 ballots to reach a decision. Two early favorites to emerge in the nomination race were New York governor Al Smith and former treasury secretary William Gibbs McAdoo of California. Smith was a favorite of the Tammany Hall organization in New York City and thus had substantial backing among the party's northern urban leaders, including future New York governor and President Franklin Roosevelt. McAdoo had ties to several Democratic strongholds—including southern states and the Ku Klux Klan, as well as his father-in-law and former boss President Wilson—making him seem an attractive potential presidential candidate.

With party leaders either pledged to another candidate or concerned about his own prospects, McAdoo chose a decidedly populist campaign strategy, drawing on his support from rank-and-file Democrats and running against the party bosses. He contested the primaries extensively, and basically dominated every contest to which he showed up, ending up with 60 percent of the total primary vote. He used those primary victories to argue that he was the one candidate with the legitimate support of the Democratic rank and file.

The subsequent Democratic National Convention, beginning on June 24th, was one for the record books. McAdoo and Smith emerged as early favorites, although neither could claim two-thirds of delegates. By the seventy-seventh ballot, calls were being made for both the candidates to drop and make way for a compromise candidate. McAdoo refused and drew on his Populist rhetorical approach, telling delegates,

> I feel that I have to carry out the mandate of the people. I feel that I must stay here and carry on this fight in order that I may not betray the trust the people imposed on me. I will cooperate with all of you in this job as quickly as possible. . . . We are here to do our duty. We have no selfish ends. We are here to serve Democracy and righteousness in this fight. (*New York Times* Staff 1924)

Historians generally describe the divisions among Democrats displayed during the convention to be crippling for the party going into the fall election. It is difficult to test this, of course, and the strong third-party candidacy by Progressive Robert M. LaFollette of Wisconsin deprived Democrats of many votes and only complicates historical comparisons to other elections. Republican Calvin Coolidge was going into his first election as president, having assumed the presidency after Warren Harding's death just a year earlier. Coolidge faced little name recognition, an administration plagued by scandal, and a modest 1.1 percent economic growth record in 1924 (Balke and Gordon 1989). He nonetheless won 54 percent of the popular vote and 382 electoral votes, with Democratic wins limited to the South. Davis only won 29 percent of the popular vote, with LaFollette claiming the remaining 17 percent. It seems reasonable to assume that Democratic Party divisions did the ticket no favors that year.

The Sanders Insurgency of 2016

Vermont senator Bernie Sanders officially entered the 2016 presidential race in April of 2015. A registered Independent who regularly caucused with Democrats in the U.S. Senate, Sanders stated his intention to run for the Democratic presidential nomination, thus becoming the most visible challenger to Hillary Clinton. By virtually all available metrics, Clinton was the preferred candidate of party elites long before 2016. Democratic members of Congress, governors, and state legislators were overwhelmingly endorsing her (Bycoffe 2016), and many former staffers for President Barack Obama and Super PACs aligned with him were supporting her (Confessore 2015).

Sanders nonetheless made significant inroads in the nomination contest, gaining rapidly in opinion polls as the early state contests approached. He substantially out-performed the early expectations of political observers, roughly tying Clinton in the Iowa caucuses and besting her by more than 20 points in the New Hampshire primary. Clinton would ultimately win the contests in 34 states and territories, with Sanders claiming 23. She won the majority of pledged delegates to the Democratic National Convention that summer, but also maintained an overwhelming advantage among the roughly 700 unpledged delegates, or "Superdelegates," that consist largely of officeholders and other party elites.

Clinton's early support from the Superdelegates and her endorsements and polling advantages in many delegate-rich states made the delegate math highly challenging for Sanders, despite his successes in early states. When urged to drop out of the race for the sake of party unity by Clinton supporters and political observers, Sanders pushed back angrily (echoing McAdoo from 92 years earlier), calling such demands "outrageously undemocratic" (Wagner 2016).

Sanders and his supporters particularly targeted the party's Superdelegates (Neidig 2016). Those Superdelegates emanating from states Sanders won by large margins, he maintained, should switch their votes to him: "If I win a state with 70 percent of the vote, you know what? I think I am entitled to those Superdelegates. I think the Superdelegates should reflect what the people of the state want" (Alcindor 2016). The Sanders campaign's efforts to woo Superdelegates already committed to Clinton bore little fruit, and may have even alienated some (Foran 2016a). But highlighting this aspect of the Democratic nominating system set off a heated debate within the party about representation and democratic legitimacy. One notable example of this campaign included an online argument between Superdelegate Kim Metcalfe, a DNC committee member from Alaska (where Sanders had won nearly 80 percent of the support of caucusgoers), and Levi Younger, a young Alaskan who had caucused for Bernie Sanders (Linkins 2016). Metcalfe explained in a Facebook discussion that she was continuing to support Clinton "because I believe Hillary Clinton would be a better president. End of conversation." Younger pushed back:

> And that's why people get angry. Bernie supporters can be quite vapid. But voting in opposition to what we voted for is only supporting the idea that Hillary and her supporting superdelegates are in the pockets of others. Bernie won in Alaska. End of story. Your personal preferences for president are represented in your vote as a citizen. Not as a representative of your state.

Metcalfe responded,

> I'm in the pocket of no one. I have no financial connections to Hillary Clinton or any other Democrat. I am a retired union representative. I put in my time

in the trenches for 40 years, and I really object to someone like you who has probably done nothing except caucus telling me what to do.[1]

Further fuel was added to the fire when WikiLeaks published thousands of emails it had hacked from DNC servers shortly before the Democratic convention. While those emails demonstrated no voter suppression or obvious forms of corruption, they did reveal DNC employees to have personal biases against Sanders. Sanders's supporters largely saw this as further evidence of the illegitimacy of Clinton's nomination (Samuelsohn et al. 2016).

Clinton's securing a majority of delegates did little to stem these arguments. Nor did the events at the Democratic convention, despite Sanders endorsing Clinton. Sanders's supporters orchestrated anti-Clinton protests, with marchers chanting "Hell, no, D.N.C., we won't vote for Hillary." One protester said he'd "rather watch the D.N.C. burn" than see Clinton nominated (Gabriel 2016b).

Arguments over party democracy, with the DNC and economic elites as twin foils, also emanated from the Sanders campaign. Sanders wrote in his book about how "the DNC announced only six debates. It was clear they wanted to give Hillary Clinton's opponents as little public exposure as possible" (Sanders 2016). Describing the significance of the Sanders campaign's use of small donations and various online organizing platforms, Andrew Chadwick and Jennifer Stromer-Galley wrote "Sanders's campaign is a reassertion of the power of the grassroots-netroots. It puts a dent in the top-down, analytics-driven, inauthentic, and disempowering side of contemporary election campaigns" (2016, 288).

Political observers often portrayed Sanders's insurgency as simply the liberal mirror of Donald Trump's campaign—an anti-establishment effort fueled largely by angry white voters dissatisfied with the state of American politics (Leland 2016). But Sanders's approach had a particular lineage in the Democratic Party. Concerns about corrupt establishment figures and unfair and undemocratic party decision-making processes, all resulting in illegitimate leadership, echoed the Populist rhetoric of the 1890s and various internal party disputes across the decades. The parallels between 1924's and 2016's Democratic contests are especially prominent. In both, a popular choice within the party knew he was coming up short in the support needed to secure the nomination and resorted to Populist appeals to activists and diatribes against party insiders.

Discussion

The cases we have presented here demonstrate that arguments for a truly democratic Democratic Party long precede 2016. Claims that the party's nomination process should represent the will of a majority of its voters or delegates (or "citizens," in democratic parlance) were on full display during McAdoo's failed candidacy in 1924, drawing on the legacy of Populism, and followed by debates over party reforms later in the century.

It was perhaps inevitable that such claims would be introduced into party discussion following the move toward mass democratic involvement in them in the late 1800s and following the introduction of the direct primary at the turn of the century. Yet as these accounts suggest, there were some costs associated with the embrace of internal party democracy. McAdoo's invocation of a mandate for his claim to the nomination may have undermined support for the party's eventual nominee and helped cost the party the fall election in 1924. The efforts of Sanders's supporters to undermine the democratic legitimacy of Hillary Clinton's nomination in 2016 surely led some to abandon the Democratic ticket and helped to produce the Trump presidency. Such concerns continue to motivate party reformers in 2018.

It is obviously problematic to describe American political parties as democracies, but it is not an altogether incorrect appellation. We may note that these organizations are not pure plebescitary democracies today, nor were they perfect oligarchies a century ago, but that they have become more democratic over time. And with this increased democratic quality has come an insistence by rank-and-file members that legitimacy rests on their consent. This may or may not improve the parties' functioning, but it suggests that the genie of democratic legitimacy is not easily returned to its bottle.

Note

1. It should be noted here that Metcalfe's interpretation of her role as a Superdelegate was entirely consistent with the goals of the Hunt Commission that created the category in the early 1980s. Superdelegates were seen as a source of nominating power retained by party establishment figures should primary voters be leaning toward a candidate who seemed to be a poor choice for the party. Superdelegates may have been useful to Walter Mondale's nomination campaign in 1984, although they generally haven't demonstrated much willingness to tip the scales toward a nominee not preferred by party voters.

7

State Party Activism in 2016

Daniel J. Coffey

THE 2016 PRESIDENTIAL NOMINATION produces divisive primaries on both sides, historically unusual in the contemporary era. Intra-party divisions, largely absent from the political system for the past two decades, were seen by some as reemerging with insurgent campaigns in both presidential nominations. The steady path to ever-more polarized parties seemed to have reached a breaking point and the 2018 nomination struggles may indicate the kind of inflection point, in which the trajectory of politics is sent in a new direction. The parties' ability to manage vast coalitions of different groups became too much to bear and the tightly-wound system spun apart under the pressure.

This interpretation is a bit of an extreme. As some research has shown, 2016 has produced largely expected county and state voting patterns, with only minor shifts in support along demographic lines (Hopkins 2017). This chapter assesses the importance of the 2016 election on the state and direction of party platforms. Historically, state party platforms have yielded considerable insight into the nature of party agendas, but also about the federal nature of the party system. Recent research, however, indicates state party agendas are becoming less distinct over time (Hopkins 2018; Schickler 2016). As such, whether the 2016 elections represent a fundamental break from intra-party homogeneity and inter-party polarity, or a continuation in the march toward nationalization of the past decades is crucial to see how 2016 stands.

As such, an empirical examination of internal party agendas is appropriate to assess whether the 2016 contests represent an inflection point on the trend of party polarization. In this chapter, I reexamine state party platforms

(Coffey 2007, 2014). I compare state party platforms by states in two group-ings for each party: on the Democratic side, comparing platforms in states won by Clinton to those won by Sanders, and on the Republican side, states in which Trump won versus those won by other, more establishment-friendly candidates. I also seek in the following analysis to understand how the parties have changed since party agendas can be shaped in ways other than the forms of the party platform. Past historical patterns suggest intra-party nomination fights leave traces in state party agendas as activists seek to have their views formally institutionalized in the party platform (Schickler 2016).

In this analysis, I find little evidence of intra-party factionalism in terms of ideology and only mild differences in issue content. Using unsupervised text analysis methods, I find that the real divisions are between and not within the parties. I conclude by examining the implications for parties and whether this finding represents evidence of stability within each coalition, or perhaps hints at changes in the forms and procedures of party representation. It may be that given the rise of new forms of mass communication, activists may no longer see the value of using formal party mechanisms to shape party ideology and legislative agendas.

Party Nationalization

The story of the 2016 presidential cycle is generally told as a breakdown of party unity. Insurgent candidates challenged party orthodoxy and, at least on the Republican side, they successfully shattered that orthodoxy with issue positions frequently directly at odds with party elites as noted by many other chapters in this book. The cycle also demonstrated potential weakness within the normal institutions' structures and processes of parties. On the Republi-can side, the establishment was largely unable to coordinate an unruly 17-candidate primary and ultimately acquiesced in the nomination of an outsider candidate. On the Democratic side, the party was unable to quell discontent among its progressive base despite strong elite support for the established candidate. Elite endorsements, normally a strong predictor of candidate success in presidential nomination contests, were an unreliable indicator of the contentiousness of the primaries (Cohen et al. 2008).

It may seem, then, that this cycle indicates high-levels of intra-party fac-tionalism, something that has been generally muted in the contemporary era, which is defined by high-levels of inter-party polarization (Abramowitz 2010). Extensive research has shown parties are becoming less heterogeneous across states (Hopkins 2018). Roll-call votes in national legislatures are already well documented as highly polarized, regardless of states or regions

(McCarty, Poole, and Rosenthal 2008). At the state level, measures of state legislatures also showed considerable inter-party polarization (Shor and McCarty 2011).

Importantly, scholars tracing party platforms over time have found that since the mid-twentieth century, party agendas have become far less variable. Hopkins (2018) traced state party agendas on 40 issues from World War I to the contemporary era and found a general decline in the uniqueness of state agendas. Instead, when party agendas vary, they do so because of changes in the national agenda: "Far more than in the past, the state parties now shift their gaze in unison, from education to terrorism or gay marriage as national politics dictate" (Hopkins 2018). Hopkins argues this is largely the result of three factors: a changing media stream directing citizen attention toward national, as opposed to local, stories; a decline in the salience of state or regional identities; and the increasingly nationalized network of interest groups and donors that provide the support for the parties. In sum, the research is clear; party and not region, define the lines of ideological conflict in the twenty-first century: a typical Northern Republican is more conservative than a Southern Democrat.

Theory

Party agendas of course change over time (Noel 2013). Previous research has shown that activist participation is highly variable and conditioned on calculations about the perceived threat to party orthodoxy and opportunities for change in policy positions or agendas (Carmines and Stimson 1990; Karol 2009; Bawn et al. 2012). Presidential nominations fit this threat/opportunity dynamic. The candidate battles are often seen as proxy wars between party factions. In the 1960s, as the process of ideological sorting was getting underway, both parties had unruly conventions in which different factions fought for control of the party. As the sorting process has largely played out, ideological battles have become more muted, while calculations of electability and character have motivated most of the nomination contests in recent years (Cohen et al. 2008). Inter-party polarization is a product of sorting, while in turn also reducing intra-party factionalism (Levendusky 2009a). In sum, activists have largely been able to have their cake and eat it too, without needing to sacrifice policy commitments in the name of electability.

The 2016 cycle presents an interesting test for this interpretation. Both parties had insurgent campaigns that seemed to tap into ideological fault lines. As Carmines, Ensley, and Wagner (2018) find in this volume, ideological conflict is in many ways two dimensional and there are up to five distinct ideological groupings of voters. On the left, Sanders was clearly to the left of Clinton. Clinton's centrism allowed Sanders to stake a position that seemed to more clearly oppose her position; Sanders could be both more populist and more liberal. Trump's position can best be described as orthogonal to the current line of cleavage between the parties, best seen as a conservative populism. Given the large number of candidates, initially the GOP field represented a wide spectrum of policy positions, but as the contest went on, the struggles were reduced in a battle between an establishment candidate, representing a middle point of party ideology, opposed by a candidate presenting a more extreme version of the party agenda.

It is also the case, however, that tonal differences attracted support of different factions. Both Trump and Sanders used more assertive language and styles. Activists, as past research has shown, weight both the electability and the ideological fidelity of the candidates they support. Additionally, affect has been shown to motivate both perceived policy differences and participation (Mason 2015; see also Kimball, Anthony, and Chance 2018 in chapter 12 of this volume). By presenting more aggressive styles, the candidates would be expected, based on past research, to trigger participation from activists calculating that opportunities existed for changes in party policy positions and ideology.

There are many examples of activists entering nomination struggles to effect changes in party agendas and overall philosophy. In the 1960s, as has been well-documented, Goldwater supporters were already present in the 1964 state party conventions, altering nomination rules and state party platforms to undermine efforts of the party establishment to elect Nelson Rockefeller (Busch 1997). At the 1964 convention, Goldwater supporters drafted a weak civil-rights platform in contrast to the more liberal 1960 version (Schickler 2016). An example of platform change that can occur is with regard to abortion policy. Entering the 1980s, many state parties either did not have planks on abortion, or took equivocal positions. For example, in Minnesota, the state Republican Party voted down a pro-life plank in 1982, but voted to accept a similar plank in 1984 (Coffey 2006). By 2000, most state Republican Party platforms had socially conservative positions (Carr, Gamm, and Phillips 2016). In sum, party activists seek to institutionalize their values to become permanent party principles. The party platforms at both the state and national level have traditionally been the vehicle for cementing new policy positions or ratifying the winner of an intra-party struggle.

As such, an investigation of the state party platforms may reveal whether the differences in candidate support represented either new intra-party cleavages or differences in party agendas. Both Trump and Sanders may have motivated the participation of activists, who in turn may have sought to institutionalize their values. The platforms may reveal ideological shifts or evidence of intra-party agenda differences.

Data and Methods

In this study, I will analyze the text of state party platforms to evaluate four factors. First, have there been major changes in state party platform ideology since 2012? Second, is there evidence of internal ideological differences between the states that supported insurgent versus ideological candidates? Third, is there evidence that intra-party conflicts are tonal in nature? Finally, did the insurgent and establishment candidates win states in which the parties emphasized different types of issues?

Given that the common interpretation of state voting patterns is that they indicate potential civil wars within each party, this analysis will proceed by dividing state parties into two groups.[1] Of course, there are limitations to this approach. First, the primaries were not all equally competitive and some of the candidate performances were due to differences in strategy or the allocation of campaign resources. Second, not all states issue platforms and so this analysis can only assess observable differences in platforms. Finally, the platforms themselves are not perfect representations of voter preferences. Ideally, state parties would issue new platforms each presidential cycle. In this case, changes in platform ideology and issue positions would be directly traceable to changes in the external political environment. In reality, many platforms are kept in place, with only minor changes in platform issue positions. In fact, in many states, platforms undergo only minor differences between election cycles.

At the same time, there are good reasons to evaluate whether the nomination battle triggered fights over party agenda and philosophy. As such, I have divided the states by those won by Clinton and those won by Sanders, and those won by Trump and those won by another Republican candidate. These divisions serve as a reasonable proxy for assessing what potential intra-party divisions the candidates tapped into. It is also the case that some of these divisions already existed and were not necessarily triggered by the nomination battle. Platforms can capture preexisting differences within the party coalitions and so even if the nomination battle triggered divisions, the observation of states voting for one candidate versus another should be indicative of both preexisting differences as well as new differences aroused by the presence of new activists. Examining party platforms can, therefore, be used to assess the degree of intra-party disagreement.

Ideology in 2012 and 2016

The dataset includes 61 platforms for states that issued platforms in both 2012 and 2016; 33 for Democrats and 28 for Republicans. To do so, I employed

Wordfish, an automated scoring, which I implemented using the Austin package in R (Slapin and Proksch 2008; Lowe 2015). Wordfish is an unsupervised text analysis method that scales political documents along a single dimension using word frequencies. In the American two-party system, with parties highly polarized along a single dimension, the technique has been shown to accurately place texts along the left-right spectrum (for an example, see Sides 2014).

The Wordfish scores reveal broad differences between, but not within, the parties across both years. Higher scores indicate more conservative platforms, while lower scores indicate more liberal platforms. In 2016, the average score for Republicans (see figure 7.1) is 1.01 and in 2012, the score is 1.00, and the Pearson correlation (.89) is statistically significant (p<.01). For Democrats, the data indicate the platforms were marginally more liberal in 2012 (− .80) than 2016 (− .83), but the scores were similar and the Pearson correlation (.60) between the two cycles is also statistically significant (p< .01). Additionally, the intra-party differences pale in comparison to the inter-party differences. Democratic platforms of insurgent states versus establishment states have virtually identical means Wordfish scores; the platforms in Sanders states are only marginally more liberal (− .83) compared to platforms issued in states won by Clinton (− .81). The Republican platforms reveal more internal variance, but the establishment states have more conservative platforms than the insurgent states and the difference is statistically significant ($p <.05$).

The conclusion is fairly clear. Whatever differences there were between

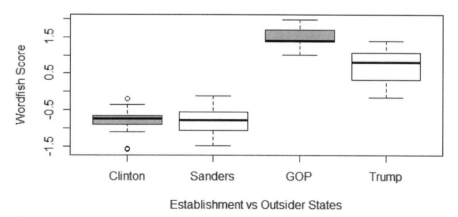

Figure 7.1
Ideological Differences between Establishment and Outsider States in 2016 Primaries.

establishment and insurgent voters, the differences between parties is much larger than the differences within the parties. This pattern is also revealed in figure 7.2. State party platforms in 2016 represented the same language and ideology of 2012. The Wordfish scores reveal some differences in that some states have moved a bit; the Wyoming Democratic 2016 platform has a more liberal platform than the 2012 version, while the South Dakota Republicans score was more moderate. Overall, however, the automated technique is unable to detect evidence that something had changed in 2016, at least in terms of ideology.

Sentiment Analysis

Another angle with which to investigate internal party differences is the emotional tone of the platforms (Hart, Childers, and Lind 2013). There is good reason to suspect that the populist nature of the insurgent campaigns drew support based on the tone, rather than the ideology or the issues that are emphasized. Indeed, as several of the chapters on public opinion in this volume suggest that partisan polarization is affective in nature, and based as much on emotion as cognitive assessments.

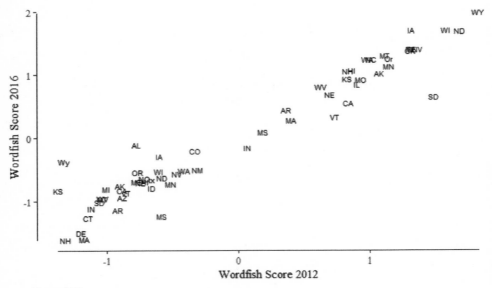

Figure 7.2
Correlation between 2012 and 2016 State Party Platforms.

Tonal differences have been shown to exist. In this case, differences in political tone may be a signal to voters about a candidate's willingness to fight or compromise to further the party agenda. So, activists drafting platforms are likely to find different types of language more appealing. One way to capture political tone is to use sentiment analysis (Liu 2015). Sentiment analysis codes texts based on a ratio of negative to positive sentiments. A positive score indicates that more positive words are used than negative words while a negative score indicates that more negative words are used than positive words. The populist nature of the campaign appeals should be more appealing to activists who draw on negative language as both Sanders and Trump tended to express more anger toward institutions and socioeconomic conditions in the country.

The results, however, are not consistent with what would be expected. Sentiment scores were calculated using the "affin" method, scoring each word as the unit of analysis. The scores range from −5 to 5, with higher scores indicating the words have more positive associations. As shown in figure 7.3, the sentiments of Sanders states were indeed more negative, but the differences (as illustrated by the boxplot) are not statistically significant, even though the Clinton state platforms tended to use the most positive language. Republican establishment states, in contrast, used the most noticeably negative language, while Trump states tended to mirror Sanders states in overall tone. It should be noted that all texts were coded with overall positive average scores and different methods of sentiment analysis yielded positive scores for the platforms. Party platforms are largely free of the vitriolic language often used in contemporary politics.

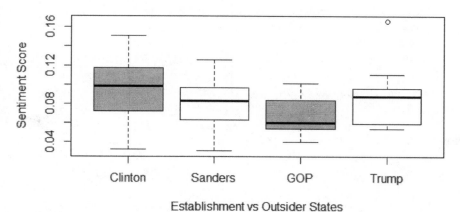

Figure 7.3
Sentiment Differences between Establishment and Outsider States in 2016 Primaries.

Issue Differences between Parties

Another possible source of conflict is over agendas, or issues priorities. My previous research (Coffey 2014) has shown that party agendas are, even if nationalizing over time, not uniform. It is important to remember that in many states, especially those with caucuses, party platforms are still written by activists at precinct meetings. The job of the state party, then, is to accumulate and refine these expressions through a process that builds consensus from the precinct, to the county, and then to the state level. In other states, party leaders, working in a committee, revise and update the platform, sometimes to reflect the agenda of the governor or the state legislature. While Hopkins (2018) provides evidence of nationalization over time, the data-generating process (i.e., how the platforms are written) still leaves room for the state "franchises" of the national party "chain" to create unique agendas. It is possible, then, some of the divisions within the parties are in terms of issue emphasis, rather than ideology or sentiment.

A review of the top words used by the platforms identifies again broader differences between the parties rather than within the parties. Democratic platforms of both types of states are more likely to use communitarian language; words such as "access," "care," "community," "equal," "health," "include," "protect," "provide," and "service" dominate the platforms. Republican platforms tend to use noticeably different language; words such as "children," "citizen," "constitution," "freedom," "family," "limit," "nation," "reduc," "respons," "strong," and "unite" signal their underlying ideology.

A common visual representation is to use word clouds, but these are often uninformative. Instead, figures 7.4 and 7.5 illustrate how the words are related to form topics for each party. The figures show how the parties each draw on different vocabularies to articulate their issue positions. Figures 7.4 and 7.5 illustrate the relationship between these words and how they hint at the topical structure of the word use.[2] Each branch is a cluster of words that correlate in terms of how often they appear together. The analysis is meant to reveal broad differences in how the parties discuss issues, but it should be noted that different specifications of the cluster model will produce different cluster patterns. Democratic platforms generally have clusters that emphasize health care and education in one node (the top node in figure 7.4), followed by less distinct clusters that focus on environmental issues, economic issues, and a related cluster that focuses on fairness and equality. Republican platforms, in contrast, focus on family and social issues in one cluster ("children," "family," and "citizen"), nationalism (top left node) and economic issues (bottom node). The clusters reveal differences in how the parties discuss issues; the Republican discussion of economic issues includes words like

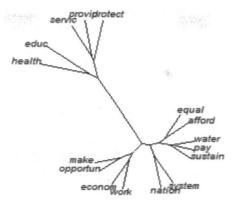

Figure 7.4
Platform Vocabulary of Democratic States.

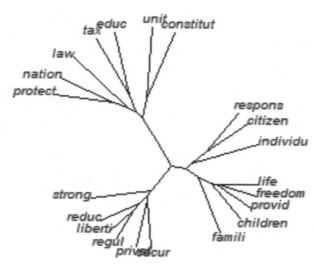

Figure 7.5
Platform Vocabulary of Republican States.

"liberty" and "security," while the Democratic discussion of economic issues includes words such as "access."

Conclusion

The analysis of this paper finds that little change occurred at the activist-level between the 2012 and 2016 cycles. There is little evidence of internal party factionalism in the state platforms in a manner that matches the division between candidates. Additionally, analysis of the sentiment of 2016 state party platforms provide some evidence of tonal differences, but in a manner contradicting expectations. Finally, a brief analysis of party vocabulary use finds that there were no clear agenda differences between state platforms won by insurgent candidates and those won by establishment candidates.

Polarization, at least in this analysis, overrides intra-party factionalism. Certainly, this study has limitations and it may simply be the case that candidate performance and the content of state party platforms are too far removed to adequately answer the research question this chapter posed. Other indictors of convention delegates, voters, and roll-call votes of legislators may be more direct measures of intra-party factionalism.

Nevertheless, as I explained above, in the past, intra-party nomination battles often triggered fights over state party organizational control and battles over the planks of state party platforms. This raises questions about the relevance of established mechanisms for instituting changes in party positions. Traditionally, party platforms represented the best way for factions within the party to formalize their positions and to compete with other factions for establishing the winning viewpoint and for attention from politicians who could enact those policies. The platform, in a sense, represented which faction had won the battle.

In the policy-demander model, the network is broad and made up of many disparate groups (Bawn et al. 2012). Policy changes are as likely to be driven by bloggers, talk show hosts and Twitter feeds as much as by interest groups and activists (Noel 2013). The platform, then, may be a relic of era, an appendix-like anachronism. A more extreme interpretation, one perhaps not at all justified by the data analysis above, but worth pondering nevertheless, is whether the traditional procedures and mechanisms of the party will survive the contemporary era. In this case, activists can achieve electoral success without the party's support. Party power has often been defined as holding monopoly control over pathways to change in both office and policy (Aldrich 2011). Cooperating with a large network of factions may not be selected as the optimal strategy given that social media allow for direct contact with candidates and an ability to sway policy positions. Of course, it is a stretch to conclude this just because the platforms in 2016 did not seem to represent anything different from the platforms of 2012. Yet, parties will have to change as modes of communication, fundraising, and mobilizing support change. A single document to represent the party ideals may be an anachronism, but this could also be a deeper signal of change to come for parties.

Perhaps a more reasonable interpretation is that the institutionalizing of party conflict has yet to occur, much the same way that Republican agendas came to reflect to co-optation of the Reform Party in the 1990s and Democratic platforms often did not fully embrace socially liberal planks until the 1970s (Rapoport and Stone 2005). The 2016 elections may have triggered new activists who, in their focus to support the outsider candidate, overlooked ways to incorporate their ideals into permanent principles.

Notes

1. The breakdown is as follows: Trump (AR, CA, HI, IL, IN, KS, MA, MI, MS, MT, NC, NE, NH, NV, OR, RI, SD, VT, WA, WV); GOP Establishment (AK, IA, ME, MN, MO, ND, OK, TX, WI, WY). For Democrats, the breakdown is Clinton (AL, AR, AZ, CA, CT, DE, GA, IA, MA, MS, NC, NM, NV, SD, TX) and Sanders (AK, CO, HI, ID, IN, KS, ME, MI, MN, MO, ND, NE, NH, OR, RI, VT, WA, WI, WV, WY).

2. I had employed a topic model, but the results were inconsistent. The graphs were created using the R package "ape" to represent a dendogram produced by hierarchal cluster analysis in the shape of a tree. The graph is for illustrative purposes and is not meant to represent the topic models.

8

#Polarized2016

Affective Campaign Rhetoric and Mass Polarization in Social Media

Eric C. Vorst

THE 2016 PRESIDENTIAL RACE was considered by many to be one of the most divisive, uncivil, and polarizing political races in recent American history. According to recent polling by Zogby Analytics, 68 percent of Americans viewed the contest between Hillary Clinton and Donald Trump as being "extremely or very uncivil" (*PR Newswire* 2016). This represented a more than three-fold increase over Americans' views regarding the "extremely or very uncivil" nature of prior presidential contests between Barack Obama and Mitt Romney in 2012 (20 percent), Barack Obama and John McCain in 2008 (18 percent), and George W. Bush and John Kerry in 2004 (15 percent). The open animosity between candidates and their campaigns was evident on the campaign trail, in political advertisements, during debates, and in television reporting. In turn, this behavior produced a super-charged political environment ripe with examples of elite polarization. Such conditions provided an excellent opportunity to study what effects, if any, elite polarization has on mass polarization.

The phenomenon of rising elite polarization has also been accompanied by a concurrent rise in the use of social media as a vehicle for political communication. A particularly popular social media platform for this type of communication is Twitter, which allows users to instantly share thoughts, opinions, and reactions via words, images, and HTML links. One of the most valuable aspects of Twitter is that it offers an immediate snapshot of a person's state of mind; reactions to external stimuli can be measured in near real-time. Just as the conditions of the 2016 presidential race provided an excellent opportunity to study possible links between elite polarization and mass polarization, the emergence of social media as a popular form of political discussion provides an extremely valuable tool for measuring such possible links.

This research examines the extent to which polarizing behavior on the part of elites translates into polarizing behavior on the part of the mass public on social media. It is relevant to the state of the parties, as it contributes to our understanding of social media as a strategic resource for political parties and their candidates. Further, this research adds to the political polarization literature by shedding new light on how the relationship between elite cues and mass polarization is modified by the dynamic environment of social media networks, while also observing how this relationship varies depending upon the mode of delivery.

Political Polarization, Elite Polarization, and Mass Polarization

Political polarization is a defining feature of the contemporary American political landscape. By most measures, polarization among political elites has reached record levels (Hetherington 2009). A primary tool for measuring polarization among elites is DW-NOMINATE (Dynamic Weighted Nominal Three-Step Estimation), originally developed by Keith T. Poole and Howard Rosenthal in the early 1980s. This tool utilizes roll-call vote records by members of Congress as a means for estimating their position on the liberal/conservative ideological continuum. Over time, a clear ideological divergence in voting behavior among political elites has emerged. Republicans are voting in a more exclusively conservative manner and Democrats are voting in a more exclusively liberal manner, while the moderate areas of liberal Republicans and conservative Democrats is progressively shrinking.

Recent research suggests polarization in Congress has become so pronounced that members sharing district borders, yet representing different parties, consistently vote in opposition to each other—even when congresspersons share heavily gerrymandered borders where one would expect some geographical common interests (Andris et al. 2015). These phenomena are indicative of increased polarization among American leaders and are widely considered to influence our political system in a way that causes more harm than good. For example, an increasingly polarized U.S. Congress faces more scenarios where compromise is difficult to achieve, leading to gridlock and, in some cases, government shut downs (Farina 2015).

The extent to which polarization manifests itself in the American electorate is still an open question. Fiorina and Abrams provide strong evidence that most voters have not been influenced by increased levels of polarization among elites (2008). At the same time, polarization can be observed through increased "sorting," where voters' ideological self-placement is aligned with their party identification (Levendusky 2009b). Polarization is also evidenced by a tendency of supporters of one party to follow to demonize supporters of the opposing party (Abramowitz 2013). Further, there is evidence to suggest mass polarization is fueled by deep-seated psychological impulses of "fear and loathing" of members in the opposing political party, especially among those who are in the "out party" (Kimball, Summary, and Vorst 2014).

Recent national polls support the conclusion that the American public is increasingly divided along party lines and, more importantly, separated by a growing gap of partisan identification. The Pew Research Center (2014b) found the percentage of Democrats who were consistently more liberal than the median Republican rose from 70 percent to 94 percent from 1994 to 2014. Similarly, the percentage of Republicans who were consistently more conservative than the median Democrat rose from 64 percent to 92 percent. During the same time span, the levels of antipathy toward members of the other political party more than doubled, with the percentage of Democrats viewing Republicans very unfavorably rising from 16 percent to 38 percent and the percentage of Republicans viewing Democrats very unfavorably rising from 17 percent to 43 percent.

Just as levels of elite polarization can be measured by observing behavior on the part of political elites such as voting records or other elite cues, levels of mass affective polarization can be measured by observing variances in mass affective rhetoric. Questions remain as to whether or not high levels of affective polarization translate into high levels of mass political polarization. However, it is reasonable to believe that such a relationship could exist, as an atmosphere filled with strong psychological divisions could be primed for divisions along other lines, given the proper elite cues are delivered.

Such a possibility appears more likely when one considers that expressions of political polarization in the form of elite cues may have a kind of framing effect on the mass public, wherein expressions of political polarization by elites influences and shapes the mass public's understanding of political reality. Broadly defined, political framing occurs when a story or issue is portrayed using a specific perspective or through a particular lens. Despite being presented with the same set of facts, a person may reach different conclusions depending upon the way an issue is framed. Framing has the potential to be a powerful persuasive tool, as it occurs in a manner that is far less obvious than the traditional means of outlining an argument based upon clearly stated premises and conclusions. If viewed from a theoretical perspective (Blumler 2015), the framing potential of elite cues would equate to elites affecting not only polarized behavior on the part of the mass public (or, "what to think about"), but also potentially affecting polarized political positions on the part of the mass public (or, "what to think about it"). Given the influence of political figures' ideological differences on affective mass polarization (Rogowski and Sutherland 2016), such a causal link is not out of the question.

Affective Rhetoric, Incivility, and Affective Polarization

An increasing body of literature is defining mass polarization in terms of affect. While related to the concept of emotion, affect is best defined as "emotion that persuades." When applied to political polarization, this perspective argues that political divisions in the mass public are driven by hostility toward the opposing party rather than being driven by political ideology. Instead of people with different party identifications opposing each other based upon ideological differences or policy disagreements, such hostility is the product of psychological mechanisms. When affect is defined as a mode of emotional persuasion, opposition rooted in affect spawns behavior that is less cerebral and more about base emotions. When such persuasion is married to party identification and infused within political debate, the results can be detrimental to reasoned discussion. Such partisan discrimination fuels levels of affective polarization that can, in some cases, be equally as strong as levels of polarization based on race (Iyengar and Westwood 2015). These tendencies are troubling, especially given what social scientists know about the myriad divisions rooted in race related issues.

Regardless of whether a causal linkage exists that flows from elite polarization, through elite cues, affective rhetoric, affective polarization, and results in mass polarization, the political communications literature can be strengthened by understanding how different types of elite cues influence affective polarization in different types of interpersonal environments. This understanding is especially important with respect to how elite cues delivered in a live, confrontational, and politically charged atmosphere contribute to affective polarization which, in turn, may be creating conditions that may foster mass polarization in online spaces.

Theoretical Model

The vast majority of prior research on elite cues, political polarization, and media effects has been conducted within the context of the traditional media environment. Prior research on causal links between elite and mass polarization has primarily relied upon evidence citing individuals' positions on public policy issues and party sorting (Fiorina and Abrams 2008; Hetherington 2009; Levendusky 2009a; Abramowitz 2013). While these are useful measures when applied to the traditional media environment, ostensible effects are often separated from their purported causes by a considerable amount of time. This time lag allows for a significant muddying of the waters, as individuals have increasingly more opportunities to be influenced by multiple intervening variables as the time horizon between cause and effect increases. Such a time lag represents significant challenges for measuring a causal relationship between elite and mass polarization in social media due to the fluid nature of social network structures.

A completely different approach is required when testing for potential causal relationships between elite and mass polarization in social media, due in large part to fundamental differences between the social media environment and the traditional media environment. Given the fluid nature of the social media communication environment, it is possible that the influence and reach of elite cues disseminated through social media sources will be different from the same elite cues that would be in traditional media sources. This is especially true with respect to the structural dynamics of social media which often redefine what it means to be a political elite, as members of the mass public can often gain significant amounts of influence within social networks (Freelon and Karpf 2015).

One major advantage of analyzing social networks is that it allows researchers to examine how interpersonal relationships and social neighborhoods form in response to political stimuli in near real time. This theoretical model proposes that potentially polarizing cues originate from elites and enter the communications environment. When the mass public is exposed to these cues, there is a likelihood of increases in mass affective rhetoric which, in turn, could contribute to increases in affective polarization. Due to the unique nature of the social media environment, the mass public can re-enter the communications environment to express polarized cues of their own—not unlike the cues originating from elites. This process may reinforce an increasingly polarized communications environment which, in turn, may create spaces where mass political polarization can thrive. In other words, social media allows for affective rhetoric to not only spread efficiently among the mass public, but to be amplified by members of the mass public as well.

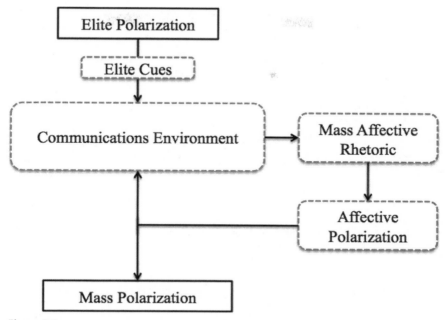

Figure 8.1
Theoretical Model: The Social Media Environment's Role in Transforming Elite Cue Influence.

The following hypotheses are used to measure the extent to which elite affect influences mass affect in social media:

H1: Increases in elite affective rhetoric lead to increases in mass affective rhetoric on social media.

H2: Social networks with high levels of affective rhetoric foster conditions conducive to mass polarization.

H3: Social networks with high levels of affective rhetoric enhance the reach and impact of strategic hashtags.

Data and Methods

This research utilizes a mixed methods approach incorporating content analysis, social network analysis, and visualization. It draws upon a large, diverse, and growing set of data measuring multiple sources of elite cues as well as mass public reactions on Twitter. The dataset used to analyze candidate language in campaign speeches was gathered via *The American Presidency Project*, which is an online source containing over 127,000 official presidential documents dating back to 1789. Social media data was collected using the Twitter REST API on a daily basis from September 1, 2016, through November 9, 2016 to collect approximately 1.5 million tweets. Content analysis was conducted using Lexicoder 3.0, a software application developed by Mark Daku, Stuart Soroka, and Lori Young at McGill University. This software was used in conjunction with the Lexicoder Semantic Dictionary (Daku, Soroka, and Young 2015), which draws upon a dictionary of approximately 5,000 words to measure the positive and negative sentiment in political texts.

When combined with content analysis, network analysis provides a picture of both the nature of political discussion and the efficiency with which this discussion spread throughout members in the network. For example, if content analysis on a specific date demonstrates a relatively high rate of affective rhetoric, but network analysis suggests a weakly connected network, one could infer that the impact of such rhetoric has been mitigated. Conversely, if content analysis alone was used in this scenario, the more likely inference would have been an overestimation of the affective rhetoric's overall impact on members in the network as a whole. Content analysis provides valuable aggregate data, but network analysis puts this aggregate data into context by introducing the critical influence of network structure.

The emergence of social media—and of Twitter in particular—has provided a wealth of new opportunities to utilize social network analysis tools as a means for studying human behavior. Social network analysis goes far beyond the ability to produce "eye candy" in the form of striking and often beautiful visualizations. Social network analysis draws upon empirical data to provide context for relationships between individuals and, in doing so, reveals insight into issue trends, influential participants, and a treasure map for learning more about their predominant characteristics. In this respect, social network is a powerful tool for organizing massive amounts of empirical data and allowing the analyst to identify and focus upon empirical data that is most germane to his or her research question. Today, social network analysis is an invaluable tool for making sense of the millions of interactions that occur on an hourly basis across multiple social network platforms.

Data Analysis

In order to achieve clarity and context in a sea of data, this study focuses on the final ten weeks of the 2016 Presidential Election. This timeframe also represents the "final stretch" of the campaign and is a time during which both the stakes and the emotions of the players are arguably at their highest. Figure 8.2

provides a summary view of aggregate elite affect expressed through tweets by @realDonaldTrump, @HillaryClinton, @GOP, and @TheDemocrats over these final ten weeks, as well as through speeches by Donald Trump and Hillary Clinton during the same time frame. Donald Trump speeches contained the highest overall rate of affective language, followed closely by Hillary Clinton speeches and tweets by @HillaryClinton. Tweets by @realDonaldTrump, @TheDemocrats, and @GOP contained comparatively lower rates of affective language. Intriguing characteristics emerge when delineating between rates of positive and negative affect. Interestingly, rates of positive and negative affect in Donald Trump speeches were roughly the same, as was the case for @GOP tweets. Perhaps even more surprising, tweets by @realDonaldTrump contained noticeably higher rates of positive affect than negative affect. Higher rates of positive affect than negative affect were also seen in tweets by @HillaryClinton and by @TheDemocrats; Hillary Clinton speeches contained nearly twice the rate of positive affect than negative affect.

Observing overall rates of affect is useful for providing a sense of the general sentiment originating from each elite source. These data take on new meaning when measured in a way that accounts for the daily ebbs and flows which occur during the final weeks of a presidential campaign. The first hypothesis predicts that increases in elite affective rhetoric lead to increases in mass affective rhetoric on social media. This hypothesis is tested by first measuring rates of combined elite affect over time originating from Democrat elite sources (Hillary Clinton campaign speeches, @HillaryClinton tweets, and @TheDemocrats tweets) and Republican elite sources (Donald Trump campaign speeches, @realDonaldTrump tweets, and @GOP tweets). Next, rates of combined elite affect are compared to rates of affect in tweets mentioning either Hillary Clinton or Donald Trump.

Figure 8.3 tests for a relationship between elite and mass affect when constrained within the same party. At first glance, the data appear to exhibit corresponding trends between combined Republican elite affect and tweets mentioning Donald Trump, especially during the final month of the election. However, similar trends are not evident when comparing combined Democrat elite affect and tweets mentioning Hillary Clinton.

Figure 8.4 tests for a relationship between elite and mass affect when applied to opposing parties. As was the case with figure 8.3, the data suggest mixed results. While there do appear to be corresponding trends between combined Republican elite affect and tweets mentioning Hillary Clinton, similar trends are not evident when comparing combined Democrat elite affect and tweets mentioning Donald Trump.

There are two likely reasons why there is lack of observable evidence of a causal relationship between elite affect and mass affect in social media as measured by these tests. First, it is possible that the dependent variables—as

Sources of Elite Affect: Rate of Affective Language per 100 Words
(9/1/2016 - 11/9/2016)

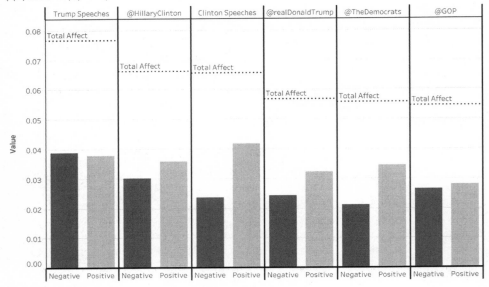

Figure 8.2
Sources of Elite Affect.

measured—lack a high enough level of accuracy with respect to actual discussion regarding the candidates. Given the random sampling mechanisms of the Twitter REST API, it is possible that the data contains inconsistent content variations from day to day, which would lead to an inaccurate measurement when observing rates of affect over time. A second possibility is that the mass public discusses candidates differently when using their full names (e.g., Donald Trump and Hillary Clinton) than they do when using their Twitter handles (e.g., @realDonaldTrump and @HillaryClinton). Future research can address these possibilities by using complete data acquired by paying for access to historical data from the Twitter Firehose.

Interesting findings emerge when focusing solely upon affect in candidate speeches. Figures 8.5 and 8.6 suggest compelling evidence of a relationship between affect in candidates' official campaign speeches and subsequent shifts in affect in tweets mentioning the candidates. This possible relationship exists for both same-party candidate mentions as well as opposing-party candidate mentions, and is especially evident from early October through the end of the election. These findings are noteworthy because they suggest the mode of delivery matters when measuring for a relationship between elite and mass affect.

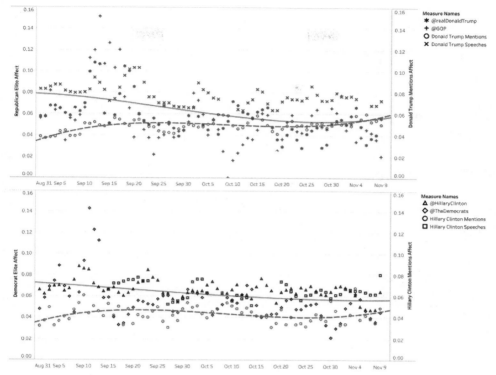

Figure 8.3
Combined Elite Affect and Same-Party Candidate Mentions.

Specifically, there is evidence that elite affect delivered through televised events (such as campaign speeches) has a stronger influence on mass affect in social media than elite affect delivered through social media.

Network Analysis and Visualization

The second hypothesis predicts that networks with high levels of affect will be more likely than networks with low levels of affect to foster the development of mass polarization. This hypothesis is tested by looking for a "Small World Effect" in networks, as indicated by densely grouped communities with few connections to other communities in the network. In such a scenario, individuals are more likely to communicate within cliques and are less likely to be exposed to other individuals in the network. Given this limited

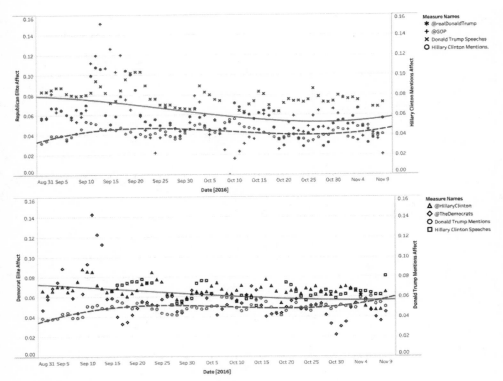

Figure 8.4
Combined Elite Affect and Opposing-Party Candidate Mentions.

exposure to others, these types of networks can foster conditions where mass polarization is more likely to develop.

Figure 8.7 tests for the Small World Effect by examining networks on days with the three highest and three lowest rates of affect in tweets mentioning each of the candidates. Two defining features of the Small World Effect are a high clustering coefficient (indicating a high incidence of network members forming dense communities) and a low average geodesic path length (indicating fewer overall "steps" from one node to the next in the network). In figure 8.7, networks placed in the top-left quadrant are more "small worldly" than networks placed in the bottom-right quadrant. Surprisingly, there was no observable relationship between high levels of mass affect and comparatively high levels of mass polarization as indicated by a Small World Effect. Rather, networks with high levels of affect tended to demonstrate less clustering and more user interaction than networks with low levels of affect. These

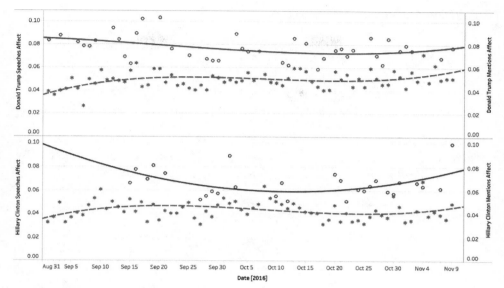

Figure 8.5
Affect in Campaign Speeches and Same-Party Candidate Mentions.

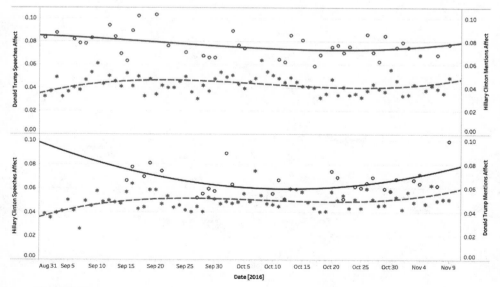

Figure 8.6
Affect in Campaign Speeches and Opposing-Party Candidate Mentions.

findings suggest that mass affect may serve a positive role in encouraging interaction between members in a network.

Despite the lack of evidence of a Small World Effect in networks with high rates of mass affect, an examination of these networks' ability to facilitate political messages still holds significant practical value. This is an area where network visualization offers a level of insight that is difficult to achieve through broad statistical measures of the overall networks. The final set of tests examines the extent to which affective rhetoric facilitates the spread of politically strategic hashtags. These tests focus on high affect and low affect networks both for tweets mentioning Hillary Clinton and tweets mentioning Donald Trump. For each of these four networks, pro-candidate and anti-candidate hashtags are isolated from a list of the top-ten hashtags for that network on that day.

In figures 8.8 and 8.9, pro-Trump and anti-Trump hashtags are highlighted in order to assess their reach and impact on the broader network. As shown above, the network with the highest rate of affective rhetoric was more effective in spreading both pro-Trump and anti-Trump hashtags than the

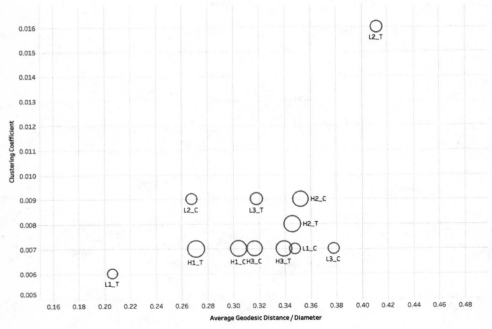

Figure 8.7
Mass Affect and the "Small World Effect."

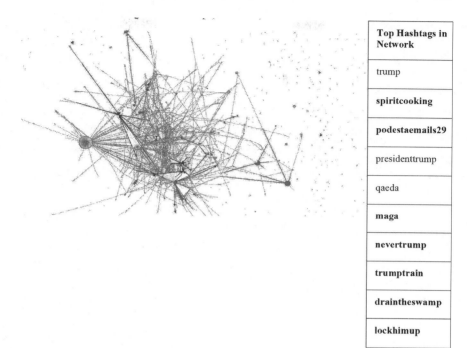

Top Hashtags in Network
trump
spiritcooking
podestaemails29
presidenttrump
qaeda
maga
nevertrump
trumptrain
draintheswamp
lockhimup

Figure 8.8
Reach and Impact of Strategic Hashtags, High Affect Network (0.713) Tweets Mentioning Donald Trump (November 4, 2016).

network with the lowest rate of affective rhetoric. Videos with 3D rendering of these networks are available at http://bit.ly/2y37vvQ and http://bit.ly/2y2poLi.

In figures 8.10 and 8.11, pro-Clinton and anti-Clinton hashtags are highlighted in order to assess their reach and impact on the broader network. As was the case with pro-Trump and anti-Trump hashtags, the network with the highest rate of affective rhetoric was more effective in spreading both pro-Clinton and anti-Clinton hashtags than the network with the lowest rate of affective rhetoric. Videos with 3D rendering of these networks are available at http://bit.ly/2ixqF6P and http://bit.ly/2h60eok.

Conclusions

The explosion in popularity of social media took most observers by surprise. This was also true in the field of political science, as researchers have scurried

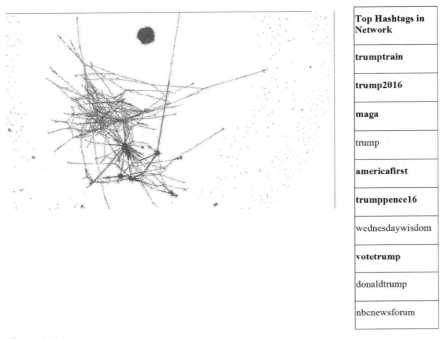

Top Hashtags in Network
trumptrain
trump2016
maga
trump
americafirst
trumppence16
wednesdaywisdom
votetrump
donaldtrump
nbcnewsforum

Figure 8.9
Reach and Impact of Strategic Hashtags, Low Affect Network (0.259) Tweets Mentioning Donald Trump (September 7, 2016).

to play "catch up" in understanding the nature and implications of this new landscape of political communication. Likewise, researchers have been forced to develop new methods and tools to measure and explain phenomena in a manner that takes into account the unique nature of the networked communication environment. The mixed methods approach presented in this research represents an important step in developing such methods and tools.

Does elite affect influence mass affect in social media? There are signs that affective rhetoric on the part of the political parties and candidates on social media does have some impact in the extent to which the mass public uses affect when discussing the candidates. There is stronger evidence that elite affect expressed in the form of campaign speeches has a much more consistent influence in how the mass public uses affect when discussing the candidates in social media. As suggested earlier, this could indicate the power of televised communication—whether this communication is received by the

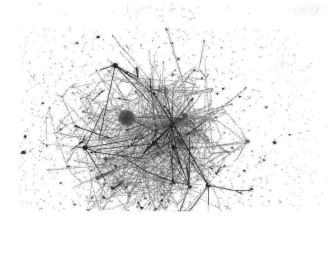

Top Hashtags in Network
spiritcooking
trump
podestaemails29
maga
presidenttrump
qaeda
draintheswamp
nevertrump
trumptrain
lockhimup

Figure 8.10
Reach and Impact of Strategic Hashtags, High Affect Network (0.679) Tweets Mentioning Hillary Clinton (November 4, 2016).

viewer on an actual television or a streaming device like a mobile phone, tablet, or computer. Regardless, these are findings that warrant future research.

The most compelling findings emerge from the network analysis portion of this study, as they present evidence that high levels of affective rhetoric in social networks is not necessarily a negative condition. Further, these findings suggest that measurements of network polarization alone are not sufficient to determine the extent to which a given message will be successful in achieving broad reach and impact in a network. If true, this would have significant implications not only to social scientists, but also to campaign managers, political strategists, and political marketing specialists.

While affective rhetoric can lead to affective polarization which, in turn, can lead to mass polarization, a great deal of this process may be dependent upon network dynamics that may be inadvertently overlooked when using

Top Hashtags in Network
hillary
maga
hillaryclinton
draintheswamp
clinton
trump
evangelicaltrump
podestaemails
imwithher
trumppence16

Figure 8.11
Reach and Impact of Strategic Hashtags, Low Affect Network (0.309) Tweets Mentioning Hillary Clinton (October 18, 2016).

traditional methods of measurement and analysis. This study has provided evidence that high levels of mass affect could be beneficial, as such an atmosphere could more effectively facilitate discussion between individuals with opposing beliefs. Further, such an atmosphere could more efficiently facilitate the reach and impact of targeted political strategies which depend upon the use of hashtags to deliver their message. These are exciting possibilities, as they challenge conventional wisdom regarding the nature and effects of political polarization.

Part III

Party Nominations

9

The State of the Primaries 2016[1]

Drew Kurlowski

T HE 2016 PRIMARY SEASON was an exciting one to follow. Both parties featured long and competitive presidential primaries—a Democratic contest between establishment favorite Hillary Clinton and Independent Bernie Sanders, and a Republican contest between 17 candidates that eventually winnowed down to an attempt by Ted Cruz and John Kasich to disrupt the seemingly inevitable nomination of outsider Donald Trump. With both parties experiencing increased intra-party factionalism and bitter nominating contests that year, one continued refrain has been the need of the party organizations to exert more control over presidential nominations.

However, it is not clear that the parties and rulemaking structures are currently well adapted to suit party needs. In this chapter, I will discuss primary rules broadly, as well as rule changes between 2012 and 2016 in order to grasp the strategies, successes, and failures of the parties in controlling the pace and outcome of their primaries. These rules, including party registration, primary sequencing, and delegate allocation, are perhaps some of the most malleable rules, and offer insight into how parties have attempted to affect change in state nomination systems.

This investigation reveals three conclusions. First, while parties have a good deal of latitude in setting primary rules, some important electoral rules are products of states and state legislatures, and are insulated from party change. Second, it is not entirely clear what effect any changes might have on the electoral process—anecdotal evidence, as well as empirical evidence from scholars is not in agreement as to the direction or magnitude of any effects. Third, and perhaps most important, it is not clear that parties know what kind of change they are seeking within the process, and intra-party factions are not always in agreement on what path to take.

Party Registration

One notable feature of the 2016 primaries was a renewed focus on party registration and rules with regard to closed primaries. Much scholarly and media attention has been paid to a continuum of primary rules, from open to closed. In the most general of terms, closed primaries restrict participation in primaries to those who are registered members of the parties; semi-closed primaries allow undecided voters as well as registered partisans to participate; semi-open primaries permit any voter to participate under the condition that they publicly state a preference; and open primaries allow all voters to participate while keeping their party choice a secret.

The lines between these systems are not always clear. An example of this comes from Michigan, which updated their primary laws in 2011 (Public Act 163 of 2011) to require voters in presidential primaries to make a *written* declaration of party membership before being allowed to vote in a primary. Some listings of primary systems, including the state itself, classified this as a closed system, asserting that the written declaration amounted to a party membership requirement. The state simultaneously asserted that no actual party membership was required to participate (Johnson 2012). This is a contradiction in terms of the definitions offered here, and is only one source of confusion. This rule also highlights the fact that presidential primaries and sub-presidential primaries can have different rules within a state. Here, the written declaration only applied to presidential primaries, not the later state-wide primary. Many states conduct closed caucuses for presidential nomination and open (or semi-open) primaries for other sub-presidential races, effectively using two separate sets of rules.

A second feature of party registration relates to the administration of closed primaries. The 2016 election shone new light on this problem vis-à-vis the pseudo-Independent candidacy of Bernie Sanders. In an interview, he himself admitted the necessity of running as a Democrat in order to overcome the institutional hurdles of an Independent candidacy (Bump 2016a). However, many of his supporters found themselves having a tougher time casting their ballots in closed primary states. Registered Independents who supported Sanders were required to reaffiliate with the Democratic Party before some set deadline in order to participate in these Democratic primaries. This hurdle is specific to registered voters, because those who are not registered to vote may register for the first time, and declare a party affiliation at a date which is often different from the party reaffiliation deadline.

The most glaring example of this rule is in New York, which cuts off reaffiliation 25 days before the *preceding* general election (for the 2016 primaries, this was October 9, 2015—25 days before the November 3, 2015 general election and 193 days before the presidential primary (New York Consolidated Laws, Election Law—ELN § 5–304)). As an interesting aside— two of Donald Trump's children, Eric and Ivanka, missed this deadline to reaffiliate, and were unable to vote for their father in the New York primary. New York is not the only example of early-registration deadlines, but it is the strictest case. Kentucky sets the new year as the deadline, requiring party registrations be changed before December 31st (KY 116.055). New Hampshire closes reaffiliation 97 days before the election (the start of the candidate filing period) but allows registered Independents to affiliate with a party at the polling place. Further, they may then immediately file paperwork to disaffiliate from the party as they exit their polling location. Another six states (CO, CT, DE, ID, NJ, and RI) have a window between 50 to 100 days before the election in which voters can change affiliation. This confusion, and the wide variance in states, makes the study of primary types particularly difficult in terms of tracking changes to laws; however, there have been some notable changes in the last few years.

Since 2012, there have been some significant changes to state primary systems. Alaska has reconfigured their Republican primary to allow unaffiliated voters while all other parties operate an open primary. The state may become a battleground for this issue as the debate has reached the state house. Early in 2017, a bill was introduced (HB200) that would completely open the primaries. Courts have recently been reluctant to uphold open or closed primaries on unwilling parties, so any changes would have to stand up to potential legal challenges. There have been court challenges on both sides of this issue, and the courts have repeatedly upheld a party's associational rights to closed (see cases in Idaho, Kansas, and Oklahoma) or open (see Connecticut) primaries. This is not to say that the courts have found a right for individuals in states to sue for a particular system (*Crum v. Duran,* a recent NM Supreme Court case, upheld their closed primary after a challenge from a citizen that argued that closed primaries do not qualify as "free and fair" elections).

Kansas has grappled with these recent legal challenges, with a new change to their primary system—the latest in a series of changes reaching back to 2004. In a case stemming from an Oklahoma controversy (*Beaver et al. v. Clingman et al.*), the Tenth Circuit Court of Appeals had ruled that states cannot impose a closed primary on unwilling parties. The Kansas secretary of state was bound by the decision (as a part of the Tenth Circuit) and reached out to the parties to ask them if they wanted to continue to hold closed primaries. Both parties had responded that they would open their primaries to unaffiliated voters (Thornburgh 2004). After an intra-party squabble, the Republican Party subsequently closed their primaries, leaving Kansas with a hybrid primary system—closed by default, but with a semi-open Democratic primary. This leads us to the most recent change. With relatively little fanfare, the Democratic Party has decided that they would be better served by closing their primary as well (Associated Press 2013). This brings the state back to its original position of a fully closed system and ending ten years of experimentation with open primaries.

The reason for this attention to party registration centers around a debate regarding the relationship between these primary systems and such factors as voter turnout or the ideological extremity of elected officials. Closed primaries are often cited as being indicative of strong party organizations, as they are able to more fully control nominations. This is reflected in the conventional wisdom that suggests that open primaries lead to more moderate legislators rather than more ideologically pure officials (Kanthak and Morton 2001). If parties were interested in protecting the ideological sanctity of their nomination processes, we would expect state parties to pursue closed systems. Another important concern is the possibility of "crossover voting" where members of one party attempt to collectively assert influence on the primary of the other party by "crossing over" to vote in the primary of the other party.

Three problems immediately arise with the study of primary systems and parties. First, recent studies have concluded that open primaries have not necessarily led to more moderate roll-call votes among legislators (McGhee et al. 2013), calling into question our conventional wisdom on primaries. Another recent study was able to leverage the recent changes in Idaho in order to see the effects of a change in primary systems. The study identified a decrease in voter turnout of roughly 4 percent after the introduction of the closed primary but little change in inter-party and intra-party competition (May 2016). Unfortunately, studies have yet to be done to assess any differences in the ideological extremity of Idahoan legislators. In addition to these concerns, concrete evidence of any effects of crossover voting remains to be found, and the problem, or worries about the problem, seem to be rooted in anecdote rather than empirical evidence.

Finally, as I have previously noted, many states are responsible for setting participation rules for the party primaries, as state voter registration is generally the mechanism for party registration. It seems reasonable to question the ability of parties to be able to affect meaningful change to state laws when these changes would need to be made statutorily. With this being said, I should also repeat another previous point that courts have generally been sympathetic to party challenges to both open and closed primary systems. This, at least, opens some avenue of action for the party organization itself, rather than relying on a state legislative delegation.

One should take away the larger point that party registration should be an issue to watch in 2018 and 2020—indeed one state has already made post-2016 changes to their primary election system. Colorado had traditionally run a closed primary system, and while some election spectators noted that it resembled a semi-closed system (in that voters could affiliate with a party on Election Day), reformers put Proposition 108 before the voters in order to allow unaffiliated voters to participate in the primaries without needing to affiliate at the polls. The proposition was passed and will take effect in the next election cycle. Other closed primary states have seen grassroots attempts to open primaries, but at this point, no efforts have garnered as much support as the Colorado movement. South Dakota attempted, unsuccessfully, to institute a top-two primary similar to that in Washington and California. The amendment failed 55–45, but there are already discussions of another attempt in 2018.

Primary Sequencing

Another one of the most discussed features of the presidential primaries is the sequencing of state contests. This sequencing is important in a "macro-electoral" sense because of the frontloading of states and the speed of a nomination contest. In a "micro-electoral" sense, the primary calendar is important because those states that hold primaries and caucuses earlier in the election cycle ostensibly exert more power over the nomination process. This perception has led parties, state legislatures, and political observers to see the primary calendar as an important tool to shape the nomination.

Perhaps the most important of these consequences, or at least the clearest to see, is the speed of the primary calendar. An easy way of measuring this speed is by looking at the proportion of delegates which delegates are allocated over time. Figure 9.1 shows the cumulative delegate allocation of Democratic delegates from 2000 to 2016 and figure 9.2 shows the Republican delegate allocation. The impressive frontloading of the 2008 calendar demonstrates how quickly delegates can be allocated; however, looking back at the actual speed of the 2008 primary, this story becomes more complicated. While delegate allocation looks fairly similar for both parties in 2008, the

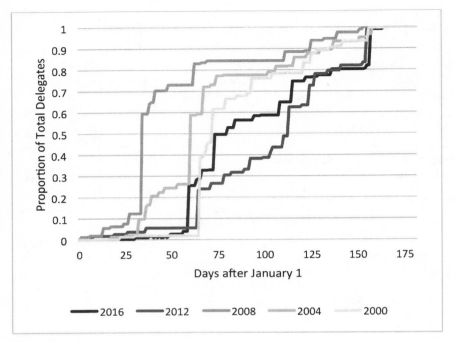

Figure 9.1
Cumulative Allocation of Democratic Delegates, 2000–2016. Source: The Green Papers.

Republican primary was decided on March 4th while the Democratic contest continued on until June 3rd. This shows that a rapid pace of delegate allocation does not necessarily yield a fast nomination. However, parties can presumably delay the process through a slower delegate allocation.

Another important consideration when looking at the primary calendar is the perception that regional or ideological interests can be brought to bear if primaries can be strategically stacked early in the process. If an ideological group or regional interest can be overrepresented early in the primary process, momentum from early wins might be able to carry a candidate to the nomination. For example, the southern Super Tuesday primary was intended to bring a more conservative element to Democratic Party nominations (Norrander 1992). In 2016, media narratives spoke of early southern states giving an advantage to the Clinton campaign, as opposed to western progressive states which favored Sanders. This narrative appeared before the primaries even began (Healy and Chozick 2015) and continued throughout the

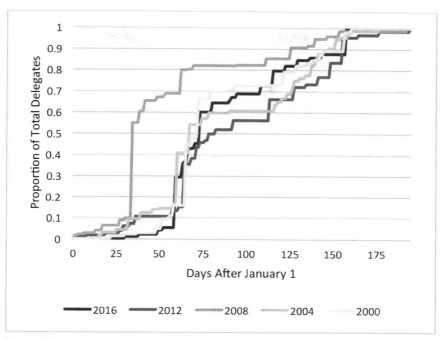

Figure 9.2
Cumulative Allocation of Republican Delegates, 2000–2016. Source: The Green Papers.

primary season (Benen 2016), with some commenters even stating that these southern primaries were "unfair" (Johnson 2016).

What is striking is that the Democratic primary calendar looks virtually the same in 2016 as it did in 2012. With the exception of the later start, which actually represents a "normal" start (early "carve out" states were forced to move their primaries to January in 2012 due to efforts by states like Florida to move their primaries into February), there are only some subtle differences in state election timing. The narrative that the party had unfairly stacked the deck in favor of Clinton with early southern primaries does not seem to bear out given the fact that many of these southern states have regularly scheduled their primaries in March. Indeed, Arkansas and North Carolina were the only pro-Clinton states to the front of the line—the remainder of the early southern primaries had not changed dates. This is not to say that there was a built-in structural advantage that helped Clinton—just that it was not manufactured for her.

This point raises another serious issue about the ability of parties to affect meaningful change in the calendar. Looking at figure 9.3, one can immediately see the similarity of both parties' calendars. What we can see from this chart is that the Republican Party got off to a slightly faster start than the Democrats, although both parties allocated the first half of their delegates within a week of each other, on March 15 and 22, respectively. This similarity tells us something important about setting the primary calendar. With the exception of caucus states (including the split primary/caucus arrangement in Kentucky for 2016) and South Carolina (which operates party primaries on successive Saturdays), state primaries are conducted on the same day for both parties. This means that any differences in this calendar come from the independent changes in caucus-state dates and because of differences in delegate allocation to the states (discussed further in the next section). This highlights the fact that primary dates are often set by state legislatures, and not the parties. To put a finer point on this, primary election dates are often

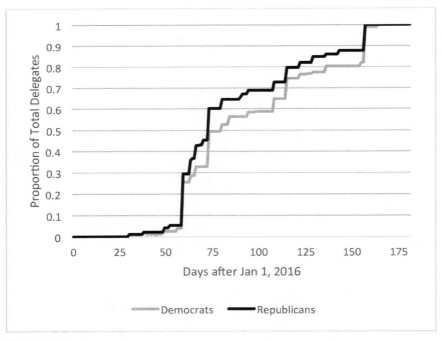

Figure 9.3
Proportion of Delegates Allocated in the 2016 Democratic and Republican Primaries.
Source: The Green Papers.

set by the *majority* party in a state. The states themselves are limited in their ability to effectively move about the primary calendar due to the timing of legislative sessions. It becomes difficult for states to one-up each other on the primary calendar if a particular state's legislative session ends before another. This has led some states to grant election-setting authority to executive branch entities, such as the governor, secretary of state, or a board of elections.

Parties are also limited in their ability to affect change to the calendar in two ways. First, the national party has no mechanism to set the election calendar beyond their ability to coerce states through the delegate allocation process. While the parties have granted special status to Iowa, New Hampshire, Nevada, and South Carolina, their ability to coerce later states is questionable. Parties are also limited by their ability to garner cooperation from the calendar-setting authority in the state—a dubious prospect in states where a party is in the minority. Returning to our previous example of Arkansas and North Carolina entering the March window and potentially stacking the deck for Clinton, it seems unlikely that the Democratic Party would have been able to solicit the assistance of two Republican trifectas (that is, Republican majority upper and lower houses, and a Republican governor) in crafting a calendar to better help their favored candidate.

Before moving on to a discussion of delegate allocation, it is worth looking at some specific changes that parties made. The DNC cleared up some language regarding start times for the four early states—allowing New Hampshire to avoid conflict with their state law, but otherwise did not meddle with timing. This is not to say that state moves did not occur, but that the party did little to compel or entice any changes to primary dates. As mentioned earlier, one carrot that the Democratic Party does have is the ability of states to gather "bonus delegates" by delaying and clustering their primaries. The Democratic Party awards states a 10 percent or 20 percent delegate bonus when states delay their primaries to April (Stage 2), or May/June (Stage 3), respectively. Additionally, the party awards a 15 percent delegate bonus when three or more contiguous states cluster their primaries on the same day.

Some states were able to take advantage of these delegate bonuses with calendar moves. Arizona, Idaho, Utah, Alaska, Hawaii, and Washington all gained a 15 percent cluster bonus in March; however, some of these states lost a previously held bonus for holding their primary in Stage 2 (Alaska, Idaho, and Washington—further, Idaho had a previous clustering bonus with Wyoming, Nebraska, and Kansas, and thus sustained a net loss in bonus delegates with their move forward in the calendar; however, their previous partners, Nebraska and Kansas, moved into early March and were no longer eligible for a clustering bonus). Delaware, Maryland, and Pennsylvania clustered in April, receiving bonuses for clustering and timing. Pennsylvania previously had partners in Connecticut, New York, and Rhode Island, but when New York moved their primary one week earlier, they disconnected Connecticut and Rhode Island from the cluster, leaving them without a bonus. Looking at these changes broadly, it is not clear that the Democratic Party enticed any changes to the calendar beyond some state clustering; and, in fact, this year's moves suggest that some states are willing to forego delegate bonuses in order to move up in the calendar.

On the Republican side of things, changes had added complexity. In 2016, states choosing to hold a primary in the first two weeks of March were required to use a proportional scheme to allocate their delegates. As we will see in the next section, states moving into this window already had proportional systems in 2012, and no non-proportional state moved into the window, meaning there were no allocation changes with this rule. While this may be an effective vehicle for delaying primaries (if states do not previously conform to the proportional rule), the lack of change makes any causal argument difficult to make.

What is clear from examining the primary calendar is that parties may not be as completely free to alter the calendar as conventional narratives or media spin may suggest. Parties must contend with the realities of party control in the states, as well as statutory limitations to their interference. One of the few tools that parties may be able to leverage in compelling states to alter the calendar may be delegate allocation, which we turn to next.

Delegate Allocation

Delegate allocation can be thought of as two complementary processes. First, is the allocation of delegates to the states by the parties. Second, is the process for awarding delegates to the winners in the various caucus and primary contests. In 2016, the rules for both of these processes changed, especially within the Republican Party.

Thinking about the first process—the allocation of delegates to the states—we can see few Democratic Party changes but some more important ones for the Republican Party. In 2016, the DNC did little to change the awarding of delegates to the states, but they did have fewer delegates to go around. Both parties award delegates to the states through a hybrid consideration of state population and party loyalty. The Democratic formula is based on the number of votes cast for the Democratic presidential candidate over the preceding three elections. This formula results in a proportion that is then multiplied by a set number of base delegates for the entire convention. While this formula did not change, the number of base delegates for the Democratic Party was reduced from 3,700 to 3,200—decreasing the total number of delegates, but not affecting the balance of power between states. One caveat to this assertion is that Superdelegates in 2016 were a slightly larger percentage of total delegates (15 percent) than in 2012 (13 percent), but still a reduction from 2008, when Superdelegates were roughly 20 percent of the delegate total. While this change would not change the outcome of the Democratic nomination, continued consternation over Superdelegates— exacerbated by the bitter primary fight between Clinton and Sanders—led to the creation of a Democratic commission tasked with studying and offering suggestions for reforming the Superdelegate process. If they are successful remains to be seen.

Across party lines, the Republican Party made one important change to their delegate allocation rules that affects both the first process—awarding delegates to the states; and the second process—awarding delegates to the candidates. Considering the first process, the Republican Party sets a universal baseline of ten at-large delegates per state (presumably to reflect five delegates per senator). On top of this is added a population-based component in the form of three delegates per congressional district. After this, bonus delegates are awarded for party loyalty—voting for the Republican presidential candidate in the previous election and for sitting Republican elected officials. This leaves each state with a set number of at-large delegates (ten + bonus delegates) and three delegates per district. While this baseline formula did not change, new penalties became part of the rules for the RNC.

In 2016, all Republican contests taking place in the first two weeks of March were required to allocate their delegates on a proportional basis. Republicans first looked at proportionality in the leadup to the 2012 election. The speed of the 2008 primaries led the party to chart a middle course between a completely hands-off approach, and a strict proportional system. In 2012, the GOP mandated that any contest taking place in the month of March would have to adhere to a proportional allocation scheme, and had scaled that back to two weeks for 2016. This rule is enforceable by the party through a delegate penalty. Previously, the RNC was able to compel some state behavior (preventing states from moving their contests into February) through a 50 percent delegate penalty. In 2016, this penalty has been increased and covers this proportionality requirement. The new penalty reduces a state's delegate count to nine, or one-third of their delegation, whichever is less. This should theoretically give the RNC much more ability to compel compliance with the calendar and with proportional delegate allocation rules.

Returning to an examination of the new proportionality window, it seems at first like a scaling back of proportionality for the party, and perhaps an attempt to slow down the primary process. This is based on the assumption that a proportional delegate allocation system favors a longer process. There is, however, an important second change that the Republicans made. In addition to mandating proportionality during this two-week window, the GOP is now mandating the particular "flavor" of proportionality that the states must utilize. The first iteration of the Republican proportionality rule did not set out any requirements for how proportionality was to be carried out, thus, states could award their at-large delegates (the state's ten baseline delegates) proportionally, yet award congressional district delegates in a winner-take-all fashion in each district. The 2016 rules changed this and mandated that both at-large and congressional district delegates needed to be awarded on a proportional basis, minimizing the ability for states to "water down" proportional voting practices. While some states like Texas have adopted a fully proportional system, others retained the at-large/congressional district distinction and now allocate both sets of delegates proportionately. In practice, this usually means that congressional district winners get two delegates and second place finishers are awarded one delegate, rather than a winner-take-all scenario. As stated before, the RNC offered little guidance on how to implement proportionality, so many flavors exist in the states.

Previous iterations of this proportionality window also lacked specific guidance on two remaining areas, the first of which is the concept of qualifying thresholds. These thresholds are minimum percentages that a candidate must receive before they qualify for a proportional share of the state's delegates. The Republican Party has now mandated that these thresholds may not exceed 20 percent (compared to an across-the-board mandate of 15 percent in Democratic primaries). By setting qualifying thresholds, many states were able to disqualify candidates that would otherwise be able to scrape together some delegates (and perhaps prompt a brokered convention in a crowded race such as 2016). Further, states may set a winner-take-all threshold, at which point the winning candidate takes all of a given state's delegates. In this case, the RNC sets a minimum threshold of 50 percent (Democrats do not allow a winner-take-all scenario like this). However, winner-take-all thresholds may not have been an important factor for Republicans in 2016, especially given high fragmentation of the vote in the early period of the race, and winner-take-all contests, by rule, late in the cycle. What this all means in practice, is that the Republican primaries are not as proportional as they may seem on the surface. What is clear, however, is that the Republican Party continues to have a complicated relationship with proportionality.

Looking Toward 2020

If anything, 2016 was an important year for rules because of an increased focus on procedure. Media, parties, candidates, and citizens alike seemed to take notice of many of the rules behind the primaries which so often go unnoticed. This increased focus may bring change, innovation, or at the very least, reconsideration of the rules that govern this most important process. Already, some states have begun to make moves affecting the 2020 elections. Some news sources have begun to comment that Nevada may lose its privileged place in the primary calendar (Cheney 2016). The Democratic Party has a unity reform commission that is currently meeting in order to hash out changes to their nominating structures, paying specific attention to the issue of Superdelegates. Maine and Minnesota have decided to move to a primary, rather than a caucus, and California has already passed legislation to move their primary into March. If this flurry of activity is suggestive of the amount of potential change to come, the 2020 primaries may look much different from those in 2016.

What is perhaps more interesting to consider, is what 2016 can tell us about the future prospects for party power over nominations. While cries for reform have come from both parties, it is unclear what the parties can do about this problem. Three immediate issues must be considered. First, and perhaps most important, is whether or not parties have the capacity to affect change in their nominating procedures. Parties have made a proverbial deal with the devil in instituting state-run primaries, in that they have lost most of their direct oversight over these processes. While the parties have experienced some success in using delegate allocation as a tool for compliance, recent examples as noted here highlight issues with the partisan composition of state legislatures, statutory limitations, and outright state disobedience. Second, is the question of whether or not these rules can actually affect the changes that parties seek in their nomination systems. As noted throughout this chapter, it is not clear that primary system type, the calendar, or delegate allocation styles are directly linked to outcomes. To be sure, rules matter; however, the relationships between these electoral rules and the outcomes that parties seek are much more complicated than meets the eye, and parties would be wise to be sure to understand the implications of change before pursuing it. Finally, and intimately related to the first two issues, is whether or not parties know what change they want to affect, and whether or not intra-party factions can agree on a path to reform.

Regardless of the power of the parties and the effects of rules, the normative desires of parties seem to change within different factions of the parties, and with each passing year. Does the Democratic Party need to open up their process, or dilute the influence of Superdelegates, or perhaps change to ensure that an establishment candidate doesn't have such a strong outside challenge? Should Republicans do more to ensure an establishment-friendly candidate? Parties would do well to think seriously about the long-term implications of these changes, and scholars should continue to investigate the confusing and often contradictory effects of these rules.

Note

1. The party rules referenced in this chapter are the authors' interpretations of the DNC Office of Party Affairs and Delegate Selection's "Delegate Selection Rules for the 2016 Democratic National Convention" and Republican National Committee's "Rules of the Republican Party."

10

Perception of the Parties and the 2016 Presidential Nominations

Caitlin E. Jewitt

EVEN AS DONALD TRUMP racked up win after win and enlivened a signifi-cant segment of the Republican primary electorate, GOP party elites were tepid, and in many cases downright disparaging, of his candidacy. By early May 2016, Trump had amassed a sizable delegate lead—large enough that his competitors had withdrawn. Despite the writing on the wall, House Speaker Paul Ryan (R-WI) announced publicly that he was "not ready" to endorse Trump and that the Republican Party needed a "standard-bearer that bears our standards" (Steinhauer and Burns 2016). Further reflective of the deep chasm existing between elites and voters, several elected Republican officials announced that they either did not support or would not vote for Trump in November (Reilly 2016).

On the Democratic side, an analogous divide between voters and elites emerged. Superdelegates were overwhelmingly supportive of Hillary Clinton, with many announcing their support for her before the primaries even began. According to Democratic Party rules, Superdelegates are unbound and free to support any candidate. In fact, they were designed, in part, to provide knowledge and expertise, acting as a counterweight to the masses. Despite this rationale, some delegates reported instances of harassment from angry Sanders supporters, including phone calls, emails, accusations of bribery, and negative reviews of their businesses (Lerer 2016). One Sanders supporter went as far as to compile a "Superdelegate Hit List," a website to share the contact information of Superdelegates so they can be pressed to switch their votes (Lerer 2016). So ubiquitous were claims of an unfair Democratic nomination that headlines such as "Is the Democratic Primary Really Rigged?" (Foran 2016b) and "Democratic Super Delegates: The Villains of a 'Rigged' System, According to Sanders's Supporters" (Weigel 2016) abounded. In fact, Sanders's supporters brought a class action lawsuit "alleging that the Democratic National Committee worked in conjunction with Hillary Clinton's 2016 campaign to keep Bernie Sanders out of the White House" (Riotta 2017). Though Clinton was expected to, and ultimately did, secure the 2016 Democratic nomination, the process was far from smooth and harmonious.

Both nominations in 2016 illustrate deep-seated disagreements rooted within the parties—not just ideological conflict but also factional divisions. Though the political parties spent decades reforming the process for choosing the presidential candidates, they have clearly not landed on a system that is able to nominate a popular, electable candidate who simultaneously pleases and inspires confidence among both party elites and rank-and-file party members.

While examples such as the actions and protests of Sanders supporters in 2016 suggest displeasure and distrust in the parties and the process, we have limited systematic understanding of how the mass public feels about the presidential nomination process. In this chapter, I investigate Americans' perceptions of the parties, their nominating processes and procedures, and the impact of Trump and Sanders on their parties. The findings suggest that even among rank-and-file members of each party, the parties do not fare particularly well, with large segments expressing only some or hardly any confidence in their party. This analysis also reveals that Americans view primaries as fairer than caucuses and open contests as fairer than closed contests. Exposure to a caucus, which can seem complicated and confusing, does not result in an increase in support for this type of nominating mechanism. Finally, though many Republican elites think that Trump's candidacy damaged the Republican Party, rank-and-file party members disagree.

The Evolution of a Complicated System

As private organizations, the parties could theoretically utilize a nomination process where citizens have no input in the selection. Of course, this would not be the wisest, or most popular, decision, as citizens have grown to expect to have a role in the selection of the nominee. Generally, there is support among Americans for "more democracy" (e.g., Achen and Bartels 2016; Stimson 2004; Dahl 1961), which for many equates to more opportunities for Americans to participate in the political process. When the people have more involvement in the selection of presidential candidates, it is in line with the representative democracy philosophy, under which power stems from the people (Steger 2015).

Despite this pervasive popular belief advancing citizen involvement in political decisions and the selection of candidates, Schattschneider (1960) acknowledges that political elites serve a crucial function in defining and restricting the choices presented to Americans. He contends that many Americans are simply not up to the tasks necessary for a functioning democracy. The parties seem to be cognizant of this limitation, as they have worked to achieve the ideal balance of citizen input and elite expertise in the nomination process.

Throughout most of American history, a small group of select individuals chose the nominee behind closed doors, but those permitted to have some formal say in the process has expanded over time. The Democratic Party's McGovern-Fraser Commission (1968–1972) tightened the connection between voters and the outcome at the Convention and shifted power away from elites and toward citizens. Throughout this reform process, an overarching goal of the Democratic Party was to create a system that consistently nominated a popular, electable candidate who could win the presidency, appeal to elites and the masses, and reflect the party's values. In an attempt to achieve this objective, the Democratic Party had to grapple, time and time again, with determining the optimal balance—between the knowledge, insight, and wisdom of party elites and the preferences and sentiments of voters.

With its alterations of the process, the Winograd Commission (1974–1978) swung the balance of power back toward elites by creating PLEOs, delegate seats reserved for party leaders and elected officials. These delegates reflected voter preferences, as they were pledged to candidates based on the results of the primary or caucus held in each state. This reform ensured that party leaders and elected officials were able to bring their "experience and knowledge as to what we [the Democratic Party] need in order to win."[1] The Winograd Commission also advocated for closed contests, hoping to limit participation to Democratic identifiers (though the actual implementation of this recommendation proved more difficult). The commission made it clear that the Democratic Party wanted elite judgment in the process as well as citizen input, as long as those citizens identified as Democrats.

Reacting to Democratic losses in recent elections, the Commission on Presidential Nominations (1981–1982), chaired by Jim Hunt, swung the pendulum of influence even more strongly back toward elites. The Hunt Commission created unbound delegate slots reserved for party elites and elected officials. These Superdelegates, as they became commonly known, are not required to make their candidate preferences known (though many do), can change their mind throughout the nomination season, and are in no way tied to citizen preferences expressed in primaries and caucuses. For the most part, Superdelegates have not played a decisive role, though their function is often questioned. The 2016 Democratic nomination, where party elites favored Clinton and impassioned Sanders's voters claimed the system was rigged against the outsider candidate, demonstrates that the balance between elites and citizens is still elusive, despite frequent adjustments to the process.

Without a doubt, the reforms originating in the 1960s created a system that gives voters more of a say in selecting the presidential nominees than ever before. However, that is not to imply that voters have the ultimate say in who becomes their party's presidential candidate. Cohen et al. (2008) argue that by essentially crowning a candidate the frontrunner during the invisible primary, elites can send a strong signal to voters about who is the preferred candidate. Jewitt (forthcoming) demonstrates that through the ability of party elites and elected officials to influence the electoral rules, they can exert powerful guidance over which candidate is nominated. Elites now play a subtler, yet still powerful, role in selecting a presidential nominee in this complicated system.

Theoretical Expectations

As the national Democratic Party reformed, and then adjusted and readjusted the newly altered rules, the states and state parties also modified their procedures. In the federalist system, as long as the states abide by the national guidelines, they are permitted to determine their own rules governing their nominating contests. Thus, some states have maintained relatively consistent rules over the course of the post-reform era while other states have less stable rules. As a result, for some citizens, the nomination process can look very different from year to year, even if they remain in a single state; the process may also be quite distinct for residents of different states, even if they are members of the same political party. Therefore, there is the possibility that exposure to various rules may influence attitudes.

I expect that most citizens will prefer a primary over a caucus. A primary is a recognizable, familiar type of Election Day activity, where people have many hours on a designated day to cast a secret ballot and the process may take mere minutes. If citizens have voted in a general election and have some basic level of political knowledge, then there is not a great deal of mystery about how a primary functions.

A caucus, on the other hand, may seem complicated, confusing, and impenetrable, especially to those who lack familiarity with the process. In 2016, the *New York Times* published, "Our Man in Iowa: How the Iowa Caucuses Work" (Gabriel 2016a) and the *Huffington Post* posted a story titled, "How Does a Caucus Work?" (Noble 2016). The mere presence of these user guides indicates that significant portions of the public may not understand the purpose and procedures of a caucus.

Caucus rules vary widely by state, and even within a state, which certainly contributes to the confusion. Generally, in a caucus, voters have to show up at a designated time, such as 7:00 in the evening, and may be required to stay for several hours, deliberate on party business, and make their candidate preference publicly known (Norrander 1992). The number of citizens willing to participate in this type of democratic exercise is likely to be much smaller than those willing to vote in a primary (Norrander 2015).

Due to the complexity and the higher costs associated with a caucus, the lack of familiarity many have with the process, and the prevalence of primary elections, I expect citizens to prefer primaries to caucuses. I also anticipate that citizens who live in states that hold caucuses and thus are more familiar with the process will see more value in caucuses than citizens who live in states that hold primaries.

However, a portion of the electorate may believe caucuses are a superior nominating mechanism. Redlawsk et al. argue that the dynamics and requirements of a caucus mean that participants are "generally more aware and involved than voters elsewhere" (2011, 8). Caucuses provide citizens an opportunity to discuss candidates and issues, as well as an opportunity to weigh in on party business and issue positions (Steger 2015; Norrander 1992). Some scholars argue that because of the demands associated with caucuses, more educated, passionate, ideologically extreme citizens are more likely to participate (Citrin and Karol 2009; Haskell 1996). Thus, stronger partisans may be more likely to find value in caucuses.

The openness of the contest also varies across states. In an open contest, any registered voter, regardless of party affiliation, is able to participate in the state's primary or caucus. In a semi-open contest, party members and Independents are allowed to participate while opposite party members are excluded. In a closed contest, only party members are allowed to voice a preference to select the presidential candidates.

The parties, and in particular the Democratic Party, have spent significant time debating the advantages and disadvantages of opening or closing the process. On the one hand, advocates of open primaries claim they allow citizens to choose which party's nominating contest is most interesting and engaging (Davis 1980). Opening up the selection of the nominee may make it more likely that the party's presidential candidate has wide appeal, rather than only having the support of a small segment of ideologically extreme partisans (Hedlund 1977–1978). On the other hand, many believe that open contests lend themselves to the possibility of raiding, or opposite party members voting insincerely for a less preferred, less electable candidate in an attempt to spoil the party's chances in the general election (Lengle 1981). These discussions continue today—with both parties considering reviewing these rules prior to the 2020 nominations (Siegel 2017; Putnam 2016a, 2016b). There have been investigations into whether openness affects turnout (e.g., Jewitt forthcoming, 2014; Kenney 1983; Ranney 1977; Norrander and Smith 1985) and how these rules influence the types of candidates selected (e.g., Kanthak and Morton 2001; Lengle 1981). However, there has been little systematic exploration into which type of rule citizens prefer or view as the fairer method.

Assuming they prefer more ideologically extreme candidates, I expect strong Republicans and strong Democrats will seek to advantage those types of candidates by closing off the process to opposite-party members and Independents, who are more likely to prefer more moderate candidates. Correspondingly, Independents should prefer the opportunity to participate; therefore, they should prefer open contests. Partisans who only lean toward the parties (but do not affiliate strongly) may be more likely to want to vote in the opposite party's primary at some point and thus should prefer open contests.

As previously mentioned, the mass public has come to expect a role in the selection of candidates through a democratic process. For that reason, combined with the negative attention they received in 2016, I expect that voters are unlikely to support the idea of Superdelegates. Strong partisans, because of their commitment to the party, its positions, and its success, may be more likely to recognize the value Superdelegates bring to the process.

Data Analysis

In order to assess Americans' perceptions of the parties and the 2016 presidential nominations, I rely on a national survey conducted by The Associated Press-NORC Center for Public Affairs Research.[2] The survey was conducted between May 12 and May 16, 2016, as the 2016 presidential nominations were ongoing, but nearing completion. At that point, all of Trump's major competitors had withdrawn from the race, leaving him as the de facto nominee. However, Trump had still not secured a majority of delegates,[3] so there was still some discussion about the (increasingly unlikely) possibility of blocking his nomination at the convention. The 2016 Democratic nomination was still technically competitive in mid-May, as Sanders had not withdrawn and Clinton had not yet secured the necessary delegates, though she was getting close.[4]

I begin by examining confidence in the parties, by party identification of the respondents (figure 10.1). As one would expect, Republicans have very little confidence in the Democratic Party; about 75 percent of Republicans report having hardly any confidence in the Democratic Party and less than 3 percent report having a great deal of confidence in the Democratic Party. Using the seven-point party identification scale, the trend is as one would anticipate—stronger Republicans have less confidence in the Democratic Party than Republican leaners. Independents are also not overly enthusiastic, with 48 percent having hardly any confidence, 47 percent expressing only some confidence, and less than 5 percent reporting a great deal of confidence

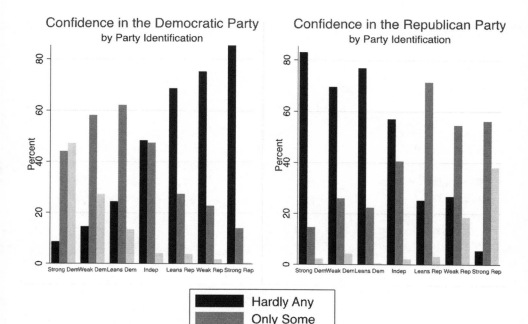

Figure 10.1
Confidence in Parties, by Party ID.

in the Democratic Party. Democrats are more confident in their own party, but even then, there is not overwhelming confidence. Here 13.5 percent of Democratic leaners, 27 percent of weak Democrats, and 47 percent of strong Democrats express a great deal of confidence in their party. Nearly a quarter of Democratic leaners indicate that they have hardly any confidence in the Democratic Party.[5]

Americans' confidence in the Republican Party is even more tepid (figure 10.1, right panel): 75 percent of Democrats and 57 percent of Independents report hardly any confidence in the Republican Party, and less than 3 percent of Democrats and Independents report a great deal of confidence in the Republican Party. More specifically, about 83 percent of strong Democrats, 70 percent of weak Democrats, and 77 percent of Democratic leaners have hardly any confidence in the Republican Party. Republicans have more confidence in their own party, but there are sizable segments of Republican identifiers expressing a lack of confidence in the GOP. About a quarter of Republican leaners indicate they have hardly any confidence in the Republican Party; about 71 percent of Republican leaners indicate they have some confidence in the party. Only 3 percent of Republican leaners indicate they have a great deal of confidence in their party. Weak Republicans are more supportive with about 19 percent indicating they have a great deal of confidence; 38 percent of strong Republicans profess a great deal of confidence in their party.[6] Overall, Americans are generally not very confident in the parties, with the Republican Party faring a bit worse.

Americans are also not satisfied with the nominating processes used to select the presidential candidates (figure 10.2). About 39 percent of respondents indicate hardly any confidence in the Democratic nominating process, with 18 percent expressing a great deal of confidence. Nearly 45 percent of Americans (a plurality) report hardly any confidence in the Republican nominating process, and only 12 percent indicate a great deal of confidence. Of course, it is vital to examine confidence in the nominating processes by party identification, which is done in figure 10.3.

As is to be expected in these polarized times, Republicans have little confidence in the Democratic nominating process. Republican leaners are the least enthusiastic in the Democratic nominating process, with nearly 60 percent indicating they have hardly any confidence. Weak and strong Republicans are not much more confident in the Democratic process, with 56 percent and 54 percent respectively, proclaiming hardly any confidence. For Republican identifiers, depending on the strength of their affiliation, between 6 percent and 10 percent indicate a great deal of confidence in the Democratic Party's nominating process. Independents are not as negative as Republicans, but they are also not very confident. Half of Independents

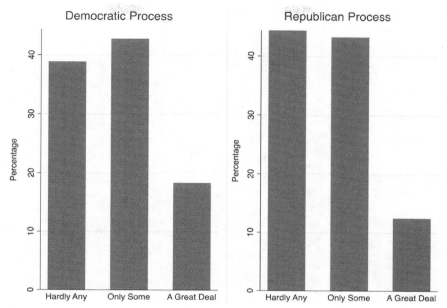

Figure 10.2
Confidence in the Parties' Nominating Processes.

express only some confidence in the Democratic Party's nominating process, and 46 percent report hardly any confidence, with less than 4 percent indicating they have a great deal of confidence. Despite higher overall levels, even Democratic identifiers do not have overwhelming levels of confidence. A majority (52 percent) of weak Democrats and (55 percent) of Democratic leaners profess only some confidence in the party's nominating process. However, a majority (51 percent) of strong Democrats indicate a great deal of confidence in their party's nominating process.[7] Americans are not very confident in the process that was utilized to select Hillary Clinton as the Democratic presidential candidate, but Democrats have more faith in the system.

Mirroring trends regarding the parties generally, confidence in the Republican Party's nominating process is lower than that of the Democratic Party's. About half of Democratic identifiers (50 percent of strong Democrats, 48 percent of weak Democrats, and 54 percent of Democratic leaners) indicate that they have hardly any confidence in the GOP's process. Between 13 and 14 percent of strong and weak Democrats indicate a great deal of confidence in the Republican nominating process, reflecting higher levels of confidence

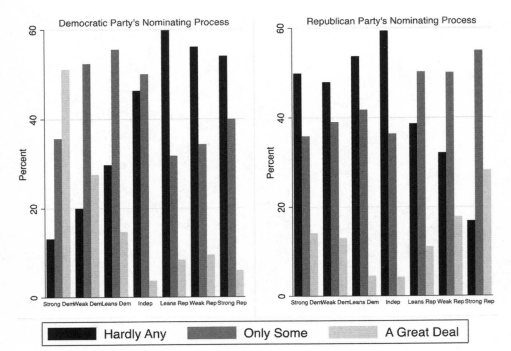

Figure 10.3
Confidence in the Parties' Nominating Processes, by Party ID.

than Republicans had in the Democratic process. A majority (59 percent) of Independents have hardly any confidence in the process used to select Republican presidential candidates; less than 5 percent of Independents report having a great deal of confidence. The majority of each category of Republican identifiers profess only some confidence in their party's nominating process (50 percent of Republican leaners and weak Republicans; 55 percent of strong Republicans). Less than 29 percent of strong Republicans report a great deal of confidence in their party's nominating process—this stands in sharp contrast to the 51 percent of strong Democrats who declared a great deal of confidence in their party's nominating process.[8] Even among the party faithful, the Republican process, used to nominate Donald Trump, does not inspire much faith.

Clearly, Americans are not enamored with the parties' nominating procedures. Perhaps this is not surprising given that the post-reform nomination systems are exceedingly complex. In an attempt to understand these opinions more fully, I next investigate attitudes toward specific aspects of the nominating processes, including whether Americans favor primaries or caucuses, how they feel about open and closed contests, and their beliefs about Superdelegates.

Americans overwhelmingly think primaries are fairer than caucuses (figure 10.4). Only 17 percent declared caucuses as the fairer type of nominating contest. Though many caucus proponents promote the aspects of deliberative democracy, with the opportunity for debate, discussion, and party-building in caucus meetings, Americans prefer the more familiar, commonly used primary format. The analysis also shows that Americans strongly prefer open contests (figure 10.4), with about 70 percent of respondents believing it is fairer to allow any registered voter to participate.

These straightforward depictions of Americans' preferences may obscure information that would be valuable to the parties when evaluating their rules. Therefore, figure 10.5 explores respondents' attitudes toward nominating procedures, controlling for party identification. Given that caucuses are a

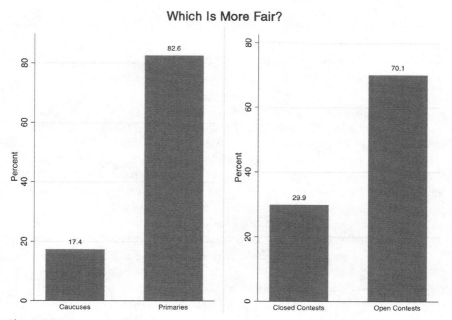

Figure 10.4
Attitudes toward Nominating Procedures.

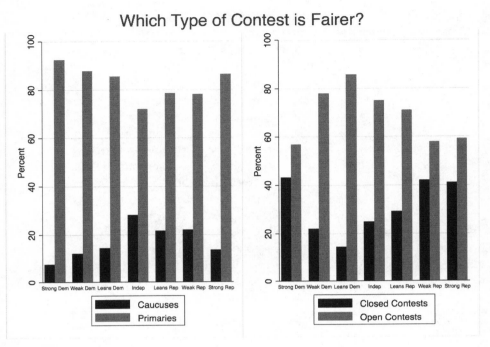

Figure 10.5
Attitudes toward Nominating Procedures, by Party ID.

place to conduct party business and typically attract a smaller, more committed pool of participants, I suspected strong partisans would be the most likely
to laud their advantages. This expectation is not supported by the data.
Strong partisans are the most supportive of primaries, and Independents are
the most likely to believe that caucuses are the fairer type of contest. Here 92
percent of strong Democrats and 86 percent of strong Republicans consider
primaries fairer, compared to only 72 percent of Independents.[9]

I expect Independents should prefer open contests because it would allow
them an opportunity to participate if they so desire. Strong partisans should
be more likely to want to close off the process, to ensure that a more ideological, strongly committed group of voters is choosing their party's presidential
candidate. The results (shown in figure 10.5), more or less, support this
line of thinking; 57 percent of strong Democrats and 59 percent of strong
Republicans think open contests are fairer than closed contests, whereas 75
percent of Independents profess this opinion. The relationship is not exactly
as anticipated, as a higher percentage of weak Democrats (78 percent) and

Democratic leaners (86 percent) than Independents believe open contests are the fairer procedure. Nevertheless, it is clear that strong partisans are the most likely to support closed contests, and Independents are more likely than strong partisans to favor open contests.[10]

In an effort to further explain people's attitudes toward nominating procedures, I also explore the relationship between exposure to various rules and opinions of the fairness of the type and openness of the contest. I expect that voters who have been exposed to a caucus (through living in a state that holds a caucus), should be more likely to understand the procedures, and thus may be more apt to see them as fairer than primaries. As is shown in figure 10.6, this expectation is not confirmed. People living in a state where a caucus was held in 2016 are less likely to think a caucus is the fairer procedure than people who live in a state where a presidential primary was held in 2016.[11] Of people who were not exposed to a caucus, 19 percent think a caucus is the fairer procedure; of people who were exposed to a caucus, 11 percent think a caucus is the fairer procedure.[12] It appears that exposure to a caucus does not improve people's opinions about the fairness of the selection method—in fact, it has the opposite effect.

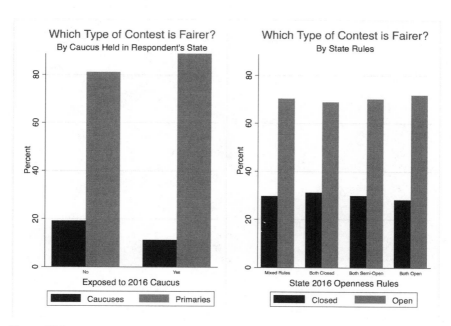

Figure 10.6
Attitudes toward Nominating Procedures, by Exposure to Those Rules.

As can be seen in figure 10.6, there is no evidence of statistically significant differences in attitudes about the fairness of open and closed contests, regardless of whether respondents live in a state where both parties held open, semi-open, or closed contests, or whether respondents live in a state where the parties employ different rules.[13] It may be that attitudes about fairness of inclusion or exclusion of various segments of the electorate are broader and more tied to people's views of democracy than their personal experiences and state rules. It is also possible that voters, particularly partisans, may not be aware of whether Independents and opposite party members are permitted to participate in their state, and so it has no impact on their opinions.

An aspect of the nomination process that may be more known to Americans, particularly given the context of the 2016 Democratic nomination, is the use of Superdelegates. As is evidenced in figure 10.7, only 5 percent of respondents report that Superdelegates are a very good idea and only about 13 percent indicate they are a somewhat good idea. A little less than a third (29 percent) feel neutrally toward Superdelegates. Most believe they are not a good idea; a plurality (32 percent) of Americans feel that Superdelegates

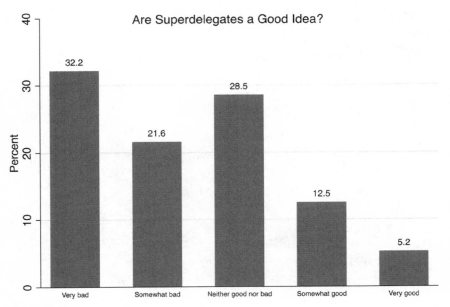

Figure 10.7
Attitudes toward Superdelegates.

are a very bad idea, with another 22 percent of respondents expressing that they are a somewhat bad idea. It is not only Sanders' supporters decrying the practice of Superdelegates; on the whole, Americans are decidedly against Superdelegates.

Figure 10.8 shows attitudes toward Superdelegates (utilizing a collapsed, three-category ordinal variable), broken down by party identification. This analysis illustrates interesting partisan dynamics. Republicans are more emphatically against Superdelegates than Democrats, and Independents feel the most neutral to these unpledged party and elected officials serving as delegates. More specifically, about 20 percent of strong Republicans and 11 percent of weak Republicans and Republican leaners think Superdelegates are a good idea, as opposed to less than 9 percent of Independents. A majority of Independents report that they feel neither good nor bad regarding the use of Superdelegates. Democrats are clearly more in favor of the practice, though not overwhelmingly so, with about 23 percent of Democratic leaners and weak Democrats and 32 percent of strong Democrats thinking Super-delegates are a good idea. Strong Democratic identifiers are the most support-ive of the idea of Superdelegates. This may be because they are more likely

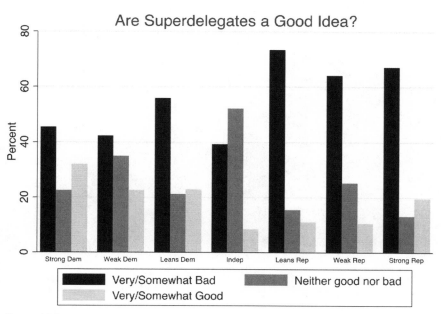

Figure 10.8
Attitudes toward Superdelegates, by Party ID.

to understand how elite input could ensure that their nominee reflects the values and positions of the party and the party faithful.

In 2016, there were discussions about whether the Republican Party would benefit from having Superdelegates, as illustrated in a *Chicago Tribune* headline declaring, "Superdelegates Exist for a Reason. Just Look at the Republicans" (Lane 2016). Given these conversations and the elite outcry over Trump's success, Republican respondents are not as supportive of Superdelegates as I expected. Consequently, below, I examine the impact of the two more controversial, surprisingly well-performing candidates, Donald Trump and Bernie Sanders, on their parties.

Trump was perceived to have a much more negative impact on the Republican Party than Sanders was viewed as having on the Democratic Party (figure 10.9). Only about 17 percent of respondents said Sanders had a very bad or somewhat bad impact on the Democratic Party; this stands in sharp contrast to the almost 51 percent of respondents reporting that they believe Trump had a very bad or somewhat bad impact on the Republican Party. A

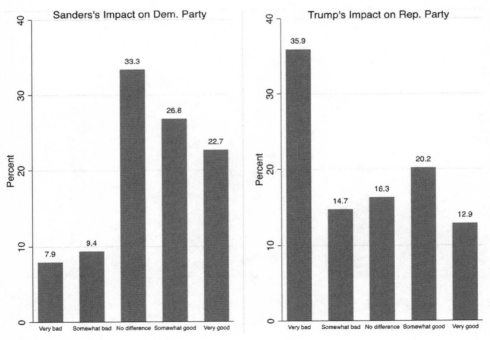

Figure 10.9
Perceived Impact of Sanders and Trump on Their Parties.

plurality of respondents (33 percent) suggested that Sanders had a neutral (or no) impact on the Democratic Party. A much smaller percentage (16 percent) said the same about Trump. These results raise the question—if Trump is perceived as having such a negative impact on his party, how did he become the nominee?

Looking at the perceived impact of the candidates on their parties across partisan identification lends some insight. Democrats and Republicans feel very differently (figure 10.10). Republicans believe that Trump had a good impact on the Republican Party, while Democrats overwhelmingly think Trump had a very bad impact on the Republican Party: 68 percent of Strong Democrats, 51 percent of weak Democrats, and 56 percent of Democratic leaners think Trump had a very bad impact. In contrast, only 18 percent of Republican leaners, 16 percent of weak Republicans, and 9 percent of strong Republicans report Trump has having a very bad impact on the party. Strong Republicans are the most positive about Trump's impact on the GOP,

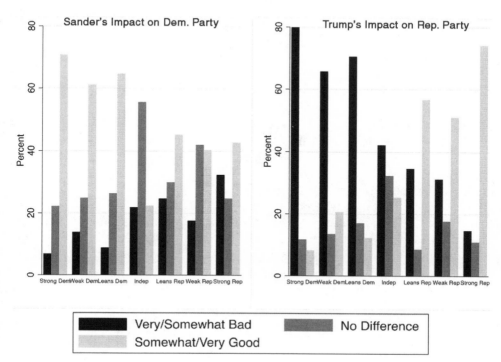

Figure 10.10
Perceived Impact of Sanders and Trump on Their Parties, by Party ID.

with 46 percent reporting he had a very good impact, and another 28 percent reporting he had a somewhat good impact on the GOP. Independents were more mixed, with a plurality (42 percent) reporting that Trump had a very bad or somewhat bad impact, and only about a quarter reporting his impact was very good or somewhat good.[14] Republican elites may not have been pleased with the Trump candidacy and its effect on the Republican Party; Democratic identifiers would tend to agree. This sentiment, however, is not mirrored among rank-and-file Republicans.

The partisan differences in attitudes about Trump's impact on the GOP are much more pronounced than those that exist about Sanders's impact on the Democratic Party. All segments of Democrats overwhelmingly felt that Sanders had a somewhat good or very good impact on the Democratic Party. Independents were neutral about Sanders's impact, with a majority feeling that he had no difference on the party. Republicans were less enthusiastic about Sanders's impact on the Democratic Party, but overall, they still felt he had a positive to neutral impact on the party. About 43 percent of strong Republicans reported that Sanders had a very or somewhat good impact on the Democratic Party, with only 21 percent indicating he had a very bad impact on the party.[15] Republicans were certainly less negative about Sanders than Democrats were about Trump.

Conclusion

Neither party's 2016 presidential nomination can be described as smooth or unifying: it was not a year where party leaders and elected officials rallied around candidates in the invisible primary to then have the electorate enthusiastically support the chosen candidate throughout the primaries and caucuses. Instead, discord between party elites and rank-and-file party members were evident within both parties.

Certainly, it is not solely because of the events that took place in 2016, but it is undeniable that Americans have a fairly pessimistic view of and lack confidence in the parties and the processes they use to select presidential candidates. Based on the analysis presented here, the Democratic Party inspires slightly more confidence than does the Republican Party. However, even among rank-and-file members of each party, the parties do not fare particularly well, with large segments expressing only some or hardly any confidence in their party. This analysis also reveals that Americans view primaries as fairer than caucuses and open contests as fairer than closed contests. Strong partisans are actually the most supportive of primaries, and Independents are the most likely to say that caucuses are the fairer type of contest. Exposure to a caucus, which can seem complicated and confusing, does not result in an increase in support for this type of nominating mechanism. Instead, people who live in a state that held a caucus in 2016 are less likely to think that a caucus is the fairer mechanism than people who live in a state that held primaries in 2016.

When it comes to open contests, Independents are more likely to favor open contests than strong partisans, who are more likely to believe that closed contests are the fairer method. Exposure to various openness rules does not appear to impact attitudes. Americans are also not enamored with the idea of Superdelegates, with more than half of respondents stating that they are a very or somewhat bad idea. Only about 17 percent report that they are a somewhat or very good idea. Democrats, and particularly strong Democrats, were the most likely to see the advantages of Superdelegates.

When assessing the impact of Sanders and Trump, Trump was seen as having a much more negative impact on the Republican Party than Sanders had on the Democratic Party. In fact, the vast majority of respondents believe that Sanders had a positive or neutral impact on the Democratic Party, whereas a majority reported that Trump had a very or somewhat bad impact on the Republican Party. Republican identifiers, however, broke sharply with their Democratic counterparts in their feelings toward Trump's impact, with Republicans supportive of his impact and Democrats harshly negative of it. Republican elites may think that Trump's candidacy damaged the Republican Party, but rank-and-file party members disagree—and they selected him to be the nominee.

In light of what transpired in 2016, the parties will, once again, make adjustments to the nomination system, hoping to create a process in 2020 that chooses a popular, electable candidate, who represents the party on its issue priorities, and pleases and energizes both party elites and rank-and-file party members. The Democratic Party is attempting to do so through the Unity Reform Commission, which will try to bridge the divide between the Clinton and Sanders camps. The commission will consider (among other aspects of the nomination system) the role of Superdelegates, the delegate allocation procedures, and the participation of citizens, particularly as it applies to the openness of contests (Putnam 2016a, 2017; The Democratic Party 2017; Siegel 2017).

At the 2016 National Convention, the Republican Party also left the door open for reforms. It created a temporary committee that is expected to examine aspects of the nomination process from the scheduling of contests, to delegate allocation rules, to which voters should be allowed to participate in the process (Putnam 2016b). When reviewing and revising the process, the parties may wish to take the attitudes of Americans into account if they want to increase confidence in the parties or in their nominating process. Of course, the parties may have other goals—namely, selecting a popular, electable candidate that reflects the party's values—that they prioritize over inspiring confidence and faith among the American public.

Notes

1. Winograd Commission, Democratic National Committee, Hearing Transcript, June 24, 1977, Washington, D.C. Pages 34–35.

2. The publicly available dataset and accompanying materials can be found on the AP-NORC website: http://www.apnorc.org/projects/Pages/the-frustrated-public -americans-views-of-the-election.aspx. The sample includes 1,060 adults, who are part of a larger AmeriSpeak Omnibus survey. Respondents were selected based on a "probability based panel designed to be representative of the U.S. household population" (AP-NORC 2016, 13). 761 respondents completed the survey online, while the other 299 were contacted via phone. The weighted data, which is representative of U.S. adults, was utilized in the analyses that follow. AP-NORC also provided me an amended dataset that includes the state each respondent lives in. Due to re-identification risk and the terms of the data supplier, each respondent's state of residence cannot be disclosed. I greatly appreciate the assistance of the AP-NORC staff, particularly Dan Costanzo, in obtaining this expanded dataset.

3. He would do so on May 26, 2016.

4. She would do so on June 7, 2016.

5. The relationship between party identification (seven-point scale) and confidence in the Democratic Party is statistically significant, with an uncorrected chi-squared statistic of 412.98, and $F_{(10.95,\ 11268.79)} = 22.32$, p<.001.

6. The relationship between party identification (seven-point scale) and confidence in the Republican Party is statistically significant, with an uncorrected chi-squared statistic of 353.70, and $F_{(10.59,\ 10961.99)} = 19.09$, p<.001.

7. The relationship between party identification (seven-point scale) and confidence in the Democratic Party's nominating process is statistically significant, with an uncorrected chi-squared statistic of 231.25, and $F_{(11.63,\ 11977.18)} = 10.81$, p<.001.

8. The relationship between party identification (seven-point scale) and confidence in the Republican Party's nominating process is statistically significant, with an uncorrected chi-squared statistic of 75.08, and $F_{(11.59,\ 11946.59)} = 3.60$, p<.001.

9. The relationship between party identification (seven-point scale) and attitudes toward the fairer type of contest is statistically significant, with an uncorrected chi-squared statistic of 30.04, and $F_{(5.46,\ 5587.46)} = 3.07$, p = .007.

10. The relationship between party identification (seven-point scale) and attitudes toward the openness of the contest is statistically significant, with an uncorrected chi-squared statistic of 50.33, and $F_{(5.95,\ 6093.72)} = 4.49$, p = .002.

11. The operationalization of caucus exposure presented simply codes for whether a caucus was held by either party in 2016. In ten states, both parties held a caucus. In another six states, one of the parties held a caucus and one party held a primary. Thus, any respondent living in one of these sixteen states was coded as having been

exposed to a caucus. I also operationalized caucus exposure by party, where I considered the party identification of respondents living in the six states where one party uses a primary and the other uses a caucus. For instance, in Washington, the Democratic Party held caucuses whereas the Republican Party used a primary. Therefore, I categorized Washington respondents identifying as Democratic as having been exposed to a caucus, but Republican respondents were coded as not having been exposed to a caucus. One of the limitations of this operationalization is that it requires omitting Independents who lived in these mixed states. The results under this operationalization did not differ substantively, so I chose to present the more straightforward operationalization that utilizes the largest number of cases.

12. The relationship between caucus exposure and attitudes toward the type of contest is statistically significant, with an uncorrected chi-squared statistic of 7.03, and $F_{(1,\ 11031)} = 4.6$, p = .032.

13. Similarly to the analysis conducted for exposure to primaries and caucuses, I also operationalized the openness rules in the state based on whether the respondent's party held an open, semi-open, or closed contest in his or her state. This operationalization reduces the sample size, as it excludes Independents. Regardless of which version of the variable is employed, no statistically significant relationship between exposure to various openness rules and attitudes about the fairness of these rules emerges.

14. The relationship between party identification (seven-point scale) and attitudes about Trump's impact is statistically significant, with an uncorrected chi-squared statistic of 329.87, and $F_{(22.01,\ 22916.21)} = 8.10$, $p < .001$.

15. The relationship between party identification (seven point scale) and attitudes about Sanders's impact is statistically significant, with an uncorrected chi-squared statistic of 168.32, and $F_{(21.67,\ 22538.6)} = 3.90$, $p < .001$.

11

Populist Waves in the 2016 Presidential Nominations

Another Limit to the Party Decides Thesis

Wayne Steger

Bernie Sanders and Donald Trump ran anti-establishment populist campaigns for their parties' presidential nominations. Sanders railed against billionaires, CEOs, Wall Street, and the political party establishments that he accused of serving their interests at the expense of the ninety-nine percent. Trump targeted government officials, saying, "we are led by very, very, stupid people," who are "corrupt" and "beholden to special interests."[1] Both candidates sought to mobilize discontented people to upend the party establishments in Washington D.C. Sanders called on people to join "a revolution" while Trump promised to "drain the Swamp." Sanders and Trump posed serious challenges to existing party coalitions. Despite that threat, party leaders seemed limited in their ability to stem the populist tide.

Cohen, Karol, Noel, and Zaller's (2008) *The Party Decides* argued that party insiders, groups, and activists that form the stakeholders of the party coalition greatly influence the selection of presidential nominees by coordinating their support early in the nomination process. Steger (2013, 2015) qualified that thesis, arguing that party insider influence is conditional on the unity of the party coalition and the availability of a candidate with majority support in national opinion polls three years before the caucuses and primaries begin. Populism poses an additional challenge to the thesis by reducing the influence of party insiders and enabling populist leaders to challenge the policy orthodoxy of the party coalitions. The elevation of new players in party networks and the challenge to the party ideology have the potential to redefine the coalitions and policies of both political parties.

Explanations for the rise of populist sentiments focus on declining economic opportunity, and/or cultural backlash against sociocultural change (Grattan 2016; Inglehart and Norris 2016; Mudde and Kaltwasser 2012). This chapter presents evidence for both the economic and the cultural backlash arguments. Specifically, the growth of left-wing populist sentiment seems to center on the problems of economic inequality and the political power of the very wealthy, while right-wing populism is fueled by a mixture of declining economic opportunity and economic mobility (but not inequality) and cultural backlash.

The strength of populist attitudes has considerable potential to redefine the coalition and policies of the political parties. Populism also matters because of the implications for the political system more generally. On the positive side, populist movements serve as a wake-up call to the political class that they have been overly attentive to special interests and must correct course to serve a forgotten middle (Grattan 2016). Populism also threatens the institutions and values liberal democracy. Populists want the will of the people to prevail, even if that means overriding the interests of and constitutional protections afforded to minorities (Mudde and Kaltwasser 2012). Overriding such institutions may upset the precarious balance of majority and minority interests that maintain social and political stability (Riker 1988).

Two Veins of Populism

Populism has a variety of meanings in popular and academic discourse, but the common threads are an anti-elite or an *anti-establishment framework* in which candidates or political parties seek to *mobilize "the people" against corrupt elites* in order to *disrupt status quo, politics-as-usual* (e.g., Kazin 1998; Canovan 1999; Mudde 2004). Beyond these common threads, left- and right-wing populist diverge. Populism is a "thin ideology" that attaches to a traditional thick ideology such as progressivism or conservatism (Mudde 2004). Sanders's left-wing populism fused anti-establishment appeals with a progressive economic agenda and culturally inclusive social values. Trump's right-wing populism fused anti-establishment appeals with a blend of traditional economic conservativism, economic nationalism, and culturally exclusive social values.

Sanders's Brand of Left-Wing Populism

Sanders's populist rhetoric was *primarily* anti-elite with respect to Wall Street, corporate managers, and the one-percenters who gained an outsized share of the economic growth that has occurred since the 1970s. Sanders emphasized the need to limit the economic and political power of the 1 percent and he sought to use government to reduce economic inequality. Sanders opposed, on a *secondary level*, the political "establishment" that serves the interests and priorities of these economic elites. Sanders and the digital media outlets that supported his brand of politics, portrayed the Clintons as neoliberal enablers of Wall Street and Corporate America. Sanders proposed a progressive economic agenda that included reigning in big banks, pro-union policies, increased minimum wage, expanded Social Security, a single-payer health care system, tuition-free college education, protectionist trade policy, and a more progressive tax system.

The cultural dimension of Sanders's left-wing populism reflects a cosmopolitan value system that embraces cultural diversity and inclusive social values (e.g., Inglehart 1977). Inglehart and Norris (2016) argue that the cosmopolitan value system appeals to more educated and urban populations that are more accepting of the need for social justice for historically disadvantaged groups. It should be noted that Clinton also embraced cosmopolitan and social justice themes, so there were only nuanced distinctions between the two candidates on this dimension.

In general, these themes aligned with the attitudes, issue preferences, and priorities of Sanders's supporters as indicated by the ANES Pilot Survey.[2] Sanders's portrayal of Clinton as a neoliberal appears to have influenced his supporters. Sanders supporters rated Clinton as more centrist, $\mu = 2.92$, than they rated the Democratic Party, $\mu = 2.48$, or Barack Obama, $\mu = 2.54$ on a seven-point scale from very liberal to very conservative. By comparison, Clinton supporters rated her as more centrist, $\mu = 3.15$ but close to their rating of the Democratic Party, $\mu = 3.04$. The perception that Clinton was a neoliberal also shows up in Sanders's supporters' responses in the 2016 exit polls during the caucuses and primaries (see below). While many Sanders supporters saw Clinton as too moderate for the party, there was no significant difference in the ideological self-placement of the candidates' supporters. Clinton supporters had a mean self-placement of 3.32 while Sanders supporters had a mean self-placement of 3.29 on the same seven-point scale.

Sanders's supporters were similar to Clinton's in many of their attitudes and policy preferences, especially in regard to questions about social identity and social policy. Supporters of both candidates held similar feelings toward Blacks, Hispanics, feminists, Muslims, LGBTQ, and transgender populations. Sanders's supporters were significantly more likely to agree that "the way people talk needs to change with the times to be more sensitive to people from different backgrounds." Sanders's supporters were significantly less likely to view race and "being an American" as important to their social identity. Sanders's supporters thus appear to have been somewhat more cosmopolitan in their cultural orientation, but both groups of supporters held socially inclusive views.

There were a few more differences in supporters' issue preferences and priorities, with Sanders's supporters closer to the left-wing populist profile described earlier. Sanders's supporters were significantly more likely to identify income inequality and limiting campaign spending—two of Sander's signature issues, as important for choosing a candidate. Sanders's supporters were less supportive of free trade agreements and of sending troops to fight ISIS in Syria, consistent with Sanders's protectionist and isolationist foreign policy. Clinton's supporters gave gun control, crime, women's rights, immigration, unemployment, and economic growth greater priority than did Sanders's supporters, though the differences were not substantial. Clinton supporters were significantly more supportive of expanding legal immigration, and significantly more likely to agree that whites have advantages and they were more supportive of government action to redress racial inequalities. These differences likely reflect the racial, ethnic, and gender differences of the candidates' supporters—Clinton had far more black and Hispanic supporters, while Sanders's supporters were mostly white. Clinton also had an advantage among women.

Notably, Sanders's supporters were significantly less favorable in their retrospective (and prospective) evaluations of economic conditions over the past year (for the coming year), compared to Clinton supporters. Sanders's supporters also were: (1) less optimistic about the opportunity in America today for the average person to get ahead; (2) more pessimistic about people's ability to improve their financial well-being; and (3) saw it as significantly harder to climb up the income ladder compared to Clinton supporters. The differences between the Democratic candidates' supporters were greater on questions of economic inequality and economic mobility/opportunity than on other attitudinal or policy areas. These distinctions are consistent with explanations of populism as a response to economic dislocations and declining economic opportunity (Inglehart and Norris 2016; Rothwell and Rosell 2016; Mudde and Kaltwasser 2012; Steger forthcoming).

Trump's Brand of Right-Wing Populism

Trump's right-wing populism is multi-faceted in its anti-elitism. Trump and other right-wing populists blame government for "rigging the system" in ways that disadvantage middle- and working-class Americans in favor of "special interests" above *and* in favor of "undeserving" poor, minorities, and especially immigrants. Trump and his supporters were *primarily* anti-establishment with respect to government officials consistent with decades of conservative rhetoric. Trump and digital media outlets that backed him attacked, on a *secondary level*, "special interests" including Wall Street and hedge-fund managers *and* policies for ethnic or racial minorities, and immigrants. Trump and his digital media supporters also stoked antipathy toward urban and intellectual elites whose cultural values and promotion of diversity conflict with traditional values—a conflict defines a central cleavage between Democrats and Republicans (Hetherington and Weiler 2009).

Trump's "Make America Great Again" themes fused anti-establishment rhetoric with a blend of neoliberal economics (i.e., lower taxes, less regulation) with economic nationalism and culturally exclusive social values. Economic nationalism is an economic strategy of protectionism conjoined with the emotional affect of patriotism and nativism. Trump promised to end the Trans Pacific Partnership (TPP) agreement, renegotiate NAFTA, and penalize American manufacturers that move jobs out of the country. On the domestic front, Trump promised a massive infrastructure program to create jobs and to protect social welfare programs for "deserving" people—those who have paid Social Security and Medicare taxes and which may not include immigrants and welfare recipients. In many ways, Trump campaigned more as an identity conservative than as an economic conservative (Noel 2016a). The cultural dimension targets both the "other" as well as cosmopolitans whose cultural values and promotion of diversity conflict with traditionalism and self-identification as "real Americans." Trump demonized Mexicans and Muslims and promised to build a wall along the Mexican border, deport illegal immigrants, and ban Muslim immigrants. Trump called for tougher law enforcement to deal with violent crime, a problem that he attributed to illegal immigrants and people in inner cities—references that prime people to think about Latinos and African-Americans (Ball 2016; Hurwitz and Peffley 2005). Trump responded to criticisms of his rhetoric by attacking "political correctness." Trump's attacks on political correctness targeted feminists and university professors, groups that Trump supporters viewed even more negatively than African Americans and Hispanics. Trump's attacks on political correctness also solidified his anti-elitist credentials. He demonstrated his resolve to challenge elites by saying what others would not (Dreher 2016).

These themes and positions enabled Trump to appeal to constituencies that were attitudinally distinct on a number of dimensions from the supporters of other Republican candidates. Trump's supporters held similar views as other Republicans but they were more extreme in their attitudes on social identity. Compared supporters of other Republican candidates (averaged for the rest of the field), Trump supporters were significantly less favorable in their thermometer ratings toward blacks, Hispanics, feminists, LBGTQ, transgendered, and especially Muslims. Trump supporters exhibited more favorable feelings toward whites than did the supporters of other Republicans. Trump supporters were also significantly more likely to view being an "American" as important to their identity. Trump's attacks on political correctness seemed to have resonated. Trump's supporters were much more likely to agree that "the way people talk" has "already gone too far and many people are just too easily offended," compared to the supporters of other Republican candidates.

Trump's aggressive attacks on President Obama and Hillary Clinton also resonated with his supporters. ANES Pilot Study Thermometer ratings indicate that Trump supporters, were on average, more cool toward Obama ($\mu = 22.7$) and Clinton ($\mu = 25.2$) than were the supporters of other Republican candidates ($\mu = 43.6$ for Obama and $\mu = 39.2$ for Clinton). Another indication that Trump's supporters were right-wing populists is that his supporters were significantly more likely to believe that Barack Obama was a Muslim and they were more confident in this belief—supporting Hofstadter's (2008) view that right-wing populists are prone to conspiracy theories.

In terms of issue priorities and preferences, Trump supporters were more isolationist and were less supportive of sending troops to fight ISIS in Syria than were the supporters of other Republican candidates. Trump supporters also were significantly more opposed to the United States making free-trade agreements with other countries compared to supporters of other Republican candidates. They also were significantly more likely to believe that the United States would experience a terrorist attack in the United States that kills more than 100 people and were more worried that such an attack would occur in the area that they live. Perhaps the biggest policy difference between Trump supporters and other Republicans was that Trump supporters were much more opposed to legal and illegal immigrants than supporters of other Republican candidates, and most were opposed to allowing Syrian refugees into the United States.

Also consistent with the economic backlash theory of populism, Trump supporters were significantly less favorable in their retrospective (and prospective) evaluations of economic conditions over the past year (for the coming year), compared to supporters of other Republican candidates—who as a whole, were on average much more pessimistic than were Democrats in early 2016. As with Sanders's supporters, Trump supporters were (1) less optimistic about the opportunity in America today for the average person to get ahead; (2) more pessimistic about people's ability to improve their financial well-being; and (3) saw it as significantly harder to climb up the income ladder compared to the supporters of other Republican candidates. Overall, the attitudinal differences between the supporters of Trump and the other Republican candidates were more pronounced on questions of economic opportunity and economic mobility than on most questions relating to social identity. Trump's supporters, however, were most distinctive in their responses to questions about immigrants, terrorism, and especially Muslims. All of this is consistent with the characterization of Trump's appeal on the grounds of economic nationalism and his socially exclusive white identity politics.

Thus Sanders, Trump, and their respective supporters fit the profiles of left- and right-wing populists. While both candidates and their supporters look like populists, why did Sanders's campaign fall short while Trump's campaign succeeded? The next section focuses on some of the reasons for those different outcomes.

Conditional Arbiters and The Populist Challenge

Sanders and Trump were able to run particularly strong campaigns because they had the opportunity and the means to do so. First, both candidates had opportunities because the rules governing the selection of presidential nominees enable outsider candidates to compete. Political parties are the arbiters of representative democracy because they put candidates on the ballot (Schattschneider 1960; Bawn et al. 2012). Reforms of the presidential nomination process during the early 1970s democratized the selection of presidential nominees, with both political parties empowering rank-and-file party voters to express their preferences for candidates in binding caucuses and primaries (Ceaser 1979; Polsby 1983). Power over the nomination shifted from party insiders to party activists who cast the decisive ballots in the caucuses and primaries, the outcomes of which determine candidates' allotment of delegates to the national nominating conventions. This process opened the door for outsider candidates to compete for the nomination by appealing directly to political activists and groups.

While outsider candidates can compete for a presidential nomination, they rarely succeed. A major reason is that political party insiders have the capacity to rally behind a candidate that serves party coalition partners' interests. Cohen, Karol, Noel, and Zaller (2008) argue that party insiders can advance their preferred candidate by coordinating their support behind that candidate during the invisible primary—the phase of the campaign occurring before the beginning of the caucuses and primaries. Essentially, party insiders and group leaders can coordinate their support and rally behind a preferred candidate and thereby structure the choices of caucus and primary voters. Party insider support helps a candidate financially, organizationally, and in image because party insiders shape media narratives by talking up their preferred candidate while downplaying the qualities and chances of other candidates.

Party insiders, however, are conditional arbiters of presidential nominations. Their ability to influence the outcome is conditional on the extent of their participation in trying to influence the race, the timing of their involvement, and their degree of convergence on a candidate.[3] Party insiders unify sooner and they participate in the process more extensively when (1) the party coalition is stable and unified, *and* (2) there is a candidate in the race with demonstrable national support in polls three years before the election (Steger 2013, 2015).

There have been two patterns of presidential nominations since the 1980s (Steger 2013). One is the *The Party Decides* party-centric pattern in which party insiders and groups coordinate and signal their support to the media, donors, activists, groups, and rank-and-file party identifiers which candidate is viable, electable, and preferable on political and policy grounds. The other is a more candidate- and campaign-centric pattern that occurs when party insiders fail to engage and unify behind a candidate during the invisible primary. In this case, the outcome is impacted more heavily by momentum during the caucuses and primaries.

The 2016 Democratic presidential nomination epitomizes the pattern articulated in *The Party Decides*. Hillary Clinton had the endorsements of 97 percent of elite party officials by the end of the invisible primary.[4] Since 86.9 percent of elite elected Democratic officials made an endorsement during the invisible primary, Clinton received the endorsements of 84.4 percent of all of the possible elite endorsements that could have occurred during the invisible primary. Both conditions identified by Steger (2013, 2015) were met in this race. Clinton had consistently received the support of a majority of respondents in national polls of Democratic Party identifiers and leaners between 2013 and 2015, despite withering attacks from Republicans on the right and from Bernie Sanders and progressive digital media on the left. While the Democratic Party coalition is diverse ideologically and by social identification, the divisions were, at the beginning of the 2016 nomination cycle, less extensive than the divisions in the Republican Party. The unity in the Democratic coalition was illustrated in the above discussion about the relative lack of attitudinal and policy differences between the supporters of Clinton and Sanders. Another critical factor clearing Clinton's path was that prominent Democratic politicians like Vice President Joe Biden and Senator Elizabeth

Warren decided not to run. The presence of a strong front-runner in national polls tends to deter potential candidates from entering the race (Adkins et al. 2015). With strong poll numbers, a relatively unified party, and an absence of traditionally strong opponents, Clinton gained the most widespread set of endorsements received by a Democratic presidential candidate in the post-reform era. Since all of these endorsers would become Superdelegates to the Democratic Convention, Clinton began the race with a nearly insurmountable lead in the delegate count. She also gained a substantial advantage in early fundraising, built a massive campaign organization, and she received most of the news coverage of the Democratic campaign. Sanders faced an enormous up-hill climb to the nomination.

As important, the breadth of populist/progressive support was more limited in the Democratic race. There were fewer populist and progressive voters in the Democratic race, especially in Southern states where Clinton won by large margins. Party loyalists favored Clinton. In the 28 states in which CNN conducted exit polls, Clinton won 63 percent of self-identified Democrats who constituted almost 74 percent of the voters in these states. Sanders won over 58 percent of the vote of self-identified Independent voters in these states, but these voters constituted only 23.5 percent of the electorate according to the 2016 exit polls. Sanders also won over two-thirds of the first-time nomination voters, but these constituted only 17 percent of caucus and primary voters.[5]

Despite Sanders's appeal to progressive voters, Sanders and Clinton split the votes of self-identified "very liberal" voters, 49.6 percent to 49.4 percent, respectively. Self-identified, "very liberal" voters constituted only a quarter of the Democratic nomination electorate. Clinton won increasingly larger percentages of self-identified "somewhat liberal," "moderate," and "conservative" voters, who were relatively larger proportions of the voters in Southern states. In terms of issue priorities, Sanders beat Clinton only among voters identifying income inequality as the most important issue influencing their decision, winning only 51.1 percent of these voters. Importantly, this segment of voters—who exhibited the issue concern most important to left-wing populists—constituted less than a quarter of voters in the 2016 exit polls. Clinton ran ahead of Sanders among respondents identifying health care, the economy or jobs, and terrorism as the most important issue.

Compared to the Republican race, there were fewer Democratic exit polls that included questions that could be used to make direct inferences about populism. In nine states, the exit polls included a question asking Democratic voters if they were satisfied, dissatisfied, or angry with the federal government. Sanders won only among voters expressing anger with the federal government (with just over 53 percent of these voters), but this block was only

14.4 percent of the respondents—less than a third of the figure for the Republican race (see below). Sanders won over 80 percent of the votes of respondents who felt that the next president should come from outside the establishment, but this group formed only 15.3 percent of the respondents in the fifteen states in which this question was asked. Sanders won 79 percent of voters who felt that Clinton was "too pro-business" but this group of respondents formed 25 percent of voters; while Clinton won 87 percent of voters who felt that Sanders was "too anti-business," a group that formed 28 percent of voters.[6] Although this is a less-than-complete picture, the available evidence indicates that the progressive, populist-oriented voters did overwhelmingly support Sanders, but these voters formed a relatively small fraction of voters in the Democratic caucuses and primaries.

As a final note, if party establishment engagement and convergence on a candidate matter for the nomination, then voting in the caucuses and primaries should not evidence the kind of campaign momentum identified by Aldrich (1980) and Bartels (1988). Rather, Clinton was expected to maintain her lead even if Sanders won an upset victory or a few such wins in the early caucuses and primaries. That is basically what happened across the primaries (see figure 11.1). Clinton won most of the caucuses and primaries, especially the larger states with more convention delegates. Sanders won enough states to stay in the race, but he did not substantially gain or sustain the momentum needed to win the race (see figure 11.1). Across the caucuses and primaries, Clinton won 56.1 percent of the popular vote to Sanders's 43.8 percent. The left-wing populist movement was not sufficiently large in 2016 for Sanders to win the nomination.

On the other side of the partisan divide, the race looked very different in each of these respects. First, the Republican race began very differently, essentially as the antithesis of *The Party Decides* pattern. Only a third of Republican governors, senators, and representatives endorsed any candidate, and no candidate received more than 27 percent of the endorsements made before the Iowa Caucus. The most endorsed Republican candidate, Jeb Bush, had the support of only 9.25 percent of the elite Republican elected officials who could have made an endorsement. When insiders divide or remain uncommitted, caucus and primary voters gain influence over the nomination because they have a larger number of viable candidates to select among, and they exercise a more independent voice. Candidate and campaign-centric factors like candidate appeal, campaign spending, media coverage, and campaign momentum become relatively more important for determining the nominee (Steger 2016).

Republican insiders failed to engage in the race and unify behind a candidate during the invisible primary for two central reasons (Steger 2016). First,

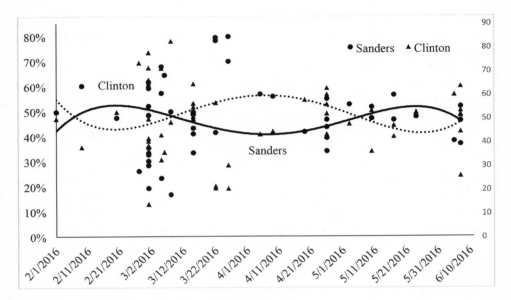

* The figure does not show the relative weights of the states.

Figure 11.1
Leading Candidate Vote Shares in 2016 Democratic Caucuses and Primaries.

party elites refrain from making endorsements when there is uncertainty about the popular appeal of candidates (Ryan 2011; Whitby 2014). The Republican Party lacked a clear front-runner in 2013–2014. None of the Republican candidates polled above 20 percent during these years and nine different candidates led in national polls leading up to the caucuses and primaries. With no clear leader at the onset of the race, a large number of ambitious Republican office holders and former office holders entered the race, making it harder for party insiders to discern which candidate would resonate with party activists and identifiers. The large number of candidates also helped divide the primary vote, a factor that helped Trump gain momentum (see below).

More importantly, the Republican Party is internally divided along ideological and populist/establishment lines. These ideological divisions are evident among party elites (Noel 2016b) and among party voters (Olsen and Scala 2015). The division between the Tea Party and establishment Republicans, however, is probably more consequential than the party's ideological divisions. Tea Party Republicans organized to challenge "establishment" Republicans who held moderate positions or who compromised with Barack

Obama (Skocpol and Williamson 2013). While the Tea Party movement faded as an organized political force by 2016, the underlying anti-establishment sentiments remain. A Pew Research Center survey found that 42 percent of politically engaged Republicans were "angry with government."[7] In the same survey, 89 percent of Republican identifiers and leaders responded that they "can seldom, if ever, trust the federal government," and 75 percent agreed that government needs "major reform." In short, these bits of evidence suggest that the potential right-wing populist electorate in the Republican nomination race was much greater than in the Democratic race.

The breadth and intensity of dissatisfaction among Republican identifiers indicates another limit to party insiders' capacity to influence nominations. Partisans who are angry with the party establishment are less likely to follow elite cues. Indeed, widespread anti-establishment sentiment among Republican voters disadvantaged experienced politicians like former Florida governor Jeb Bush. As the candidate most associated with the establishment wing of the party, Bush lost badly despite greatly outspending his opponents in the primaries that he contested. Recognizing the power of the anti-establishment sentiment, Ben Carson, Carly Fiorina, Governor Chris Christy, and Senator Ted Cruz all sought to become the candidate who would take on the establishment. None proved as effective as Donald Trump in attracting support from anti-establishment Republicans (see below).

Given the absence of an early front-runner, greater party disunity, and a big candidate field, the race was wide-open with numerous competitive candidates. In this kind of race, there should be evidence that the winner is the candidate that gains campaign momentum as identified by Aldrich (1980) and Bartels (1988). Figure 11.2 presents the Republican candidates vote shares across the caucuses and primaries. Voters in the early caucuses and primaries divided their vote among a large number of candidates and Trump prevailed in most of these contests with a narrow plurality of the vote. Across the primaries, trailing candidates dropped out of the race and Trump's share of the caucus and primary vote grew until he locked up enough delegates to win the nomination. Trump won the nomination with a 45 percent plurality of the national popular vote—a vote total padded by his winning by large majorities in the last 15 states when other candidates ceased campaigning. Trump was able to build momentum across the primaries, knocking off rivals until he could claim the Republican nomination.

Divisions in the Republican Party helped Trump by enabling Trump to gain momentum by winning narrow pluralities of the vote in the early states. Recent Republican presidential nominations have had four factions with differing preferences for candidate characteristics and policy—a declining faction of "moderates," a large faction of "somewhat conservatives," and a

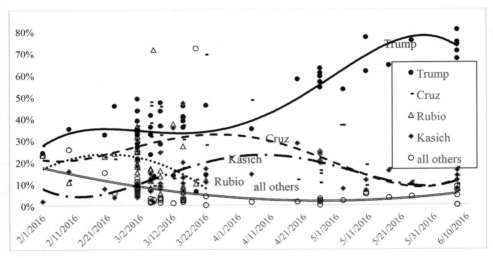

Figure 11.2
Leading Candidate Vote Shares in 2016 Republican Caucuses and Primaries.

sizable faction of "very conservatives" who further divide into religious and secular branches (Olsen and Scala 2015). Most of the candidates sought, to varying degrees, to establish themselves as the preferred candidate of one of these preferential groups. Trump emerged as the first choice of Republicans across all of these ideological groups. Trump narrowly beat Cruz among very conservative voters, but he beat Cruz by large margins among somewhat conservative and moderate Republican voters. Kasich finished second among moderate voters, but Kasich had almost no support from more conservative voters.

This pattern still leaves the question of why pluralities of Republican voters across the ideological spectrum preferred Trump to the other candidates. The critical factor appears to have been widespread dissatisfaction with the establishment among Republican caucus and primary voters. Populism, lacking a thick ideological content, spanned the ideological factions of the Republican Party. An indication of the scope of the populist vote in Republican primaries is evident in the 2016 exit poll questions asking whether they were satisfied, dissatisfied, or angry with government. Almost 90 percent of Republican voters expressed dissatisfaction or anger with the federal government. Trump won 45.6 percent of Republican respondents who were dissatisfied with the federal government and 52.9 percent of those who were angry with government. No other candidate came close to those margins. The extent of dissatisfaction and anger with government was far greater than was the case in the Democratic caucuses and primaries.

Republican polls also showed that almost 54 percent of Republican voters preferred a candidate who was "outside the establishment." Trump won over 65 percent of the votes from these anti-establishment Republicans—constituting 80 percent of his support in the caucuses and primaries. None of the other candidates came close to matching Trump's support among these voters. Trump won the support of only 8.3 percent of the votes from the 40 percent of Republicans who preferred a candidate with experience in government. These voters, however, divided their support among the other candidates so none of Trump's rivals could offset his advantage among voters preferring a candidate outside the establishment.

Republican voter preferences for candidate characteristics also distinguished Trump from other candidates in ways that reflect the populist versus establishment divide among Republicans. Of the 20 percent of Republican voters who identified "telling it like it is" as the most important candidate characteristic, 77 percent voted for Trump. Trump won over 51 percent of the vote from the 31 percent of Republican voters who said they wanted someone who could bring change as their most important candidate characteristic. Trump drew the least support (15 percent) from "values voters" comprising 34 percent of respondents in the exit polls. Values voters tend to be religious conservatives who prioritize family values and social conservatism. Values voters formed the largest block of supporters for Ted Cruz who remained in the race the longest as Trump's main rival. Finally, voters who preferred a candidate "who can win" divided their support among Rubio, Kasich, and Donald Trump in the early nominating elections. Trump's support grew among these voters as the primary season progressed and Trump's momentum grew. Trump increasingly came to be perceived as "electable" the more he won.

In terms of issues, media portrayals of immigration as a driving factor in Trump's campaign may be overstated. Trump did win 60.7 percent of the votes of people identifying immigration as the most important problem, but this constituted only 10.6 percent of respondents in the Republican exit polls. It was a critical issue for Trump, but the economy and jobs were the most important problem to a larger, 35 percent of respondents; Trump won a plurality of 42.5 percent of these voters. Trump also won pluralities of the votes of Republican voters identifying terrorism and government spending, though with narrower margins over his closest rival in each case. Trump's proposed ban on Muslim immigration was important because it blended fears of terrorism, anti-immigrant sentiment, and identity politics. In the 18 states where 2016 exit polls included a question about the ban, over 69 percent of Republican respondents agreed with the ban and Trump won almost 50 percent of these votes. The take away is that Trump won across Republican voters from different ideological factions and across voters with different issue priorities. The issues that most distinguished Trump were those most closely associated with right-wing populism.

Concluding Thoughts

Sanders and Trump both ran strong populist campaigns. Sanders's ability to win the nomination was limited in part by the unified front of party elites and loyal partisan voters, particularly African Americans and moderate Democrats who preferred Clinton to Sanders. Sanders also appears to have been limited by the proportions of Democratic voters who exhibited left-wing populist attitudes. There simply were fewer dissatisfied and angry Democrats to fuel a left-wing populist revolution. Clinton essentially matched Sanders on the cultural dimension of progressive, left-wing politics so he was unable to gain the kind of multi-faceted bases of support that Donald Trump achieved in the caucuses and primaries. Sanders failed to draw support from across the ideological spectrum of Democratic voters. Sanders's campaign, however, has energized and activated progressives in the Democratic Party in ways that appear to mirror the Tea Party faction of the Republican Party. The emergence of new, left-wing populist and progressive activists and groups likely mean a much greater, more intense nomination fight for the Democrats in 2020.

Trump won the Republican Party nomination by running as a populist candidate at a time when a large portion of the Republican electorate was sympathetic to populist appeals—reflecting a backlash to declining economic opportunity and mobility and to cultural backlash centered on immigrants and the politically correct ethos of cosmopolitan elites. He ran an unorthodox campaign and he capitalized on widespread anti-establishment sentiment among Republican Party identifiers with his rhetoric, style, and policy positions that deviated substantially from Republican Party policy orthodoxy. Trump received support from across the ideological and policy spectrum of the Republican Party while his rivals drew support from narrower niches of the party. He gained momentum during the caucuses and primaries while his opponents divided the remaining votes until one by one, they dropped out of the race.

Both Sanders and Trump threaten the ideological and policy profiles of the two major parties. Sanders's candidacy energized the left wing of the

Democratic Party in ways that omen poorly for "third-way" Democrats in the party. At a minimum, Democratic insiders have to reckon with the powerful wakeup call posed by the Sanders campaign. The progressives are increasingly angry, activated, and demanding of policy. The invigoration of these activists will move the Democratic coalition to the left. Trump's ascension to the White House makes him and his populist supporters a much more disruptive force. Presidents have considerable potential to reshape the ideological profile of their party (Skowronek 1993; Herrera 1995). Given the extent to which Trump's economic nationalism and identity politics diverge from traditional Republican orthodoxy, the expectation is that the Republican Party coalition is amid a dramatic reconfiguration as well.

Notes

1. https://www.youtube.com/watch?v=-UvgCwOmD80. September 9, 2015.

2. The following discussion uses data from the 2016 ANES Pilot Survey, taken right before the onset of the caucuses and primaries. Responses are grouped by support for a candidate. All values for the ANES Pilot Survey are weighted sample values for SPSS.

3. *The Party Decides (TPD)* analyzed the timing and convergence of endorsements, but did not consider participation rates. Accounting for participation changes the picture.

4. This analysis uses endorsements by elite elected party officials, which is a less inclusive measure than that used by Cohen et al. (2008). The two measures, however, correlate highly because party elites and group leaders and activists generally endorse the same candidate, with most differences resulting in less consensus in the endorsement patter (e.g., Steger 2016).

5. The question identifying first time voters was asked in only 15 states.

6. This question was asked in only Mississippi, Florida, Missouri, and Ohio. Another question, asking if "Wall Street helped or hurt the economy" was asked in six other states. Sanders won 54 percent of the 62 percent of the voters identifying "hurt" but Clinton won 74 percent of the 30 percent of voters identifying "help."

7. See studies by the Pew Research Center, "Beyond Distrust: How Americans View Their Government," November 2015, p. 9; "Campaign Exposes Fissures Over Issues, Values and How Life Has Changed in the U.S.," March 2016; and "2016 Campaign: Strong Interest, Widespread Dissatisfaction," July 2016.

Part IV

Party in Electorate

12

Political Identity and Party Polarization in the American Electorate

David C. Kimball, Joseph Anthony, and Tyler Chance

ARTISAN POLARIZATION has become a defining feature of contemporary American politics. Evidence of ideological polarization among party elites has fueled a debate about the nature and extent of polarization among the American public. While much of the early debate focused on an ideological definition of polarization, recently, attention has shifted to psychological dimensions of polarization. Increased partisan disagreement among politicians and activists has fostered a more attentive electorate and a stronger sense of partisan identity among the mass public. Polarized politics encourages the public to view party competition in zero-sum terms and to denigrate their political opponents more than in the past.

One manifestation of partisan conflict is increased fear and loathing of political opponents among the mass public, often termed "affective polarization" or "negative partisanship" (Webster and Abramowitz 2017; Lelkes, Sood, and Iyengar 2017). Supporters of both parties express increasing levels of contempt toward the opposite party and its presidential candidates, with the 2016 election cycle producing record levels of out-party demonization. Polarized ratings of the two major parties have many roots, but identity politics rooted in partisanship and group-based attitudes remain the most powerful predictors of affective polarization. Furthermore, affective polarization highlights a mismatch between how politics is practiced at the elite level and how politics is understood by the mass public. Among elites, such as politicians, lobbyists, and party activists, political conflict is often waged in terms of competing ideologies or policy programs, but the public tends to see politics in terms of group identities and group conflict. Donald Trump exploited this disjuncture by appealing to group-based biases to win the GOP nomination and the 2016 presidential election. Using data from the American National Election Studies, we find that partisanship and other group attitudes are more closely associated with the growth of affective polarization in the mass public. In something of a departure from previous elections, we also find that group-based attitudes outperform ideological measures in explaining the choice for president in 2016. The forces producing affective polarization show no signs of abating and identity politics is in full flower in the Trump era.

The Growth of Affective Polarization

The increased frequency of elite-level partisan conflict primes partisan loyalties among the mass public and leads to growing contempt for opposing partisans. One piece of evidence comes from feeling thermometer ratings of political parties and presidential candidates, according to national surveys conducted by the American National Election Studies (ANES).[1] The thermometer questions ask respondents to rate groups or political figures on a scale from 0 to 100, with higher values indicating warmer feelings and lower scores indicating more animosity toward the group or political figure. As these data show, during the past forty years, Republicans and Democrats have consistently rated their own party positively, at an average rating of approximately 70 degrees, with a modest decline during the most recent decade. However, ratings of the opposite party have dropped substantially during the same period, particularly since the turn of the twenty-first century. Mean ratings of the opposite party were close to 50 degrees in 1980 but have dropped to 31 degrees in 2016, a record low for the series. The absolute difference between thermometer ratings of the two major parties has become a fairly common measure of "affective polarization." As the solid curve in figure 12.1 shows, the average gap in affection for each of the major political parties has increased from 21 degrees in 1978 to roughly 35 degrees in 2012 and 2016.

Evidence of affective polarization is even more compelling when we examine thermometer ratings of presidential candidates. Over the past several decades, we see the same pattern of consistent positive ratings for the candidate of one's own party but sharply declining ratings of the opposite party's candidate. The negative ratings of presidential candidates plumbed new depths in the 2016 presidential election, when 30 percent of respondents rated Donald Trump at 0 degrees and 23 percent rated Hillary Clinton at 0 degrees. To put these numbers in perspective, the only prior candidates to

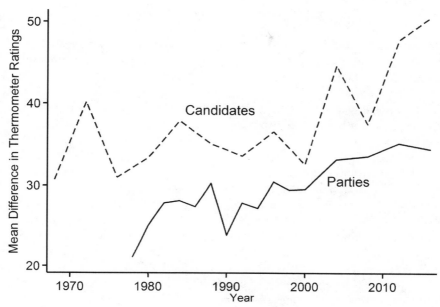

Figure 12.1
Growth in Affective Polarization, 1968–2016.
Source: ANES 2016, 2017.

reach double digit percentages for a 0 degree thermometer rating are Barack Obama in 2012 (11 percent), Mitt Romney in 2012 (13 percent), and George W. Bush in 2004 (13 percent). As the dashed line in figure 12.1 shows, the mean difference in thermometer ratings for the two major party candidates increased from 31 degrees in 1968 and 1976 to 51 degrees in 2016, a record level of affective polarization for the series.

There is further evidence of affective polarization in the American public. Substantial portions of each party report feeling angry about the opposing party and its candidates (Mason 2015; Miller and Conover 2015). Strong party identifiers are also more likely to endorse the use of unsavory tactics to win an election or policy debate (Miller and Conover 2015). Americans are less trusting of members of the opposite party (Iyengar and Westwood 2015), and people discriminate against members of the opposing party in hiring decisions, employee behavior, and consumer choices (Iyengar and Westwood 2015; McConnell et al. 2018). Finally, a growing number of Americans say they would be "displeased" if one of their children married someone from the opposite party (Iyengar, Sood, and Lelkes 2012). Evidence of bias and hostility toward out-partisans is growing.

Explaining Affective Polarization

One perspective holds that ideology is an important source of affective polarization. In a straightforward application of the median voter theorem (Downs 1957), some argue that when the opposite party and its candidates adopt more extreme ideological positions then other voters tend to dislike them more (Rogowski and Sutherland 2016; Webster and Abramowitz 2017). This explanation is plausible, since there is clear evidence of elite ideological polarization in the United States (e.g., McCarty, Poole and Rosenthal 2008). This view of affective polarization in service of ideology casts polarization and the American public in a more favorable light.

We are skeptical of the claim that ideology is a major force behind affective polarization. Seminal studies, old and new, conclude that much of the American public is largely "innocent of ideology" (Converse 1964). Few Americans demonstrate a command of ideological concepts, and roughly half of American adults identify as moderates or do not place themselves on an ideological scale at all. Furthermore, most Americans do not hold consistent policy preferences across different issues, and policy preferences are not very stable over time (for more recent evidence, see Lewis-Beck et al. 2008; Kinder and Kalmoe 2017). Party sorting (a growing correlation between partisanship and ideological identification) has indeed occurred, and this process is an important element of polarized politics in the United States. However, sorting occurs mainly because people are shifting their ideology and policy positions to make them consistent with their party identification, not the other way around (Levendusky 2009a; Layman et al. 2010). Constituents often change their policy opinions in response to the announced positions of their elected representatives or politicians they like (Broockman and Butler 2017). A recent study finds that many Republican voters are willing to change their policy preferences to align them with positions adopted by President Trump, even when Trump advocates liberal policies (Barber and Pope 2017). Furthermore, strong Republicans were more susceptible to Trump opinion leadership than weak and leaning Republicans. Among the mass public ideology seems to be a product of other attitudes and behavior rather than a causal variable.

Instead, we argue that group identities and group attitudes are the driving force behind the growing affective polarization in American politics. Several recent studies evaluate a lot of evidence and conclude that group-based theories, rather than ideological reasoning, better explain mass political behavior (Achen and Bartels 2016; Kinder and Kalmoe 2017; Mason 2018). People tend to understand politics in terms of group interests and group identities, and voters often act on group-based attitudes. This is consistent with social identity theory, which argues that people derive their own sense of self from their membership in groups. The motivation to identify with an in-group that is distinct from a perceived out-group is powerful. Social identity theory predicts that group conflict strengthens group identities and fosters in-group favoritism and hostility toward out-groups (Tajfel and Turner 1979). For example, a recent study found that Hillary Clinton's defeat in the 2016 presidential election strengthened the political and gender identities of her supporters (Gomez et al. 2017). Group differences in resources and advantages often form the basis for enduring social and political conflicts (Tilly 1998). Furthermore, public evaluations of a variety of public policies tend to be "group-centric" (Nelson and Kinder 1996)—that is, support for a particular policy is shaped by public attitudes toward the groups most affected by the policy (e.g., Schneider and Ingram 1993).

The most important group identity in politics is party identification. The authors of *The American Voter* developed the concept of party identification to resemble other social group identities, like religion (Campbell et al. 1960). Strong partisans stand out from other partisans in terms of their robust social identity with a political party, which produces higher levels of voter loyalty and political activism (Green, Palmquist, and Schickler 2002; Miller and Conover 2015). Partisan identity and hostility toward the opposing party are deeply ingrained and automatic impulses that precede reflection and reasoning (Iyengar and Westwood 2015; Theodoridis 2017). Futhermore, exposure to political campaigns and partisan media can increase the salience of party identification and other group identities and prime associated group biases in the mass public (Gerber, Huber, and Washington 2010; Iyengar, Sood, and Lelkes 2012; Lelkes, Sood, and Iyengar 2017; Druckman, Peterson, and Slothuus 2013; Huddy, Mason, and Aarøe 2015; Levendusky 2013).

Finally, party identification shapes other political attitudes and behavior. A strong party identifier "tends to see what is favorable to his partisan orientation" (Campbell et al. 1960, 133). Strengthened party identification causes a shift in policy preferences and evaluations of public officials (Gerber, Huber, and Washington 2010; Lodge and Taber 2013). In addition, partisans are motivated to believe things that make their party look good, even when those beliefs are factually incorrect (Bartels 2002; Jerit and Barabas 2012). As Mason puts it, a partisan is "more like a sports fan than like a banker choosing an investment" (2015, 129). Some argue that ideological labels are simply additional group identities that provide clues about one's partisan identity (Kinder and Kalmoe 2017). For example, while most Americans do not seem to understand ideological concepts, most do know that the GOP is the more conservative party (72 percent answered this question correctly in the 2016

ANES survey). For these reasons, we expect group identities and attitudes to be stronger predictors of affective polarization than ideology.

Figure 12.2 provides a comparison of partisanship and ideology as predictors of affective polarization, based on ANES election surveys conducted from 1978 to 2016. The vertical axis in the figure measures the difference in thermometer ratings of the two major parties. The left panel of the figure depicts the mean party thermometer differences by strength of party identification. As the graph shows, the thermometer measure is very effective at discriminating between various levels of strength of partisanship. Strong partisans produce significantly more polarized ratings of the two parties than weaker partisans, and the difference between strong partisans versus each of the weaker partisan groups has grown by about five to ten degrees over the past 38 years. The differences between weak and leaning partisans are not as pronounced, but weak partisans consistently hold more polarized evaluations of the two parties than leaning partisans. For strong partisans, the difference in party thermometer ratings increased from roughly 39 degrees in 1978 to roughly 55 degrees in 2012 and 2016. Affective polarization has risen for weak and leaning partisans as well, while pure Independents have remained in a low (5–10 degree) range throughout this period. The evidence suggests that party identification has become more salient during this time period.

The right-hand panel in figure 12.2 depicts the same measure of affective polarization for different categories of ideological identification over the same period. We measure ideology with the ANES question that asks respondents to place themselves on a seven-point scale from extremely liberal at one end to extremely conservative at the other end. Roughly 28 percent of ANES respondents in this sample did not place themselves on the seven-point ideology scale, yet those non-respondents are on par with weak partisans when it comes to their polarized ratings of the two parties, including an increase in affective polarization over time. Moderates, who placed themselves at the midpoint of the ideology scale (23 percent of the sample), are fairly similar to leaning partisans in the trend and levels of affective polarization. If ideology is a driving force behind affective polarization, then it is not clear why moderates and non-respondents rate the two parties so differently. Ideologues, who placed themselves on the liberal or conservative side of the ideology scale, comprise a bit less than half of the ANES sample, and their ratings of the two parties are more polarized than the other two groups, and ideologues have become more polarized over time. Nevertheless, ideologues are only 8 to 15 degrees more polarized, on average, than the other two less ideological groups.[2] When it comes to affective polarization, party is the more important group identity than ideology.

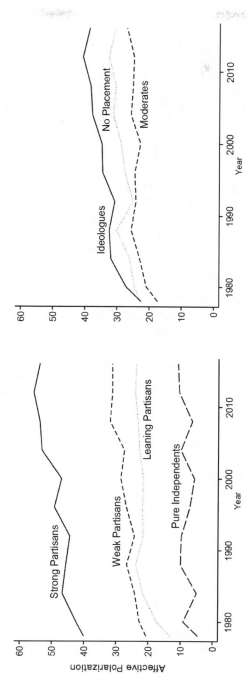

Figure 12.2
Affective Polarization by Strength of Partisanship and Ideology.
Source: ANES 2016, 2017.

2016: A Group Attitudes Election

The growth of negative partisanship culminated in the 2016 presidential campaign, which gave new meaning to the term "identity politics." The Democrats nominated the more moderate of the two front-running candidates and Republican voters eschewed several more traditional conservative candidates in favor of Donald Trump. A Cruz versus Sanders general election campaign could have been an ideological battle royale. Instead, Trump versus Clinton provided a different campaign that highlighted numerous group identities and attitudes. For example, Hillary Clinton became the first woman in American history to be a major party nominee for president, raising the salience of the role of women in society during the campaign.

Furthermore, while Donald Trump has behaved as a more traditional conservative as president, during the presidential campaign (including the nomination phase) he staked out decidedly non-conservative positions on several issues, including foreign policy, trade, entitlements, and eminent domain. During one of the primary debates, Trump even said that "millions of women" have been "helped greatly" by Planned Parenthood (Paquette 2016). Donald Trump did not offer a consistent conservative ideology on the campaign trail. What Trump did serve up to GOP voters, in heaping portions far exceeding what any competitor could provide, was red meat. No Republican candidate disparaged as many groups that annoy GOP voters—the Clintons, President Obama, the media, Muslims, immigrants, protesters, people of color, labor unions—with as much gusto as Trump. While conventional wisdom holds that campaign appeals to prejudice need to be subtle and implied, Trump eschewed the dog whistle for the bullhorn. We expect group-based attitudes to matter in 2012 too, since the 2012 election featured the nation's first African-American president running for reelection. However, the 2012 campaign did not feature the daily onslaught of outrages that stoked group identities and grievances like the 2016 campaign. In these two campaign environments how do group attitudes and ideological measures fare in explaining the choice for president?

To answer this question, we estimate a regression model of the vote for president in the 2012 and 2016 elections, comparing a set of group attitudes and a set of ideology measures as predictors. The ANES data include a wide range of public opinion measures for this comparison. Our group attitudes include the familiar seven-point party identification scale, and it is coded so that higher values denote Republicans.

For another set of group attitudes, we average the thermometer ratings of groups associated with each party coalition to create a Democratic-aligned group measure and a Republican-aligned group measure. The group measure for Democrats includes thermometer ratings of environmentalists, feminists, gays and lesbians, transgender people, liberals, labor unions, people on welfare, and Black Lives Matter (α = .77 in 2012; α = .85 in 2016). The group measure for Republicans includes ratings of big business, rich people, Christian fundamentalists, the military, the Tea Party, and conservatives (α = .80 in 2012; α = .79 in 2016).[3] Many of the groups aligned with each party were frequent targets of charged rhetoric during the 2016 campaign. We expect voting for the Republican candidate for president to be negatively associated with the Democratic Party group measure and positively associated with the Republican Party group measure.

It is an understatement to say that racially infused rhetoric was a common feature of the 2016 campaign. Before he was a presidential candidate, Donald Trump may have been best known in politics as the champion of "birtherism"—the false claim that President Obama was not born in the United States. Trump regularly retweeted messages from white supremacists during the campaign and he was slow to distance his campaign from the support of David Duke, a former Ku Klux Klan leader. Trump frequently denigrated the Black Lives Matter movement, included a "law and order" refrain in his stump speech, and he hired as a key campaign advisor Steve Bannon, the Breitbart News executive and self-professed leader of the Alt-Right movement (Shear, Haberman, and Schmidt 2016). Hillary Clinton also brought attention to the concept of implicit racial bias during the campaign.

While overt racism in American public opinion has declined over time, "racial resentment" has emerged as a powerful variable in the wake of the civil rights movement. Racial resentment centers on a belief that a lack of work ethic accounts for inequality between black and white Americans. Since there are substantial differences between black and white voters in their support for the two major parties, we expect racial resentment to be associated with polarized ratings of the parties. Racial resentment gained potency in public opinion during the presidency of Barack Obama, the first black president in American history (Tesler and Sears 2010). Racial resentment has not diminished over the last two decades and it is associated with a variety of policy attitudes and voting choices (Kinder and Sanders 1996; Tesler and Sears 2010). We measure racial resentment based on four questions that ask respondents the degree to which they agree or disagree with statements about the status of blacks in society (Tesler and Sears 2010, 19). Responses to these four items are averaged together to create the racial resentment index and we rescale it to range from 0 to 1 (α = .80 in 2012; α = .84 in 2016). Thus, we expect racial resentment to be positively associated with the vote for president.

Immigrants may have been an even more frequent rhetorical target than

African Americans during the 2016 campaign. Donald Trump owned the immigration issue and he launched his presidential campaign by denigrating Mexican-American immigrants, calling them "rapists." He led chants of "build the wall" while on the campaign trail. Trump referenced the Mexican heritage of a federal judge in criticizing the judge's ruling against him. Trump proposed banning Muslims from entering the United States and he falsely claimed that thousands of Muslims in New Jersey celebrated the attacks against the World Trade Center on September 11, 2001. Thus, we also expect that attitudes toward immigrants help explain the vote for president, particularly in 2016. We create a measure of hostility to immigrants based on responses to four ANES questions that ask whether immigrants (1) increase crime, (2) harm America's culture, (3) take away jobs, and (4) are good for America's economy. Each item was recoded to a 0–1 scale, with higher values indicating greater antipathy toward immigrants, and the four variables were averaged together to form an immigrant attitude scale (α = 0.81).[4] We expect the immigration measure to be positively correlated with a vote for the Republican presidential candidate.

Finally, the 2016 presidential campaign included charged rhetoric about the role of women in politics and society. The Clinton campaign frequently invoked equal rights for women and nodded toward the historic nature of her bid as the first woman running as a major party nominee for president. Trump faced allegations of sexual assault from several women after the "Access Hollywood" tape was made public. In addition, the campaign featured familiar debates over abortion, contraception, equal pay, and workplace rights for women. There is a consistent gender gap in voting and party identification, and exit polls indicate that the 2016 presidential election produced the largest gender gap in the polling era. Thus, beliefs about the role of women are likely to be another group attitude influencing vote choice in 2016. Our group attitude measure is modern sexism, a concept that taps beliefs about changing gender roles and discrimination against women (Glick and Fiske 2011). Six ANES items ask about media coverage of sex discrimination, work and homemaking roles for men versus women, whether women demanding equality seek special favors, whether complaining about sex discrimination creates more problems, whether a working mother can bond with her children, and whether it is important to elect more women to office. We averaged responses to the six questions to create a modern sexism scale (α = .65).[5] Higher values indicate more traditional views about women in society and should be associated with a greater likelihood of voting for the GOP presidential candidate.

In addition to group attitudes, we amass a series of ideological measures as predictors of the vote for president. One is the seven-point ideological placement measure described above. Higher scores indicate more conservative respondents, so the ideology measure should be positively correlated with a Republican vote for president. We include two additional measures that tap separate economic and cultural dimensions of political preferences. One is a measure of social welfare policy preferences, based on eight items. Four items are seven-point scales that ask for preferences on (1) government aid to blacks, (2) government versus personal responsibility for jobs and living standards, (3) the government services and spending scale, and (4) support for the Affordable Care Act. The other four items measure preferences for increased or decreased federal spending on (1) poor people, (2) child care, (3) public schools, and (4) welfare programs. All eight items were recoded to a common scale and then averaged together to create a social welfare policy scale (α = .85 in 2012; α = .72 in 2016).

To measure cultural values, we use a measure of moral traditionalism that focuses on "the degree to which conservative or orthodox moral standards should guide the public and private life of the nation" (Goren 2013, 5). Moral traditionalism undergirds several policy debates in the United States, including abortion and gay rights; and moral traditionalism has been a source of partisan conflict since the 1960s. We measure moral traditionalism using four questions that ask respondents the degree to which they agree or disagree with statements about newer lifestyles, changing moral behavior, traditional family values, and tolerance for different moral standards. Responses were averaged together to create a moral traditionalism scale ($\alpha = .77$ in 2012; α = .71 in 2016). Higher values indicate a stronger preference for traditional moral values. Social welfare preferences and moral traditionalism are coded so that they should be positively related to voting for the Republican candidate for president.

We examine the value of egalitarianism as another ideological predictor of the vote for president. Egalitarianism, which emphasizes equal opportunity and treatment regardless of personal characteristics, is closely related to a range of policy preferences (Feldman 1988) and undergirds some of the racial differences in opinion on several policies (Kinder and Sanders 1996). We create a measure of egalitarianism based on responses to four questions in the 2016 ANES survey that ask about (1) the need for equal opportunity, (2) whether it is a problem that some don't have an equal chance in life, (3) whether we should worry less about equality, and (4) whether there would be fewer problems if people were treated more fairly. Each item was recoded to a 0–1 scale, with higher values indicating greater support for equality, and the four variables were averaged together to form an egalitarianism scale (α = 0.68).[6] We expect the egalitarianism measure to be negatively correlated with a vote for the GOP presidential candidate.

Finally, some have argued that Trump was successful at appealing to the aspirations and fears of white working-class people facing economic troubles, while the Clinton campaign failed to reach these voters (e.g., Confessore and Cohn 2016). Since the 2012 and 2016 elections came during Democratic tenure in the White House, perhaps voters facing economic stresses were amenable to GOP appeals. To test this hypothesis, we rely on three items in the 2016 ANES data about financial vulnerabilities. These questions ask respondents whether they (1) can afford to pay all of their health care costs, (2) worry about their financial situation, and (3) are able to make their housing payments. Each item was recoded to a 0–1 scale, with higher values indicating higher levels of economic anxiety, and the three variables were averaged together to form an economic anxiety scale ($\alpha = 0.70$).[7] We expect economic anxiety to be positively associated with a vote for the Republican presidential candidate.

We use logistic regression to estimate the vote choice model, with the dependent variable coded 0 for the Democratic candidate and 1 for the Republican. The independent variables are not all coded on the same scale, and some have skewed distributions. Thus, we use the model estimates to calculate how much the expected probability of voting for the GOP candidate changes, on average, when moving from the 10th percentile to the 90th percentile on each independent variable. These calculations are summarized in figure 12.3.[8]

The results in both panels of figure 12.3 show that group attitudes are more potent than ideology measures in explaining presidential vote choice. Partisanship and evaluations of social groups are the strongest predictors in both elections. Holding other factors constant, shifting from low to high scores on ratings of groups aligned with each party is associated with a 10–20 point change in the predicted probability of voting for the GOP presidential candidate. In addition, racial resentment and attitudes toward immigrants are statistically significant predictors of vote choice in both elections as well. By comparison, among ideological measures only social welfare preferences and moral traditionalism are statistically significant correlates of the vote for president, and those effects tend to be a bit weaker than each of the group attitudes. Furthermore, after controlling for group attitudes we find that economic anxiety is neither statistically nor substantively associated with the choice for president in either election.[9] An economic anxiety explanation of Donald Trump's victory in the 2016 presidential election is not supported by the ANES data.

Comparing the two panels in figure 12.3 also shows how group attitudes were more influential in 2016. Comparing the 2012 and 2016 results reveals two important differences in voting predictors in the last two presidential

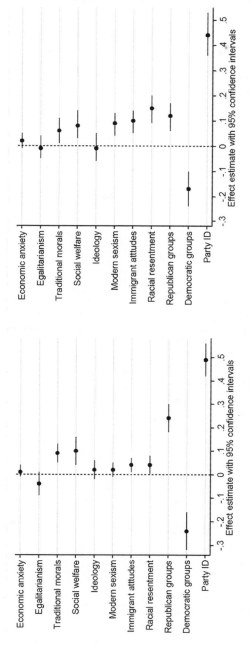

Note: The estimated effect (change in the predicted probability of voting for the GOP candidate) is computed by moving from the 10th to 90th percentile on each independent variable.

Figure 12.3
Predictors of Voting for the Republican Presidential Candidate in 2012 and 2016.
Source: ANES, 2013, 2017.

elections. First, two core ideological measures (moral traditionalism and social welfare preferences) are more strongly associated with the vote for president in 2012 than in 2016. Second, three group attitude measures (modern sexism, attitudes toward immigrants, and racial resentment) barely register as predictors of the vote for president in 2012 but are powerfully associated with vote choice in 2016, with each associated with at least a 10-point shift in support for Trump. It is worth noting that racial resentment is more closely correlated with the vote for president in 2016, when President Obama was no longer on the ballot. While this comparison is limited to the last two presidential elections, it suggests that the 2016 campaign was unique in raising the salience of group-based attitudes among American voters. In explaining the choice for president in 2016 group attitudes trump ideology.

Conclusion

Identity politics are ascendant. Party conflict in the United States has increased in frequency and intensity over the past few decades, making partisanship and other politically relevant group identities more salient to the mass public. This environment encourages partisans to view politics as a zero-sum "us versus them" struggle, and it motivates partisans to engage in biased processes of information seeking and reasoning. As a result, Americans express growing levels of contempt for members of the opposite party, with the 2016 cycle setting new records for polarized public assessments of the two major parties and their presidential candidates. Polarized ratings of the political parties derive from many sources, but group attitudes and identities are the most powerful sources of affective polarization.

Many scholars note the increasing association between ideology and party identification in American politics (Levendusky 2009a; Webster and Abramowitz 2017). It is not just ideological preferences that have become more sorted with partisanship over the last few decades. Group identities and attitudes have become sorted with party identification as well (Mason 2018; Abramowitz 2017). For example, the 2016 sample produces the largest difference between Democrats and Republicans in racial resentment scores and thermometer ratings of groups aligned with the two major parties over the entire ANES series. Our definition of party sorting should be broadened to include a growing association between partisanship and group-based identities and attitudes.

The increased hostility toward opposing political groups among the mass public offers a target-rich environment for campaigns eager to mobilize the base of either party. Appeals that emphasize fear and threats from political opponents are more effective at motivating mass political activity than positive proposals (Miller 2013). Politicians can appeal to feelings of contempt, anger, and fear to draw citizens into the political arena. Since group identities and attitudes come in many hues, campaigns fashioning appeals to encourage revulsion of the opposition can draw from a rainbow palette of public attitudes. It should not be a surprise that Russian efforts to influence the 2016 election included phony social media campaigns playing to both sides in group conflicts over race, immigration, and religion in the United States (Glaser 2017; Entous, Timberg, and Dwoskin 2017). In political campaigns that have taken place after 2016, we see no evidence of leaders in either party pulling back from appeals to group-based prejudices.

Increasing levels of affective polarization in the mass public create mounting challenges for policymaking. Having repeatedly stoked contempt for the opposition among party supporters, it can be dangerous for politicians to shift to governing, which requires negotiation and compromise. Polarization has boosted the reliable base of supporters in each party and reduced the number of voters that respond to short-term political forces. Thus, there is less incentive for politicians to attend to the pragmatic needs of unattached voters. Each party's core supporters, who dislike the opposite party the most, may signal to politicians that they do not want to compromise with the other side. This is a bigger problem for Republicans than for Democrats. In the 2016 ANES data, 74 percent of Democrats but only 54 percent of Republicans say they prefer government officials who compromise. Similarly, 43 percent of Republicans but just 29 percent of Democrats agree that compromise means selling out one's principles. Furthermore, both thermometer measures of affective polarization are positively associated with opposition to compromise among Republicans, but not among Democrats.

Relatedly, contempt for the out-party is not a governing agenda. If a party coalition is most united around disdain for the opposition rather than a policy program, then legislating will be more difficult than people may think. For example, Republican candidates for national office have promised, almost uniformly, to repeal and replace the Affordable Care Act for many years. Yet after winning the White House and majority control of both chambers of Congress, repeal efforts in 2017 failed even when using reconciliation rules that required no Democratic votes to pass the repeal legislation. The rise of affective polarization will not make governing any easier nor will it make political campaigning any more civil.

Notes

1. To maintain consistency with prior ANES surveys, for analyses of historical trends we only use the face-to-face samples of the 2012 and 2016 surveys. We apply

Chapter 12

sampling weights and we treat Independents who lean toward a party as partisans in all of the analyses.

2. Similar patterns hold with the thermometer ratings of presidential candidates. In multivariate analyses, we find that evaluations of social groups associated with each party are stronger predictors of affective polarization than ideological positions or core values.

3. When we analyze all of the group thermometer items, they form two factors that confirm our hypothesized party coalitions. For the ratings of Republican groups, the 2012 data includes thermometer ratings of the military. For evaluations of Democratic groups, the 2012 measure does not include ratings of BLM and transgender individuals but does include ratings of people on welfare.

4. Among immigration items, only the jobs question was included in the 2012 ANES survey. We created an immigration measure from the 2012 data based on the jobs item plus the feeling thermometer rating of illegal immigrants and four questions about immigration levels, path to citizenship, status checks, and immigration policy. These items form a reliable scale of immigration attitudes (α = .75).

5. In the 2012 ANES data, the modern sexism scale (α = .66) is based on six questions, but only three items overlap with the 2016 ANES data.

6. The 2012 egalitarianism scale (α = .78) is based on the same four items included in the 2016 ANES survey, plus two more questions.

7. The economic anxiety scale for 2012 (α = .68) is based on the same three items from the 2016 ANES survey plus a question asking whether respondents put off medical care in the past year because of the cost.

8. The predicted probabilities reported in figure 12.3 are "as observed" —calculated while leaving other independent variables at observed values and then averaging over all cases in the sample (see Hanmer and Kalkan 2013). The coefficient estimates and standard errors are available from the authors.

9. If we limit the sample to white voters, then all of the group attitudes are statistically correlated with support for Trump in 2016, but moral traditionalism is the only ideology measure that reaches statistical significance.

13

The Angry American Voter

Negative Partisanship, Voter Anger, and the 2016 Presidential Election

Alan I. Abramowitz and Steven W. Webster

IN THE TWENTY-FIRST CENTURY, partisanship in the American mass public has been shaped by two seemingly contradictory trends. First, opinions of both major parties have become increasingly negative. According to data from the American National Election Studies (ANES), on a feeling thermometer scale running from 0 through 100 degrees, the average rating of the Democratic Party fell from 59 degrees in 2000 to 49 degrees in 2016 while the average rating of the Republican Party fell from 54 degrees in 2000 to 43 degrees in 2016. The percentage of Americans with favorable opinions of both parties is now the lowest it has been since the ANES began asking this question in 1978.

While both major parties are less popular than at any time in recent history, party loyalty in voting has reached record levels. Thus, according to the 2016 ANES only 68 percent of voters identified with one of the two major parties but another 23 percent described themselves as Independents who usually felt closer to one of the two parties. Less than one voter in ten felt no attachment at all to either the Democrats or the Republicans. Moreover, in recent elections, partisanship has had a stronger influence on vote choice than at any time since the 1950s. In 2016, despite the unpopularity of both major party nominees, 89 percent of Democratic identifiers and 81 percent of Independents who leaned toward the Democratic Party voted for Hillary Clinton while 88 percent of Republican identifiers and 80 percent of Independents who leaned toward the Republican Party voted for Donald Trump.

The growing impact of partisanship can also be seen in the dramatic decline in ticket-splitting by voters. During the 1970s and 1980s, according to ANES surveys, about a quarter of voters split their tickets—voting for presidential and congressional candidates of different parties. In recent elections, however, only about one voter in ten has cast a split-ticket ballot. The result has been a growing nationalization of elections below the presidential level: the outcomes of elections for U.S. Senate, U.S. House, and even state and local offices are now largely consistent with the outcome of the presidential election. Thus, in 2016, all 34 Senate elections and 400 of 435 U.S. House elections were won by the party winning the presidential election in the state or district.

Partisanship also has a powerful influence on Americans' opinions of political leaders including the president. As the Gallup Poll has documented, the party divide in evaluations of presidential performance has increased dramatically since the 1960s. Under both George W. Bush and Barack Obama, that divide reached record levels and the most important factor in the growing partisan divide in public evaluations of presidential performance has been a sharp drop in approval by those identifying with the opposing party. Recent presidents have typically received approval ratings from supporters of their own party that are comparable to those received by presidents during the 1950s, 1960s, and 1970s. However, while presidents like Eisenhower, Kennedy, and even Nixon frequently enjoyed approval ratings of 40 percent or higher from supporters of the opposing party, recent presidents have rarely received approval ratings as high as 20 percent from opposing partisans.

The party divide in evaluations of presidential performance has reached new heights under Donald Trump. During his first few months in office, Trump has received extraordinarily low approval ratings for a new president. In fact, he was the first president in the history of the Gallup Poll, going back to Harry Truman, to begin his presidency with an approval rating below 50 percent. However, what is especially striking about opinions of Trump's presidency has been the extraordinarily large divide in approval between supporters of the two parties—a divide that was evident immediately after his inauguration. After only one week in office, President Trump's approval rating in the Gallup tracking poll was 89 percent among Republicans but only 12 percent among Democrats. By February of 2018, according to the Gallup Poll, not much had changed: 87 percent of Republican identifiers continued to approve of President Trump's job performance compared with only 7 percent of Democratic identifiers.

The Rise of Negative Partisanship

The patterns of public opinion toward recent presidents, including President Trump, reflect a long-term shift in the attitudes of Americans toward the two major parties and their leaders—the rise of negative partisanship (Abramowitz and Webster 2016). Until 2016, opinions of partisans toward their own party and its leaders have been fairly stable; since the 1970s, however, opinions toward the opposing party and its leaders have become much more negative. This trend is very clear in figures 13.1 and 13.2 which display changes in average feeling thermometer ratings by party identifiers and leaners of their own party and presidential candidate and the opposing party and presidential candidate based on ANES data. The party feeling thermometer ratings go back to 1980 while the presidential candidate ratings go back to 1968.

The data displayed in figures 13.1 and 13.2 show that between 1980 and

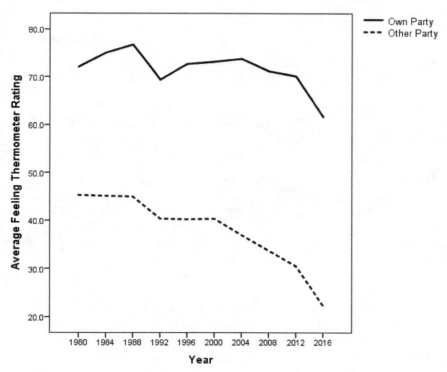

Figure 13.1
Average Feeling Thermometer Ratings of Own Party and Opposing Party, 1980– 2016.

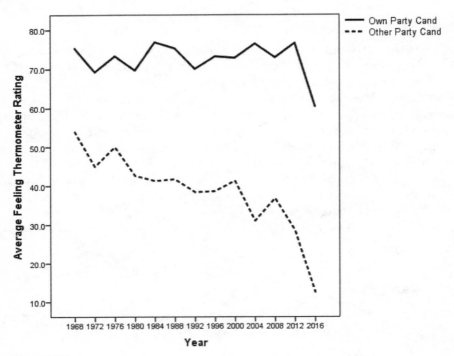

Figure 13.2
Average Feeling Thermometer Ratings of Own Party and Opposing Party
Presidential Candidates, 1968–2016.

2012, ratings by party identifiers and leaners of their own party fluctuated within a fairly narrow range between the upper 60s and low 70s. Similarly, between 1968 and 2012, ratings by party identifiers and leaners of their party's presidential candidate showed little evidence of change—hovering around the mid-70s. Over the same time period, however, the data show that ratings of the opposing party and its presidential candidate fell sharply. Ratings of the opposing party fell from just under 50 degrees (the neutral point) in 1980 to about 30 degrees in 2012 while ratings of the opposing party's presidential candidate fell from close to 50 degrees between 1968 and 1976 to just below 30 degrees in 2012.

The data in this figure show that something remarkable happened in 2016—ratings by voters of the opposing party and candidate and of their own party and candidate fell sharply. In fact, the average ratings by voters of their own party, the opposing party, their own party's presidential candidate, and the opposing party's presidential candidate were the lowest ever recorded in ANES surveys. And this pattern was true for both Democrats and Republicans. On average, voters gave their own party an average rating of only 62 degrees on the feeling thermometer scale while they gave the opposing party an average rating of only 23 degrees. And the declines in ratings of the presidential candidates were even more dramatic. On average, voters gave their own party's nominee an average rating of only 60 degrees while they gave the opposing party's nominee an average rating of only 11 degrees. In fact, well over half of Democratic and Republican voters gave the opposing party's nominee a rating of zero on the feeling thermometer which is the lowest possible score.

The data in figures 13.1 and 13.2 show that record numbers of voters in 2016 were dissatisfied with their own party's presidential nominee and the opposing party's nominee—and that these negative feelings carried over to some degree to the parties themselves. Donald Trump and Hillary Clinton were the most unpopular major party candidates for president since the ANES introduced the feeling thermometer scale in 1968 and probably in the entire postwar era. Many Democratic voters, especially among those who had supported Bernie Sanders in the Democratic primaries, were less than enthusiastic about Hillary Clinton's candidacy. Twenty percent of all Democratic voters and 26 percent of Sanders's primary voters gave Clinton a neutral or negative rating on the feeling thermometer scale. Likewise, many Republican voters, especially among those who had supported mainstream Republicans like John Kasich and Marco Rubio in the Republican primaries, were less than enthusiastic about Donald Trump's candidacy. Twenty-seven percent of all Republican voters and 37 percent of Republicans who voted for candidates other than Trump in the Republican primary gave Trump a neutral or negative rating on the feeling thermometer scale.

However, in terms of understanding the current state of partisanship in the United States, the most important finding that emerges from figure 13.1 is that large majorities of Democrats and Republicans truly despised the opposing party's nominee. Given these results, it is hardly surprising that despite the qualms that many Democrats and Republicans felt about their own party's candidate, very few ultimately defected to the opposing party in the presidential election.

Consequences of Negative Partisanship
for Voting Behavior

Thus far, we have documented a dramatic increase in negative partisanship within the American electorate. Though this growth in negative affect is important in its own right, it has also had major consequences for American political behavior. Perhaps the most important effect of the rise of negative partisanship has been a dramatic increase in party loyalty and straight-ticket voting. Figure 13.3 displays the trend in consistent party loyalty in voting between 1980 and 2012. Consistent party loyalty means voting for your own party's candidates for president, U.S. House, and U.S. Senate. The data show that consistent party loyalty has become increasingly prevalent in U.S. elections since the 1990s. Moreover, the data in this figure show that the trend toward increased loyalty is found across all categories of party identification including Independents leaning toward a party. By 2012, both leaning Independents and weak party identifiers were as loyal in their voting decisions as strong party identifiers during the 1970s and 1980s.

In the 2012 elections, about 80 percent of voters were consistently loyal: supporting their party's candidates for president, U.S. House, and U.S. Senate. This pattern was the highest level of consistent loyalty in the history of

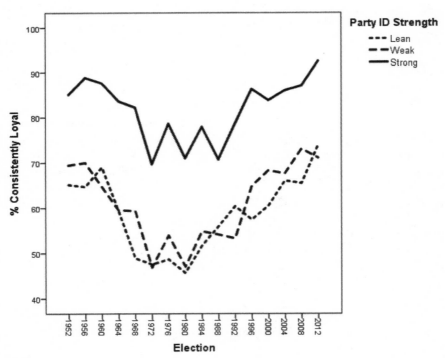

Figure 13.3
Trends in Consistent Party Loyalty by Strength of Party Identification, 1952–2012.

the ANES. It is striking that party loyalty remained very high in the 2016 election despite the unpopularity of both Donald Trump and Hillary Clinton. Data from the 2016 ANES indicate that partisans were still overwhelmingly likely to vote for their own party's candidates, including its presidential candidates. Party loyalty in presidential voting declined only slightly compared with 2012 with close to 90 percent of party identifiers choosing their own party's nominee. Based on our findings for earlier elections, negative partisanship appeared to be a likely explanation for these results.

To assess the relationship between negative partisanship and partisan loyalty at the presidential level, we utilized data from the 2016 ANES and regressed an indicator variable for party loyalty (e.g., voting for the candidates of one's own party at the presidential level) on feeling thermometer ratings of the opposing political party's candidate. As control variables, we also included a series of dummy variables for strong partisans and weak partisans (with Independent leaners as the contrast category), and feeling thermometer ratings toward an individual's own party and the opposing party. The results of this logistic regression are shown in table 13.1.

Unsurprisingly, the results of this analysis indicate that individuals were

TABLE 13.1
Explaining Loyalty in Presidential Voting in 2016

	(1) Vote Loyal
FT own candidate	0.078***
	(0.022)
FT opposing candidate	-0.151***
	(0.033)
FT own party	0.080**
	(0.029)
FT opposing party	-0.038
	(0.025)
Strong partisan	-1.745
	(0.892)
Weak partisan	0.166
	(0.834)
Constant	-2.545*
	(1.176)
N	2,233
AIC	271.4

Note: Standard errors in parentheses
* p<0.05, ** p<0.01, ***p<0.001

more likely to vote for their own party's candidate when they had positive feelings toward that candidate. In addition, positive ratings of one's own party on the feeling thermometer score is also associated with a higher likelihood of partisan loyalty. However, the dummy variables for strong partisans and weak partisans had no statistically significant relationship, nor did ratings of the opposing party on the feeling thermometer scale.

According to the data in table 13.1, the most important factor in predicting party loyalty in the 2016 presidential election was how voters felt about the opposing party's presidential candidate. In fact, this measure was twice as important in predicting loyalty as feelings toward the candidate from one's own party. Thus, even though both major party nominees in 2016 were quite unpopular, partisan loyalty remained very high because both Democratic and Republican identifiers overwhelmingly viewed the opposing party's candidate with deep hostility.

Voter Anger in the 2016 Presidential Election

The rise of negative partisanship within the American electorate implies that in the current era of polarized politics, negative feelings toward the opposing party and its candidates, rather than positive feelings toward one's own party and its candidates, is the most important factor in maintaining partisan loyalty. One of the most important ways that these negative feelings are expressed is voter anger toward leaders of the opposing party and especially toward its presidential candidate. And while signs of rising anger toward the opposing party's presidential candidates were clearly evident in 2012 and other recent elections, the 2016 election and the candidacies of Donald Trump and Hillary Clinton seemed to accelerate this trend.

According to data from the 2012 ANES, 33 percent of Democrats and 43 percent of Republicans reported feeling angry toward the opposing party's presidential candidate "always" or "most of the time." By 2016, these numbers had increased dramatically. For Democrats, an overwhelming majority, 72 percent, felt angry toward the Republican nominee "always" or "most of the time." Among Republicans, the corresponding figure was 66 percent. This increase in anger over four years can be seen very clearly in figure 13.4.

Increasing voter anger is closely connected to ideological polarization. As our previous work has shown (Webster and Abramowitz 2017), voters' issue positions are strongly related to feelings of anger toward the opposition party—very liberal Democrats and very conservative Republicans are generally much angrier than more moderate supporters of each party. During the age of Trump, this trend has continued. To illustrate the relationship between

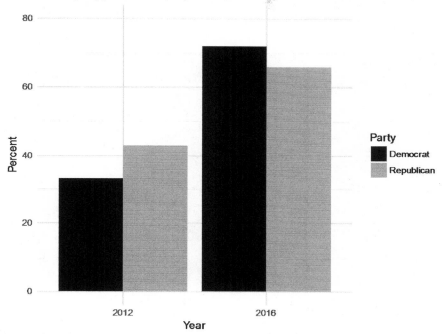

Figure 13.4
Partisans Are Increasingly Angry at the Other Side.

issue positions and negative affect, we performed regression analyses of anger toward Donald Trump and Hillary Clinton on attitudes toward the size and role of government in American society, attitudes toward immigrants and immigration, attitudes toward gay rights, attitudes toward gun control, and a series of demographic control variables. The role of government, immigration, and gay rights policy scales are all coded such that higher values indicate a more conservative outlook. Finally, to assess the extent to which anger is also a function of partisanship itself, we included the seven-point party identification scale as a control. The results are shown in table 13.2.[1]

The results of the regression analyses indicate that, while partisan identification plays a role in engendering anger toward the opposing party's presidential candidate, issue positions also strongly influence feelings of anger. Conservative views on immigration, gun control, and the role of government in society are associated with anger toward the Democratic presidential

Chapter 13

TABLE 13.2
Explaining Voter Anger toward the Presidential Candidates

	Clinton	Trump
Republican ID	.219***	-.203***
	(.020)	.019)
Oppose Gov't Activism	.028***	-.025***
	(.006)	(.006)
Anti-Immigration	.042***	-.053***
	(.005)	(.006)
Oppose Gay Rights	.006	-.023**
	(.007)	(.008)
Oppose Gun Control	-.292***	.251***
	(.067)	(.070)
Constant	-.103	3.359
	(.246)	(.476)
N	2,212	2,212
Adjusted R2	.48	.48

Note: Standard errors in parentheses
* p<0.05, ** p<0.01, ***p<0.001

candidate among Republicans. Similarly, liberal views on immigration, same-sex marriage, gun control, and the role of government in society are associated with anger toward the Republican presidential candidate among Democrats. Thus, the high levels of anger toward the opposing party's presidential candidate among Republican and Democratic voters had a clear, rational foundation: anger was closely related to disagreement with the policies of the opposition party and its candidate.

This growth in anger within the American electorate has had important consequences for voter behavior. With the rise of negative partisanship and its attendant reorientation of the ways in which Americans affiliate with the two major political parties, what is becoming increasingly important in producing party loyalty is not encouraging positive feelings among supporters toward their own party and its candidates, but inciting anger toward the opposing party and its candidates.

To illustrate the growing importance of anger as a tool for increasing party loyalty, we regressed an indicator variable for party loyalty in the 2016 presidential election on a series of variables measuring affective evaluations of parties and candidates. These included anger at the opposing party's presidential candidate, ratings of your own party and your own party's presidential candidate, and a dummy variable for those who identified as strong partisans. To facilitate an easier comparison of the relative magnitude of the coefficients, all of our independent variables were scaled to range from 0–1.

The results from the logistic regression in table 13.3 show that affective evaluations play a large role in shaping vote choice. The most important predictor of party loyalty is feelings toward your own party's presidential candidate. However, anger toward the opposing party's presidential candidate is only slightly less powerful. Perhaps most impressively, anger toward the opposing party's presidential candidate is nearly 3.5 times as powerful as evaluations of your own party. Further analysis indicates that anger has an especially strong influence on party loyalty when partisans have reservations about their own party's candidate, as was common in 2016. This relationship is shown graphically in figure 13.5.

The results in figure 13.5 show that for those voters who held positive views of their own party's presidential candidate, anger at the opposing party's candidate had little influence on voting decisions. Even among those

TABLE 13.3
Logistic Regression Analysis of Presidential Loyalty in 2016

	(1) Party loyalty
Frequency of anger	4.819***
	(0.414)
FT own party	1.442*
	(0.447)
FT own party candidate	5.886***
	(0.607)
Strong partisan	-0.135
	(0.398)
Constant	-3.615
	(0.414)
N	2,248
AIC	568.2

Note: Standard errors in parentheses
* p<0.05, ** p<0.01, ***p<0.001

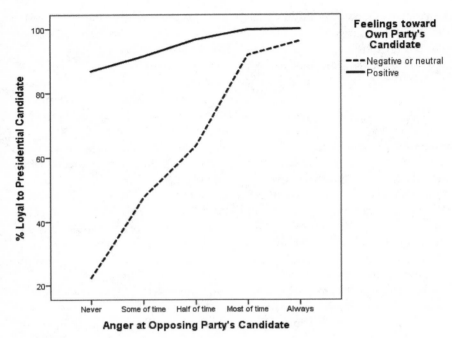

Figure 13.5
Loyalty in Presidential Election by Anger toward Opposing Party Candidate and Feelings toward Own Party's Candidate.

who reported that they never felt angry toward the opposing party's candidate, fully 87 percent cast a vote for their party's presidential candidate. Loyalty increased to 100 percent among those who liked their own party's candidate and reported frequently feeling angry at the opposing party's candidate.

By contrast, the relationship between anger at the opposing party's presidential candidate and loyalty to one's own party is very strong among voters who held negative or neutral views of their own party's candidate. Among these voters, only 23 percent of those who reported that they never felt angry toward the opposing party's candidate were loyal to their party's nominee. For those who were negative or neutral about their own party's candidate but reported feeling angry toward the opposing party's presidential candidate "half of the time," 63 percent voted for their own party's candidate. What is most striking is that, among those with reservations about their own party's candidate, 95 percent voted for their own party's presidential candidate if they reported "always" feeling angry toward the opposing party's candidate.

Thus, increasing anger toward the opposing party's candidate appeared to cause individuals who did not care for their own party's candidate to support that candidate at a level comparable to that of voters who felt very positively toward their party's nominee.

Conclusion

The behavior of the American electorate has changed dramatically over the past 25 years. Today, electoral politics in the United States is defined by negative partisanship: decisions are based more on which party or candidate voters dislike than on which party or candidate they like. In this chapter, we have shown that anger is a key element of negative partisanship. When dislike is combined with anger, it can strongly influence voting behavior. Along these lines, our results showed that anger was one of the most important factors in maintaining party loyalty in the 2016 presidential election, especially among voters who had reservations about their own party or its candidate. This was especially important in 2016 due to the unusually large proportions of partisans who were less than enthusiastic about their party's presidential candidates. It remains to be seen whether 2016 was exceptional in this regard or whether voting for "the lesser of two evils" will become the norm in future elections.

We believe that the rise of anger-fueled negative partisanship poses a potential danger to the stability of American democracy. Willingness to accept the outcomes of elections as legitimate, even when one's preferred candidate loses, is crucial to the survival of democratic institutions. In recent years, however, and especially in 2016, we have seen the legitimacy of election results increasingly questioned by those on the losing side. Indeed, 2016 even saw the legitimacy of the results questioned by the victorious presidential candidate when Donald Trump repeatedly, and without evidence, claimed that Hillary Clinton only won the popular vote due to millions of ballots cast by illegal immigrants. If voters come to believe that the results of elections are fraudulent and that the political opposition is illegitimate, there is a real danger that political leaders will feel empowered to enact policies aimed at undermining democratic institutions including free and competitive elections.

Note

1. For the sake of clarity in presentation, demographic control variables are not shown.

14

The Role of Populists in the 2016 U.S. Presidential Election and Beyond

Edward G. Carmines, Michael J. Ensley,
and Michael W. Wagner

THE ELECTION OF DONALD TRUMP IN 2016 took many political observers, academics, and pundits by surprise. Despite election forecasts from political scientists that predicted a close race by focusing on fundamental political and economic conditions, there is a sense that Trump's election is qualitatively different. Notably, he received a surge in support from white, less-educated voters in rural areas, particularly in the Midwest region of the country, as compared to previous Republican candidates. In this chapter, we analyze the sources of Trump's support based on a multidimensional conception of ideology in the American electorate that classifies citizens based on their positions on economic and social-welfare issues, as well as cultural issues that have defined much of the recent partisan conflict in American politics. Building off of our previous work that studied Trump's support in the 2016 Republican presidential primaries (Carmines et al. 2016), we find an increase in support for Republicans from white voters who fit our label of Populists, those who possess a liberal orientation on economic issues but a conservative orientation on cultural issues, was a key factor in Trump's surprising victory. We also show that the behavior of other ideologically heterodox voters (Libertarians and Moderates) were also crucial to Trump's victory.

Despite a presidential election season that broke many of the rules of modern electoral campaigns, most political scientists' forecasts of the 2016 elections results were within one point of the popular vote result (Campbell

2016b). Moreover, both exit polls and more sophisticated measures of American public opinion revealed that, as always, the vast majority of Americans voted for the presidential candidate with whom they shared a partisan affiliation.

However, the 2016 election season was one in which several atypical outcomes were experienced—by candidates and the voting public. In Donald Trump, the Republican Party nominated a political novice who was widely rejected by party elites who have historically controlled the nomination outcome (Cohen et al. 2008). Trump outpaced more than a dozen serious contenders for the GOP nomination—most of whom (1) claimed records of conservative governing, and (2) had experience winning statewide elections in Electoral College swing states. Trump's appeal to news reporters covering the campaign (Wells et al. 2017) and his appeal to primary voters who were highly nationalistic, authoritarian, and anti-elitist (Oliver and Rahn 2016) helped propel him to the nomination. However, none of these factors on their own sufficiently explain how Trump captured the White House in the general election.

Our focus in this chapter applies our work examining how the ideological heterogeneity of the American electorate (Carmines, Ensley, and Wagner 2011, 2012a, 2012b, 2014, 2016) helps us understand voting behavior in the 2016 general election. Considering recent work highlighting the growing importance of Populists, we show that ideologically Populist Americans—those who have preferences that tend to be liberal on economic issues but conservative on social issues—were an important factor in Trump's victory. Specifically, our analysis provides some evidence for those arguing that less-educated white Populists contributed to Trump's rise as we show that this group was strongly for Trump as compared to their support for Republicans in previous elections. However, our analysis also shows that the movement of additional white voters to the Republican column—among Populists to be sure, but also among Libertarians and Moderates—is a central explanation for Trump's Electoral College victory.

Ideological Heterogeneity in the American Electorate and Its Consequences

Contemporary scholarship in American politics has been locked in a decades-long battle over whether the citizenry is as polarized as the nation's elected officials. Certainly partisan elected officials are deeply polarized along a single left–right ideological continuum (McCarty, Poole, and Rosenthal

2008). In contrast, research exploring whether the public has followed suit is divided.

On the one hand, there is evidence of increasing mass partisanship (Hetherington 2001) and growing ideological extremity (Abramowitz 2010) in nontrivial pockets of the electorate. Moreover, evidence of "affective partisanship," the notion that partisan divides are also rooted in deeply ingrained hostile feelings toward the opposing party, is growing (Iyengar and Westwood 2015). Thus, there is evidence that partisan antipathy abounds in contemporary American politics because of the widening chasm between policy attitudes among partisans and negative feelings each side holds about the other.

On the other hand, while each party is home to some ideological extremists, many Americans are ideologically moderate (Fiorina and Abrams 2009). There is evidence for party sorting—the increased correlation between policy views and party identification—but voters finding their appropriate partisan home is not evidence of a growing ideological distance between partisans (Levendusky 2009a).

Our view is that both perspectives reveal important truths about contemporary divisions in American politics. However, each perspective also conceives of public divisions on issues as being arrayed across a single, left–right ideological continuum. The American public is made of polarized liberals and conservatives to be sure, but it is also made up of Libertarians, Populists, and Moderates who not only face a party system with no natural home, but one that systematically cross-pressures them issue by issue and election by election.

A unidimensional conception of ideology results in the obscuring of important differences among self-identified moderates (Carmines, Ensley, and Wagner 2012b). Crucial to understanding who is not truly a Moderate, but rather a Libertarian or Populist, is to allow for a second dimension of public attitudes to help explain American public opinion. There is a growing body of evidence that Americans organize their policy attitudes across at least two ideological dimensions, one primarily economic in nature and the other primarily social (Hillygus and Shields 2009; Shafer and Claggett 1995; Klar 2014). Economic issues deal with questions related to the government's intervention in the economy while social issues generally are concerned with moral questions of right and wrong.

Citizens might have views that share the orthodoxy of the preferences of partisan elites. For example, Liberals in the electorate have preferences that mirror the positions of Democratic Party politicians. They favor government involvement in the economy through taxation, education, health care, and similar policies while also generally preferring that the government stay out of questions such as which adults can marry, who can have an abortion, and so forth. Conservatives in the electorate have preferences that match the opposite set of issue positions advocated by Republicans in government: fewer economic regulations and more aggressive regulation of traditional social behavior. However, many citizens have perfectly defensible and thoughtful policy preferences that are heterodox with respect to the menu of issue positions offered by the two major political parties. Libertarians prefer the government stay out of managing the economy and social behavior. Populists prefer a more active governmental hand at regulating the economy and legislating more traditional social behaviors (Carmines, Ensley, and Wagner 2011, 2012a).

Our previous research reveals deep divides in contemporary American politics—not just between Liberal Democrats and Conservative Republicans —or between an active ideological minority and a less active non-ideological majority—but also between ideologically orthodox and ideologically heterodox citizens (Carmines, Ensley, and Wagner 2012a). Moderates, in our definition, hold middle-of-the-road and/or ambivalent views across both issue dimensions.

The entrenched ideological heterogeneity in the American electorate has led to two simultaneous but diametrically opposing developments in contemporary American politics. Because orthodox Liberals and Conservatives share the economic and social issue preferences of Democratic Party elites and Republican Party elites respectively, they have become significantly more entrenched, and indeed polarized in the contemporary party system. These individuals are usually stable partisans, straight-ticket party voters with comparatively strong attachments to their respective parties while just as actively opposing the opposition party (Carmines, Ensley, and Wagner 2012a). Though they do not vote at higher rates than others, they do participate in more campaign-related activities which no doubt enhances their political influence (Carmines, Ensley, and Wagner 2011). Ideologically orthodox citizens exemplify the influence of party elites that reach into the wellsprings of the American electorate. Populists and Libertarians, along with Moderates, are not as deeply connected to the two major parties and are less likely to engage in political activities. They are being shoved aside in established two-party politics, leaving them with a classic "exit or voice" choice (Hirschman 1970): not participating in politics, become the primary force of swing and split-ticket voting, or forming and voting for third parties.

Why Populists?

Several popular and scholarly accounts of the 2016 election have focused on the potentially pivotal role played by Populist voters (Inglehart and Norris

2016). A common narrative about the 2016 presidential contest is that Donald Trump's "Make America Great Again" campaign ignited a group of voters that felt ignored, disrespected, and left behind by contemporary politics and modern politicians. That said, electoral accounts placing the behavior of Populists at center stage have largely ignored Populist views about issues of government economic regulation and traditional social mores. It is important to note that our own account of contemporary public preferences does not claim that there are only two issue dimensions structuring American politics. Rather, we have argued that the economic and social issue dimensions serve as primary anchors that individuals can use to help align themselves with the party that most closely articulates their desires.

The 2016 primaries introduced a variety of issues into contemporary political discussion that do not clearly fit into either the social and economic issue dimensions. Donald Trump began his campaign by promising to build a wall between the United States and Mexico, placing center stage an immigration issue that had been dividing party elites—especially in the Republican Party—for several years. Trump's rhetoric also highlighted strong anti-free trade nationalistic views through opposing the North American Free Trade Agreement and the Trans-Pacific Partnership while advocating anti-elite perspectives via attacks on politicians and the news media (Azari 2016b) and engaging in an authoritarian campaign style containing boasts that he and he alone could solve the problems facing the country. Oliver and Rahn (2016) found that Trump voters, as compared to supporters of the other Republican primary candidates, preferred more authoritarian leadership styles. Trump supporters were also more nationalistic than supporters of other Republican candidates and held stronger anti-elitist attitudes than other Republican candidates, though Bernie Sanders voters in the Democratic primaries shared anti-elitist characteristics with Trump supporters.

Cramer's (2016) elucidation of the concept of rural consciousness and its relation to a general politics of resentment in Wisconsin has been extrapolated to pockets of the electorate at large in 2016. A wide swath of voters, many of them rural and white, has felt as though conventional politics generally and the parties in particular have ignored their needs. They see a growing economy in the abstract, but not one that reaches their own lives. Rather, Cramer reveals how many of these voters believe that those who are benefiting from government aid are not deserving of the assistance, especially when large cities and state governments are perceived as ignoring the needs of more rural citizens.

Nationalist, authoritarian, anti-elitist, and rural consciousness-oriented attitudes do not fall neatly in our two-dimensional portrait of the electorate. As such, we sought in previous work to examine whether Populists, as we define them, were more likely to hold attitudes that other scholars demonstrated were important in voters' 2016 electoral decision. Our analysis, relying on the ANES 2012 general election survey and 2016 survey of primary voters, discovered that white Populists in 2012 expressed a strong sense of national identity, and more nationalist issue preferences about immigration, outsourcing, and torture than Liberals, Libertarians, and Moderates (Carmines, Ensley, and Wagner 2016).

In the 2016 primary elections, Populists and Conservatives were the two groups expressing strong nationalist views on issues ranging from allowing Syrian refugees into the country, concerns about a local terrorist attack, support to fight ISIS in Syria and Iraq, and support for legal immigration (Carmines, Ensley, and Wagner 2016). These were also the two ideological groups expressing the most support for Donald Trump in the primary election season. In this chapter, we seek to clarify the role that Populists and indeed how all heterodox voters—Libertarians, Populists, and Moderates—contributed to the presidential election results.

Measuring Ideological Heterogeneity in the American Electorate

To create empirically our five ideological categories, we conducted confirmatory factor analysis (CFA) on American National Election Studies (ANES) questions on citizen's issue positions from 1972 to 2016.[1] We identified questions that mapped onto the economic and social ideological dimensions and used those questions to identify citizens' underlying, latent positions on each dimension. Since the number of complete cases is diminished when all the issue questions are used simultaneously, we chose to impute missing values before performing the CFA.[2] We created five datasets through multiple imputation. Next, we performed the CFA to estimate each individual's position on each dimension.[3] The scores were standardized so that they have a mean of 0 and a standard deviation of 1. A high (i.e., positive) score indicates a conservative orientation and a low (i.e., negative) score indicates a liberal orientation on the dimension of interest.[4] All of the estimates obtained using these measures are the average effect based on the five imputed datasets (see King et al. 2001).

We have defined ideological groups by dividing the two-dimensional policy space into five distinct areas. Each dimension is set to have a mean of 0 and the standard deviation is 1, so the origin (0, 0) is roughly the center of the space. Moderates are defined as those respondents that are within a one-half of a standard deviation of the origin in any direction. That is, Moderates are those who are located in the circle of figure with a diameter of 1 where the center of the circle is located at the point (0, 0). The other groups are defined in terms of which quadrant they are located in, excluding those that fall in the Moderate category. We classify those that have a positive (negative) value on both dimensions as Conservative (Liberal). Those respondents that have a positive (negative) value on the economic dimension and a negative (positive) value on the social dimension are considered Libertarian (Populist).

Measuring Republican and Democratic Presidential Coalitions

To examine the changing composition of the ideological coalitions that constitute the Republican and Democratic Parties, we use an analytic model that calculates the contribution that different groups make to a party's electoral coalition. Axelrod (1972) defines the group's contribution as the proportion of a party's total votes provided by a given group's size, turnout, and loyalty. A group's contribution to the party's coalition is greater if the group is large, its turnout is high, and its vote is lopsided for a single party. Conversely, a group's contribution to a presidential candidate's coalition is less when it is small in size, has low turnout, and its members evenly split their vote between the two parties. Since these components can differ substantially both across and within groups and can change over time, Axelrod's formula allows us to evaluate the contribution that any group makes to a party's electoral coalition.

Axelrod developed his model to calculate the contribution of various demographic groups to the Democratic and Republican electoral coalitions but the model can readily be applied to ideological groups. Thus, it is straightforward to calculate the contribution that Liberals, Conservatives, Moderates, Libertarians, and Populists make to each party's electoral coalition.[5]

Results in the 2016 Presidential Election

Table 14.1 and table 14.2 report the turnout, size, loyalty, and contribution to Republican and Democratic coalitions among our five ideological groups in 1976, 1996, and 2016.[6] In 2016, table 14.1 reveals that Populists made their smallest overall contribution to the Democratic Party in at least 40 years, tying the 9 percent contribution Populists made to Bill Clinton's winning coalition in 1996. At first blush, this result appears alarming for Democrats.

TABLE 14.1
Size, Turnout, Loyalty, and Contribution to Democratic Presidential Coalition

Year	Turnout	Loyalty	Size	Contribution
		Liberal		
1976	74%	65%	25%	33%
1996	72%	93%	29%	46%
2016	89%	93%	36%	63%
		Conservative		
1976	73%	43%	29%	25%
1996	84%	22%	28%	12%
2016	90%	3%	26%	2%
		Moderate		
1976	76%	45%	23%	22%
1996	72%	61%	22%	23%
2016	84%	49%	20%	18%
		Libertarian		
1976	74%	40%	13%	10%
1996	79%	60%	11%	12%
2016	91%	34%	9%	6%
		Populist		
1976	60%	66%	9%	10%
1996	54%	72%	10%	9%
2016	74%	69%	8%	9%

However, it is also the case that Populists comprised the smallest portion of the electorate of any ideological group in 2016. Moderates slightly increased their contribution to the party while Conservative and Libertarian contributions to the Democrats were also at 44-year low points. Liberals' overall contribution to the Democratic Party coalition jumped from 40 percent in 2012 to 63 percent in 2016. Even though their contribution to the Democratic Party and their overall size in the electorate were at historic lows, it is also worth noting that Populist turnout increased 8 percent from 2012 to 2016.

On the Republican side, the overall contribution to Populists made to the GOP was down from 6 percent in 2012 to 5 percent in 2016. How could the overall contribution of Populists go down for both parties? Again, the size column reveals that Populists were a slightly smaller part of the electorate in 2016 than in previous years. While their overall contribution to Republicans was down, Populist loyalty to Republicans continued its slow and steady

Chapter 14

TABLE 14.2
Size, Turnout, Loyalty, and Contribution to Republican Presidential Coalition

Year	Turnout	Loyalty	Size	Contribution
		Liberal		
1976	74%	35%	25%	18%
1996	72%	7%	29%	4%
2016	89%	7%	36%	5%
		Conservative		
1976	73%	57%	29%	34%
1996	84%	78%	28%	59%
2016	90%	97%	26%	57%
		Moderate		
1976	76%	55%	23%	27%
1996	72%	39%	22%	20%
2016	84%	51%	20%	21%
		Libertarian		
1976	74%	60%	13%	16%
1996	79%	40%	11%	11%
2016	91%	66%	9%	14%
		Populist		
1976	60%	34%	9%	5%
1996	54%	28%	10%	5%
2016	74%	31%	8%	5%

increase since 2008 on the right side of the aisle. Meanwhile, Moderate's contribution to the Republican coalition jumped from 10 percent in both 2008 and 2012 to 21 percent in 2016.

Overall, the data in tables 14.1 and 14.2 do not make a persuasive case that Populists were critically central to Donald Trump's victory in 2016. However, about 30 percent of Populist Americans are black, making Populists the most racially diverse of our five categories of ideological citizens. Though not reported here, we also restricted to white voters our calculations of our five ideological group's contributions to each party's electoral coalition. Keep in mind that the calculations are thus limited to white voters and their contributions to the 2016 electoral coalitions. They are not revealing the contribution of white voters to the overall 2016 vote. It is clear that white Populists are abandoning the Democratic Party. Their loyalty to the Democrats in 2016 was down to a 44-year low point of 28 percent and they comprised only 2 percent of their 2016 coalition among white voters, down from 12 percent in 2004. It is interesting to note that the contribution of white voters among Populists has been dropping since 2008. White liberals were 69 percent of the Democratic coalition in 2016, up from 42 percent in 2012. Conservatives, Libertarians, and Moderates respectively provided 1, 8, and 17 percent of the Democrats' coalition in 2016.

Despite being three percent less of the electorate in 2016 than in 2012, White Populists in 2016 equaled their 2012 contribution to white voters in the GOP coalition. For Republicans, Populist loyalty among whites was at a 44-year high point, though the contribution white Populists made to the Republican Party was consistent with their behavior in 2012. White Libertarian loyalty increased from 56 to 70 percent from 2012 to 2016, but the contribution of white Libertarians to all of white voters' support for Republicans was down from 2012. White Moderate support was a larger part of Donald Trump's vote share than Mitt Romney's while Conservative support was fairly steady across the last three presidential elections.

When examining the loyalty column for the Democratic coalition (again, not reported here for space concerns), it becomes immediately evident that white Populist loyalty to Democrats is half of what it was when Bill Clinton was reelected in 1996. White Populist support for Democrats began dropping in the Obama years, reaching their low point (by more than 10 percentage points) in 2016. Consistent with explanations of ideological sorting, Conservative loyalty to Democrats was at 2 percent in 2016, another low point for the years we are able to study.

With respect to the overall impact on the election results, white Populist turnout is a bit more complicated to interpret. On the one hand, white Populist turnout was considerably lower than self-reported turnout of the other four ideological categories. On the other hand, white Populist turnout jumped nearly 20 percentage points from 2012 to 2016. It is possible to conclude that Trump's campaign activated some voters who felt as though the contemporary party system had left them behind while also concluding that the number of white Populists voting were not enough to take credit for giving the White House to Trump.

White Populists have been moving toward the Republican column since the turn of the century. The decline in white Populist's loyalty to the Democrats and their concomitant increase in loyalty to the GOP are cardinal features of the 2016 election. Yet, the support of white Populists is not enough to explain how Donald Trump tipped the electoral scales in his favor. Additionally, white Libertarian and white Moderate loyalty to Republicans was at 30-year high points in 2016. Once again, it appears that heterodox voters —most especially white heterodox voters—were central to Trump's success in the primaries and his Electoral College victory.

Discussion

Many scholars, journalists, pundits, and campaign operatives have written about the determinative role that Populist voters played in swinging the 2016 presidential election to Donald Trump. We have presented evidence that while Populists in the aggregate behaved substantially as they did in every presidential election since 1976; white Populists began slowly, but steadily abandoning the Democratic Party in 2000. This culminated in the strongest display of loyalty to Republicans and the lowest level of support for Democrats from white Populists in the 44 years of ANES data we analyzed.

It would be tempting to clap our hands together and report that yes, the Populists did it. However, our examination of white heterodox voters showed significant jumps in loyalty to the Republican Party from Populists, Libertarians, and perhaps most importantly, Moderates. Except for white Liberals, more white heterodox voters sided with the Republican candidate than is typical. Though the election only took place two years ago, much has already been written about the central role of race in 2016 (Schaffner, MacWilliams, and Nteta forthcoming). Our results encourage the continued exploration of this explanation of presidential election results.

One explanation for our findings has to do with the way that we define Populists. In published work over the past six years, we have defined Populists as individuals who preferred government intervention on both economic and social issues. However, much of the current research on Populism's role in the American elections, the Brexit vote, and other phenomena occurring in western democracies define Populism differently than we do. Many of these definitions focus on Populist views about governance, elites, nationalism, geography, and other factors that are far removed from our definition. We have sought to address this issue in previous work by demonstrating that our category of Populist voters hold stronger nationalist attitudes than Libertarian, Populist, Moderate, and Liberal voters (Carmines, Ensley, and Wagner 2016). Thus, research seeking to cast a revealing light on Populists' impact on the 2016 vote should carefully consider what a Populist is. A virtue of our definition is that it allows for direct comparison of Populists to four clearly defined ideological groups over time. That said, our measure, and its focus on issue preferences, may miss some of the essence that makes Populists a distinct group in American public life.

American political parties are risk-averse organizations that tend to hold fast to the status quo. Donald Trump's behavior upended that risk aversion. Our analysis suggests that President Trump might have been successful at uniquely appealing to voters who have felt pulled between the two parties.

Notes

1. The CFA model allowed the correlation between the dimensions to vary.

2. We have used this approach in examining how individuals' location in a two-dimensional measure of ideology helps explain variation in party ID and civic engagement (Carmines, Ensley, and Wagner 2011).

3. The multiple imputation procedure was performed in SAS version 9.1 using the PROC MI procedure. Specifically, we used the MCMC algorithm and an uninformative Jeffery's prior with the default 200 burn-in iterations and the Expected Maximization algorithm for creating starting values.

4. The correlation between the two issue dimensions never exceeds 0.5 in any survey, which is crucial for our contention that there is a large proportion of the American public that does not fit into the traditional left–right continuum on both of these issue dimensions simultaneously.

5. Axelrod's formula is: Contribution = (Size x Turnout x Loyalty) / (National Turnout x National Loyalty).

6. For results for every presidential year from 1972 forward, please contact the authors.

Part V

Party Resources

15

The 2016 Money Race

The Limits of Campaign Money, and the Nature of Popular Love for the Presidential Candidates[1]

Robin Kolodny

J UST BEFORE THE South Carolina Republican primary in 2016, it became
clear that Jeb Bush—former governor of Florida, brother of one former
president, son of another,[2] and beneficiary of the largest Super PAC of the
2016 presidential primary season—was headed for certain defeat and humili-
ation. Bush seemed to have everything—establishment backing, huge name
recognition, a successful governing record, and solid formal and informal
fundraising capacity. He lacked only the interest of Republican primary voters, the excitement that seemed to go to three others: Donald Trump, Florida
U.S. senator and one-time Jeb Bush protégé Marco Rubio (Barbaro 2015),
and Texas U.S. senator Ted Cruz. Trump, who mostly self-funded and raised
and spent the least amount of money of any of the major Republican contenders, ultimately earned the love of some 40 percent of Republican primary
voters and caucus attendees.

During the general election, Trump was outspent by Hillary Clinton by
nearly half a trillion dollars. The big advantage Clinton had over Trump was
in fundraising for her personal campaign committee—$623 million to $335
million. She also had him beat soundly in terms of candidate-linked Super
PACs—$204 million to $79 million. Clinton also beat Trump in party and
joint fundraising committee receipts—$598 million to $543 million—but
this margin was far more modest (Narayanswamy, Cameron, and Gold
2017). Nevertheless, Trump prevailed in the general election.

Trump's success raises this question: Could it be that money doesn't "matter" in American elections any longer? As a scholar of campaign finance, I find it extremely odd that the attention of social scientists and journalists often focuses on the tallies of campaign funds collected by candidates and on the composition of the donor bases that produce this result. A fixation on campaign finance reduces the influence of those with money on politics to a transactional one: those who want favors from politicians "buy" them with campaign cash. This view ignores the substantial power of those who do not engage in such observable transactions. Other social scientists, especially sociologists, have done a better job of revealing the basis of the distorting power of rich people on American politics.

Money: Campaign Donations

To run for president in the United States, one needs to establish a personal campaign operation. Since 1974, the United States has prohibited the major political party organizations from running their candidate's campaign in the general election. Also, since 1972, both major political parties have embraced a nominating system that asks ordinary citizens to register their preferences for their party's nominee for president via primaries and caucuses, replacing the party elites who previously had ultimate authority. The American system of presidential nomination and election demands that candidates have their own fundraising operation.

Candidate campaign committees must report all contributions and expenditures to the Federal Election Commission (FEC). Contributions from individuals, political parties, and political action committees (PACs) are legally limited to very modest amounts because according to the Supreme Court, large, unlimited contributions would give the appearance of undue influence from a particular donor on a particular candidate. Through traditional PACs, interest groups have two major ways to influence elections: they can donate directly to candidates or political parties, or they can conduct independent expenditure campaigns (Boatright 2011). There is a widespread belief that most PACs are affiliated with corporations and flood Washington with campaign money, leading to grave concerns about corporate America's ability to corrupt the political process. However, David Hart finds that not all firms that do business with the government, and do substantial business at that, have PACs at all. On average, most PACs in the high-tech sector were rather modest in size. Also, the presence of a national lobbying office in Washington D.C. proves to be a larger factor in firm success than PAC activity (Hart 2001).

While money given directly to candidates is limited by law, the rights of others (individuals and interest groups in particular) to express their views have led to a series of clever work-arounds that essentially allow outsiders to spend unlimited amounts of money on elections. One vessel for such spending is a Super PAC, an organizational type made possible by the Supreme Court ruling *Citizens United* in January 2010. Super PACs have existed since the 2010 election cycle and have been most noticeable in U.S. Senate races. The 2012 presidential election was the first in which Super PACs were used. In 2016, most observers expected Super PACs to dominate the financing of the nominating contests and general election.

However, figure 15.1 shows that from the nomination race through to the general election, sizable Super PAC money did not help candidates win. The black bars indicate the amount of money the candidates have raised for their own campaign committees through the end of 2016. The numbers reflect

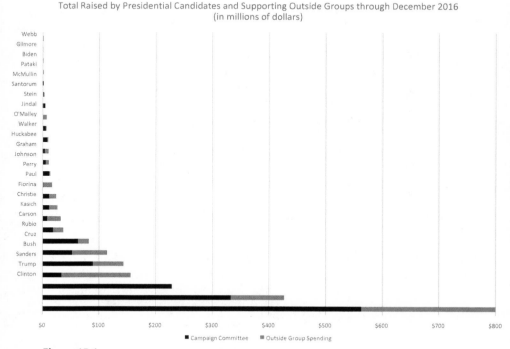

Figure 15.1
Total Raised by Presidential Candidates and Supporting Outside Groups through December 2016 (in millions of dollars).

funds raised throughout the primary and general election seasons. These amounts include all donations, including self-donations. The three candidates who raised over $200 million dollars for their campaigns are Democratic nominee Hillary Clinton, Republican nominee Donald Trump, and Vermont U.S. senator Bernie Sanders, Clinton's rival for the Democratic nomination. Of the Republican primary field, the competitive candidates with the most to the least in their candidate committee funds were Cruz, retired surgeon Ben Carson, Rubio, Bush, and Ohio governor John Kasich. Nearly every candidate has a gray bar next to their black bar, indicating the amount collected by "outside" spending groups on behalf of a candidate, but not coordinated directly with them.[3] The top three candidates benefiting most from outside spending (largely Super PACs) were Hillary Clinton, Republican primary contender Jeb Bush, and Trump. Sanders and Trump are especially notable for the popular support they attracted in 2016 with little to no reliance on Super PAC money.

In the general election campaign, Super PAC activity ran alongside traditional "outside" spending by interest groups and political party organizations on independent expenditure campaigns. The result was an unprecedented level of spending to benefit Hillary Clinton—more than $340 million compared to only $182 million spent to help elect Donald Trump (Center for Responsive Politics 2016a, 2016b). Combined with her significant campaign committee fundraising advantage, Clinton was expected to defeat Trump using the heavily tested tools of electoral politics. The relatively small amount of outside support for Trump in particular (compared to Clinton) leads some to question the importance of money in politics.

This evidence illustrates the shortcomings of the "transactional" approach to campaign finance. When we focus on the transactions of campaign donations, we reduce everything in the political world to be about the election accounts of politicians who are only interested in retaining office, which is an "insider" strategy. Likewise, Super PACs that support presidential candidates signify the interest of a very few wealthy donors in promoting a particular candidate. The assumption is that money used to dominate the airwaves in campaigns will shower (positive) attention on the Super PAC's preferred candidate, which will lead the electorate to give their support. While there is no question that financial donations illustrate an existing affection between donor and candidate, the 2016 presidential campaign shows the limitations of our previous assumptions about the power of campaign donations.

Self-Financing: Help or Hindrance?

Sometimes very wealthy candidates decide to underwrite their run for office with their own money and forego fundraising entirely. Conventional wisdom holds that self-financed candidates will have a huge advantage over candidates who need to raise money because procuring funds takes away precious time from campaigning. Jennifer Steen's extensive study of self-financed candidates eviscerates many of these assertions. Self-funded candidates do not win very often—while they discourage some competitors from running, they typically do quite poorly with voters. One reason for this is that fundraising does not, in fact, detract from a successful campaign. Instead, it is a form of campaigning itself, especially with community opinion leaders whose endorsements are sought to convince people to donate money and/or time for the candidate's campaign. Steen also finds that if a self-financed candidate wins office, the candidate never self-finances the reelection bid, having learned important lessons about what fundraising can do for a campaign (Steen 2006). Adam Brown underscores the central problem with candidate-as-donor in his study of self-financed gubernatorial candidates. He finds that donors are rather strategic when selecting which candidates will gain their contributions. They examine candidates' policy positions as well as their likelihood of winning. Brown found one exception to this rule: "[T]here is one type of donor that doesn't ever seriously ask herself which candidate to give her money to: The self-financed donor" (Brown 2012, 27).

Trump was slow to become a political fundraiser himself, planning at first to finance what campaign needs he had from his personal wealth. By the end of 2016, Trump had provided his campaign with over $66 million, nearly 20 percent of his overall receipts. He was also able to raise money from individuals, most of it from small contributors ($86 million). Still, it was hard and slow going for Trump to come to terms with the resources needed to run even a rudimentary presidential campaign. As late as June 21, 2016, Nicholas Confessore and Rachel Shorey of the *New York Times* reported that Trump was continually loaning (or ultimately donating) money to his campaign to meet basic expenses. He was also heavily relying on the Republican National Committee's infrastructure and staff. Indeed, Trump's repeated assertions that he would pay for the campaign himself was at odds with his attempts to raise money for the general election (Confessore and Shorey 2016).

Money: Buying Support from Politicians?

While there has been an enormous amount of scholarship focused on whether PAC donations buy votes in Congress (in short, they don't appear to do so), Hall and Deardorff offer a view of group influence that is largely unrelated to the size of PAC donations. Indeed, they argue that the donations received by politicians from any particular PAC are so small that politicians would be practically giving away their votes by trading them for such paltry sums. Instead, they focus on the legislative labor offered to members of Congress by professional lobbyists: "Interest groups today spend over a billion dollars a year lobbying Congress, more than they spend in PAC contributions and independent expenditures to congressional campaigns combined" (Hall and Deardorff 2006, 69).

Those who write about campaign money often overlook corporate investment in lobbying. They make the assumption that any interest that donates to politics must also have an established lobbying office. Lobbying and campaigning are thought to be two sides of the same coin. As *Politico* writer Kenneth Vogel puts it,

> Though I'd spent years watching deep-pocketed interests interface with government, big giving never struck me as a particularly effective way for billionaires to get what they wanted. Savvy CEOs with major interests before government consider lobbying a more effective way to boost or protect their interests. Lobbying, in other words, is for financial gain, while big campaign contributions are mostly for passion or ego. (Vogel 2014, 22)

One irony of Trump's past political behavior is that he has made significant donations to politicians on both sides of the aisle, though he has donated exclusively to Republicans since 2010 (Singer 2016). During the Republican primary debates, Trump claimed that politicians took donations and then did his bidding. Yet, when he began to seek donations, he did not acknowledge that he was controlled by money. His professed independence from money's (and its donors') effects up until the present has made his presidency possible.

The Making of the Pre-2016 Trump: What 2016's Money Can't Buy

What Trump lacked in campaign money, he more than compensated for with claims to great personal wealth and exhortations for capitalism and favorable markets as a panacea for America's ills. Many have written about Trump's deficiencies as a politician and his strength as a reality TV star. However, Trump attracted voter interest like no other candidate due to his constant coverage by the media. Much of the coverage is not flattering. Obviously, this makes little difference in his supporters' eyes.

Like so many reportedly self-made men, Trump's "Horatio Alger story," false though it may be in his case, attracted attention because of the common notion that anyone can make it in America. Trump has built his narrative as someone who took a little money and made a lot as a result. Michael Poca-lyko makes the case that Trump's approach is not "corporate" but that of an entrepreneur and/or a family-business CEO. For this reason, he says that Trump "is at ease with disruption in a way that corporate leaders generally never become" (Pocalyko 2017, 52). We certainly see a consistent disruptive narrative in the Trump presidency.

In Trump's long-running reality TV show, *The Apprentice*, the mogul was the judge of success, deciding each week which contestant should be elimi-nated on account of deficient business skills. In addition, Trump's ability to label someone a "loser" in a one-hour show makes the determination of complex traits of business skill look "obvious"—as they seem to be to Trump. Simplicity is a very attractive quality, and Trump perfected it then and continues it now, adding to his media allure.

Scholars of reality television and popular culture identified Trump's dis-tinctive quality some time ago. In 2007, Lisa Perks wrote of the "royal" yet relatable imagery of Trump:

> Trump's commodification has become so omnipresent that he is now referred to in popular press as "The Donald." The Donald's ability to profit from the free market's invisible hand has even elevated him to divine status (at least on the show). As he descends an escalator in his eponymous towers, "royal" trum-pets sound in the background (23 September 2004). The top of the escalator may have originated in heaven judging by the imagery shown before the final scene of the 4 November 2004 episode: Fast-moving clouds are shown jetting across the New York City skyline and a crescendoing [*sic*] chorus is heard before a tuxedoed Trump steps into the board room for the firing. As a divine figure, Trump possesses the ability to define the lives of his apprentices: In this episode, he privileges industry over workers explaining, "It's not personal, it's just busi-ness." (Perks 2007, 110)

Trump made the "just business" aspect of his success seem attainable. The show's setup implies that any person willing to work hard can achieve the wild financial success Trump enjoyed. They need only display the determina-tion the eventual winners do in the show's contrived situations.

Jim McGuigan, a scholar of cultural analysis, argues that shows like *The Apprentice* draw attention away from the classic imbalance between rich and poor, toward the "cool capitalism" view that portrays the poor as legitimate competitors with the rich:

> The public face of capitalism, however, has changed from its earlier, and some might argue its original, form in Protestant asceticism . . . to a much more hedonistic and "cool" appearance. Cool capitalism is largely defined by the incorporation of signs of disaffection and resistance into capitalism itself,

thereby contributing to the reproduction of the system and reducing opposition to it. This is a vital feature of capitalism's hegemonic dominance now. . . . A program like *The Apprentice*, then, performs an ideological role in projecting the values of free-market business in a seductive manner that disarms criticism. (McGuigan 2008, 309)

Trump's use of TV shows, products, casinos, and all other branding sold seduction in spades. If not "love," then at least an aspiration to consume like Trump became associated with him. Along the lines of the "cool capitalism" view, the journey as well as the goods matter. So, Trump has failed businesses, failed marriages, and yet always seems to come out on top. Setbacks become details. Even more interesting, the tough love displayed by business leaders on reality TV becomes an asset. As Boyle and Kelly explain while analyzing the United Kingdom's *Dragon's Den*,

[T]he viewer is regularly aligned with the viewpoints of Sugar and the "dragons" and is thus encouraged to draw upon the skills, knowledge and expertise put forward by these entrepreneurs before going on to judge the contestants and participants accordingly. It is also the case that these figures perform a certain "nasty" role that has become appealing to audiences schooled in reality TV and which is indicative of the televisual skills they have acquired. However, this does not necessarily make them appear inauthentic, as their ruthlessness is again legitimized by their off-screen achievements within the demanding world of business. (Boyle and Kelly 2010, 337)

Political scientists seem startled at the response Trump's nasty language and assertions get from some Americans. Apparently, some voters respect the "plain talk" on hot-button issues. If ruthlessness brings success, so be it.

The Voters' Vote

So, Trump had built a relatable brand. How does that translate into political support? Rapoport, Abramowitz, and Stone argue that Trump's positions are precisely what 40 percent of the Republican primary electorate want. Even supporters of other Republican candidates approved of Trump's positions. Furthermore, when it came to candidate preference, Trump rated highly among Republicans throughout the contest. He was not simply the beneficiary of a crowded field; he was getting the love (Rapoport, Abramowitz, and Stone 2016). Trump was in a strong position to win the nomination early on despite having little in the way of professional campaign staff, any real campaign experience, paid media, or praise from the free press (earned media). The more outrageous his claims, the more press coverage he got, and the more "establishment" candidates such as Bush seemed to be part of a past complacence in politics.

But there are other considerations. There is something unique about Trump's fame from *The Apprentice*. As Eric Konigsberg wrote,

> In light of Trump's candidacy, *The Apprentice*—and *The Celebrity Apprentice*, its later iteration starring famous contestants—can be viewed as an extensive Trump campaign ad, or as Goertz might say, an infomercial on steroids. Polls suggest that *Apprentice* viewers are Trump's base. David Axelrod wrote on CNN's website that Trump's poll numbers just after the second Republican debate were almost twice as high among people who watched the show than those who didn't. (Konigsberg 2015)

And so the "wisdom through wealth" sales approach led, as we have seen, to Trump's domination of "free" or "earned" media. While there is no way to reliably say how Trump's status as perpetual news items played out in the campaign, Mary Harris estimates that Trump "earned" approximately $4.96 billion in media coverage value while Clinton earned about $3.24 million. He exceeded Clinton's exposure in every media metric (online news, broadcast, blogs and forums, Twitter, and print), but especially won the Twitter war, with over 50 percent more exposure than Clinton. As we have come to know, it doesn't much matter how the coverage was earned. Harris reminds us that he earned it "from his bombastic and insulting statements, he earned it from pulling in massive crowds to his rallies, and he earned it from winning primary after primary" (Harris 2016).

Trump Wins in the General Election

In some very important ways, we have seen this appeal before in the 1992 campaign of Independent candidate Ross Perot. Perot used his business success and value to the media as a curiosity to turn an otherwise "conventional" race between a Democrat and a Republican into a three-way contest. The differences between 1992 and 2016 are significant, of course. Perot ran as an Independent candidate. He ended up earning over 19 percent of the popular vote but zero electoral votes. Trump managed to win a major party nomination and then prevailed in the Electoral College but not the popular vote. While Perot was well known, Trump was a household name. Perot was an awkward presence who came into and left the race, using thirty-minute "infomercials" to talk "commonsense" to the American public. As we have just seen, Trump was a well-seasoned media personality who used traditional and new media to promote his presumably non-political image.

Yet, the substance of many of Perot's and Trump's appeals were eerily similar. A quick look on YouTube will show how closely Perot and Trump's discussions of trade's role in the American economy mirror each other. In both cases, the candidates used their celebrity to reach voters disenchanted with American politics. Together, they mark a change in how we view the role of money in campaigns.

The next successful presidential candidate may very well come from a more traditional political background. However, the campaign must begin with a relatable relationship showcasing that candidate's expertise as Trump has done. We should expect that the conventional manner in which we have assessed political resources is on the way out, to be replaced by a return to retail politics, even if the retail moves "online."

Notes

1. An earlier version of this chapter was published as "Money Can't Buy Me Love: The 2016 Presidential Nominating Process, the Limits of Campaign Money, and the Nature of Popular Love." *Society*, 53 (5): 487–492.

2. That would be George W. Bush (brother) and George Herbert Walker Bush (Father).

3. This data, produced by the Center for Responsive Politics, includes Super PACs, Leadership PACs, and "Carey" committees.

16

Everything Is Relative

Are Political Parties Playing a Meaningful Campaign Finance Role in U.S. Federal Elections?

Diana Dwyre

Is big spending by super PACs and other non-party groups eclipsing political party spending in contemporary U.S. federal elections? Indeed, these non-party groups operate under a different set of rules that allow them to more easily raise money than the parties, and there has been significant growth in the number of and spending by non-party groups in recent elections. Moreover, how are the parties doing relative to their own past performance? Has party fundraising and spending kept pace with the competitive environment and the strategic needs of their candidates?

In this chapter, I evaluate the various changes to the rules governing federal campaign finance activities as independent variables to discover how these changes have impacted the fundraising and spending activities of the national party committees over time as well as relative to the performance of other campaign finance actors. I find that the national parties have adapted tangibly and often effectively to these changes. Yet, relative to other spenders, the formal parties' role in the overall campaign finance system has diminished significantly. This evaluation is conducted in the context of an ongoing debate about the nature of contemporary American parties, and my analysis will shed some light on this theoretical debate as well.

The Changing Campaign Finance Landscape

The Federal Election Campaign Act (FECA) and its amendments of the 1970s codified the candidate-centered character of campaign funding by limiting what could be raised and spent by parties, groups, and individuals and solidifying restrictions on the sources of campaign money. Then, in 1976, with *Buckley v. Valeo*, 42 U.S. 47 (1976), the Supreme Court redefined the contours of permissible fundraising and spending by various campaign finance actors according to the Court's relatively narrow understanding of corruption and of how First Amendment free speech rights apply to the financing of elections in the United States. In order to guard against corruption, the justices retained the limits on contributions to candidates, parties, and PACs. Yet, in the name of free speech, the court lifted the limits on candidate spending and individual independent spending (spending not coordinated with a candidate or party), as well as the ability of candidates to spend unlimited amounts of their own money. The parties were not permitted to make independent expenditures until the congressional campaign committees were given that ability in 1996 with *Colorado Republican Federal Campaign Committee v. Federal Election Commission* (518 US 604 1996) and the DNC and RNC through Federal Election Commission (FEC) approval in 2003 (Wilson 2003).

Other recent adjustments to the rules governing how elections are funded in the United States have had perceivable impacts on the campaign finance activities of political parties and other campaign finance actors. How have these changes impacted the role of political parties, particularly the role of parties relative to other campaign finance actors? I focus mostly on campaign finance activities and developments since passage of the Bipartisan Campaign Reform Act (BCRA) in 2002, for BCRA is a logical turning point in the move to a more deregulated campaign finance system that has enhanced the fundraising and spending capabilities of *non-party* campaign finance actors. Have these deregulatory changes diminished the role and influence of parties? Is it a zero-sum game whereby rules that increase the fundraising and/or spending capabilities of non-party actors decrease the fundraising and/or spending capabilities of parties? I expect that it is not that simple, because both the formal party organizations and non-party actors react and adapt to changes in the regulatory environment, and their reactions and adaptations alter the role that parties and other organizations play. For instance, parties have adapted to the restrictions on their ability to directly support their candidates with contributions and coordinated expenditures by taking advantage of their ability (since 1996) to make unlimited independent expenditures. Another adaptation is the development of robust party ally groups that enhance the parties' reach and influence as partners in the extended party network.

How we evaluate the role of parties depends on our understanding of parties. Contemporary scholars disagree about how we should define and conceptualize political parties today, and one's view of parties is likely to shape one's evaluation of the role of parties in the financing of modern campaigns. Indeed, there is disagreement about the effects of campaign finance changes on parties and non-party actors (see, for example, Stratmann 2005; Samples 2006; La Raja 2008; Cain 2014). I analyze the campaign finance activities of the national parties, as well as non-party political actors, in the wake of recent legal and regulatory changes. I aim to discover how the parties' role has changed relative to their own past performance, as well as to other campaign finance actors, and to consider whether the parties are playing a meaningful role in the contemporary federal campaign finance system.

What Is A Party?

Efforts to curb the influence of political parties in the United States are as old as the nation itself. In *Federalist No. 10,* James Madison warned about the "mischief of faction," especially majority factions—parties. In his 1976 book, *Curing the Mischiefs of Faction*, Austin Ranney documented the history of efforts to curtail what had been seen as the negative impacts of parties in the United States (Ranney 1976). One's view of the relevance and influence of parties in the modern U.S. campaign finance system depends to some extent on how one defines contemporary political parties.

Recent political science research on American political parties features a new *group theory* of parties as broad organizations that include allied partisan groups and activists in an *extended party network*. This group theory approach contrasts sharply with the characterization of American parties as organizations populated and controlled by party elites such as elected officials, candidates, and party leaders, what Aldrich called the "ambitious office holders and seekers" who are focused on winning as the proximate goal to achieving policy or other goals (Aldrich 1995). The group theory also differs from the traditional view of parties as composed of a tripod of the party-in-the-electorate, party organizations, and party-in-government (Key 1942).

Scholars have focused on different aspects of the group theory of parties. Some view parties as "networked" with interest group and activist "policy demanders" outside of the traditional party organizations, whereby these "policy demanders, rather than office holders, determine the broad agendas of political conflict" (Bawn et al. 2012, 589). Most scholars agree contemporary U.S. parties are surrounded by intense policy demanders with narrow policy goals, but some see the consequences of their activities as more detrimental to American representative democracy than others. Bawn et al. (2012) suggest possible negative consequences *because of* the nature of contemporary political parties as a collection of organized policy demanders who work, especially in nomination contests, to elect lawmakers in service to *their* policy agenda rather than the parties' interest in majority status through the election of moderate lawmakers who can appeal to the median voter.

Other scholars also note that the goals of some non-party organizations are not necessarily congruent with those of the party organizations, and that the diminished campaign finance role of parties, relative to non-party organizations, has resulted in negative consequences for the health of representative democracy itself. For instance, La Raja and Schaffner (2015) contend that limits on state party campaign finance activities have contributed to polarization, and thus to governmental dysfunction. They found that limits on party fundraising alter the flow of campaign money away from the parties and toward non-party groups, which they argue are more ideologically extreme than pragmatic party leaders. These groups, they assert, help elect more extreme candidates who then contribute to heightened partisan polarization and decreased representation in state legislatures.

Yet, Hamm et al. (2014) examined party and non-party spenders in states with and without limits on party fundraising, and they found that these campaign finance rules have had little clear impact on party and non-party spending before and after the 2010 *Citizens United* Supreme Court decision, which allowed corporations to spend unlimited amounts in elections as long as they do not coordinate with a candidate or their party. The *Citizens United* decision, along with a lower court decision and some FEC rules, led to the rise of Super PACs, which can both raise and spend money in unlimited amounts as long as they spend independently (i.e., not in coordination with candidates or parties). Hamm et al. compared party and what they call "party-affiliated" (e.g., the Republican Governors Association) and "party-allied" (e.g., Crossroads) group spending in 2006 and 2010 (before and after *Citizens United*), and they found the partisan groups most removed from the parties, the "party-allied" groups, spent little in states with limits on party fundraising in both years, and there was more spending by both types of non-party groups in both years in states with *no* party limits (2014, 313). They argue that this finding "throws a monkey wrench into the notion that limits on political party contributions are the key mechanism driving money away from the formal party organizations" (Hamm et al. 2014, 313).

Others focus on the parties as the central players in the party networks.

For instance, Herrnson views contemporary American parties as "enduring multilayered coalitions," with the parties as the central node in a wider network of allied outside groups and activists (Herrnson 2009, 1207). In the campaign finance world, certain party-allied organizations, such as some traditional PACs, 527 organizations, Super PACs and 501(c) groups, are viewed as *part of* a party's "extended party network" (Bedlington and Malbin 2003; Dwyre and Kolodny 2014a; Herrnson 2009; Koger, Masket, and Noel 2009; Kolodny and Dwyre 1998, 2018; Skinner 2005; Skinner, Masket, and Dulio 2013). These party-allied organizations are thought to often *complement* rather than contradict the parties' pursuit of majority status.

Indeed, Mann and Corrado (2014) note that the *national* parties have actually done quite well financially after the BCRA ban on party soft money and *Citizens United*, which have led to big independent spending by non-party groups. They too make the case that some "party-affiliated" Super PACs, such as Majority PAC and House Majority PAC (which they call "essentially parallel campaign organs of the Democratic congressional campaign committees"), are part of the party network, and these groups pursue the party's objectives by targeting many of the same races that the formal party committees target (Mann and Corrado 2014, 12). They do not see diminished parties in the wake of BCRA, *Citizens United*, and other campaign finance changes: "To contend that parties have been marginalized or that their role in contemporary elections is diminishing as a result of the rise of Super PACs and other non-party organizations is to view 'the party' simply as the formal party committees, rather than as a networked amalgamation of diverse organizations with common electoral goals and shared ideological predispositions" (Mann and Corrado 2014, 13).

So, what do we know about the relationship between parties and these allied groups? Skinner et al. used network analysis to examine how closely linked partisan 527 groups were to the formal party organizations by analyzing personnel connections between the parties and 527s after BCRA, and they found that "the formal parties are highly central to the network of 527s. The best-connected 527s tend to have a high percentage of employees who have also worked for formal party organizations and top presidential campaigns" (Skinner, Masket, and Dulio 2013, 141). Robin Kolodny and I also used network analysis to examine the spending of party and non-party groups in the 2014 congressional elections and discovered that partisan groups most closely ideologically allied with a party (e.g., the Chamber of Commerce with the GOP) spent most of their money on the same races that their allied party targeted, while anti-establishment groups (e.g., the Tea Party group FreedomWorks) did not generally spend in the same races as the party ideologically closest to them (Kolodny and Dwyre 2018). Evelyn Braz and I also found high levels of congruence between the parties' congressional campaign committee spending and Super PAC spending in the 2012 congressional elections (Dwyre and Braz 2015). Indeed, the national parties make it quite easy for their interest group and donor allies to know who the parties would like them to support, without actually talking to one another, which would likely be considered illegal coordination (Dwyre and Kolodny 2014a; Jacobson 2013, 80; Kolodny and Dwyre 2018). So, if party allies want to help the parties pursue winning, they can easily do so.

Of course, even party allied groups also spend to pursue their legislative goals by supporting candidates from both parties, safe incumbents, and powerful lawmakers to ensure access to politicians who are key to achieving their policy goals (Herrnson 2009, 1220; Grossman and Dominguez 2009). Indeed, Malbin argues that party and non-party organizations are not in a zero-sum game: "Increased activity by these groups in a polarized environment did not come at the *expense* of the parties. The organizations often acted together with party surrogates through independent-spending coalitions in a manner that has been more helpful to the parties than the groups' direct contributions to candidates has ever been" (Malbin 2014b, 101–102; see also Malbin 2017).

For those who view the extended party network as a positive development or at least a useful adaptation to a changing campaign finance landscape, the party organizations are the central players in the extended party network. For instance, Robin Kolodny and I contend while the parties may not do the lion's share of campaign spending, they influence, or "orchestrate" the spending strategies of their allied partners in the network (Dwyre and Kolodny 2014a; Kolodny and Dwyre 1998, 2018; see also Malbin 2017; Herrnson 2009). Yet, do the party organizations need to maintain some minimal level of campaign finance activity in order to play this orchestration role? As non-party groups have benefited from recent legal and regulatory changes that allow them to raise and spend more than the parties because they face fewer restrictions than the parties do, have the parties continued to play a meaningful role in the financing of federal elections?

National Party Fundraising

Changes to the rules have influenced how the parties raise their money. Most scholars point to the loss of soft money with passage of BCRA in 2002 as the biggest blow to the parties' bottom line in recent years, but it did not completely undermine the national party committees' ability to raise money (Dwyre and Kolodny 2014b; Malbin 2014b; Mann and Corrado 2014). Figure

16.1 shows national party committees' receipts of both hard and soft money between 1992 and 2002, and then hard money only after BCRA from 2004 to 2016 (note: all dollar amounts adjusted for inflation). The impact of soft money is clear, as especially the Hill Committees (DSCC, NRSC, DCCC, and NRCC) took advantage of their last chance to raise and spend soft money in 2002. However, the DNC raised more money *after* BCRA, reaching a fundraising peak in 2004, with a sharp decline in receipts in 2006 and only a slight recovery after that. The DCCC actually *exceeded* its pre-BCRA fundraising totals from 2006 to 2016. So, perhaps the end of soft money was not, as some had predicted, a major blow to party strength (La Raja 2003, 69–96; McConnell 2003, 143), especially Democratic Party strength (Gitell 2003).

Yet, figure 16.1 also shows that Republican Party national committee hard money receipts (RNC, NRSC, and NRCC combined) have declined since 2004. The Republican Party's reduced receipts are somewhat surprising given that BCRA raised and indexed to inflation the limits on hard money individual contributions to party committees. However, as Malbin (2014b, 97–99) and Mann and Corrado (2014, 11) note, before BCRA, the Republican Governors Association (RGA) and the Republican State Leadership Committee (RSLC) were part of the RNC, and they were spun off into independent 527 organizations after BCRA. Thus, the RGA and RSLC fundraising totals were no longer included in national party reported receipts after 2002. If this money is added back in to the RNC's totals, as Malbin did in a 2014 study, the RNC's 2004, 2006, and 2012 fundraising actually exceeded the committee's receipts before BCRA (Malbin 2014b, 98). Malbin notes, however, the Republican national committees *did* raise less during *midterms* after BCRA, particularly between 2006 and 2010, primarily due to a decline in receipts from small donors who give less than $200 (Malbin 2014b, 99). Malbin also contends that the receipts and spending of the "leadership Super PACs" should be included in parties' totals as well (the Republican Party affiliates Congressional Leadership Fund and Senate Leadership Fund, and the Democratic Party allies Senate Majority PAC and House Majority PAC) (Malbin 2017), and doing so would surely increase the party committees' receipts in recent years.

Sources of Party Funds

The parties get their money from a variety of sources. Figure 16.2 shows the sources of receipts for the national Democratic and Republican Party committees from 2000 to 2016. Soft money was an important source of funds for both parties since the 1990s until it was banned with the passage of BCRA in 2002. While both parties have always relied heavily on contributions from

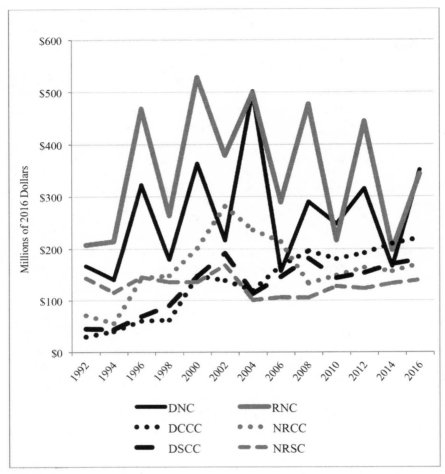

Figure 16.1
National Party Committee Receipts, 1992–2016 (in millions of 2016 dollars).

Source: Data for 1992–2014 compiled by author from Brookings Institution. 2017. *Vital Statistics on Congress: Data on the U.S. Congress,* Updated January 2017, Table 3–13 at https://www.brookings.edu/multi-chapter -report/vital-statistics-on-congress/ (accessed March 31, 2017). Data for 2016 from Federal Election Commis- sion, "2015–2016 Election Cycle Data Summaries through 12/31/16" at http://www.fec.gov/press/sum maries/2016/ElectionCycle/24m_NatlParty.shtml (accessed May 10, 2017).
Note: Totals include both hard and soft money from 1992 to 2002 and only hard money from 2004 (after the national party committees were prohibited from raising soft money by the Bipartisan Campaign Reform Act of 2002).

individuals, after BCRA, individuals became the primary source of funding for the national parties. BCRA also increased individual contribution limits and indexed them to inflation, which accounts for some of the increase in the amount parties have raised from individual donors. Transfers show up in 2010 because that is when the Federal Election Commission began to report these receipts (presumably transfers were included in the "Other Committees" category before that). Figure 16.2 shows that prior to BCRA in 2002, the GOP had a fundraising edge over the Democrats. By 2008, Democratic Party committees had almost caught up to the Republican committees, and in 2010, 2014, and 2016, Democratic Party receipts exceeded GOP receipts. As before, we see a clear impact of policy change, in this case BCRA (2002), on campaign finance activity as the types of sources on which the parties rely for funds shift from soft money to mostly hard money contributions from individuals and from PACs and other committees (note that some of the other changes in sources, such as the increase in transfers, are due more to FEC reporting changes than to policy or strategic changes).

Contributions from Individuals

Since 2004, all six national party committees (the DNC, DSCC, DCCC, RNC, NRSC, and NRCC) have raised more of their funds from individual donors than from any other source (Dwyre and Kolodny 2014b, 180–83). Donors generally prefer to give contributions directly to candidates for access reasons, ideological reasons, or for the social benefits associated with attending fundraisers and meeting candidates and lawmakers (Francia et al. 2003). Yet, many contributors also will give to the parties. Some reform-minded activists and some jurists view parties as "corrupt conduits" through which donors who want to influence lawmakers can direct contributions (Persily 2006, 213–40). This view helps explain why, for example, FECA limited direct contributions to parties, parties' contributions to candidates, and the coordinated expenditures that parties can make on behalf of their candidates, and why BCRA ended party soft money. From this perspective, a small donation from an individual is seen as the most acceptable type of contribution because it is least likely to raise corruption concerns.

Yet, since BCRA in 2002, both parties' committees, and especially the DNC and RNC, have raised a good deal of their money from individuals making *large* contributions, with many of them giving over $20,000 to the party committee in a two-year election cycle. Figure 16.3 shows different levels of individual contributions to the DNC and RNC by percentage of total individual receipts from 2000 to 2016, and it is clear, especially in the most recent election cycles, the national committees now rely heavily on donors who give very large amounts (the parties' House and Senate campaign committees have followed similar patterns in individual contributions). One possible

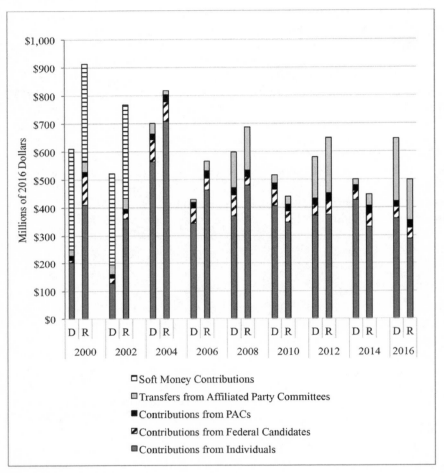

Figure 16.2
Sources of National Party Funds, 2000–2016 (in millions of 2016 dollars).

Source: Compiled by author from Federal Election Commission data.
Note: Figure includes data for all national party committees: the DNC and RNC, DSCC and NRSC, and DCCC and NRCC.

explanation for the decrease in small-donor fundraising is that BCRA raised the contribution limits to candidates and parties and indexed them to inflation, which may have motivated party leaders to focus on pursuing more of these larger donations. Yet, the parties have clearly shifted their fundraising strategies toward these large donors, a development that may be related to their increasing use of joint fundraising committees (see below).

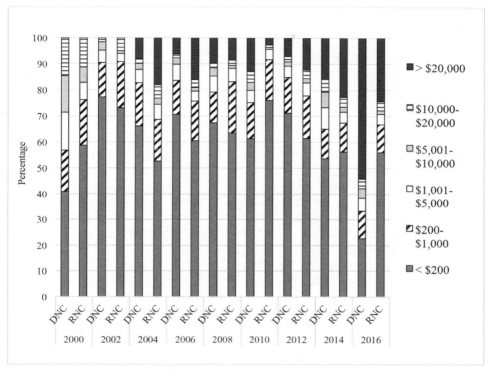

Figure 16.3 Individual Contributions to DNC and RNC by Amount, 2000–2016 (percentage).

Source: Compiled by author from FEC. 2013. "2011–2012 Election Cycle Data Summaries through 12/31/12: Party Committees" at https://transition.fec.gov/press/summaries/2012/ElectionCycle/24m_NatlParty.shtml; FEC. 2015. "2013–2014 Election Cycle Data Summaries through 12/31/14: Party Committees" at https://transition.fec.gov/press/summaries/2014/ElectionCycle/24m_NatlParty.shtml; FEC. 2017. "2015–2016 Election Cycle Data Summaries through 12/31/16: Party Committees" at https://transition.fec.gov/press/summaries/2016/ElectionCycle/24m_NatlParty.shtml (accessed October 30, 2017).

New Party Accounts

The national party committees also are now permitted to raise additional money for other specific purposes. In April 2014, Congress passed, and President Obama signed, the Gabriella Miller Kids First Research Act (P.L. 113–94), which eliminated public funding for the party's presidential nominating conventions that had been in place since 1976 and directed the funds to the "10-Year Pediatric Research Initiative Fund" for research on pediatric cancer, autism, and other childhood diseases (Overby 2014).[1] Indeed, public support for the public funding system had plummeted, and the convention grants had failed to keep pace with the cost of the conventions. Then, Congress passed, and President Obama signed, the Consolidated and Further Continuing Appropriations Act of 2015 (P.L. 113–235), what became known as the controversial "CRomnibus" Act, a combination continuing resolution (CR) and omnibus spending bill.

A bipartisan, but mostly Republican, group of lawmakers replaced the public convention funding with a new source of funding: each party's national committee may now establish a separate nominating convention account with higher contribution limits than the standard limits for individual and PAC contributions to the parties. CRomnibus also provided for two additional new party accounts, one for legal proceedings and election recounts, and another for the national party headquarters, also with higher contribution limits. So, for the 2016 election, an individual could give $33,400 to each national party committee per year (indexed to inflation)—this is the standard traditional contribution. Plus, because of the CRomnibus changes, that same donor could give additional contributions of $100,200 per year to a party's national committee for its presidential nominating convention, as well as $100,200 per year to a party's three national committees (their national committee, House campaign committee, and Senate campaign committee) for legal proceedings and election recounts, and another $100,200 to each committee for its national party headquarters (all indexed for inflation). So, a single donor could theoretically have given a grand total of $801,600 to the three committees of one national political party per year, and a total of $1,603,200 for the two-year election cycle in 2016 (Federal Election Commission 2015; Garrett 2015, 3).

Contributions from Traditional PACs

Political action committees may give limited contributions to candidates and parties (including to the new CRomnibus party committees), and they may also make independent expenditures. A multicandidate PAC (the most common type of PAC)[2] may contribute $15,000 per year directly to each national party committee (the party's national committee, House campaign committee, and Senate campaign committee), $45,000 per year to each of these committees for their legal/recount accounts, another $45,000 per year to each for their party headquarters, and $45,000 to the DNC and RNC presidential nominating convention account. Yet, unlike individual donations, multicandidate PAC contributions are not indexed to inflation. Non-multicandidate PACs can give more than twice as much to these new party accounts, and their donations *are* indexed to inflation. The 2016 election was the first election cycle with these new party accounts, and table 16.1 shows the Republican Party committees generally raised more than their Demo-

TABLE 16.1
Contributions to the New CRomnibus Accounts of the
National Party Committees, 2015–2016

	Convention	Headquarters	Recount/Legal	Total
DNC	$16,755,965	$6,953,019	$4,089,189	$27,798,171
DSCC	n/a	$7,068,150	$2,931,767	$9,999,917
DCCC	n/a	$7,321,678	$2,693,120	$10,014,799
Democratic Party Totals	**$16,755,965**	**$21,342,847**	**$9,714,076**	**$47,812,887**
RNC	$23,817,038	$26,367,459	$5,949,515	$56,134,013
NRSC	n/a	$9,408,452	$1,348,478	$10,756,929
NRCC	n/a	$10,080,459	$10,751,747	$20,832,207
Republican Party Totals	**$23,817,038**	**$45,856,371**	**$18,049,740**	**$87,723,149**

Source: Federal Election Commission, "Party Table 10: Contributions to Accounts of National Party Committees, January 1, 2015 through December 31, 2016" at https://transition.fec.gov/press/summaries/2016/tables/party/Prty10_2016_24m.pdf (accessed August 22, 2017).

cratic counterparts, and almost twice as much overall in all three of the new accounts.

The national parties collect tens of millions of dollars from PACs, but, as figure 16.2 shows, PAC contributions constitute a small portion of their overall receipts. Indeed, many PACs, particularly those tied to interest groups and industries that also lobby, are more inclined to follow an access-oriented strategy by making contributions directly to candidates, and quite often to safe incumbents of the majority party (rather than the marginal incumbents and challengers the parties target), and sometimes to both parties' candidates. Perhaps we will see more PAC money going to the new party accounts for conventions, headquarters, and legal and recount issues, which would increase the parties' reliance on PAC funds.

Joint Fundraising Committees

Another source of party funds is joint fundraising committees (JFCs), which are created by one or more candidates, party committees, and/or PACs that share the costs of fundraising and distribute the receipts according to a prearranged formula. Each donor can write one large check to give the maximum contribution to each candidate and to each party committee(s) and/or PAC(s) in the JFC. These joint fundraising arrangements can help parties raise quite a lot. In fact, in 2012, the DNC was allocated more from joint fundraising committees ($128 million) than it raised from individual donations given directly to the party committee ($119 million) (Dwyre and Kolodny 2014b, 194). Joint fundraising committees can help streamline fundraising for multiple candidates and various party committees with events featuring high-profile guests such as a presidential candidate, where each JFC participant can reap proceeds from donors who have the means to write one big check to max out their allowable contributions (Corrado 2011, 138). Joint fundraising committees also may raise funds for the new party accounts for presidential conventions, party headquarters, and legal and recount costs, so, in 2016, a single donor could write a check for over $801,600 for a party's three national committees if a JFC was set up to allocate the maximum amount to each party account, and even more if the JFC also included candidates.

The Supreme Court's 2014 decision in *McCutcheon v. Federal Election Commission* (572 US 2014) is expected to have a significant impact on party fundraising, particularly through joint fundraising committees. The *McCutcheon* decision eliminated the aggregate limit on individual donations in a two-year election cycle, meaning that a wealthy contributor, who may have rationed his or her donations to candidates, parties, and groups in the past because of the overall limit, may now spread the wealth around to as many of these as he or she wishes, within the limits for each, of course. Not surprisingly, the number of multiple party committee and candidate-party joint fundraising committees rose soon after the court's *McCutcheon* decision in 2014, just as Justice Breyer predicted in his dissenting opinion (Carney 2014; Mann and Corrado 2014, 4).

Some welcome this new avenue that may direct more money toward the parties and away from Super PACs (La Raja 2013, 2014). Others assert that the *McCutcheon* decision might open up a wider avenue for undue influence, and that the court's narrow view of what constitutes corruption (i.e., only *quid pro quo* corruption warrants concern) will encourage such behavior (Malbin 2014b). With the ability to raise so much money from a single donor, party leaders and office holders can use JFCs to attract wealthy donors seeking access and policy results. Figure 16.4 shows the national party committees' receipts from joint fundraising committees from 2008 to 2016. Both parties' national committees, but especially the DNC, are taking advantage of this vehicle for raising funds, with the DNC raising more each successive presidential election cycle since 2008. In 2016, the DNC raised 40 percent ($148.7 million) of its total receipts ($372.2 million) from JFCs, while the RNC raised 32 percent ($109.7 million) of its total receipts ($343.4 million) from JFCs (Center for Responsive Politics 2017a, 2017b).

The amounts in figure 16.4 reflect only what each party was allocated directly from JFCs according to the prearranged allocation formulas. Yet, since party committees may transfer unlimited amounts of federal (hard) money to other party committees, the funds allocated to state parties from JFCs are often later transferred to the national party committees, significantly enhancing the national party committees' take from the JFC arrangement.

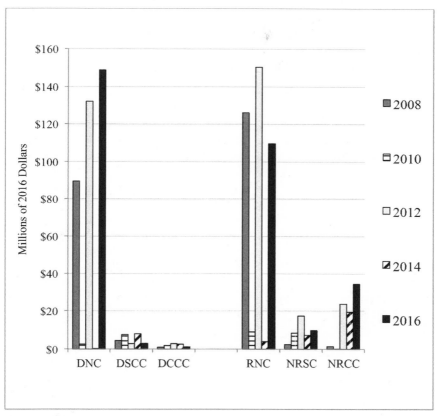

Figure 16.4
National Party Receipts from Joint Fundraising Committees, 2008–2016 (in millions of 2016 dollars).

Source: Compiled by author from Center for Responsive Politics data. See Center for Responsive Politics, "Joint
Fundraising Committees Recipients" at https://www.opensecrets.org/jfc/top.php?type = R&cycle = 2016 (accessed June 20, 2017).

For instance, in 2016, the Hillary Victory Fund JFC raised $529.9 million, with $158.2 million allocated to the Clinton campaign and $107.5 million to the DNC. Yet, much of the $112.4 million that was allocated to the 38 state parties was then transferred to the DNC, permitting "a small number of elite Democratic donors to give hundreds of thousands of dollars to the DNC for the purpose of affecting the presidential campaign" (Biersack 2016). Thus, a single donor could, in effect, direct far more via a JFC to a single federal party committee than the $33,400 per year allowed by giving up to $10,000 per year to any (or many) state party committees that then forward those funds to the party's national committee, in effect circumventing the limits on how much a contributor may give to a national party committee.

Member Contributions to Their Party Committees

Parties also raise money from their own elected officials and candidates. Federal candidates and officeholders may transfer unlimited amounts from their own campaign committee and $15,000 per year from their leadership PAC to a national party committee (11 CFR 113.2). In the 1970s and 1980s, federal lawmakers gave little to their parties or to fellow partisans running for Congress (Heberlig and Larson 2012, 9; Bedlington and Malbin 2003; Jacobson 1985; Kolodny and Dwyre 1998; Wilcox 1989). This began to change in 1994, when control of Congress was seriously in contention for the first time in decades. Heberlig and Larson argue that this uncertainty allowed the congressional campaign committees "to induce their members to leverage money from their own networks of donors on behalf of the party's collective electoral fortunes" (2012, 16). Transfers from members of Congress to the House and Senate campaign committees grew again in 2004, after passage of the Bipartisan Campaign Reform Act, which prohibited the national parties from raising soft money (Currinder 2009, especially chapter 6; Heberlig and Larson 2012, 5).

Figure 16.5 shows the increase in member giving to their parties. The competitive political context gave House party leaders the ability to aggressively raise increasing amounts from the party's incumbents and to successfully encourage members to give directly to the party's candidates in the closest races that could determine majority control. Congressional party leaders assess dues and set fundraising quotas for their members (especially committee chairs and other leaders), and party leaders use their control over institutional positions of power such as committee and subcommittee leadership posts and important party positions to encourage member participation. Elected party leaders, committee chairs, and majority party members are expected to and more inclined to give more to their party committees and candidates than other incumbents since their positions make it easier to raise money from access-seeking PACs and policy oriented individual donors (Heberlig and Larson 2012, chapter 5; Heberlig and Larson 2014).

Figure 16.5 shows that the House campaign committees were particularly good at raising money from their House members, and their receipts track with partisan control of the chamber, especially after 2004. The DCCC's fundraising from federal candidates dropped in 2010 and 2012, but the NRCC raised more from their candidates in those years, as the GOP was riding a congressional electoral tide even as Democrat Obama was reelected president, suggesting that these party fundraising trends are quite sensitive

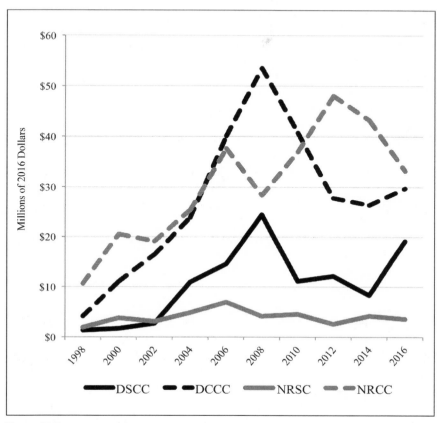

Figure 16.5
Member Contributions to Their Congressional Party Committees, 1998–2016 (in millions of 2016 dollars).

Source: Compiled by author from Federal Election Commission data.

to the partisan political context (Dwyre and Kolodny 2014b; see also Herrnson 2012, 108). Note also that figure 16.5 shows the DSCC raised more than it had in the three previous election cycles from Senate Democrats in 2016 as many thought the Democrats could take majority control of the chamber.

As competition for majority status remains intense, the CCCs are likely to continue their aggressive efforts to convince their incumbents to share some of their campaign funds with their parties and fellow candidates in close races. Yet, incumbent fundraising in service of their party's collective interest of majority pursuit has raised concerns about the source of the funds being raised. The need to support their parties' collective interests has likely intensified the money chase for incumbents and increased the amount of time they spend raising money, and the additional money incumbents are raising to pass on to their parties and fellow candidates in competitive races is mostly from access-oriented business PACs and large individual contributors (Heberlig and Larson 2012, 216; Jacobson 2010, 397). However, money originally given to gain access to lawmakers is being redistributed by the parties to many non-incumbent candidates, a process that could potentially increase the number of competitive contests. As Jacobson notes, "[L]aundering donations through the parties may diffuse and soften whatever effect interested contributions have on the behavior of individual members, reinforcing the parties' character as broad coalitions of economic and social interests" (2010, 397). La Raja and Schaffner (2015) agree that the parties can serve to place some distance between intense policy-demanding contributors and lawmakers as well as to moderate the impact of money given by ideologically extreme donors, and consequently they recommend more money be channeled through the party organizations.

National Party Spending

Parties spend money in different ways to help their candidates win, and contemporary party committees distribute their money efficiently by directing most of it to close races to maintain or pick up seats (Jacobson 2010, 383). As with fundraising, the rules in place and the political environment impact how the parties spend money. When the political tide is running against a party, as it was for the GOP in 2008 and the Democrats in 2010, parties do what they can to shore up endangered incumbents and focus less on challengers. Of course, all of the money in the world may not help if the political winds are not blowing one's way.

Direct Contributions to Candidates and Coordinated Party Expenditures

A national party committee may contribute $5,000 per election (primary and general election) directly to a federal candidate. This is a very small amount of what it takes to run for office, especially for president. This low limit on party contributions to candidates stems from the concern that parties could act as "corrupt conduits" for big contributors to influence elected officials (Persily 2006, 213–40). Yet, the 1974 FECA amendments included a provision to allow parties, but not others, to also spend *on behalf of* their candidates in coordination with them on polls, voter list development, advertising, opposition research, and other campaign expenses. Lawmakers were concerned "that campaign finance regulation might further marginalize institutions once so central to electoral politics" if parties were permitted to give their candidates only as much as a PAC could give (Jacobson 2010, 383). These *coordinated expenditures,* originally limited to $10,000 in 1974, are adjusted for inflation, and by 2016, the party coordinated expenditure limit for House candidates was $48,100 for House nominees in most states ($96,000 for House nominees in states with only one representative) and from $96,100 to $2,886,500 for Senate nominees (depending on the state's population) (Federal Election Commission 2016).

With direct contributions and coordinated expenditures, parties can give significant financial support to a congressional candidate, amounting to $126,000 for a House candidate in 2016. Yet, this is generally "no more than 20 percent of what it typically costs to mount a competitive campaign" (Jacobson 2013, 79). Most congressional candidates receive no national party assistance at all, and party contributions and coordinated expenditures amounted to only 1 percent of the funding for *all* House candidates and only 4 percent of Senate candidate funding in 2016, with most of their funds coming from individuals (52 percent for House candidates and 71 percent for Senate candidates) and from PACs (34 percent for House candidates and 16 percent for Senate candidates) (compiled by author from Federal Election Commission data).

Party Independent Expenditures

The parties now spend far more without coordinating with their candidates at all. The Supreme Court's 1996 decision in *Colorado Republican Federal Campaign v. Federal Election Commission* (518 U.S. 604) allowed the national party congressional campaign committees to make unlimited independent expenditures in federal elections, as long as these expenditures are made from publicly disclosed funds raised in limited amounts from permissible sources (i.e., "hard" money), and the spending is not coordinated with the candidate. As figures 16.6a and 16.6b show, independent expenditures are now the primary means of party spending in congressional elections, particularly in races for the House of Representatives (see figure 16.6b).

These figures show that as campaign finance rules changed, the parties reacted and adapted to the new regulatory environment by shifting their spending strategies. After the 1996 *Colorado* decision, both parties, but especially the GOP, shifted some of their spending to independent expenditures in Senate races, and by 2004 the vast majority of both parties' spending in House and Senate races was dedicated to independent expenditures. This shift to independent expenditures did not happen sooner because from the 1990s until the 2002 passage of the Bipartisan Campaign Reform Act, the

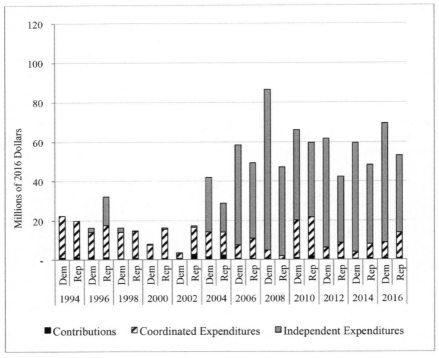

Figure 16.6a
Party Spending on Senate Candidates, 1994–2016 (in millions of 2016 dollars).

national parties relied more on soft money to help federal candidates, which they could raise in unlimited amounts from virtually any source, including corporations and unions, and transfer to state party committees to spend in unlimited amounts (Dwyre 1996). Indeed, the parties were spending quite a lot more from 1994 to 2002 than figures 16.6a and 16.6b indicate, because they were transferring so much soft money to state parties that spent it to help the party's targeted federal candidates. Thus, the national congressional campaign committees' shift to independent expenditures was slightly delayed after the 1996 *Colorado* decision that allowed them to engage in such spending, because the national party committees could get more bang for their buck using soft money until it was banned with BCRA in 2002.

The national committees (the DNC and RNC) have been permitted to make independent expenditures since 2003 (Wilson 2003). Yet, the DNC and RNC have not wholeheartedly shifted to independent expenditures as the

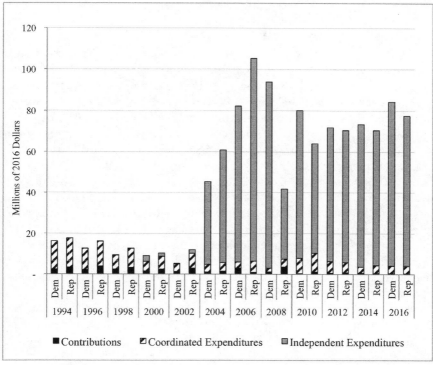

Figure 16.6b
Party Spending on House Candidates, 1994–2016 (in millions of 2016 dollars).

Source: Compiled by authors from: Brookings Institution. 2017. *Vital Statistics on Congress: Data on the U.S. Congress,* updated January 2017, at https://www.brookings.edu/multi-chapter-report/vital-statistics-on-con gress/ (accessed March 31, 2017); and Federal Election Commission. 2017. "2015–2016 Election Cycle Data Summaries through 12/31/16: Party Committees" (accessed May 9, 2017).

Hill Committees have. Indeed, until 2012, at least one major party presidential nominee accepted the public funding, impacting the national party committees' ability to spend on their races. In 2016, the DNC made no independent expenditures and the RNC spent only $321,531 (Federal Election Commission 2017). However, the RNC did transfer $42,601,302 and the DNC transferred $116,029,801 to state and local party committees, most likely to party organizations in battleground states, while neither national committee had transferred any funds to state and local parties in the previous four presidential election cycles. These transfers indicate a possible shift in spending strategy for the national committees. It will be interesting to see if the national committees continue this new spending strategy of transfers to state party committees in future presidential elections.

Is Everything Relative? Party and
Non-Party Campaign Finance

The analyses above show how changes in campaign finance law, court rulings, and regulatory decisions, as well as changes in the political environment, have affected the parties and how they have adapted over time. Some of these changes have challenged the parties' ability to raise and spend money, and the most obvious example is the shift in the sources of party receipts after the loss of soft money with passage of BCRA in 2002 (see figure 16.2). Overall, through various changes in both the regulatory and political landscapes, party fundraising has remained somewhat stable, with some of the Hill Committees raising more funds than they had before soft money was banned in 2002 (see figure 16.1). Moreover, three of the four Hill Committees (all but the NRSC) have successfully institutionalized their efforts to raise campaign funds from their own members (see figure 16.5). These changes in party campaign finance indicate that the parties have adapted to the various changes in the rules governing their activities, and relative to their own past performance, the national party committees have generally remained on a steady course.

Yet, how have the parties fared relative to *other* players in the changing campaign finance environment? As figure 16.7 shows, outside of the heady soft money years (1992–2002), the parties' financial role is now smaller than the role of non-party spenders, as party spending, as a share (percentage) of overall spending, has decreased over time. In 2016, party contributions, coordinated expenditures, and independent expenditures amounted to only 13.3 percent of reported spending by the various campaign finance actors, down from a post-BCRA high of 29.7 percent in 2006 and a high of 64.6 percent of all spending (57.9 percent in soft money and 6.7 percent hard money) in 2000. The rise of newer non-party groups, such as 527 and 501(c) organizations, and especially Super PACs, has reduced the *relative* amount of formal party committee money in the overall mix. This is a big change from 1996 to 2002, when party hard and soft money spending was over half of all reported spending in federal elections (see figure 16.7).

Yet, the parties spend their money differently than many non-party organizations and individuals. The parties' expenditures are generally focused on winning and thus concentrated on a few close contests, while much of the non-party spending is dispersed widely across many contests and motivated by a variety of goals. For instance, many Super PACs are established to assist a single candidate. Access-oriented PACs give primarily to incumbents and ideological groups, and individuals work to elect only true believers. Scholars who view the parties more broadly as networked with non-party groups

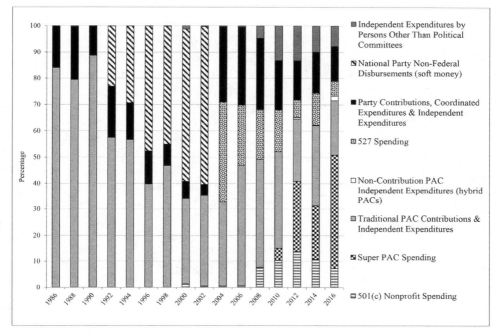

Figure 16.7
Noncandidate Spending in Federal Elections by Percentage, 1986–2016.

Source: Compiled by author from Federal Election Commission and Center for Responsive Politics data, various dates.

Note: A non-contribution PAC, also called a hybrid PAC or Carey committee, is a type of committee that resulted from *Carey v. Federal Election Commission* (Civil Action No. 2011–0259, D.C. 2011). A hybrid PAC can make limited contributions directly to candidates and other committees, as traditional PACs do, *and* it can raise and spend unlimited amounts to expressly advocate for the election or defeat of a candidate, as Super PACs can, but it cannot use those unlimited donations for its traditional PAC contributions.

might include some of these non-party groups, such as the Democratic Party Super PAC, ally House Majority PAC, and the Republican Party ally Senate Leadership Fund, in calculations of party influence. Malbin reports that when party spending is combined with the spending of these close party allies, overall party spending (parties plus leadership Super PACs) was actually higher than non-party spending in both 2014 and 2016 (Malbin 2017). Indeed, Mann and Corrado argue, "[I]t is a mistake to assume that all or most non-party independent spending committees are separate from the parties" (Mann and Corrado 2014, 12; see also Bedlington and Malbin 2003; Hamm et al. 2014; Herrnson 2009; Kolodny and Dwyre 2018; Malbin 2014b).

Some of the early research on parties as extended party networks focused on understanding the contours of these party networks (Grossman and

Dominguez 2009; Herrnson 2009). Herrnson (2009), Hamm et al. (2014), Magleby (2014), Mann and Corrado (2014), and Dwyre and Braz (2015) classify Super PACs and other non-party organizations and test, for example, whether they are more or less party-connected based on their spending behavior. Robin Kolodny and I attempted to map each House congressional campaign committee's extended party network with case studies of the spending patterns of party and non-party groups using network analysis (Kolodny and Dwyre 2018). We contend that the formal party organizations (the DCCC and NRCC in this case) can, and do, effectively "orchestrate" the campaign activities of their closely allied groups (Kolodny and Dwyre 1998; Dwyre and Kolodny 2014a; Kolodny and Dwyre 2018). The changing nature of these networks (and of the political environment) makes it difficult, however, to get a clear picture of who is inside and outside of a party's network beyond a single election cycle. Moreover, other scholars see the direction of influence reversed. For instance, Bawn et al. (2012) see the non-party groups as orchestrating the parties by influencing, in particular, which candidates get nominated to run for office under the party's banner.

What is clear is that the *relative* role of the formal party organizations (the national committees and the congressional campaign committees) has declined over recent years. Yet, a close examination of figure 16.7 shows that the parties' role relative to other campaign finance actors is very similar to what it was before the extensive use of party soft money in 1992. Thus the introduction and elimination of party soft money may have actually impacted the relative share of party spending more than the entry of new campaign spenders such as 501(c) nonprofits and Super PACs. Moreover, this is not a zero-sum situation, as the overall amount of money in the system can and has changed. Thus, if some non-party groups are indeed following campaign finance strategies more congruent with their party allies than not, then party influence in the campaign finance system may be more significant than these party and non-party spending patterns can reveal.

Conclusion

Political parties have long endured in the United States in part because of their ability to successfully adapt to often-dramatic changes in their environment. This examination of the campaign finance activities of the contemporary national parties offers further evidence of the parties' ability to adapt and adjust. In recent years, the parties have worked to adapt to a number of changes in the rules governing federal campaign finance activities, and to the presence of new campaign finance actors (i.e., 527 organizations, 501(c) nonprofits, and Super PACs) who have fewer restrictions on their campaign finance activities than the parties do. There is some evidence that the parties are adapting to this new environment by guiding or "orchestrating" the activities of some of these non-party actors most closely allied with them in an extended party network, even though the parties are not permitted to actually coordinate with many of their allied groups (Kolodny and Dwyre 2018). The extent to which the parties are able to count on these network allies to pursue the parties' goals will affect how successfully the parties adapt to a campaign finance landscape that has left them with less flexibility than non-party campaign finance actors. To fully comprehend the extent to which non-party groups follow party strategies, however, we need more research to gain a better understanding of the boundaries of the parties' extended party networks and the activities of those in the network.

In the future, Congress, or perhaps the Supreme Court, may act to loosen restrictions on party campaign finance, by, for example, allowing the national party committees to make unlimited coordinated expenditures from money raised in small amounts, an idea supported by scholars at the nonpartisan Campaign Finance Institute, the left-leaning Brookings Institution, and the conservative American Enterprise Institute (Malbin 2014a). Indeed, the Supreme Court's very narrow understanding of what constitutes corruption, laid out most recently in the *McCutcheon* decision, may result in a reexamination of the notion that parties act as "corrupt conduits" through which interested money can influence lawmakers' policy decisions (Malbin 2014b; Persily 2006). Such a shift in opinion would potentially put parties on a more level playing field with non-party groups. Having more party money in the mix would possibly focus even more money on the small number of competitive races, but with more money to spend, the parties also might target their funds to *more* races and thus potentially actually increase the number of competitive contests, a development many observers of American electoral politics would welcome.

Notes

1. Note Congress did, however, keep the separate appropriation for convention security costs, which totaled $100 million for the major parties' nominating conventions in 2016.

2. A multicandidate PAC has been registered with the FEC for at least six months, collected contributions from at least 50 people, and made contributions to at least five federal candidates. Before these criteria have been met, the committee is a non-multicandidate PAC (Garrett 2015, 5).

17

The Impact of Organizational Characteristics on Super PAC Financing

Paul S. Herrnson, Jennifer A. Heerwig, and Douglas M. Spencer[1]

S UPER PACs ARE AMONG the most influential participants in contemporary elections. Having spent billions of dollars since 2010, these relative new-comers to the political scene have had a conspicuous presence in many competitive House, Senate, and presidential contests. Nevertheless, remarkably little is known about these groups' goals, strategies, or other organizational attributes, and even less is known about what enables some of them to raise the millions of dollars that fuel their television advertisements and other campaign efforts. In this study, we use a new dataset comprising information about the Super PACs that participated in the 2010 through 2016 federal elections to address the question: What is the impact of Super PACs' organizational characteristics and strategic objectives on their financing? Following a brief overview of their history and attributes, we analyze the impact of Super PACs' organizational characteristics and strategies on their revenues. The results demonstrate that a group's mission, financial transparency, age, participation in elections for various levels of office, and support for different types of candidates have a major impact on its ability to raise money.

An Overview of Super PACs

Super PACs emerged on the political scene in the aftermath of the U.S. Supreme Court's ruling in *Citizens United v. Federal Election Commission* (2010) and the D.C. Circuit's subsequent holding in *SpeechNow.org v. Federal*

Election Commission (2010). These rulings and several agency decisions substantially altered the ways in which individuals and groups can participate in elections. Combined, they eliminated prohibitions that previously prevented corporations, labor unions, trade associations, and other groups from using their general treasuries to finance independent expenditures that explicitly advocate the election or defeat of a federal candidate. They also enabled individuals and groups to use new types of spending organizations, including Super PACs, for this purpose. Referred to as "independent expenditure-only committees" in federal regulations, Super PACs differ from traditional political action committees (PACs), political parties, and candidate committees in that they can raise unlimited sums from virtually any source. Although the *Citizens United* ruling was announced more than halfway into the 2010 midterm election cycle, Super PACs raised more than $89 million and spent almost $63 million before Election Day. Between 2010 and 2016, Super PACs raised about $3.4 billion and spent in excess of $2.1 billion in federal elections.

Super PACs differ from other outside spending groups in a number of respects. Super PACs differ from "traditional" PACs in that they cannot directly contribute to federal candidates or the federal accounts party committees and other groups use to contribute to federal candidates. They differ from social welfare groups registered as 501(c)(4) organizations under the Internal Revenue Code and trade associations registered as 501(c)(6) organizations in that Super PACs are required to disclose the sources of donations of $200 or more. However, unlike the 501(c) groups, Super PACs can use all of their funds to finance independent expenditures.[2]

Often depicted as working to promote the interests of a wealthy and narrow segment of society, Super PACs vary on several dimensions, including their mission, transparency, age, and the elections in which they participate. For example, single-candidate Super PACs exist for the sole purpose of advancing the career of an individual politician, participate in one contest per election cycle, and many disband once the election is over. Multi-candidate Super PACs, on the other hand, seek to advocate a specific issue, interest, political party, or ideology, participate in more than one election per election cycle, and many are active in several election cycles.

Super PACs also differ in their financing. Over the course of the last four election cycles, a surprisingly large number raised no funds at all, while the wealthiest—Restore Our Future, which backed Mitt Romney's 2012 bid for the White House—collected almost $154 million. Between 2010 and 2016, Super PACs spent about 58 percent of their funds on TV ads and other independent communications intended to affect the outcomes of closely contested elections. The remainder was used to finance political research, voter mobilization, fundraising, salaries, and other aspects of organizational maintenance (Dwyre and Braz 2015). Roughly 69 percent of all Super PAC independent expenditures were spent in opposition to candidates, indicating these groups have contributed to the negativity of federal elections (Herrnson 2016, 2017). Super PACs relied heavily on organizations for their financing during their initial foray into campaign politics in 2010. However, individuals became the dominant source of Super PAC funding in ensuing elections. Over the course of the 2010 through 2016 elections, individuals accounted for 62 percent of all Super PACs receipts.

Super PAC Characteristics and Fundraising

Super PACs are similar to traditional PACs in that there is substantial variation in the sums they raise. One of the most interesting facts about Super PACs is roughly 63 percent of those registered with the Federal Election Commission (FEC) during the last four election cycles raised no money. The plethora of inactive groups is attributable to some degree to the minimal cost and effort needed to create a Super PAC. Another 6 percent of all Super PACs raised less than $1,000. The top five fundraisers collected $701.9 million, more than 38.3 percent of all Super PAC receipts, and the next ten groups raised $676.3 million, or 36.9 percent. The 72 groups that raised $10 million or more each (less than 2 percent of the total number of Super PACs) accounted for two-thirds of all Super PAC receipts, while the 3,838 groups that raised less than $10,000 (74 percent of all Super PACs) collected less than 1 percent of total Super PAC funds. What explains this variation in Super PAC receipts? We hypothesize that much of it can be explained by a group's most salient organizational characteristics (see table 17.1).

The most notable nonfinancial distinction among Super PACs concerns their mission. As noted earlier, single-candidate groups (SCGs) exist to advance the fortunes of a single politician, and multicandidate groups (MCGs) seek to influence the election prospects of more than one candidate.[3] MCGs constituted 64 percent of all active Super PACs during the 2010 through 2016 election cycles, while SCGs accounted for 36 percent. SCGs associated with high-profile candidates, particularly incumbents or those for high office, have significant advantages over other outside spending groups. Most are organized or staffed by a candidate's former political aides, major donors, or political consultants knowledgeable about the candidate's policy stances, public image, financial supporters, and electoral constituency. Although these groups cannot coordinate electioneering efforts with a candidate, a candidate committee, or anyone who directly participates in the candidate's campaign, the candidate can participate in some of the Super PAC's

TABLE 17.1
Predictors of Super PAC Fundraising and Our Hypotheses

Predictors	Hypotheses
Mission	SCGs that support a presidential candidate, a senate candidate, or an incumbent raise more money than MCGs, followed by SCGs that support a challenger
Transparency	Super PACs that accept donations from organizations that do not fully disclose their sources raise more money than Super PACs that are financially transparent
Hybrid	Hybrid committees raise less money than other Super PACs
Age	The number of elections in which a Super PACs has participated should have a positive impact on the money it raises
Office	Super PACs that make independent expenditures in a variety of elections raise the most money, followed by those that only participate in presidential elections, those that only participate in Senate elections, those that only participate in House elections, and those that make no independent expenditures
Incumbency	Super PACs that make independent expenditures in a variety of elections raise more money than those that only help incumbents, followed by those that only help open-seat candidates, those that only help challengers, and those that make no independent expenditures
Partisanship	Super PACs that make independent expenditures to help only one party's general election candidates should raise more money than those that make independent expenditures to help candidates of both parties, followed by those that make no independent expenditures
Election cycle	Super PACs should raise more in presidential election cycles (2012 and 2016) than congressional election cycles (2010 and 2014), and the amounts raised should increase over time

Notes: With the exception of age, an interval variable, all of the variables are dummy variables.

activities, including headlining fundraising events—as long as the candidate is not present when the solicitations are made. Moreover, some SCGs have begun to take on tasks usually carried out by traditional campaign organizations (e.g., Magleby 2017). The shared relationships and mutual understandings between a candidate's campaign staff and SCG's staff facilitate the "orchestration" of some of these organizations' campaign efforts, which enables a SCG to disseminate television ads and other communications that complement the candidate's message.

Although the sharp focus of SCGs probably gives them some advantages over MCGs in many aspects of campaigning, the advantages in fundraising are likely conditional on the candidate a SCG supports. Prominent politicians, particularly presidential and Senate candidates and current officeholders, routinely raise huge sums while most House challengers raise a pittance. Given these dynamics and the strategic factors discussed below, one would expect SCGs that support a presidential candidate, Senate candidate, or an incumbent for any office to raise the most money of all outside spending groups. SCGs that support congressional challengers are likely to raise less money than MCGs because the latter groups' finances probably benefit from their support of several recognizable candidates, which may include a presidential candidate or one or more powerful congressional incumbents. Our first hypothesis, regarding a group's mission, is that Super PACs associated with one presidential candidate, one Senate candidate, or one congressional incumbent raise the most money, followed by MCGs, and then SCGs that support a House challenger. This ordering parallels the media coverage of independent expenditures and the visibility of their advertising (Fowler, Franz, and Ridout 2016).

Almost 90 percent of all active Super PACs raised the entirety of their funds from sources that were fully transparent. Their financiers include individuals, corporations, and limited liability companies (LLCs) with legitimate business interests (as opposed to LLCs created to shield their backers' identities). Another 2 percent of active Super PACs collected their receipts exclusively from "dark money" groups, including 501(c)(4) organizations, such as the American Crossroads-affiliated Crossroads GPS; 501(c)(6) organizations that include the U.S. Chamber of Commerce; and quasi (or shell) LLCs that allow individuals or groups to stealthily participate in elections. The remaining 9 percent of all Super PACs, considered partially transparent, raised 5 percent or more of their funds from groups that did not disclose their sources. Given that groups with limited or no transparency enable donors to avoid public recognition, while at the same time allowing for private acknowledgement by the Super PAC's organizers, beneficiaries, and other contributors, we anticipate these groups raise more money than others.

Another relevant dimension of Super PAC organizational characteristics concerns their relationship to traditional PACs. Hybrid committees, sometimes referred to as "Carey committees" after the court case that sanctioned them, accounted for about 8 percent of all active Super PACs.[4] Most hybrids originated as traditional PACs and then created a segregated independent expenditure account in response to changes in campaign finance regulations.

Hybrid committees raise so-called "hard money" within the traditional federal campaign finance framework, and these funds can be contributed directly to federal candidates, party committees, and PACs. They also raise "soft money" outside the federal framework that can be used to finance independent expenditures for one or more candidates. The bifurcated mission of hybrid committees—raising hard money for contributions and soft money for independent expenditures—poses some unique fundraising challenges. Potential donors interested in supporting candidates may be averse to being identified with groups that make negative independent expenditures. Moreover, appeals designed to raise small contributions from many individuals differ from appeals intended to attract hefty contributions from businesses, labor unions, lobbying firms, and their executives (e.g., Francia et al. 2003). As such, we expect hybrids to raise less money than other Super PACs.

A Super PAC's age (the number of election cycles in which it has participated) may also be relevant to its finances. 48 percent of active Super PACs took part in only one cycle, 29 percent in two, 16 percent in three, and 7 percent in four. Groups that have participated in several election cycles can be expected to raise more money than those with less experience. Continued participation raises a group's visibility among potential contributors, provides opportunities to increase the size of its donor base, and enables it to better hone and target the messages it uses to mobilize contributors. Because older groups have less need to prospect for new donors, they are able to raise money efficiently.

Some of the most important distinctions among Super PACs concern their participation in political campaigns. Most accounts of Super PACs focus on their independent expenditures, especially televised campaign ads. Nevertheless, more than 41 percent of all active Super PACs eschew independent expenditures in favor of less noticeable undertakings. Some of these groups resemble think tanks, consulting firms, party committees, or leadership PACs in that they specialize in research, voter mobilization, or raising funds for redistribution to other organizations; other groups spend their money primarily on fundraising, salaries, or additional aspects of organizational maintenance (e.g., Dwyre and Braz 2015). Most of these groups have little appeal to individuals and organizations that prefer their contributions support a visible campaign activity. None of these activities comes even close to independent expenditures in drawing public attention. This informs the hypothesis that Super PACs that make independent expenditures enjoy a significant fundraising advantage over others.

Three strategic considerations are likely to influence a Super PAC's finances. One is the types of elections in which a group participates. During the 2010 through 2016 election cycles, 18 percent of all active Super PACs made independent expenditures exclusively in House races, 13 percent participated solely in Senate elections, and 11 percent limited their participation to presidential contests. Another 17 percent spent funds in some combination of these races and, as noted above, 41 percent made no independent expenditures. The extraordinary power, visibility, and symbolism of the Office of the President, leads to the hypothesis that Super PACs that focus their efforts solely on presidential elections will raise more money than groups that concentrate on other offices, despite the relatively small number of candidates who run for the White House. The greater power attributed to individual senators, the Senate's six-year terms, the higher costs incurred in Senate elections, and the greater competition for control over the upper chamber suggest that Senate-oriented Super PACs should possess fundraising advantages over groups that focus exclusively on the House. Nevertheless, we expect the most successful fundraisers will be groups that participated in elections for more than one level of office. Their ability to appeal to partisan donors interested in helping their party elect as many candidates as possible, regardless of the specific office, should be a substantial fundraising asset.

A second strategic consideration that could affect how much money a Super PAC raises concerns the electoral status of the candidates it supports. Individuals and groups motivated by economic considerations make large contributions to gain access to politicians positioned to influence their profits (Langbein 1986; Hall and Wayman 1990; Nownes 2013; Holyoke 2014). Not surprisingly given their high reelection rates, congressional incumbents are the major beneficiaries of these contributions. Because money is drawn to power, congressional party leaders, committee chairs, and policy entrepreneurs have substantial fundraising advantages over others (Denzau and Munger 1986; Romer and Snyder, Jr. 1994; Francia et al. 2003). They are able to collect huge sums for leadership PACs and party committees, as well as their own principal campaign committees (Heberlig, Hetherington, and Larson 2006; Cann 2008). Challengers collect substantially fewer funds from access-oriented donors and in general. For these reasons, one might expect active Super PACs that support only incumbents (about 10 percent of all groups) to raise more funds than active Super PACs that solely support open-seat candidates (about 10 percent of all groups) which, in turn, would be expected to raise more funds than active Super PACs that support only challengers (about 16 percent of all groups). However, as previously discussed, we anticipate the 22 percent of groups that support some combination of incumbents, challengers, or open-seat candidates will probably raise the most funds because of their ability to appeal to ideological and issue-oriented contributors whose overriding goal is to help elect their preferred party's candidates.

A third strategic consideration that could affect how much money Super PACs raise is partisanship. Approximately 19 percent of all groups help only Democratic candidates in the general election. That is, they make independent expenditures in support of these candidates, against their opponents, or do both. Another 34 percent back only Republican candidates and 5 percent are bipartisan in their spending. The partisanship of the remaining 41 percent of groups cannot be determined because they make no independent expenditures. A substantial portion of all individual and organizational donors make most, if not all, of their contributions to one party's candidate organizations (e.g., Brown, Powell, and Wilcox 1995; Francia et al. 2003; Wright 1989, 1990; Heerwig 2018). Among the most partisan are ideological donors and labor unions. Business interests seeking access to powerful policymakers account for the vast majority of donors that make contributions across party lines. The partisan hypothesis is rooted in the polarized nature of contemporary politics—MCGs that support only one party's candidates are expected to enjoy fundraising advantages over others.

Data and Methods

Which types of Super PACs raise the most money? We address this question using data from the Center for Responsive Politics (CRP), the FEC, and other sources.[5] The data record each Super PAC's receipts, expenditures, organizational characteristics, and the types of candidates whose elections the Super PAC sought to influence. Given that many Super PACs' electoral participation was trivial or nonexistent, the analysis includes only active Super PACs—those that raised or spent $1,000 in one of the election cycles under study.

We analyze the data using an ordinary least squares linear model with standard errors clustered on the group. Because the distribution of Super PAC receipts is heavily skewed toward groups that raised little money and includes several outliers comprising groups that each raised more than $100 million, the dependent variable is the log of Super PAC receipts for each election cycle. We estimate two separate models to examine Super PAC financing—one for all groups combined and one conditional on making independent expenditures. We do this for two reasons. First, as we show below, there is a vast difference in overall fundraising between groups that make independent expenditures and those that do not. Second, the strategic considerations that influence Super PAC financing apply only to those groups that make independent expenditures.

Rich Super PAC, Poor Super PAC

What influences Super PAC fundraising? Organizational characteristics are very important. The results show group mission, transparency, age, political spending, and many of the strategic variables are significantly related to the sums Super PACs raise (see table 17.2, column 1).

First, MCGs raise more money than SCGs. This result is driven by groups that make no independent expenditures. Overall, there is no statistically significant difference in the receipts collected by SCGs and MCGs that spend money on political advertisements. Second, Super PACs that collect at least some funds from organizations that do not disclose their backers are much better financed than Super PACs that are fully transparent. This effect is particularly strong among groups that make independent expenditures because their financial disclosure documents typically face more public scrutiny. Third, experience counts: the number of election cycles within which a Super PAC participated is strongly correlated with its receipts—older, more experienced groups raised more than three times as much as groups that participated in only one election cycle.

Fourth, strategic considerations affect Super PAC fundraising. Groups that make independent expenditures collect almost twice the money as the others. The types of candidates they back also matters (see table 17.2, column 2). Most notably, MCGs that make independent expenditures to help a variety of candidates by participating in elections for different offices, backing a combination of incumbents and non-incumbents, or by spending funds in support of candidates of more than one party raise far more funds than MCGs that follow an incumbent-oriented or party-centered strategy. Among Super PACs that back one or more candidates for a single office, those that focus solely on the presidency or Senate raise more than twice as much money as groups that focus on House races. These findings all support the idea that organizational characteristics affect Super PAC fundraising. Finally, the control variable for election cycle shows the amounts Super PACs raise has increased over time.

Next, we translate the findings from the log-linear models into predicted values for the amounts different types of Super PACs raise in a given election cycle. We use the coefficients in table 17.2 to calculate the predicted receipts for specific types of Super PACs. Figure 17.1 vividly illustrates the impact of organizational characteristics on how much a Super PAC raises. MCGs typically raise more than $1 million compared to about $800,000 for SCGs. Super PACs with limited or no financial transparency raise over $1.6 million per cycle and those that are fully financially transparent raise half as much. Age is very strongly related to Super PAC fundraising. Groups that participated

Table 17.2
The Impact of Organizational Characteristics and Strategic Considerations on Super PAC Receipts, 2010–2016

	1: All groups			2: Groups that make Indep. Exps.		
	Estimate	% change	one-tailed p-value	Estimate	% change	one-tailed p-value
No independent expenditures	-2.444 (0.144)	-91.3%	<0.001	—	—	
Organizational characteristics						
Multicandidate	0.432 (0.148)	54.0%	0.002	0.114 (0.233)	12.0%	0.313
Fully transparent	-0.858 (0.203)	-57.6%	<0.001	-0.644 (0.229)	-90.4%	0.003
Hybrid	0.375 (0.227)	45.5%	0.050	-0.061 (0.303)	-5.9%	0.421
2 election cycles	0.345 (0.145)	41.2%	0.009	0.395 (0.183)	48.5%	0.015
3 election cycles	0.768 (0.203)	115.4%	<0.001	0.633 (0.232)	88.4%	0.003
4 election cycles	2.092 (0.392)	709.9%	<0.001	1.538 (0.373)	365.5%	<0.001
Office						
House only				-0.693 (0.294)	-50.0%	0.009
Senate only				0.260 (0.291)	29.7%	0.186
President only				0.183 (0.340)	20.1%	0.295

Table 17.2 (Continued)

	1: All groups			2: Groups that make Indep. Exps.		
	Estimate	% change	one-tailed p-value	Estimate	% change	one-tailed p-value
Partisanship						
Democratic ally				-1.186 (0.327)	-69.4%	<0.001
Republican ally				-1.200 (0.323)	-69.9%	<0.001
Incumbency						
Helps incumbents only				-0.603 (0.335)	-45.3%	0.036
Helps challengers only				-0.700 (0.302)	-50.3%	0.010
Helps open races only				-0.601 (0.320)	-45.2%	0.031
Helps a variety: office, partisan, and/or incumbency				0.212 (0.431)	23.6%	0.312
Cycle						
2010	-0.393 (0.216)	-32.5%	0.034	-0.506 (0.220)	-39.7%	0.011
2014	0.193 (0.114)	21.3%	0.045	-0.047 (0.144)	-4.6%	0.371
2016	0.430 (0.121)	53.7%	<0.001	0.357 (0.157)	42.9%	0.012
R^2	0.31			0.24		
Adj. R2	0.31			0.22		
Num obs.	1,605			939		

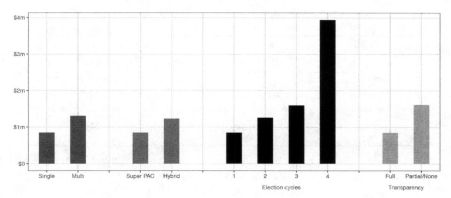

Figure 17.1
The Impact of Organizational Factors on Super PAC Receipts.

in all four elections collected nearly $4 million in 2016 (their fourth election cycle), about five times more than groups that participated in only one cycle. Contrary to expectations, hybrid committees typically raise more than other groups.

The results in figure 17.2 show that strategic factors can have a substantial impact on Super PAC financing. MCGs that make independent expenditures to support or oppose a variety of candidates typically raise more than $1 million per cycle. Super PACs that participate only in presidential races, which include some MCGs and SCGs, also typically raise approximately $1 million. The same is the case for Super PACs that specialize in Senate elections. By contrast, Super PACS that limit their participation to House

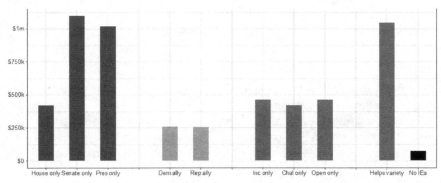

Figure 17.2
The Impact of Strategic Considerations on Super PAC Receipts.

contests average only $425,000. Partisanship has little impact on Super PAC fundraising: on average, groups that back Democrats and groups that back Republicans average about $250,000 in receipts per election cycle. Super PAC finances are not heavily affected by the incumbency component of their spending strategies. Groups that spend funds solely to reelect current office-holders and those that only back candidates for open-seats collect slightly more funds than those that only back challengers. As expected, Super PACs that follow strategies that do not include independent expenditures raise a mere fraction of the funds collected by others.

Some organizational and strategic characteristics combine to have a large impact on Super PAC financing. This is the case for group mission and financial transparency. MCGs with limited or no financial transparency raise, on average, about $2.5 million—almost twice as much as MCGs that are financially transparent. Similarly, SCGs that accept at least some dark money average almost $1.6 million, almost twice as much as financially transparent SCGs.

The type of candidate a SCG was created to support has a substantial impact on its finances. Presidential SCGs collected, on average, $1 million and Senate SCGs $1.1 million dwarfing the less than $423,000 the typical House SCGs raised. The effects of incumbency were less pronounced, but also significant: incumbent SCGs and open-seat candidate SCGs typically raised about $463,000, more than $40,000 than challenger SCGs.

Finally, a Super PAC's mission combines with its most basic strategic decision—whether to make independent expenditures—to have a huge impact on its fundraising. MCGs that make independent expenditures average $1.3 million in receipts, more than ten times the amount raised by the average for MCGs that spend funds only on lower profile activities. Similarly, independent spending SCGs typically raise about ten times more than SCGs that make no independent expenditures.

Conclusion

Super PACs have had a tremendous impact on elections. They have raised and spent billions of dollars in federal elections, influenced the dialog in the last two presidential elections, and their spending has overshadowed that of one or both candidates in dozens of congressional contests (e.g., Herrnson 2016). Super PACs have assumed some of the roles previously ascribed to political parties and traditional political action committees, including aggregating funds collected from individuals, helping to set the national political agenda, and providing some of the information voters rely on when choosing candidates. Given the many factors that influence election outcomes and the impossibility of fully disentangling their effects, it is impossible to state with certainty whether Super PAC spending was a decisive factor in any candidate's election or defeat. Nevertheless, few politicians or political observers would deny that Super PACs are a force to be reckoned with in American politics.

However, not all Super PACs are created equal. Super PACs differ in many respects, including in their abilities to raise funds. This study has demonstrated that organizational characteristics, including a Super PAC's mission, financial transparency, and its history of participating in previous election cycles, affect its ability to raise money. It also has shown that strategic considerations, such as the decision to make independent expenditures and the types of candidates a group supports, also affect a Super PAC's ability to collect donations. Perhaps most relevant to the conduct of elections, it has shown that SCGs that support incumbents or open-seat candidates raise more money than those that support challengers. Given that SCGs are particularly adept at waging shadow campaigns to advance the careers of their champions, one of the major implications of the emergence of Super PACs is that entrenched politicians and their supporters now enjoy yet another advantage in an election system that tilts in their favor.

Notes

1. We wish to acknowledge the financial support of the Democracy Fund and the Flora and William Hewlett Foundation and the research assistance of Kyle Adams, Van Augur, and Christian Caron.

2. 501(c) groups are not required to publicly disclose their backers. They also cannot make political activity their primary mission and, as a rule of thumb, must spend less than 50 percent of their funds on partisan campaigning.

3. Groups were classified as single-candidate after researching their identity and spending behavior. They include groups that use a website, media advisory, or some other means to publicly identify that their mission is to support or oppose a single candidate. They also include groups that do not publicly state their mission is to support or oppose a single candidate, but make independent expenditures in support of only one candidate, in opposition to that candidate's opponents, or in opposition to only one candidate in one election cycle. Groups that resemble SCGs in the aforementioned respects but are directly connected to a sponsoring (or parent) organization that has a broader mission than electing or opposing a single candidate (such as a corporation, trade association, or labor union) are treated as exceptions and are coded as multicandidate. Groups that publicly state their mission is to support one candidate but supported more than one candidate in a given election cycle are classified as MCGs. Note that we include both hybrid and non-hybrid Super PACs in

our analyses below to fully describe the universe of groups that make independent expenditures. Therefore, our estimates of single- and multicandidate groups also include single-candidate and multicandidate hybrid committees.

4. *Carey v. FEC*, 791 F.Supp.2d 121 (D.D.C 2011).

5. Because the original campaign finance data contained significant data entry and coding errors, they were subjected to extensive cleaning and recoding prior to the analysis (see Herrnson 2017, 5–6). The figures for hybrid committees include both soft and hard money contributions.

18

What Happened to the Ground Game in 2016?*

Paul A. Beck, Richard Gunther, and Erik Nisbet

A s THE 2016 PRESIDENTIAL CAMPAIGN progressed through the first early voting opportunities to Election Day, attention was paid to the unconventional nature of not only the Trump candidacy but also the Trump campaign. Buoyed by the incessant "free" media the Republican nominee was receiving, the Trump campaign seemingly had turned its back on core elements of the conventional strategy of a presidential campaign. It apparently was investing much less than recent campaigns in paid television advertising and in putting a substantial number of "boots on the ground" to mobilize potential supporters. By contrast, the Clinton campaign was seen to be pursuing conventional campaign strategies with substantial "air war" spending on television advertising and a robust "ground game." Most observers concluded that Clinton would be advantaged by these investments, particularly in the key battleground states, thereby giving her an added edge toward winning the presidency.

Of course, the expected Clinton victory did not materialize. Out of 130 million votes cast, a tiny margin of less than 80,000 votes in the key battleground states of Michigan, Pennsylvania, and Wisconsin proved to be the difference between a Trump and Clinton presidency. Even her vaunted advantage in conventional campaign strategy appeared not to be enough to carry Clinton to victory. There is a long catalogue of reasons why Donald Trump is president rather than Hillary Clinton, and numerous scholars and pundits have identified and debated them (see Sides, Tesler, and Vavreck 2018, for a comprehensive account). They include doubts that a conventional television spending strategy was able to overcome the "free media" that Trump attracted in getting messages to voters. But, aside from reports on fewer Clinton field offices than in 2012 (Darr 2017), little attention has been paid to the presumed Clinton advantage in the ground game—the direct contacts with voters made by campaigners on behalf of the presidential nominees.

This chapter examines the 2016 ground game from a unique perspective. Rather than record the activity reported by the campaigns or the media covering them, it focuses on voter reports of contacts by a party or candidate representative during the presidential campaign. To be sure, neither perspective can completely capture party contacts. A number of groups engage in ground game activity during a presidential campaign—including, *inter alia*, the presidential campaigns themselves, the political parties, pro-candidate political action committees, and independent groups. These activities often are, by law, independent of the candidate campaigns—and in some cases, are not publically reported. In 2016, for example, it appears that the Republican National Committee provided much of the ground game support that the Trump campaign was ignoring. Building a comprehensive account from these divergent sources is well-nigh impossible. An obvious alternative is to rely on perceptions of the recipients of the various campaign contacts. This too is challenging because of the myriad ways people can be contacted and the myriad groups that may be making the contacts—from the party and candidate campaigns to, among other things, labor unions, churches, or the National Rifle Association. People may have difficulty recalling with precision the contacts they have received or differentiating among their sources. But we think that they can reliably report whether they have been contacted at all by representatives of a particular presidential candidate. It is these reports that provide the basis for this chapter.

Our voter reports come from national surveys of the American electorate by the Comparative National Election Project (CNEP). From 1991 through 2017, the project has asked comparable party contact questions in over 50 elections across the democratic world (see Gunther, Beck, Magalhães, and Moreno 2016).[1] This chapter relies on CNEP surveys for the 2016 and 2012 U.S. presidential elections. The previous presidential election provides a useful benchmark for comparison—an election in which both the Democratic and Republican campaign organizations dedicated considerable resources to the ground game.

The 2012 and 2016 CNEP surveys were both post-election surveys conducted via the internet—by YouGov in 2016 and GfK Knowledge Networks in 2012. The 2016 survey included a national sample of 1,600 respondents plus an oversample of 350 white, non-college educated respondents in rural areas of six key battleground states (Iowa, Michigan, North Carolina, Ohio, Pennsylvania, and Wisconsin), interviewed within two months after the election. This oversample enables us to "drill down" into patterns of party contacting in areas that produced surprising levels of support for Trump, and plausibly won him the election. YouGov used propensity score matching to yield representative samples of the populations it was covering. The 2012 GfK survey yielded a national sample of 1,289 respondents, preselected from a large and demographically representative panel of telephone respondents and supplied with devices to connect them to the web questionnaire if they were not already internet users.

Overall Party Contacting in 2016 and 2012

Our analysis begins with the overall levels of perceived party contact reported by respondents in 2016 and 2012. Prior to the 2004 presidential election, the frequencies of party contacts, as reported since 1956 in the American National Election Study's (ANES) continuing series, had remained more or less level and were not differentiated by party or by whether the state was a competitive presidential "battleground" or safe for one party. Since then, ANES surveys show that party contacting has grown substantially, especially in the dozen or so key battleground states (Beck and Heidemann 2014a; see also Francia and Panagopoulos 2009; Panagopoulos 2016). The presidential campaigns have realized that the ground game could make a difference in these competitive states and concentrated their party contacting efforts there. Similar differential investments were made in campaign advertising in the battleground states as well—for 2012 see, *inter alia*, Sides and Vavreck (2013). In the two immediately preceding elections, 2004 and 2008, furthermore, Democrats outpaced Republicans in their party contacting. This edge did not carry over to 2012 (Beck and Heidemann 2014a, 2014b), but it was expected to return in 2016.

Figure 18.1 contains a wealth of information from survey respondents' reports of party contacts during the presidential campaigns. Reading from left to right, columns 1 and 2 show the percentages reporting contacts by the Democrats and Republicans, respectively. Panel three shows the percentages reporting contacts by both parties. Panel four contains the overall percentages who were contacted by either party, Democratic or Republican. Within each of the four panels, the bar charts compare 2016 with 2012 and battleground with non-battleground states.[2] The latter differentiation is important because, as shown in the ANES data, recent campaign strategies have concentrated ground game efforts in the elections' battleground states, which is

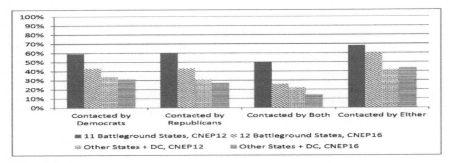

Figure 18.1
Reported Party Contacts, 2012 and 2016, by Party and Battlegrounds versus Non-Battlegrounds.

where they are expected to affect the election outcomes, rather than in their much more numerous less competitive counterparts.

Beginning with panel 4, it is clear that overall contacting fell off somewhat from 2012 to 2016 in the battlegrounds but remained about the same in non-battleground states. From an estimated 68 percent of the electorate in 2012, it declined to 60 percent in the battleground states, where we would expect the most extensive party efforts. Starting at a much lower level, it hovered slightly above 40 percent in both years in the non-battlegrounds. Despite a hotly contested election, which ended up with a narrow victory for Donald Trump, our data show that the ground game overall reached fewer voters in 2016 than it had four years before.

As panels 1 and 2 show, the difference between 2012 and 2016 appears to be the result of a diminution in activity by both party campaigns, especially in the battleground states. The reduced Republican ground game in 2016 comes as no surprise; it was widely reported during the campaign. What is surprising is that there seems to have been a parallel diminution of effort by the Clinton campaign and its allies. Furthermore, this decline in Democratic contacts from 2012 to 2016 brings it into parity with the Republicans, as it surprisingly also was in 2012. One of the post-election debates within Democratic circles has focused on the elevation of data analytics over more conventional campaign activities, such as polling and grassroots contacts. These results echo such a shift in Democratic campaign tactics. Its apparent effect was to erase whatever edge the Democrats might have enjoyed in the 2016 ground game.

One of the intriguing results of an earlier analysis of party contacting in the 2012 election was that half of voters in the battleground states reported contacts from both political parties (Beck and Heidemann 2014b). This figure belied the conventional wisdom that the parties concentrated their efforts mostly on mobilizing their base, maximizing the turnout of these supposedly loyal voters. It raises a question about how inefficient voter mobilization efforts may have been in that earlier election, sometimes even tapping potential voters for the opposition party. As is shown in panel three, contacts by both parties were cut in half (to 26 percent) from 2012 to 2016 in the battleground states. The falloff was almost as substantial in the non-battlegrounds, albeit starting at a much lower level. One big difference between 2012 and 2016, then, is that the parties appeared to be focusing much more on their base in 2016.

Personal Party Contacting in 2016 and 2012

There is considerable evidence from a variety of studies that the most effective contacts in get-out-the-vote efforts are personal in nature—mainly door-to-door and by phone—rather than via more impersonal leaflets, mail, email, robocalls, or the media (see Green and Gerber 2008, 139). To capture those efforts, the CNEP surveys have asked about different types of contacts, initially (including in 2012) asking separately about in person, telephone, mail, and email contacts, then in 2016 only by separating in person from other kinds of contacts. Personal contacts are challenging, requiring a level of effort that campaigns are hard-pressed to muster. They typically rely on volunteer canvassers, organized through presidential campaign field offices (Darr and Levendusky 2014), party headquarters, or allied groups such as labor unions or religious organizations.

The responses suggest interesting differences between the two elections in *personal* contacting. As figure 18.2 shows, personal contacts reached only a small minority of respondents in both years and were more prevalent in the battlegrounds, as would be expected. What is perhaps unexpected is that they were more frequent in 2016 than in the preceding presidential election in both battleground and non-battleground states—and for both Democrats and Republicans. Republican attempts to mobilize new voters in 2016, particularly among those unmotivated to vote in previous elections, may underlie the surprising upsurge in Republican personal contacts compared to 2012.

The difference in personal contacting between 2012 and 2016 of course could be an artifact of question changes. On more solid ground are the interparty comparisons in each year, which cannot be affected by question wording. The expected Democratic contacting edge materializes for personal contacts in both years. Because Democratic voter demographic characteristics

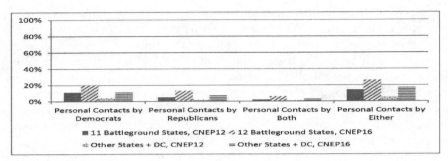

Figure 18.2
Reported Party Contacts in Person, 2012 and 2016, by Party and Battlegrounds versus Non-Battlegrounds.

often are related to lower motivations to vote, it is plausible that the Democratic campaigns need to rely on personal contacts more than do the Republicans, although it is possible that some of the Trump constituency needed mobilization. Nonetheless, it is here in both battleground and non-battleground states that the expected Democratic advantage was manifested. But it was a small advantage, based on limited contacts of a personal nature: 7 percent in 2016 and 6 percent in 2012 in the battlegrounds, even less in the non-battleground states.

Party Contacting in "Trump Country"

It is well known from both exit polls and the overall vote results that the outcome of the 2016 election was strongly influenced by the support Trump received in key battleground states from white rural voters who lacked a college education. With this in mind, the 2016 CNEP survey added a special oversample of 350 people from six battleground states—Iowa, Michigan, North Carolina, Ohio, Pennsylvania, and Wisconsin—who lived in rural areas and small towns and did not have a college degree. Donald Trump won all six of these states and built huge leads outside of their metropolitan areas. Among them, only North Carolina had voted Republican in 2012, so Trump's wins here were decisive in putting him in the White House.

It has been unclear what kind of special effort either campaign, but particularly the Republicans and their allies, focused on this particular slice of the electorate. Recent revelations of the Russian disinformation campaign suggest that these voters may have received special attention via Internet advertising and other below-the-radar methods. Our study allows us to estimate whether the Trump campaign received a special boost from an edge in contacts with respondents in our oversample. By most accounts, these locales were neglected by the Clinton campaign, which focused its efforts on the metropolitan areas where its voter base was most concentrated (Darr 2017). Did the white, rural, non-college-educated voters in these key battleground states receive substantial attention from the Trump campaign and its allies?

Figure 18.3 parallels figures 18.1 and 18.2 for the oversample of white, rural, non-college-educated voters in the six battleground states. Because we do not have a comparable sample from 2012, it focuses only on 2016—as is appropriate in testing the hypothesis that extra Republican campaign attention and Democratic campaign neglect there may have paid off in support for Trump. Clearly, these white, rural/small town, less educated voters were not neglected during the 2016 campaign. Almost as many respondents reported overall party contacts in the oversample as in the 12 battleground states overall (compare panel 4 in figure 18.3 versus figure 18.1). This perhaps comes as a surprise, because the "conventional wisdom" of campaign specialists suggested that party contacting was concentrated more in the metropolitan areas and on better-educated voters. Moreover, reflecting the Republican advantage in party identifiers among this group, more respondents reported contacts from the GOP than from the Democrats, and their edge was proportionately even more substantial in personal contacts (compare panels 1 and 2 in figure 18.3 and figure 18.1). The Trump campaign appears to have invested substantially in mobilizing its base in "Trump country."

Figure 18.4 explores party contacts in the oversample more fully by comparing Democratic, Republican, and Independent party identifiers. Almost equal percentages of Democrats and Republicans reported contacts by their own party's campaign. Because Republicans significantly outnumbered

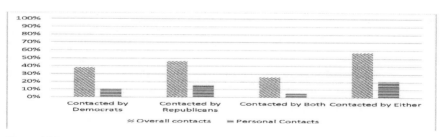

Figure 18.3
Reported Party Contacts and Party Contacts in Person, 2016, for White, Rural/Small Town Non-College-Graduate Respondents in Six Battleground States.

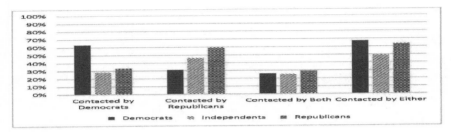

Figure 18.4
Reported Party Contacts by Respondent Party ID, 2016, for White, Rural/Small Town Non-College-Graduate Respondents in Six Battleground States.

Democrats in this group, the advantage went to the Republicans. An added Republican advantage came from party efforts with Independents, who were much more likely to report Republican than Democratic contacts. One of the underappreciated aspects of the 2016 presidential contest is how much the Trump campaign and its allies were able to reach out to these white, rural, less-educated voters, both Republican loyalists and Independents.

As figure 18.3 showed, this Trump campaign contacting advantage was even more substantial among the small minority of voters in the oversample who reported being contacted *personally*. As figure 18.5 shows, not only were Republicans more successful than Democrats in personally contacting their own identifiers as would be expected, but they also made more inroads than Democrats with opposition identifiers and Independents. The story of Trump's appeal to these white, rural/small town, non-college-educated Americans has many explanations, of course, but it is quite likely that one of them involves a more effective Republican than Democratic ground game beneath the radar.

Correlates of Party Contacting

A more comprehensive picture of party contacting in 2016 can be gained by examining in detail who was contacted overall and by each party. The likely correlates readily emerge from previous research (see, Gershtenson 2003; Wielhouwer 2003; Panagopoulos and Wielhouwer 2008; Beck and Heidemann 2014b; Panagopoulos 2016). Each of these possibilities is explored by correlating party contacts (overall and by each party) with these variables, usually in dichotomous form. The results for the national sample ($N = 1600$) are presented in table 18.1, with coefficients entered only when the relationship was significant at least at the .05 level using a two-tailed test.

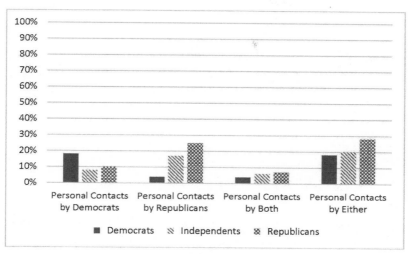

Figure 18.5
Reported Party Contacts in Person by Respondent Party ID, 2016, for White, Rural/ Small Town Non-College-Graduate Respondents in Six Battleground States.

Two distinct patterns appear in the parties' contacts as reported by voters. First, there are voter types that both parties appear to have targeted: older, higher income, college educated, high interest, regular, and primary voters. These may be thought of as the "low-hanging fruit" for the ground game: groups with exceptionally high turnout in elections and who are easy to find. Interestingly, where their partisan proclivities are not easily identifiable (as they usually are from registration rolls), they are not reached differentially via personal contacts. As shown before, those residing in the twelve battleground states also are more likely to report contacts from both parties.

Second, there are voter types that are targeted by only one party. As expected, blacks, union members, Democrats, Democratic activists, and Democratic primary voters were more likely to be canvassed by Democrats, but not by Republicans. Conversely, Republican contacts were concentrated on born-again Christians, Republicans, Republican activists, and Republican primary voters. There is clear evidence here that both presidential campaigns were reaching out to their "base" as a crucial activity in their ground games (on earlier elections, see Panagopoulos 2016). In most cases, this is easy to do, as public registration records and the parties' voter files will contain the names and locational information for these voters, making them easy to reach—for both all kinds of contacts and the more difficult but more effective personal contacts.

TABLE 18.1
Correlates of Party Contacts, 2016 (coefficients significantly different from .00 only)

	Party Contact	Contact by Democrats	Personal Contact by Democrats	Contact by Republicans	Personal Contact by Republicans
Age	.20	.14		.25	
Income	.14	.08		.15	
College degree	.09	.11		.11	
Female				-.06	
Rural resident		-.09	-.05		
White	.07		-.14	.18	
Minority	-.06			-.18	
Black	-.06.	.12	-.14	-.07	
Hispanic	-.07			-.09	
Born-Again Christian	.07			.09	.10
Interested	.28	.20	.06	.22	.06
Union member	.07	.09	.05		
Democrat	.09	.25	.13	-.10	-.07
Republican	.12	-.11	-.09	.27	.12
Nonpartisan	-.22	-.15		-.16	
Dem. Party worker	.16	.28	.23		
Rep. Party worker	.15			.21	.24
Regular voter	.41	.26	.09	.35	.13
Primary voter	.38	.25	.10	.29	.11
Dem. primary voter	.19	.31	.19	-.06	
Rep. primary voter	.24		-.08	.40	.17
Battleground 12	.15	.13	.10	.16	.10

A parallel analysis was conducted for only the six-state oversample. Table 18.2 presents its results for a smaller set of predictor variables, excluding characteristics used to select the oversample in the first place, again with coefficients entered only when the relationship was significant at least at the .05 level. By and large, the results parallel those reported in table 18.1. Not only was ground game activity focused more on these voters, albeit more by Republicans than Democrats in this more Republican group, but it targeted both the "low-hanging fruit" of likely high turnout voters and the parties' partisan bases.

Several results in tables 18.1 and 18.2 warrant special comment. First, given the importance of women and Hispanics in the Democratic base, it is puzzling that the Democratic campaign did not contact them more. Hispanics were slightly more likely than non-Hispanics to be contacted

TABLE 18.2
Correlates of Reported Party Contacts, 2016 for White, Rural/Small Town,
Non-College Respondents from Six Battleground States
(coefficients significantly different from .00 only)

	Party Contact	Contact by Democrats	Personal Contact by Democrats	Contact by Republicans	Personal Contact by Republicans
Age	.20	.22		.31	
Income			-.15	.14	
Female					
Born-Again Christian	.12	-.11		.20	.22
Interested	.25	.19	.19	.19	.13
Union member			.11		
Democrat		.30	.12	-.16	-.19
Republican	.12			.19	.17
Nonpartisan	-.11	-.13			
Dem. Party worker	.13	.22	.38	-.11	
Rep. Party worker	.20			.13	.16
Regular voter	.26	.22	.14	.22	
Dem. primary voter	.14	.31	.20		-.13
Rep. primary voter		-.11		.17	.17

and contacted personally by the Democrats in both battleground and non-battleground states—and correspondingly less likely to be reached by Republicans. But the differences are small, and small sample sizes restrict their significance. More puzzling are the results by gender. Men were slightly more likely to report Democratic rather than Republican contacts, whereas women were slightly more likely to say that more Republicans than Democrats contacted them. For whatever reason, the Democratic campaign's ground game probably underperformed when it came to trying to mobilize women and Hispanics, groups expected to have pro-Clinton predispositions.

Second, union members were somewhat more likely to report contacts by Democrats in the oversample group than in the national sample, evidence perhaps that the campaign realized that it had a special challenge in 2016 in hoping to keep less-educated white union workers in the fold. Third, while nonpartisans (almost all of them self-proclaimed Independents) were an important "swing group" in 2016, and were won significantly by Trump, they received little attention via the ground game. We surmise that this is because they are more difficult to identify for party canvassing—less likely to turn up as likely supporters in voter registration databases or even the voter files collected by the campaigns.

How Much Does Party Contacting Matter?

Our attention to party contacting assumes that it matters for the final election outcome. An old tradition of research on the efficacy of the party canvass concludes that the party or candidate that enjoys a grassroots contact advantage is able to add a small percentage to their vote total. Systematic empirical analysis found that ground game efforts often added enough to the contacting party's vote total to swing a local election in its favor (Gosnell 1937; Cutright 1963; Katz and Eldersveld 1961). There are no systematic estimates of their efficacy in presidential campaigns. Nonetheless, the increasing attention to the ground game in the 2000s suggests that campaign strategists had come to appreciate their value (Hershey 2017, chapter 11; Issenberg 2012; Panagopoulos 2016) and a recent study found that the presence of field offices advantaged the Obama campaign in 2012 (Masket, Sides, and Vavreck 2015).

To test this assumption, we have estimated the effects of Democratic and Republican Party contacts on the 2016 presidential vote in a multivariate Logistic regression model. It focuses on the Clinton versus Trump vote, ignoring votes for third-party and Independent candidates. The model includes the predictors of vote choice that seemed to figure most prominently into the 2016 results: party identification, age, gender, education (college degree versus no degree), born again religious identity, rural versus urban residence, ethnicity (black versus white and Hispanic versus white). All variables were entered as dichotomies except age, where a continuous measure could be employed.

The results of our analysis are presented in table 18.3 for overall contacting in the national sample. For the purposes of this chapter, we are interested only in whether Democratic and Republican Party contacts were related to vote choice *after controls* for the major predictors of the presidential vote in 2016. Even against this stiff competition, being contacted by both parties had a significant effect on the vote. Democratic contacts increased the likelihood of a vote for Clinton, while Republican contacts increased the likelihood of a vote for Trump. In short, *ceteris paribus*, overall party contacting mattered in the 2016 presidential contest. It also mattered for personal party contacts in the national sample, with both personal Democratic and personal Republican contacts emerging as significant in a multivariate Logistic regression analysis (results not shown here). Based on experimental research (Kalla and

TABLE 18.3
Logistic Regression of 2016 Trump (= 1) versus Clinton (= 0)
Vote on Party Contacts and Key Controls

	Unstandardized b	Standard error	Odds ratio	Significance level
Constant	-.78	.63	.46	.22
Dem. contact	-1.26	.27	.28	.00
Rep. contact	1.99	.28	7.32	.00
Dem. Party ID	-2.42	.51	.09	.00
Rep. Party ID	3.44	.53	31.28	.00
No major party ID	1.09	.47	2.96	.02
Age	.01	.01	.03	.03
Gender	-.32	.23	.15	.15
Born-Again Christian	.49	.25	.05	.05
Rural resident	-.18	.23	.43	.43
College degree	-.78	.26	.46	.00
Black	-2.61	.50	.07	.00
Hispanic	-.76	.32	.47	.02

Broockman 2018), it is likely that party contacts led to mobilization rather than persuasion, something that our data cannot address.

Conclusion

What happened to the ground game in 2016? Despite claims that it was only a minor part of the Republican presidential game plan and that the Democratic campaign's attention was focused more on "big data" modeling than canvassing, it was alive and well. Based on our national CNEP survey, a sizable majority reported a party contact in the battleground states and two in five reported it outside of the battlegrounds. Even in the "Trump country" oversample of rural non-college-educated whites in six battleground states, a majority said that they had been contacted by a party. The presumably more challenging yet efficacious personal contacts understandably fell far below these numbers, but they reached one in five voters in both the national sample and the oversample.

However, the picture is more mixed in comparison with just four years before. Overall contacts declined from 2012 to 2016 for both the Democratic and Republican Parties. And the decline appears to have been, surprisingly, just as large on the Democratic as on the Republican side. In 2016 as in 2012, reported party contacts reached the same levels for both parties, surely unexpected given the coverage of the campaigns. By contrast, personal contacts appear to have increased for both parties in 2016 relative to 2012, preserving the Democratic advantage that they had enjoyed four years before. However, such personal contacts reach only a small slice of the electorate, despite their presumed efficacy.

The oversample of white, non-college rural residents in six battleground states, all lost by Hillary Clinton, sheds additional light on party canvassing in 2016. Similar percentages reported party contacts there as in the national sample overall, but the advantage went to the Republicans. This is perhaps not surprising given the higher percentage of Republican identifiers in the oversample group. But it belies the impressions that there was little attention to ground game voter mobilization in rural and small town America by the Trump campaign. Anyone driving through small towns and rural areas in the Midwest and encountering the proliferation of Trump signs along the roads, however, could attest to the prominence of the Trump campaigns there—even if the national radar did not track it. That the Trump effort is echoed in our party contacting data, therefore, should come as little surprise.

Our analysis of the correlates of party contacting yielded an interesting picture of what guides the respective party efforts. As is typically claimed by political observers, they focus on mobilizing their base of easily identifiable partisan supporters. Even greater party contacting might pay dividends among, for example, Hispanics and women for the Democrats, and born-again Christians for the Republicans. But, the parties share a focus on what we have called the "low-hanging fruit" of voters—those who by age, income, education, and turnout in previous elections are most likely to participate in the election.

Does it matter what happened to the ground game in 2016? Our estimate of significant Democratic and Republican Party contacting effects *in a model with controls for the major predictors of the vote* clearly suggests that it does. Echoing results from earlier studies of local elections and the conventional wisdom of many (though hardly all) campaign operatives, party contacting matters—at the critical margins. And in 2016, the margins were especially thin. One wonders whether the decline in contacting on the Democratic side from 2012 to 2016 may have cost Hillary Clinton the presidency. Correspondingly, more attention to the ground game by the Trump campaign and its allies might have narrowed his popular vote deficit and perhaps even increased his Electoral College margin.

Notes

* We are grateful to William P. Eveland and Carroll Glynn for their valuable contributions to the 2016 CNEP U.S. survey and to Joshua Darr and Seth Masket for their comments on an earlier version of this paper.

1. In 2016, respondents were asked two questions: Did a representative of any of the following parties or candidates contact you *in person* during the campaign? Did a representative of any of the following parties or candidates contact you in any other way during the campaign? In 2012, the second question was asked separately for telephone, mail, or other printed literature, and email or other electronic contacts. These separate non-personal contacts were combined in 2012 for comparison with the 2016 figures.

2. For 2012, eleven states were classified as battlegrounds: Colorado, Florida, Iowa, Michigan, Nevada, New Hampshire, North Carolina, Ohio, Pennsylvania, Virginia, and Wisconsin. For 2016, twelve states were included as battlegrounds: these eleven plus Arizona. The results are essentially the same when the number of battleground states is expanded to fifteen in 2016.

References

Abramowitz, Alan I. 2010. *The Disappearing Center: Engaged Citizens, Polarization, and American Democracy.* New Haven: Yale University Press.
———. 2013. *The Polarized Public?* New York: Longman.
———. 2017. "It Wasn't the Economy, Stupid: Racial Polarization, White Racial Resentment, and the Rise of Trump." In *Trumped: The 2016 Election that Broke all the Rules,* edited by Larry J. Sabato, Kyle Kondik, and Geoffrey Skelley, 202–210. Lanham, MD: Rowman & Littlefield.
Abramowitz, Alan I., and Steven W. Webster. 2016. "The Rise of Negative Partisanship and the Nationalization of American Elections in the 21st Century." *Electoral Studies* 41: 12–22.
Achen, Christopher, and Larry Bartels. 2016. *Democracy for Realists: Why Elections Do Not Produce Responsive Government.* Princeton, NJ: Princeton University Press.
Action for a Progressive Future. 2017. "Autopsy: The Democratic Party in Crisis." Action for a Progressive Future, October 30, 2017. https://democraticautopsy.org/wp-content/uploads/Autopsy-The-Democratic-Party-In-Crisis.pdf.
Adkins, Randall E., Andrew J. Dowdle, Greg Petrow, and Wayne Steger. 2015. "Progressive Ambition, Opportunism, and the Presidency, 1972–2012." Paper for the annual meeting of the Midwest Political Science Association, Chicago, IL.
Agiesta, Jennifer. 2016. "Clinton Wins, Trump Exceeds Expectations, but Few Move." CNN, October 10. https://www.cnn.com/2016/10/10/politics/hillary-clinton-donald-trump-debate-cnn-poll/index.html.
Aisch, Gregor, Adam Pearce, and Bryant Rousseau. 2017. "How Far Is Europe Swinging to the Right?" *The New York Times,* October 23. https://www.nytimes.com/interactive/2016/05/22/world/europe/europe-right-wing-austria-hungary.html.
Akkerman, Tjitske, Sarah L. de Lange, and Matthijs Rooduijn. 2016. *Radical Right-Wing Populist Parties in Western Europe: Into the Mainstream?* New York: Routledge.
Alcindor, Yamiche. 2016. "Bernie Sanders Says Superdelegates Should Follow Voters' Will in Landslide States." *New York Times.*
Aldrich, John. 1980. *Before the Convention.* Chicago: University of Chicago Press.

———. 1995. *Why Parties: The Origin and Transformation of Party Politics in America.* Chicago: University of Chicago Press.

———. 2011. *Why Parties? A Second Look.* Chicago: University of Chicago Press.

Alexander, Jeffrey C. 2010. *The Performance of Politics: Obama's Victory and the Democratic Struggle for Power.* New York: Oxford University Press.

Allen, Jonathan, and Amie Parnes. 2017. *Shattered: Inside Hillary Clinton's Doomed Campaign.* New York: Crown.

Allison, Bill, Mira Rojanasakul, Brittany Harris, and Cedric Sam. 2016. "Tracking the 2016 Presidential Money Race." *Bloomburg Politics* (December 9). https://www.bloomberg.com/politics/graphics/2016-presidential-camp.

Almeida, Paul, and Nella Van Dyke. 2014. "Social Movement Partyism and the Tea Party's Rapid Mobilization." In *Understanding the Tea Party Movement,* edited by Nella Van Dyke and David S. Meyer, 55–71. Surrey, UK: Ashgate Publishing.

American National Election Studies (ANES; www.electionstudies.org). 2017. The ANES 2016 Time Series Study [dataset]. University of Michigan and Stanford University [producers].

———. 2013. The ANES 2012 Time Series Study [dataset]. Stanford University and University of Michigan [producers].

———. 2016. American National Election Study Cumulative Data File, "Guide to Public Opinion." Accessed April 3, 2018 at http://www.electionstudies.org/nesguide/nesguide.htm.

Andris, Clio, David Lee, Marcus J. Hamilton, Mauro Martino, Christian E. Gunning, and John Armistead Selden. 2015. "The Rise of Partisanship and Super-Cooperators in the U.S. House of Representatives." *PLoS ONE* 10.

AP-NORC. 2016. "The Frustrated Public: Views of the 2016 Campaign, the Parties, and the Electoral Process." The Associated Press-NORC Center for Public Affairs Research. Accessed October 31, 2017. http://www.apnorc.org/projects/Pages/the-frustrated-public-americans-views-of-the-election.aspx.

Associated Press. 2013. "Kansas Democrats Vote to Limit Primaries." *The Topeka Capital-Journal,* February 24, 2013. http://cjonline.com/news/2013–02–24/kansas-democrats-vote-limit-primaries.

Atkins, David. 2016. "Trump May Be Sexist and Racist, but That's Not the Only Reason He Won." *The American Prospect* (November 11). http://prospect.org/article/trump-may-besexist-and-racist-%E2%80%99s-not-only-reason-he-won.

Axelrod, Robert. 1972. "Where the Votes Come From: An Analysis of Electoral Coalitions, 1952–1968." *American Political Science Review* 66: 11–20.

Azari, Julia. 2016a. "Weak Parties and Strong Partisanship Are a Bad Combination." *Vox,* November 3, 2016. https://www.vox.com/mischiefs-of-faction/2016/11/3/13512362/weak-parties-strong-partisanship-bad-combination.

———. 2016b. "How the News Media Helped Nominate Trump." *Political Communication* 33(4): 677–680.

Baldassarri, Delia, and Barum Park. 2016. "Was There a Culture War? Polarization and Secular Trends in U.S. Public Opinion." Paper presented at the annual meeting of the American Political Science Association. Philadelphia: September.

Baldwin, Richard. 2016. *The Great Convergence: Information Technology and the New Globalization.* Cambridge, MA: Harvard University Press.

Balke, Nathan S., and Robert J. Gordon. 1989. "The Estimation of Prewar Gross National Product: Methodology and New Evidence." *Journal of Political Economy* 97: 38–92.

Ball, Molly. 2016. "The Resentment Powering Trump." *The Atlantic*, March 15. https://www.theatlantic.com/politics/archive/2016/03/the-resentment-powering -trump/473775/.

Barbaro, Michael. 2015. "2016 Ambitions Turn Marco Rubio, Jeb Bush Protégé, Into Rival." *The New York Times*. http://www.nytimes.com/2015/04/10/us/politics/ expected-presidential-bid-puts-marco-rubio-at-odds-with-a-mentor-jeb-bush.html.

Barber, Michael, and Jeremy C. Pope. 2017. "Does Party Trump Ideology? Disentangling Party and Ideology in America." Unpublished manuscript, Brigham Young University.

Barnett, Jessica C., and Marina S. Vornovitsky. 2016. *Health Insurance Coverage in the United States: 2015 Current Population Reports*. Issued September, P60–257(RV).

Bartels, Larry M. 1988. *Presidential Primaries and the Dynamics of Public Choice*. Princeton, NJ: Princeton University Press.

———. 2002. "Beyond the Running Tally: Partisan Bias in Political Perceptions." *Political Behavior* 24: 117–150.

———. 2016. *Unequal Democracy: The Political Economy of the New Gilded Age*. Princeton, NJ: Princeton University Press.

Bawn, Kathleen, Marty Cohen, David Karol, Seth Masket, Hans Noel, and John Zaller. 2012. "A Theory of Parties: Groups, Policy Demands, and Nominations in American Politics." *Perspectives on Politics* 10(3): 571–597.

Baylor, Christopher. 2017. *First to the Party: The Group Origins of Political Transformation*. Philadelphia: University of Pennsylvania Press.

Beaver et al. v. Clingman et al., 363 F.3d 1048 (10th Cir. 2004).

Beck, Paul A., and Erik D. Heidemann. 2014a. "Changing Strategies in Grassroots Canvassing: 1956–2012." *Party Politics* 20: 261–274.

———. 2014b. "The Ground Game from the Voter's Perspective: 2012 and Before." In *The State of the Parties: The Changing Role of Contemporary American Parties*, 7th ed., edited by John C. Green, Daniel. J. Coffey, and David B. Cohen, 251–269. Latham, MD: Rowman & Littlefield.

Bedlington, Anne, and Michael Malbin. 2003. "The Party as an Extended Network: Members Giving to Each Other and to Their Parties." In *Life after Reform: When the Bipartisan Campaign Reform Act Meets Politics*, edited by Michael Malbin, 121–37. Lanham, MD: Rowman & Littlefield.

Benen, Steve. 2016. "Sanders Says Southern Primaries 'Distort Reality.'" MSNBC, April 4, 2016. http://www.msnbc.com/rachel-maddow-show/sanders-says-southern -primaries-distort-reality.

Berelson, Bernard R., Paul F. Lazarsfeld, and William N. McPhee. 1954. *Voting: The Study of Opinion Formation in a Presidential Campaign*. Chicago: University of Chicago Press.

Berman, Sheri. 2017. "Populism Is a Problem. Elitist Technocrats Aren't the Solution." *Foreign Policy*, December 20, 2017. http://foreignpolicy.com/2017/12/20/pop ulism-is-a-problem-elitist-technocrats-arent-the-solution/.

Bibby, John F. 2002. "State Party Organizations: Coping and Adapting to Candidate-Centered Politics and Nationalization." In *The Parties Respond: Changes in American Parties and Campaigns*, 4th ed., edited by L. Sandy Maisel, 19–46. Boulder, CO: Westview Press.

Biersack, Bob. 2016. "How the Parties Worked the Law and Got Their Mojo Back." *OpenSecrets* (blog). https://www.opensecrets.org/news/2016/02/how-the-parties -worked-the-law-and-got-their-mojo-back/.

Bishop, Bill. 2009. *The Big Sort: Why the Clustering of Like-Minded America is Tearing Us Apart*. New York: Mariner Books.

Blumler, Jay G. 2015. "Core Theories of Political Communication: Foundational and Freshly Minted." *Communication Theory* 25: 426–38.

Boatright, Robert G. 2011. *Interest Groups and Campaign Finance Reform in the United States and Canada*. Ann Arbor: University of Michigan Press.

———. 2013. *Getting Primaried: The Changing of Congressional Primary Challenges*. Ann Arbor: University of Michigan Press.

Bonikowski, Bart, and Paul DiMaggio. 2016. "Varieties of American Popular Nationalism." *American Sociological Review* 81(5): 949–80.

Borchers, Callum. 2016. "We Need More Questions Like This One from Jake Tapper to Debbie Wasserman Schultz [video]." *Washington Post* online, February 12, 2016. https://www.washingtonpost.com/news/the-fix/wp/2016/02/12/we-need-more-ques tions-like-this-one-from-jake-tapper-to-debbie-wasserman-schultz-video/.

Boulianne, Shelley. 2014. "Does Internet Use Affect Engagement? A Meta-Analysis of Research." *Political Communications*, 26(2).

Boyle, Raymond, and Lisa W. Kelly. 2010. "The Celebrity Entrepreneur on Television: Profile, Politics and Power." *Celebrity Studies* 1(3): 334–50.

Brazile, Donna. 2017. "Inside Hillary's Secret Takeover of the DNC." *Politico*, November 2, 2017. https://www.politico.com/magazine/story/2017/11/02/clinton-brazile -hacks-2016-215774.

Brewer, Mark D., and Jeffrey M. Stonecash. 2015. *Polarization and the Politics of Personal Responsibility*. New York: Oxford University Press.

Broockman, David E., and Daniel M. Butler. 2017. "The Causal Effects of Elite Position-Taking on Voter Attitudes: Field Experiments with Elite Communication." *American Journal of Political Science* 61: 208–221.

Brooks, Arthur C. 2010. *The Battle: How the Fight between Free Enterprise and Big Government Will Shape America's Future*. New York: Basic Books.

Brooks, David. 2017. "The Abbie Hoffman of the Right: Donald Trump." *New York Times*, September 26.

Brown, Adam R. 2012. "Does Money Buy Votes? The Case of Self-Financed Gubernatorial Candidates, 1998–2008." *Political Behavior* 35(1): 21–41.

Brown, Clifford W., Lynda W. Powell, and Clyde Wilcox. 1995. *Serious Money: Fundraising and Contributing in Presidential Nomination Campaigns*. New York: Cambridge University Press.

Bump, Philip. 2016a. "How Bernie Sanders is hijacking the Democratic Party to be elected as an independent." *Washington Post*, March 15, 2016. https://www.wash ingtonpost.com/news/the-fix/wp/2016/03/15/how-bernie-sanders-is-hijacking-the -democratic-party-to-be-elected-as-an-independent/.

———. 2016b. "Trump Got the Most GOP Votes Ever—Both for and against him—and Other Fun Facts." *Washington Post*, June 8.

Burnham, Walter Dean. 1970. *Critical Elections and the Mainsprings of American Politics.* New York: W.W. Norton.

Busch, Andrew. 1997. *Outsiders and Openness in the Presidential Nominating System.* Pittsburgh: University of Pittsburgh Press.

Bycoffe, Aaron. 2016. "The Endorsement Primary." https://projects.fivethirtyeight.com/2016-endorsement-primary/.

Cain, Bruce E. 2014. *Democracy, More or Less: America's Political Reform Quandary.* New York: Cambridge University Press.

Campbell, Angus, Philip E. Converse, Warren E. Miller, and Donald E. Stokes. 1960. *The American Voter.* New York: John Wiley and Sons, Inc.

Campbell, James E. 2016a. "Seeing the Forest for the Trees: Presidential Election Forecasts and the Fundamentals." Sabato's Crystal Ball, September 22. http://www.centerforpolitics.org/crystalball/articles/seeing-the-forest-for-the-trees-presidential-election-forecasts-and-the-fundamentals/.

———. 2016b. "How Accurate Were the Political Science Forecasts of the 2016 Presidential Election?" http://www.centerforpolitics.org/crystalball/articles/how-accurate-were-the-political-science-forecasts-of-the-2016-presidential-election/.

Campbell, James E., B. J. Dettrey, and H. Yin. 2010. "The Theory of Conditional Retrospective Voting: Does the Presidential Record Matter Less in Open-Seat Elections?" *Journal of Politics* 72: 1083–1095.

Cann, Damon. 2008. *Sharing the Wealth: Member Contributions and the Exchange Theory of Party Influence in the U.S. House of Representatives.* Albany: State University of New York Press.

Canovan, Margaret. 1999. "Trust the People! Populism and the Two Faces of Democracy." *Political Studies* 47: 2–16.

Caplan, Bryan. 2007. *The Myth of the Rational Voter: Why Democracies Choose Bad Policies.* Princeton, NJ: Princeton University Press.

Carmines, Edward G., Michael J. Ensley, and Michael W. Wagner. 2011. "Issue Preferences, Civic Engagement, and the Transformation of American Politics." In *Facing the Challenge of Democracy: Explorations in the Analysis of Public Opinion and Political Participation*, edited by Paul M. Sniderman and Benjamin Highton, 329–54. Princeton, NJ: Princeton University Press.

———. 2012a. "Who Fits the Left-Right Divide? Partisan Polarization in the American Electorate." *American Behavioral Scientist* 56 (December): 1631–53.

———. 2012b. "Political Ideology in American Politics: One, Two, or None?" *The Forum*, 10(4): 1–18.

———. 2014. "Why Americans Can't Get beyond the Left-Right Divide." In *The State of the Parties: The Changing Role of Contemporary Parties*, 7th ed., edited by John C. Green, Daniel Coffey, and David Cohen, 55–72. Lanham, MD: Rowman & Littlefield.

———. 2016. "Ideological Heterogeneity and the 2016 Republican Primaries." *The Forum* 14(4): 385–397.

———. 2018. "The Role of Populists in the 2016 U.S. Presidential Election and Beyond." In *The State of the Parties 2018: The Changing Role of Contemporary*

American Parties, edited by John C. Green, Daniel J. Coffey, and David B. Cohen, 198–209. Lanham, MD: Rowman & Littlefield.

Carmines, Edward G., and James A. Stimson. 1990. *Issue Evolution: Race and the Evolution of American Politics.* Princeton, NJ: Princeton University Press.

Carnes, Nicholas, and Noam Lupu. 2016. "It's Time to Bust the Myth: Most Trump Voters Were Not Working Class." *Washington Post,* June 5.

Carney, Eliza Newlin. 2014. "Costly Midterms Fuel Hundreds of Joint Fundraising Committees." *Beltway Insiders* (blog), *Roll Call.* http://blogs.rollcall.com/beltway-insiders/fundraising-campaign-committee-kay-hagan-mitch-mcconnell/?dcz=.

Carr, Matthew A., Gerald Gamm, and Justin H. Phillips. 2016. "The Origins of the Culture War: Social Issues in State Party Platforms, 1960–2014." Paper prepared for presentation at the annual meeting of the American Political Science Association, Philadelphia, PA, September 2016.

Case, Anne, and Angus Deaton. 2015. "Rising Morbidity and Mortality in Midlife among White Non-Hispanic Americans in the 21st Century." *PNAS,* 112(49). December 8.

Ceaser, James W. 1979. *Presidential Selection: Theory and Development.* Princeton, NJ: Princeton University Press.

Center for American Women and Politics. 2017. "Gender Differences in Voter Turnout." Eagleton Institute of Politics, (July 20), Rutgers University.

Center for Responsive Politics. 2016a. "Independent Expenditures, Donald Trump, 2016 Cycle." *OpenSecrets.* https://www.opensecrets.org/pres16/outside-spending?id=n00023864.

———. 2016b. "Independent Expenditures, Hillary Clinton, 2016 Cycle." *OpenSecrets* (blog). https://www.opensecrets.org/pres16/outside-spending?id=n00000019.

———. 2017a. "Joint Fundraising Committees." *OpenSecrets.org.* Accessed June 20, 2017. https://www.opensecrets.org/jfc/top.php?type=R&cycle=2016.

———. 2017b. "Political Parties: 2016." *OpenSecrets.org.* Accessed June 20, 2017. https://www.opensecrets.org/parties/.

———. 2017c. "Behind the Candidates: Campaign Committees and Outside Groups." https://www.opensecrets.org/pres16/raised-summ.

Chadwick, Andrew, and Jennifer Stromer-Galley. 2016. "Digital Media, Power, and Democracy in Parties and Election Campaigns: Party Decline or Party Renewal?" Los Angeles, CA: SAGE Publications.

Chaturvedi, Richa. 2016. "A Closer Look at the Gender Gap in Presidential Voting." *Facttank,* (July 28). Pew Research Center. http://www.pewresearch.org/fact-tank/2016/07/28/a-closer-look-at-the-gender-gap-in-presidential-voting.

Chen, Victor Tan. 2016. "All Hollowed Out: The Lonely Poverty of America's White Working Class." *The Atlantic,* Jan 16.

Cheney, Kyle. 2016. "GOP Likely to Revoke Nevada's Early-State Status." *Politico.* May 8, 2016. https://www.politico.com/story/2016/05/nevada-gop-early-state-status-222929.

Citizens United v. Federal Election Commission. 2010. 558 U.S. 310.

Citrin, Jack, and David Karol. 2009. "Introduction." In *Nominating the President: Evolution and Revolution in 2008 and Beyond,* edited by Jack Citrin and David Karol, 1–26. Lanham, MD: Rowman & Littlefield.

Coffey, Daniel. 2006. *State Party Agendas: Representation in an Era of Polarized Parties.* Unpublished Dissertation.

———. 2007. "State Party Activists and State Party Polarization." In *The State of the Parties: The Changing Role of Contemporary American Parties,* 5th ed., edited by John C. Green and Daniel J. Coffey, 75–91. Lanham, MD: Rowman & Littlefield.

———. 2014. "Federal Parties and Polarization." In *The State of the Parties: The Changing Role of Contemporary American Parties,* 7th ed., edited by John C. Green, Daniel J. Coffey, and David B. Cohen, 137–55. Lanham, MD: Rowman & Littlefield.

Cohen, Marty, David Karol, Hans Noel, and John Zaller. 2008. *The Party Decides: Presidential Nominations Before and After Reform.* Chicago: University of Chicago Press.

———. 2016. "Party versus Faction in the Reformed Presidential Nominating System." *PS: Political Science & Politics* 49: 701–708.

Cohen, Nate. 2015. "Hillary Clinton Is More Vulnerable in 2016 Than You Think." *New York Times* (March 9).

Committee on Party Renewal. 1977. "Professional Notes," *PS* 10(1977): 494–495.

Confessore, Nicholas. 2015. "Huge 'Super PAC' Is Moving Early to Back Clinton." *New York Times,* January 23.

Confessore, Nicholas, and Nate Cohn. 2016. "Donald Trump's Victory was Built on Unique Coalition of White Voters." *New York Times,* November 9. https://www.nytimes.com/2016/11/10/us/politics/donald-trump-voters.html.

Confessore, Nicholas, Jonathan Martin, and Maggie Haberman. 2015. "Democrats See No Choice but Hillary Clinton in 2016." *New York Times* (March 11).

Confessore, Nicholas, and Rachel Shorey. 2016. "Trump Campaign Is in Deep Hole on Fund-Raising." *New York Times,* June 21: 1.

Confessore, Nicholas, and Karen Yourish. 2016. "$2 Billion Worth of Free Media for Donald Trump." *New York Times,* March 15.

Consumer Finance Protection Bureau. 2017. "CFPB's First National Survey on Financial Well-Being Shows More Than 40 Percent of U.S. Adults Struggle to Make Ends Meet." September 26.

Converse, Philip E. 1964. "The Nature of Belief Systems in Mass Publics." In *Ideology and Discontent,* edited by David E. Apter, 206–61. New York: Free Press.

Cooper, Joseph. 2017. "The Balance of Power between the Congress and the President: Issues and Dilemmas." In *Congress Reconsidered,* 11th ed., edited by Lawrence C. Dodd and Bruce I. Oppenheimer, 357–98. Thousand Oaks, CA: CQ Press.

Cooper, Marilyn. 2017. "Is Democracy Broken?" *Moment Magazine,* March 14.

Corrado, Anthony. 2011. "Financing the 2008 Presidential General Election." In *Financing the 2008 Election,* edited by David Magleby and Anthony Corrado. Washington, DC: Brookings Institution Press.

Cox, Daniel, Rachel Lienesch, and Robert P. Jones. 2017. "Beyond Economics: Fears of Cultural Displacement Pushed the White Working Class to Trump." PRRI/*The Atlantic Report,* May 9.

Cramer, Katherine J. 2016. *The Politics of Resentment: Rural Consciousness in Wisconsin and the Rise of Scott Walker.* Chicago: University of Chicago Press.

Currinder, Marian. 2009. *Money in the House: Campaign Funds and Congressional Party Politics,* 1st ed. Boulder, CO: Westview Press.

Cutright, Philipps. 1963. "Measuring the Impact of Local Party Activity on the General Election Vote." *Public Opinion Quarterly* 27: 372–386.

Dahl, Robert A. 1961. *Who Governs? Democracy and Power in an American City,* 2nd ed. New Haven, CT: Yale University Press.

Daku, Mark, Stuart Soroka, and Lori Young. 2015. "Lexicoder, Version 3.0."

Darr, Joshua P. 2017. "The Incredible Shrinking Democratic Ground Game." *Vox: Mischiefs of Faction* blog. https://www.vox.com/mischiefs-of-faction/2017/11/16/16665756/shrinking-democratic-ground-game.

Darr, Joshua and Matthew Levendusky. 2014. "Relying on the Ground Game: The Placement and Effects of Campaign Field Offices." *American Politics Research* 42: 529–548.

Davis, James W. 1980. *Presidential Primaries.* Westport, CT: Greenwood Press.

Denzau, Arthur T., and Michael C. Munger. 1986. "Legislators and Interest Groups: How Unorganized Interests Get Represented." *American Political Science Review* 80(1): 89–106.

DeSilver, Drew. 2017. "Most Americans Unaware That as U.S. Manufacturing Jobs Have Disappeared, Output Has Grown." Pew Research Center, July 25.

Dionne, Jr., E. J. 1996. *They Only Look Dead.* New York: Simon and Schuster.

DiTomaso, Nancy. 2017. "Parties, Political Coalitions, and the Democratic Party: Making Sense of the 2016 Election." Paper presented at the annual meeting of the American Sociological Association. Montreal.

Dovere, Edward-Isaac. 2016. "How Clinton Lost Michigan—and Blew the Election." *Politico,* December 14. http://www.politico.com/story/2016/12/michigan-hillary-Clinton-trump-232547.

Downs, Anthony. 1957. *An Economic Theory of Democracy.* New York: Harper and Row.

Draper, Robert. 2017. "A Post-Obama Democratic Party in Search of Itself." *The New York Times Magazine,* November 1.

Dreher, Rod. 2016. "Trump: Tribune of Poor White People." *The American Conservative,* July 22. http://www.theamericanconservative.com/dreher/trump-us-politics-poor-whites/.

Druckman, James N., Erik Peterson, and Rune Slothuus. 2013. "How Elite Polarization Affects Public Opinion Formation." *American Political Science Review* 107: 57–79.

Drutman, Lee. 2016. "How Race and Identity Became the Central Dividing Line in American Politics." *Vox,* August 30.

Dwyre, Diana. 1996. "Spinning Straw into Gold: Soft Money and U.S. House Elections." *Legislative Studies Quarterly* 21(3): 409–24.

Dwyre, Diana, and Evelyn Braz. 2015. "Super PAC Spending, Strategies, and Goals." *The Forum* 13(2): 245–67.

Dwyre, Diana, and Robin Kolodny. 2014a. "Political Party Activity in the 2012 Elections: Sophisticated Orchestration or Diminished Influence?" In *The State of the Parties: The Changing Role of Contemporary American Parties,* 7th ed., edited by John C. Green, Daniel J. Coffey, and David B. Cohen, 207–230. Lanham, MD: Rowman & Littlefield.

———. 2014b. "Party Money in the 2012 Elections." In *Financing the 2012 Election*, edited by David Magleby. Washington, DC: Brookings Institution Press.

Eberstadt, Nicholas. 2012. *A Nation of Takers: America's Entitlement Epidemic.* West Conshohocken, PA: Templeton Press.

———. 2017. "Our Miserable 21st Century." *Commentary Magazine.* February 15.

Edsall, Thomas B. 2017a. "President Trump Is the Enemy of Their Enemies." *New York Times*, May 4, 2017. https://www.nytimes.com/2017/05/04/opinion/president-trump-is-the-enemy-of-their-enemies.html.

———. 2017b. "Has the Democratic Party Gotten Too Rich for Its Own Good?" *New York Times*, June 1.

———. 2017c. "How Fear of Falling Explains the Love of Trump." *New York Times*, July 20.

———. 2017d. "The Trump Voter Paradox." *New York Times,* September 28.

Edsall, Thomas B., with Mary D. Edsall. 1991. *Chain Reaction: The Impact of Race, Rights, and Taxes on American Politics.* New York: Norton.

Edwards, Lee. 1999. *The Conservative Revolution: The Movement That Remade America.* New York: Free Press.

Ehrenreich, Barbara. 2016. "Dead, White, and Blue: The Great Die-Off of America's Blue Collar Whites." *Vox Populi.*

Eichenwald, Kurt. 2016. "Don't Blame Trump: American Democracy Was Broken Before He Muscled In." *Newsweek*, May 3.

Enders, Adam M., and Jamil S. Scott. 2018. "White Racial Resentment Has Been Gaining Political Power for Decades." Monkey Cage, *Washington Post*, January 15.

Entous, Adam, Craig Timberg, and Elizabeth Dwoskin. 2017. "Russian Operatives Used Facebook Ads to Exploit America's Racial and Religious Divisions." *Washington Post*, September 25. https://www.washingtonpost.com/business/technology/russian-operatives-used-facebook-ads-to-exploit-divisions-over-black-political-activism-and-muslims/2017/09/25/4a011242-a21b-11e7-ade1-76d061d56efa_story.html?utm_term=.c60f31b7da0a.

Epstein, Leon D. 1986. *Political Parties in the American Mold.* Madison: University of Wisconsin Press.

Evans, Geoffrey, and Mark Pickup. 2010. "Reversing the Causal Arrow: The Political Conditioning of Economic Perceptions in the 2000–2004 U.S. Presidential Election Cycle." *The Journal of Politics* 72: 1236–1251.

Fairbanks, Amanda M. 2008. "Hillary Supporters Split." *The New York Times*, August 27.

Farina, Cynthia R. 2015. "Congressional Polarization: Terminal Constitutional Dysfunction?" *Columbia Law Review* 115: 1689–738.

Federal Election Commission. 2015. *Contribution Limits for 2015–2016 Federal Elections.* http://www.fec.gov/pages/brochures/contrib.shtml#Contribution_Limits.

———. 2016. *2016 Coordinated Party Expenditure Limits.* http://www.fec.gov/info/charts_cpe_2016.shtml.

———. 2017. *2015–2016 Election Cycle Data Summaries through 12/31/16: National Party 24-Month Data Summaries.* Washington, DC: Federal Election Commission. http://www.fec.gov/press/summaries/2016/ElectionCycle/24m_NatlParty.shtml.

Feldman, Stanley. 1988. "Structure and Consistency in Public Opinion: The Role of Core Beliefs and Values." *American Journal of Political Science* 32: 416–440.

Ferguson, Thomas, Paul Jorgensen, and Jie Chen. 2013. "Party Competition and Industrial Structure in the 2012 Elections: Who's Really Driving the Taxi to the Dark Side?" *International Journal of Political Economy* 42: 3–41.

Finchelstein, Federico. 2017. *From Fascism to Populism in History*. Berkeley: University of California Press.

Fingerhut, Hannah. 2015. "In Politics, Most Americans Feel They're on the Losing Side." Pew Research Center, November 25.

Fiorina, Morris P., and Samuel J. Abrams. 2008. "Political Polarization in the American Public." *Annual Review of Political Science* 11: 563–88.

———. 2009. *Disconnect: The Breakdown of Representation in American Politics*. Norman, OK: University of Oklahoma Press.

Fischer, Claude S., and Michael Hout. 2006. *Century of Difference: How America Changed in The Last One Hundred Years*. New York: Russell Sage Foundation.

Florida, Richard, and Aria Bendix. 2016. "Mapping the Most Distressed Communities in the U.S." *CITYLAB*. https://www.citylab.com/equity/2016/02/mapping-dis tressed-communities-in-the-US/471150.

Foran, Clare. 2016a. "Can Bernie Win over the Establishment?" *The Atlantic*, March 15.

———. 2016b. "Is the Democratic Primary Really Rigged?" *The Atlantic*. May 17, 2016. Accessed October 6, 2017. https://www.theatlantic.com/politics/archive/2016 /05/is-the-democratic-primary-really-rigged/483168/.

Fournier, Ron. 2013. "Talkin' About Revolution: 6 Reasons Why the Two-Party System May Become Obsolete." *The Atlantic*, January 14, 2013. https://www.theatlan tic.com/politics/archive/2013/01/talkin-about-revolution-6-reasons-why-the-two -party-system-may-become-obsolete/461667/.

Fowler, Erica Franklin, Michael M. Franz, and Travis N. Ridout. 2016. *Political Advertising in the United States*. Boulder, CO: Westview Press.

Fowler, Erika Franklin, Travis N. Ridout, and Michael M. Franz. 2017. "Political Advertising in 2016: The Presidential Election as Outlier?" *The Forum* 14: 445–469.

Francia, Peter L., John C. Green, Paul S. Herrnson, Lynda W. Powell, and Clyde Wilcox. 2003. *The Financiers of Congressional Elections: Investors, Ideologues, and Intimates*. New York: Columbia University Press.

———. 2005. "Limousine Liberals and Corporate Conservatives: The Financial Constituencies of the Democratic and Republican Parties." *Social Science Quarterly* 86: 761–78.

Francia, Peter, and Costas Panagopoulos. 2009. "Grassroots Mobilization in the 2008 Presidential Election." *Journal of Political Marketing* 8: 315–333.

Frank, Thomas. 2004. *What's the Matter with Kansas?: How Conservatives Won the Heart of America*. New York: Owl Books.

Freelon, Deen, and David Karpf. 2015. "Of Big Birds and Bayonets: Hybrid Twitter Interactivity in the 2012 Presidential Debates." *Information, Communication & Society* 18: 390.

Friedman, Milton. 1962. *Capitalism and Freedom*. Chicago: University of Chicago Press.

Friedman, Thomas L. 2010. "Third Party Rising." *New York Times*, October 3, 2010.

Frum, David. 2016. "The Great Republican Revolt." *The Atlantic*, January/February.

Fry, Richard, and Rakesh Kochhar. 2014. "America's Wealth between Middle-Income and Upper-Income Families Is Widest on Record." Pew Research Center, December 17.

Fuller, Roslyn. 2016. "Why Is American Democracy So Broken, and Can It Be Fixed?" *The Nation.* June 9.

Gabriel, Trip. 2016a. "Our Man in Iowa: How the Iowa Caucuses Work." *The New York Times.* February 1, 2016. Accessed October 17, 2017. https://www.nytimes.com/2016/02/02/us/politics/iowa-caucuses-faq-our-man.html.

———. 2016b. "Bernie Sanders Backers March against Hillary Clinton in Philadelphia." *New York Times,* July 24.

Galvin, Daniel J. 2012. "The Transformation of Political Institutions: Investments in Institutional Resources and Gradual Change in the National Party Committees." *Studies in American Political Development* 26(April): 50–70.

Galvin, Daniel J., and Chloe N. Thurston. 2017. "The Democrats' Misplaced Faith in Policy Feedback." *The Forum* 15: 333–43.

Garrett, R. Sam. 2015. *Increased Campaign Contribution Limits in the FY2015 Omnibus Appropriations Law: Frequently Asked Questions.* Washington, DC: Congressional Research Service. https://fas.org/sgp/crs/misc/R43825.pdf.

Gehl, Katherine M., and Michael E. Porter. 2017. "Why Competition in the Politics Industry Is Failing: A Strategy for Reinvigorating Our Democracy." Harvard Business School, September 2017.

Geismer, Lily. 2014. *Don't Blame Us: Suburban Liberals and the Transformation of the Democratic Party.* Princeton, NJ: Princeton University Press.

Gerber, Alan S., Gregory A. Huber, and Ebonya Washington. 2010. "Party Affiliation, Partisanship, and Political Beliefs: A Field Experiment." *American Political Science Review* 104: 720–744.

Gerring, John. 1998. *Party Ideologies in America, 1828–1996.* Cambridge, UK; New York, NY: Cambridge University Press.

Gershtenson, Joseph. 2003. "Mobilization Strategies of the Democrats and Republicans, 1956–2000." *Political Research Quarterly* 56: 293–308.

Gilens, Martin, and Benjamin Page. 2014. "Testing Theories of American Politics: Elites, Interest Groups, and Average Citizens." *Perspectives on Politics* 12(3).

Gitell, Seth. 2003. "The Democratic Party Suicide Bill." *The Atlantic.* https://www.theatlantic.com/magazine/archive/2003/07/the-democratic-party-suicide-bill/378549/.

Gladwell, Malcom. 2010. "Small Change: Why the Revolution Will Not Be Tweeted." *New Yorker,* October 4.

Glaser, April. 2017. "Russia's Election Meddling Targeted Activists and People of Color, Too." *Slate,* November 3. http://www.slate.com/blogs/future_tense/2017/11/03/russia_s_election_meddling_targeted_activists_and_people_of_color.html.

Glick, Peter, and Susan T. Fiske. 2011. "Ambivalent Sexism Revisited." *Psychology of Women Quarterly* 35: 530–535.

Gomez, Eric M., Danielle M. Young, Alexander G. Preston, Weigh S. Wilton, Sarah E. Gaither, and Cheryl R. Kaiser. 2017. "Loss and Loyalty: Change in Political and Gender Identity among Clinton Supporters after the 2016 U.S. Presidential Election." *Self and Identity,* http://dx.doi.org/10.1080/15298868.2017.1391873.

Goren, Paul. 2013. *On Voter Competence*. New York: Oxford University Press.

Gosnell, Harold Foote. 1937. *Machine Politics: Chicago Model*. Chicago: University of Chicago Press.

Grattan, Laura. 2016. *Populism's Power: Radical Grassroots Democracy in America*. New York: Oxford University Press.

Green, Donald P., and Alan S. Gerber. 2008. *Get Out the Vote: How to Increase Voter Turnout*. Washington, DC: The Brookings Institution.

Green, Donald P., Bradley Palmquist, and Eric Schickler. 2002. *Partisan Hearts and Minds: Political Parties and the Social Identity of Voters*. New Haven, CT: Yale University Press.

Green, John C., and Daniel J. Coffey. 2007. *The State of the Parties: The Changing Role of Contemporary American Parties*, 5th ed. Lanham, MD: Rowman & Littlefield.

———. 2011. *The State of the Parties: The Changing Role of Contemporary American Parties*, 6th ed. Lanham, MD: Rowman & Littlefield.

Green, John C., Daniel J. Coffey, and David B. Cohen. 2014. *The State of the Parties: The Changing Role of Contemporary American Parties*, 7th ed. Lanham, MD: Rowman & Littlefield.

Green, John C., and Rick Farmer. 2003. *The State of the Parties: The Changing Role of Contemporary American Parties*, 4th ed. Lanham, MD: Rowman & Littlefield.

Green, John C., and Daniel M. Shea. 1996. *The State of the Parties: The Changing Role of Contemporary American Parties*, 2nd ed. Lanham, MD: Rowman & Littlefield.

———. 1999. *The State of the Parties: The Changing Role of Contemporary American Parties*, 3rd ed. Lanham, MD: Rowman & Littlefield.

Green, Joshua. 2017. *Devil's Bargain: Steve Bannon, Donald Trump, and the Storming of the Presidency*. New York: Penguin Press.

Greenblatt, Alan. 2015. "The Waning Power of State Political Parties." *Governing*, December 2015.

Gross, Daniel. 2000. *Bull Run: Wall Street, the Democrats, and the New Politics of Personal Finance*. New York: Public Affairs.

Grossman, Matthew, and Casey Dominguez. 2009. "Party Coalitions and Interest Group Networks." *American Politics Quarterly* 37(5): 767–800.

Grossmann, Matthew, and David A. Hopkins. 2016. *Asymmetric Politics: Ideological Republicans and Group-Interest Democrats*. Oxford: Oxford University Press.

Gunther, Richard, Paul A. Beck, Pedro C. Magalhães, and Alejandro Moreno, eds. 2016. *Voting in Old and New Democracies*. New York: Routledge.

Gutmann, Amy, and Dennis Thompson. 2002. "Deliberative Democracy beyond Process." *Journal of Political Philosophy* 10: 153–74.

Hacker, Jacob S., and Paul Pierson. 2010. *Winner-Take-All Politics: How Washington Made the Rich Richer—And Turned Its Back on the Middle Class*. New York: Simon & Schuster.

———. 2014. "After the Master Theory: Downs, Schattschneider, and the Rebirth of Policy Focused Analysis." *Perspectives on Politics* 12: 643–662.

———. 2015. "Confronting Asymmetric Polarization." In *Solutions to Political Polarization in America*, edited by Nathaniel Persily, 59–70. New York: Cambridge University Press.

———. 2016. *American Amnesia: How the War on Government Led Us to Forget What Made America Prosper*. New York: Simon & Schuster.

Hahl, Oliver, Minjae Kim, and Ezra W. Zuckerman Sivan. 2018. "The Authentic Appeal of the Lying Demagogue: Proclaiming the Deeper Truth about Political Illegitimacy." *American Sociological Review* 83(1): 1–33.

Hall, Richard L., and Alan V. Deardorff. 2006. "Lobbying as Legislative Subsidy." *American Political Science Review* 100(1): 69–84.

Hall, Richard L., and Frank W. Wayman. 1990. "Buying Time: Moneyed Interests and the Mobilization of Bias in Congressional Committees." *American Political Science Review* 84(3): 797–820.

Hamm, Keith, Michael Malbin, Jaclyn Kettler, and Brendan Glavin. 2014. "Independent Spending in State Elections, 2006–2010: Vertically Networked Political Parties Were the Real Story, Not Business." *The Forum* 12(2): 305–28.

Hanmer, Michael J., and Kerem Ozan Kalkan. 2013. "Behind the Curve: Clarifying the Best Approach to Calculating Predicted Probabilities and Marginal Effects from Limited Dependent Variable Models." *American Journal of Political Science* 57: 263–277.

Harris, Fred R. 1973. *The New Populism.* New York: Saturday Review Press.

Harris, Mary. 2016. "A Media Post-Mortem on the 2016 Presidential Election—MediaQuant." *Media Quant: The Numbers Behind the News.* https://mediaquant.net/2016/11/a-media-post-mortem-on-the-2016-presidential-election/.

Hart, David M. 2001. "Why Do Some Firms Give? Why Do Some Give a Lot?: High-Tech PACs, 1977–1996." *The Journal of Politics* 63(04): 1230–1249.

Hart, Roderick P., Jay P. Childers, and Colene J. Lind. 2013. *Political Tone: How Leaders Talk and Why.* Chicago: University of Chicago Press.

Haskell, John. 1996. *Fundamentally Flawed: Understanding and Reforming Presidential Primaries.* Lanham, MD: Rowman & Littlefield.

Hatch, Rebecca S. 2016. "Party Organizational Strength and Technological Capacity: The Adaptation of the State-Level Party Organizations in the United States to Voter Outreach and Data Analytics in the Internet Age." *Party Politics* 22: 191–202.

Healy, Patrick, and Amy Chozick. 2015. "Hillary Clinton Relying on Southern Primaries to Fend Off Rivals." *New York Times,* September 6, 2015. https://www.nytimes.com/2015/09/06/us/politics/hillary-clinton-relying-on-southern-primaries-to-fend-off-rivals.html.

Heberlig, Eric, Mark Hetherington, and Bruce Larson. 2006. "The Price of Leadership: Campaign Money and the Polarization of Congressional Parties." *Journal of Politics* 68: 992–1005.

Heberlig, Eric S., and Bruce Larson. 2012. *Congressional Parties, Institutional Ambition, and the Financing of Majority Control.* Ann Arbor: University of Michigan Press.

———. 2014. "U.S. House Incumbent Fundraising and Spending in a Post-*Citizens United* and Post-*McCutcheon* World." *Political Science Quarterly* 129(4): 613–42.

Hedegaard, H., M. Warner, and AM Miniño. 2017. "Drug Overdose Deaths in the United States, 1999–2016." NCHS Data Brief, No. 294. Hyattsville, MD: National Center for Health Statistics.

Hedlund, Ronald D. 1977–1978. "Cross-Over Voting in a 1976 Open Presidential Primary." *Public Opinion Quarterly* 41(4): 498–514.

Heerwig, Jennifer. 2018. "Money in the Middle: Contribution Strategies Among

Affluent Donors to Federal Elections, 1980–2008." *American Journal of Sociology* 123: 1004–1063.

Hemmer, Nicole. 2016. *Messengers of the Right: Conservative Media and the Transformation of American Politics*. Philadelphia: University of Pennsylvania Press.

Herrera, Richard. 1995. "The Crosswinds of Change: Sources of Change in the Democratic and Republican Parties." *Political Research Quarterly* 48(2): 291–312.

Herrnson, Paul S. 2009. "The Roles of Party Organizations, Party-Connected Committees, and Party Allies in Elections." *Journal of Politics* 71(4): 1207–1224.

———. 2012. *Congressional Elections: Campaigning at Home and in Washington*, 6th ed. Thousand Oaks, CA: CQ Press.

———. 2016. *Congressional Elections: Campaigning at Home and in Washington*, 7th ed. Washington, DC: CQ Press.

———. 2017. "The Impact of Organizational Characteristics on Super PAC Financing and Independent Expenditures." Presented at the Meeting of the Campaign Finance Task Force, Bipartisan Policy Center, Washington, DC, April 21. Available at https://bipartisanpolicy.org/wp-content/uploads/2018/01/The-Impact-of-Organizational-Characteristics-on-Super-PAC-Financing-and-Independent-Expenditures.pdf.

Hershey, Marjorie Randon. 2017. *Party Politics in America*. New York: Routledge.

Hetherington, Marc J. 2001. "Resurgent Mass Partisanship: The Role of Elite Polarization." *American Political Science Review* 95(3): 619–631.

———. 2009. "Putting Polarization in Perspective." *British Journal of Political Science* 39: 413–48.

Hetherington, Marc J., and Jonathan D. Weiler. 2009. *Authoritarianism and Political Polarization in America*. Cambridge, MA: Cambridge University Press.

Hibbing, John R., and Elizabeth Theiss-Morse. 2002. *Stealth Democracy: Americans' Beliefs about How Government Should Work*. New York: Cambridge University Press.

Hillygus, D. Sunshine, and Tod G. Shields. 2009. *The Persuadable Voter: Wedge Issues in Presidential Campaigns*. Princeton, NJ: Princeton University Press.

Hirschman, Albert O. 1970. *Exit, Voice, and Loyalty: Responses to Declines in Firms, Organizations, and States*. Cambridge, MA: Harvard University Press.

Hochschild, Arlie R. 2016. *Strangers in Their Own Land*. New York: The New Press.

Hochschild, Jennifer L. 1996. *Facing Up to the American Dream: Race, Class, and the Soul of the Nation*. Princeton, NJ: Princeton University Press.

Hofstadter, Richard. 2008. *The Paranoid Style in American Politics*. New York: Vintage Books.

Holyoke, Thomas T. 2014. "Why Lobbyists for Competing Interests Often Cooperate." In *New Directions in Interest Group Research*, edited by Matt Grossmann, 105–21. New York: Routledge.

Hopkins, Daniel J. 2018. *The Increasingly United States: How and Why American Political Behavior Nationalized*. Chicago, IL: University of Chicago Press.

Hopkins, David. 2017. "Party Coalitions in the 2016 Election." Paper Prepared for Presentation at the Midwest Political Science Association Conference, Chicago, IL, April 6–9, 2017.

Hout, Michael, and Daniel Laurison. 2014. "The Realignment of U.S. Presidential

Voting, 1948–2004." In *Social Stratification: Race, Class, and Gender in Sociological Perspective*, 4th ed., edited by David Grusky, 1037–45. Boulder, CO: Westview Publishers.

Huddy, Leonie, Lilliana Mason, and Lene Aarøe. 2015. "Expressive Partisanship: Campaign Involvement, Political Emotion, and Partisan Identity." *American Political Science Review* 109: 1–17.

Hurwitz, Jon, and Mark Peffley. 2005. "Playing the Race Card in the Post-Willie Horton Era: the Impact of Racialized Code Words on Support for Punitive Crime Policy." *Public Opinion Quarterly* 1(1): 99–112.

Inglehart, Ronald F. 1977. *The Silent Revolution.* Princeton, NJ: Princeton University Press.

Inglehart, Ronald F., and Pippa Norris. 2016. "Trump, Brexit, and the Rise of Populism." Paper presented at 2016 meeting of the American Political Science Association.

Issenberg, Sasha. 2012. *The Victory Lab: The Secret Science of Winning Campaigns.* New York: Crown Publishers.

Iyengar, Shanto, Guarav Sood, and Yphtach Lelkes. 2012. "Affect Not Ideology: A Social Identity Perspective on Polarization." *Public Opinion Quarterly* 76: 405–31.

Iyengar, Shanto, and Sean J. Westwood. 2015. "Fear and Loathing across Party Lines: New Evidence on Group Polarization." *American Journal of Political Science* 59(3), 690–707.

Jacobson, Gary C. 1985. "Party Organization and the Distribution of Campaign Resources: Republicans and Democrats in 1982." *Political Science Quarterly* 100: 603–25.

———. 2010. "A Collective Dilemma Solved: The Distribution of Party Campaign Resources in the 2006 and 2008 Congressional Elections." *Election Law Journal* 9(4): 381–97.

———. 2013. *The Politics of Congressional Elections.* 8th ed. Boston: Pearson.

Jerit, Jennifer, and Jason Barabas. 2012. "Partisan Perceptual Bias and the Information Environment." *Journal of Politics* 74: 672–684.

Jewitt, Caitlin E. 2014. "Packed Primaries and Empty Caucuses: Voter Turnout in Presidential Nomination Contests." *Public Choice* 160: 295–312.

———. Forthcoming. *The Primary Rules: Parties, Voters, and Presidential Nominations.* Ann Arbor: The University of Michigan Press.

Johnson, David V. 2016. "The Southern-Fried Primary Is Unfair: Column." *USA Today*, March 22, 2016. https://www.usatoday.com/story/opinion/2016/03/22/southern-primaries-frontloaded-unfair-clinton-sanders-trump-column/82094230/.

Johnson, Ruth. 2012. "Questions and Answers: Michigan's Feb. 28, 2012 Presidential Primary." State of Michigan Department of State. http://www.michigan.gov/documents/sos/Public_FAQ_2–13–12_376851_7.pdf.

Junger, Sebastian. 2016. *Tribe: On Homecoming and Belonging.* New York: Twelve Books.

Kabaservice, Geoffrey. 2017. "The Great Performance of Our Failing President." *New York Times,* June 9.

Kalla, Joshua L, and David E. Broockman. 2018. "The Minimal Persuasive Effects of Campaign Contact in General Elections: Evidence from 49 Field Experiments." *American Political Science Review* 112: 148–166.

Kanthak, Kristin, and Rebecca Morton. 2001. "The Effects of Electoral Rules on Congressional Primaries." In *Congressional Primaries and the Politics of Representation*, edited by Peter F. Galderisi, Marni Ezra, and Michael Lyons, 116–131. Lanham, MD: Rowman & Littlefield.

Karol, David. 2009. *Party Position Change in American Politics: Coalition Management*. Cambridge, MA: Cambridge University Press.

———. 2015. "Party Activists, Interest Groups, and Polarization in American Politics." In *American Gridlock: The Sources, Character, and Impact of Political Polarization*, edited by James A. Thurber and Antoine Yoshinaka, 68–85. New York: Cambridge University Press.

Katz, Donald, and Samuel P. Eldersveld. 1961. "The Impact of Local Party Activity upon the Electorate." *Public Opinion Quarterly* 25: 1–24.

Katz, Josh. 2016. "Who Will Be President?" The Upshot, *New York Times*, November 8. https://www.nytimes.com/interactive/2016/upshot/presidential-polls-forecast.htm.

Katz, Richard S., and Peter Mair. 2018. *Democracy and the Cartelization of Political Parties*. Oxford: Oxford University Press.

Kazin, Michael. 1998. *The Populist Persuasion: An American History*, 2nd ed. Ithaca, NY: Cornell University Press.

Kemble, Penn, and Josh Muravchik. 1972. "The New Politics and the Democrats." *Commentary*, December: 78–84.

Kenney, Patrick J. 1983. "Explaining Turnout in Gubernatorial Primaries." *American Politics Research* 11: 315–26.

Key, V. O. 1942. *Politics, Parties and Pressure Groups*. New York: Crowell.

Kimball, David C., Joseph Anthony, and Tyler Chance. 2018. "Political Identity and Party Polarization in the American Electorate." In *The State of the Parties 2018: The Changing Role of Contemporary American Parties*, 8th ed., edited by John C. Green, Daniel J. Coffey, and David B. Cohen, 169–184. Lanham, MD: Rowman & Littlefield.

Kimball, David C., Bryce Summary, and Eric C. Vorst. 2014. "Political Identity and Party Polarization in the American Electorate." In *The State of the Parties: The Changing Role of Contemporary American Parties*, edited by John C. Green, Daniel J. Coffey, and David B. Cohen, 7th ed, 37–54. Lanham, MD: Rowman & Littlefield.

Kinder Donald R., and Nathan P. Kalmoe. 2017. *Neither Liberal Nor Conservative: Ideological Innocence in the American Public*. Chicago: University of Chicago Press.

Kinder, Donald R., and Lynn M. Sanders. 1996. *Divided by Color: Racial Politics and Democratic Ideals*. Chicago: University of Chicago Press.

King, G., J. Honaker, A. Joseph, and K. Scheve. 2001. "Analyzing Incomplete Political Science Data: An Alternative Algorithm for Multiple Imputation." *American Political Science Review* 95(1), 49–69.

Klar, Samara. 2014. "A Multidimensional Study of Ideological Preferences and Priorities Among the American Public." *Public Opinion Quarterly* 78(S1): 344–59.

Klein, Ezra. 2016. "Hillary Clinton and the Audacity of Political Realism." *Vox*, January 28. https://www.vox.com/2016/1/28/10858464/hillary-clinton-bernie-sanders-political-realism.

Klinkner, Philip. 2016. "The Easiest Way to Guess if Someone Supports Trump? Ask If Obama Is a Muslim." *Vox*, June 2.

Kloppenberg, James T. 2014. "Barack Obama and Progressive Democracy." In *Making the American Century: Essays on the Political Culture of Twentieth Century America*, edited by Bruce Schulman. New York: Oxford University Press.

Koger, Gregory, Seth Masket, and Hans Noel. 2009. "Partisan Webs: Information Exchange and Party Networks." *British Journal of Political Science* 39(3): 633–53.

———. 2016. "No Disciplined Army: American Political Parties as Networks." In *The Oxford Handbook of Political Networks*, edited by Jennifer Nicoll Victor, Alexander H. Montgomery, and Mark Lubell. Oxford: Oxford University Press.

Kolodny, Robin, and David A. Dulio. 2003. "Political Party Adaptation in U.S. Congressional Campaigns: Why Political Parties Use Coordinated Expenditures to Hire Political Consultants." *Party Politics* 9: 729–746.

Kolodny, Robin, and Diana Dwyre. 1998. "Party-Orchestrated Activities for Legislative Party Goals." *Party Politics* 4: 275–95.

———. 2018. "Convergence or Divergence? Do Parties and Outside Groups Spend on the Same Candidates, and Does It Matter?" *American Politics Research.* 46(3): 375–401.

Konigsberg, Eric. 2015. "How the Apprentice Explains Donald Trump's Campaign." *Bloomberg.com.* https://www.bloomberg.com/news/features/2015–10–15/how-the -apprentice-explains-donald-trump-s-campaign.

La Raja, Raymond J. 2003. "State Parties after BCRA." In *Life After Reform: When the Bipartisan Campaign Reform Act Meets Politics*, edited by Michael Malbin. Lanham, MD: Rowman & Littlefield.

———. 2008. *Small Change: Money, Political Parties, and Campaign Finance Reform.* Ann Arbor: University of Michigan Press.

———. 2013. "The Supreme Court Might Strike Down Overall Contribution Limits. And That's Okay." The Monkey Cage, *Washington Post.* https://www.washington post.com/news/monkey-cage/wp/2013/10/09/the-supreme-court-might-strike-down -overall-contribution-limits-and-thats-okay/.

———. 2014. "CRomnibus Pays Off for Parties." *MassPoliticsProfs / WGBH.org* (blogs). http://blogs.wgbh.org/masspoliticsprofs/2014/12/17/cromnibus-pays-parties/.

La Raja, Raymond J., and Jonathan Rauch. 2016. "The State of State Parties—and How Strengthening Them Can Improve Our Politics." Brookings Institution, March 2016. https://www.brookings.edu/wp-content/uploads/2016/07/states.pdf.

La Raja, Raymond J., and Bryan F. Schaffner. 2015. *Campaign Finance and Political Polarization: When Purists Prevail.* Ann Arbor: University of Michigan Press.

Lane, Charles. 2016. "Superdelegates Exist for a Reason. Just Look at the Republicans." *Chicago Tribune*, June 9. Accessed October 26, 2017. http://www.chicagotri bune.com/news/opinion/commentary/ct-bernie-sanders-superdelegates-gripe-201 60609-story.html.

Langbein, Laura I. 1986. "Money and Access: Some Empirical Evidence." *Journal of Politics* 48(4): 1052–1062.

Laurison, Daniel. 2017a. "The Field of Political Production: Campaign Staff and Consultants in American National Elections." Paper presented at the annual meeting of the American Sociological Association. Montreal.

————. 2017b. Personal communication. October 7.

Layman, Geoffrey C., Thomas M. Carsey, John C. Green, Richard Herrera, and Rosalyn Cooperman. 2010. "Activists and Conflict Extension in American Politics." *American Political Science Review* 104: 324–46.

Lee, Frances. 2016. *Insecure Majorities: Congress and the Perpetual Campaign*. Chicago: University of Chicago Press.

Leland, John. 2016. "Bernie Sanders and Donald Trump Voters Share Anger, but Direct It Differently." *New York Times*, January 31. A1.

Lelkes, Ypthach, Gaurav Sood, and Shanto Iyengar. 2017. "The Hostile Audience: The Effect of Access to Broadband Internet on Partisan Affect." *American Journal of Political Science* 61: 5–20.

Lengle, James I. 1981. *Representation and Presidential Primaries: The Democratic Party in the Post-Reform Era*. Westport, CT: Greenwood Press.

Leonhardt, David. 2014. "The Great Wage Slowdown of the 21st Century." *New York Times*, October 7.

Lerer, Lisa. 2016. "Clinton Backers 'Feel the Bern' of Angry Sanders Supporters." AP News. April 28. Accessed October 6, 2017. https://apnews.com/c6d6f8e915384 38298ad78b7022ee8f2/clinton-backers-feel-bern-angry-sanders-supporters.

Levendusky, Matthew. 2009a. *The Partisan Sort: How Liberals Became Democrats and Conservatives Became Republicans*. Chicago: University of Chicago Press.

————. 2009b. "The Microfoundations of Mass Polarization." *Political Analysis* 17: 162–76.

————. 2013. *How Partisan Media Polarize America*. Chicago: University of Chicago Press.

Levin, Yuval. 2016. *The Fractured Republic: Renewing America's Social Contract in the Age of Individualism*. New York: Basic Books.

Lewis-Beck, Michael S., Helmut Norpoth, William G. Jacoby, and Herbert F. Weisberg. 2008. *The American Voter Revisited*. Ann Arbor: University of Michigan Press.

Linkins, Jason. 2016. "Why Don't Supedelegates Vote According to the Will of Voters?" *Huffington Post*, April 1.

Lipka, Michael. 2016. "U.S. Religious Groups and Their Political Leanings." Pew Research Center (Feb. 23). http://www.pewresearch.org/fact-tank/2016/02/23/u-s -religious-groups-and-their-political-leanings/.

Liu, Bing. 2015. *Sentiment Analysis: Mining Opinions, Sentiments and Emotions*. New York: Cambridge University Press.

Lodge, Milton, and Charles S. Taber. 2013. *The Rationalizing Voter*. New York: Cambridge University Press.

Lowe, Will. 2015. "Austin: Do Things with Words. Version 0.2.2." http://github.org/ conjugateprior/austin.

Lupia, Arthur, and Mathew McCubbins. 1998. *The Democratic Dilemma: Can Citizens Learn What They Need to Know?* New York: Cambridge University Press.

Magleby, David B. 2014. "Classifying Super PACs." In *The State of the Parties: The Changing Role of Contemporary American Politics*, 7th ed., edited by John C. Green, Daniel Coffey, and David B. Cohen, 231–250. Lanham, MD: Rowman & Littlefield.

————. 2017. "The Role of Interest Groups and Outside Money in Federal Elections:

What We Know and What We Don't Know." Presented at the Meeting of the Campaign Finance Task Force, Bipartisan Policy Center, Washington, DC, April 21, 2017.

Mair, Peter. 2013. *Ruling the Void: The Hollowing of Western Democracy.* London: Verso.

Malbin, Michael. 2014a. "CFI's Malbin Calls for 'A Third Approach' to Party Coordination." Campaign Finance Institute. http://www.cfinst.org/press/releases/14–12 –08/CFI's_Malbin_Calls_for_Third_Approach_to_Party_Coordination.aspx.

———. 2014b. "*McCutcheon* Could Lead to No Limits for Political Parties—With What Implications for Parties and Interest Groups?" *New York University Law Review Online* 89(92): 92–104.

———. 2017. *Political Parties and Candidates Dominated the 2016 House Elections While Holding Their Own in the Senate.* Washington, DC: Campaign Finance Institute. http://www.cfinst.org/Press/PReleases/17–04–13/POLITICAL_PARTIES_AND _CANDIDATES_DOMINATED_THE_2016-HOUSE-ELECTIONS_WHILE_HOLD ING_THEIR_OWN_IN_THE_SENATE.aspx.

Mandelbaum, Robb. 2017. "The $83,000 Question: How Much Do Regulations Really Cost Small Businesses?" *Forbes*, January 24.

Manjoo, Farhad. 2016. "How the Internet Is Loosening Our Grip on the Truth." *New York Times.* November 2.

Mann, Thomas, and Anthony Corrado. 2014. "Party Polarization and Campaign Finance." Brookings Institution. http://www.brookings.edu/research/party-polari zation-campaign-finance/.

Mann, Thomas E., and Norman J. Ornstein. 2016. *It's Even Worse Than It Looks: How the American Constitutional System Collided with the Politics of Extremism*, rev. ed. New York: Basic Books.

Manza, Jeff, and Clem Brooks. 1999. *Social Cleavages and Political Change: Voter Alignments and U.S. Party Coalitions.* New York: Oxford University Press.

Manza, Jeff, and Ned Crowley. 2017. "Trump as Working Class Hero? Interrogating the Social Bases of the Rise of Trumpism." *The Forum* 15(1): 3–28.

Marantz, Andrew. 2016. "Trolls for Trump: How the Alt-right Spread Fringe Ideas to the Mainstream." *The New Yorker* (October 31): 42–47.

Masket, Seth, John Sides, and Lynn Vavreck. 2015. "The Ground Game in the 2012 Presidential Election." *Political Communication* 33: 169–187.

Mason, Lilliana. 2015. "'I Disrespectfully Agree': The Differential Effects of Partisan Sorting on Social and Issue Polarization." *American Journal of Political Science* 59: 128–45.

———. 2018. *Uncivil Agreement.* Chicago: University of Chicago Press.

Mast, Jason L. 2017. "Legitimacy Troubles and the Performance of Power in the 2016 U.S. Presidential Election." *American Journal of Cultural Sociology* 5(3): 460–80.

May, Matthew Ryan. 2016. "Closed Primary, Exposed Preferences Idaho's Primary System and the Bureaucratic Dilemma." PhD Diss., Boise State University.

Mayer, Jane. 2016. *Dark Money: The Hidden History of the Billionaires behind the Rise of the Radical Right.* New York: Doubleday.

McCarty, Nolan, Keith T. Poole, and Howard Rosenthal. 2008. *Polarized America: The Dance of Ideology and Unequal Riches.* Cambridge, MA: MIT Press.

McConnell, Christopher, Yotam Margalit, Neil Malhotra, and Matthew Levendusky. 2018. "The Economic Consequences of Partisanship in a Polarized Era." *American Journal of Political Science* 62: 5–18.

McConnell, Mitch. 2003. "The Role of Federal Officials in State Party Fund-Raising." In *Inside the Campaign Finance Battle: Court Testimony on the New Reforms,* edited by Anthony Corrado, Thomas Mann, and Trevor Potter. Washington, DC: Brookings Institution Press.

McElwee, Sean, Brian Schaffner, and Jesse Rhodes. 2016. "Whose Voice, Whose Choice?: The Distorting Influence of the Political Donor Class in Our Big-Money Elections." Demos, December 8, 2016. http://www.demos.org/sites/default/files/publications/Whose%20Voice%20Whose%20Choice_2.pdf.

McGeough, Paul. 2016. "Forget Clinton and Trump—America's Democracy is Broken and They Can't Fix It." *Sydney Morning Herald.* November 5.

McGhee, Eric, Seth Masket, Boris Shor, Stephen Rogers, and Nolan McCarty. 2013. "A Primary Cause of Partisanship?" *American Journal of Political Science* 58(2): 337–51.

McGuigan, Jim. 2008. "Apprentices to Cool Capitalism." *Social Semiotics* 18(3): 309–19.

Mellnik, Ted, John Muyskens, Kim Soffen, and Scott Clement. 2017. "That Big Wave of Less-Educated White Voters? It Never Happened." *The Washington Post* (May 10). https://www.washingtonpost.com/graphic/politics/census-elections-turnout.

Merry, Robert M. 2017. "Removing Trump Won't Solve America's Crisis: The Elites Are the Problem." *The American Conservative.* May 18.

Michels, Robert. 1915. *Political Parties: A Sociological Study of the Oligarchical Tendencies of Modern Democracy.* New York: Dover Publications, Inc.

Milkis, Sidney M., and John Warren York. 2017. "Barack Obama, Organizing for Action, and Executive-Centered Partisanship." *Studies in American Political Development* 31: 1–23.

Mill, John Stuart. 1861. *Consideration on Representative Government.* London: Parker, Sons, & Bourn.

Miller, Joanne. 2013. "The Motivational Underpinnings of Political Participation." In *New Directions in American Politics,* edited by Raymond J. La Raja. New York: Routledge.

Miller, Patrick R., and Pamela Johnston Conover. 2015. "Red and Blue States of Mind: Partisan Hostility and Voting in the United States." *Political Research Quarterly* 68: 225–239.

Milligan, Susan. 2016. "The Fight on the Ground." *U.S. News and World Report,* October 14.

Miroff, Bruce. 2007. *The Liberals' Moment: The McGovern Insurgency and the Identity Crisis of the Democratic Party.* Lawrence: University Press of Kansas.

Mitchell, Joshua. 2017. "A Renewed Republican Party." *American Affairs* Spring: 7–30.

Molyneux, Guy. 2017. "A Tale of Two Populisms: The Elite the White Working Class Loathes is Politicians." *American Prospect,* June 1.

Moretti, Enrico. 2013. *The New Geography of Jobs.* New York: Mariner Books.

Mouffe, Chantal. 2005. *On the Political.* London: Routledge.

Mudde, Cas. 2004. "The Populist Zeitgeist." *Government & Opposition* 39: 541–63.

Mudde, Cas, and Cristobal R. Kaltwasser. 2012. "Populism and (Liberal) Democracy: a Framework for Analysis." In *Populism in Europe and the Americas*, edited by Cas Mudde and Cristobal R. Kaltwasser, 1–26. Cambridge, MA: Cambridge University Press.

———. 2013. "Populism." In *The Oxford Handbook of Political Ideologies*, edited by Michael Freeden and Marc Stears. Oxford: Oxford University Press.

Muirhead, Russell. 2014. *The Promise of Party in a Polarized Age.* Cambridge, MA: Harvard University Press.

Müller, Jan-Werner. 2016. *What Is Populism?* Philadelphia: University of Pennsylvania Press.

Muro, Mark, and Jacob Whiton. 2017. "Big Cities, Small Cities—and the Gaps." Brookings (The Avenue), October 17. https://www.brookings.edu/blog/the-avenue/2017/10/17/big-cities-small-cities-and-the-gaps/.

Murray, Charles. 2012. *Coming Apart: The State of White America, 1960–2010.* New York: Crown Forum.

Mus, Publius Decius (Michael Anton). 2016. "The Flight 93 Election." *Claremont Review of Books*, September 5, 2016. http://www.claremont.org/crb/basicpage/the-flight-93-election/.

Narayanswamy, Anu, Darla Cameron, and Matea Gold. 2017. "How Much Money Is behind Each Campaign?" *Washington Post.* https://washingtonpost.com/graphics/politics/2016-election/campaign-finance/.

Nardulli, Peter. 2005. *Popular Efficacy in the Democratic Era.* Princeton, NJ: Princeton University Press.

Neidig, Harper. 2016. "Sanders: 'Extremely Undemocratic' to Call Clinton the Nominee at This Point." *The Hill*, May 3.

Nelson, Thomas E., and Donald R. Kinder. 1996. "Issue Frames and Group-Centrism in American Public Opinion." *Journal of Politics* 58: 1055–1078.

New York Times Staff. 1924. "Rousing Rally for McAdoo." *New York Times*, July 7. 1.

Niemi, Richard, and Herbert Weisberg. 1993. *Controversies in Voter Behavior.* Washington, DC: Congressional Quarterly Press.

Niemi, Richard, Herbert F. Weisberg, and David Kimball. 2010. *Controversies in Voting Behavior,* 5th edition. Washington, DC: Congressional Quarterly Press.

No Labels. 2011. *Make Congress Work! A No Labels Action Plan to Fix What's Broken.* No Labels, December 2011. https://2o16qp9prbv3jfk0qb3yon1a-wpengine.netdna-ssl.com/wp-content/uploads/2017/04/MCW_Pages.pdf.

———. 2012. *Make the Presidency Work!* No Labels, October 2012. https://www.nolabels.org/wp-content/uploads/2017/04/MPW_Pages.pdf.

Noble, Gloria. 2016. "How Does a Caucus Work?" *Huffington Post.* January 31. Accessed October 17, 2017. https://www.huffingtonpost.com/gloria-noble/how-does-a-caucus-work_b_9126904.html.

Noel, Hans. 2013. *Political Ideologies and Political Parties in America.* Cambridge, MA: Cambridge University Press.

———. 2016a. "Maybe Faux Conservatives Are Still Conservatives." *Vox*, January 25. http://www.vox.com/mischiefs-of-faction/2016/1/25/10828656/faux-conservatives-trump-national-review.

————. 2016b. "Ideological Factions in the Democratic and Republican Parties." *The ANNALS of the American Academy of Political and Social Science* 667: 166–88.

Norquist, Grover G., and John R. Lott, Jr. 2012. *The Great Debacle: Obama's War on Jobs and Growth and What We Can Do to Regain Our Future.* New York: John Wiley.

Norrander, Barbara. 1992. *Super Tuesday: Regional Politics and Presidential Primaries.* Lexington, KY: University Press of Kentucky.

————. 2015. *The Imperfect Primary: Oddities, Biases, and Strengths of U.S. Presidential Nomination Politics,* 2nd ed. New York: Routledge.

Norrander, Barbara, and Gregg W. Smith. 1985. "Type of Contest, Candidate Strategy, and Turnout in Presidential Primaries." *American Politics Research* 13: 28–50.

Nownes, Anthony J. 2013. *Interest Groups in American Politics.* New York: Routledge.

Nussbaum, Emily. 2017. "Guilty Pleasure: How TV Created Donald Trump." *The New Yorker* (July 31): 22–6.

Oliver, J. Eric, and Wendy M. Rahn. 2016. "Rise of the *Trumpenvolk*: Populism in the 2016 Election," *The ANNALS of the American Academy of Political and Social Science* 667: 189–206.

Olsen, Henry, and Dante J. Scala. 2015. *The Four Faces of the Republican Party and the Fight for the 2016 Presidential Nomination.* New York: Palgrave Macmillan.

Ornstein, Norman J., and Thomas Mann. 2016. "The Republicans Waged a 3-Decade War on Government. They Got Trump." *Vox,* July 18.

Orton, J. D., and Karl Weik. 1990. "Loosely Coupled Systems: A Reconceptualization. *Academy of Management Review* 15(2): 203–223.

Ostrogorski, Mosei, and Frederick Clarke. 1902. *Democracy and the Organization of Political Parties.* New York: Macmillan. Microform.

Overby, Peter. 2014. "Say Goodbye to the Taxpayer-Funded Political Convention." NPR.org. http://www.npr.org/2014/03/26/294383506/say-goodbye-to-the-taxpayer -funded-political-convention.

Page, Benjamin, and Martin Gilens. 2017. *Democracy in America?: What Has Gone Wrong and What We Can Do About It.* Chicago: University of Chicago Press.

Panagopoulos, Costas. 2016. "All About That Base: Changing Campaign Strategies in U.S. Presidential Elections." *Party Politics* 22: 179–190.

Panagopoulos, Costas, and Peter Wielhouwer. 2008. "The Ground War in 2000–2004: Strategic Targeting in Grassroots Campaigns." *Presidential Studies Quarterly* 38: 347–362.

Paquette, Danielle. 2016. "Donald Trump's Incredibly Bizarre Relationship with Planned Parenthood." *Washington Post,* March 2. https://www.washingtonpost .com/news/wonk/wp/2016/03/02/donald-trumps-incredibly-bizarre-relationship -with-planned-parenthood/?utm_term = .c03 88254b5fd.

Parker, Kim, and Renee Stepler. 2017. "As U.S. Marriage Rate Hovers at 50%, Education Gap in Marital Status Widens." Pew Research Center, September 14.

Perks, Lisa Glebatis. 2007. "The Nouveau Reach: Ideologies of Class and Consumerism in Reality-Based Television." *Studies in Language and Capitalism* 2: 101–18.

Perlstein, Rick. 2012. "The Long Con: Mail-order Conservativism." *The Baffler* 21, November.

Persily, Nathaniel. 2006. "The Law of American Party Finance." In *Party Funding and Campaign Financing in International Perspective.* Portland, OR: Hart Publishing.

———. 2015. "Stronger Parties as a Solution to Polarization." In *Solutions to Political Polarization in America*, edited by Nathaniel Persily, 123–35. New York: Cambridge University Press.

Petrocik, John R., and Fredrick T. Steeper. 2010. "The Politics Missed by Political Science." *The Forum* 8(3).

Pew Research Center. 2012. "The Lost Decade of the Middle Class: Fewer, Poorer, Gloomier." August 22.

———. 2014a. http://assets.pewresearch.org/wp-content/uploads/sites/5/2014/06/6–12–2014-Political-Polarization-Release.pdf.

———. 2014b. "Political Polarization in the American Public." http://www.people-press.org/2014/06/12/political-polarization-in-the-american-public/.

———. 2014c. "Political Polarization and Media Habits." October 21.

———. 2016. "Partisanship and Political Animosity in 2016." June 22.

Pfeffer, Jeffrey, and Gerald Salancik. 1978. *The External Control of Organization: A Resource Dependence Perspective*. New York: Harper & Row.

Phillips-Fein, Kim. 2011. "Conservatism: A State of the Field." *Journal of American History* 98: 723–43.

Piketty, Thomas. 2017. *Capital in the Twenty-First Century*. Cambridge, MA: Harvard University Press.

Pildes, Richard H. 2014. "Romanticizing Democracy, Political Fragmentation, and the Decline of Government." *Yale Law Journal* 124: 804–52.

Pocalyko, Michael. 2017. "The Businessman President." *Survival* 59(1): 51–57.

Polsby, Nelson W. 1983. *Consequences of Party Reform*. New York: Oxford University Press.

Popkin, Samuel L. 1994. *The Reasoning Voter: Communication and Persuasion in Presidential Campaigns*. Chicago: University of Chicago Press.

Populist Party. 1892. "Populist Party Platform of 1892."

Postel, Charles. 2007. *The Populist Vision*. Oxford; New York: Oxford University Press.

PR Newswire. 2016. "2016 Presidential Campaign Reveals Chilling Trend Lines for Civility in U.S. Politics: New Zogby Survey from Allegheny College Finds Americans Significantly More Accepting of Personal Attacks in Politics since Last Survey in 2010."

Przeworski, Adam. 1999. "Minimalist Conception of Democracy: A Defense." *Democracy's Value* 23.

Putnam, Josh. 2016a. "The Democrats' Unity Reform Commission." *Frontloading HQ*. July 24. Accessed July 26, 2017. http://frontloading.blogspot.com/2016/07/the-democrats-unity-reform-commission.html.

———. 2016b. "How the Republican Party Made it Harder for Convention Delegates to Vote against Trump." The Monkey Cage, *The Washington Post*. July 17. Accessed July 26, 2017. https://www.washingtonpost.com/news/monkey-cage/wp/2016/07/17/how-the-republican-party-made-it-harder-for-convention-delegates-to-vote-against-?utm_term = .f0a688bff728.

———. 2017. "Democratic Unity Reform Commission, Meeting 1, Day 1." *Frontloading HQ*. May 5. Accessed July 26, 2017. http://frontloading.blogspot.com/2017/05/democratic-unity-reform-commission.html.

Putnam, Lara, and Theda Skocpol. 2018. "Middle America Reboots Democracy." *Democracy: A Journal of Ideas*, February 20.

Rampell, Catherine. 2016. "When the Facts Don't Matter, How Can Democracy Survive?" *Washington Post*, October 17.

Ranney, Austin. 1976. *Curing the Mischiefs of Faction: Party Reform in America.* Berkeley: University of California Press.

———. 1977. *Participation in American Presidential Nominations, 1976.* American Enterprise for Public Policy Research.

Rapoport, Ronald B., Alan I. Abramowitz, and Walter J. Stone. 2016. "Why Trump Was Inevitable." *New York Review of Books* 63(11): 8–10.

Rapoport, Ronald B., and Walter J. Stone. 2005. *Three's a Crowd: The Dynamic of Third Parties, Ross Perot, and Republican Resurgence.* Ann Arbor: University of Michigan Press.

Rauch, Jonathan. 2015. *Political Realism: How Hacks, Machines, Big Money, and Back Room Deals Can Strengthen American Democracy.* Washington, DC: Brookings Institution.

Redlawsk, David P., Caroline J. Tolbert, and Todd Donovan. 2011. *Why Iowa? How Caucuses and Sequential Elections Improve the Presidential Nominating Process.* Chicago: University of Chicago Press.

Reilly, Katie. 2016. "Meet the Republican Officials Who Aren't Voting for Donald Trump." *Time.* August 10. Accessed October 6, 2017. http://time.com/4444832/re publicans-not-voting-donald-trump/.

Reiter, Howard L. 1993. *Parties and Elections in Corporate America.* White Plains, NY: Longman.

Riker, William H. 1988. *Liberalism against Populism: A Confrontation between the Theory of Democracy and the Theory of Social Choice.* Prospect Heights, IL: Waveland Press.

Riordan, William L. 1963. *Plunkitt of Tammany Hall: A Series of Very Plain Talks on Very Practical Politics.* New York: E.P. Dutton.

Riotta, Chris. 2017. "Was the Election Rigged against Bernie Sanders? DNC Lawsuit Demands Repayment for Campaign Donors." *Newsweek.* May 15. Accessed October 6, 2017. http://www.newsweek.com/bernie-sanders-rigged-hillary-clinton-dnc -lawsuit-donald-trump-president-609582.

Rodgers, Daniel T. 2011. *Age of Fracture.* Cambridge, MA: Belknap Press of Harvard University Press.

Rogowski, Jon C., and Joseph L. Sutherland. 2016. "How Ideology Fuels Affective Polarization." *Political Behavior* 38: 485–508.

Romer, Thomas, and James M. Snyder, Jr. 1994. "An Empirical Investigation of the Dynamics of PAC Contributions." *American Journal of Political Science* 38: 745–69.

Roscoe, Douglas D., and Shannon Jenkins. 2016. *Local Party Organizations in the Twenty-First Century.* Albany: SUNY Press.

Rosenblum, Nancy L. 2008. *On the Side of the Angels: An Appreciation of Parties and Partisanship.* Princeton, NJ: Princeton University Press.

Rosenfeld, Sam. 2018. *The Polarizers: Postwar Architects of Our Partisan Era.* Chicago: University of Chicago Press.

Rothwell, Jonathan T., and Pablo Diego Rosell. 2016. "Explaining Nationalist Political Views: The Case of Donald Trump." Working paper. http://pelg.ucsd.edu/2 .rothwell_2016.pdf.

Rudalevige, Andrew. 2016. "The Obama Administrative Presidency: Some Late-Term Patterns." *Presidential Studies Quarterly* 46: 868–890.

Ryan, Josh M. 2011. "Is the Democratic Party's Superdelegate System Unfair to Voters?" *Electoral Studies* 30: 756–70.

Samples, John. 2006. *The Fallacy of Campaign Finance Reform.* Chicago: University of Chicago Press.

Samuelsohn, Darren, Burgess Everett, Daniel Strauss, and Katie Glueck. 2016. "Sanders Supporters Reject Democrats' Unity Plea." *Politico*, July 25.

Sanders, Bernie. 2016. *Our Revolution: A Future to Believe In.* N.p.: Macmillan.

Sarasohn, David. 1989. *The Party of Reform: Democrats in the Progressive Era.* Jackson: University Press of Mississippi.

Schaffner, Brian F., Matthew MacWilliams, and Tatishe Nteta. Forthcoming. "Understanding White Polarization in the 2016 Vote for President: The Sobering Role of Racism and Sexism." *Political Research Quarterly.*

Schattschneider, E. E. 1942. *Party Government.* New York: Holt, Rinehart, and Winston.

———. 1960. *The Semisovereign People: A Realist's View of Democracy in America.* New York: Holt, Rinehart, and Winston.

Schickler, Eric. 2016. *Racial Realignment: The Transformation of American Liberalism, 1932–1965.* Princeton Studies in American Politics: Historical, International, and Comparative Perspectives. Princeton, NJ: Princeton University Press.

Schlozman, Daniel. 2015. *When Movements Anchor Parties: Electoral Alignments in American History.* Princeton, NJ: Princeton University Press.

———. 2016. "The Lists Told Us Otherwise." *n + 1*, December 24, 2016. https:// nplusonemag.com/online-only/online-only/the-lists-told-us-otherwise/.

Schlozman, Daniel, and Sam Rosenfeld. 2018. "Prophets of Party in American Political History." *The Forum* 15(4): 685–709.

Schlozman, Kay L., Sidney Verba, and Henry E. Brady. 2012. *The Unheavenly Chorus: Unequal Political Voice and the Broken Promise of American Democracy.* Princeton, NJ: Princeton University Press.

Schneider, Anne, and Helen Ingram. 1993. "Social Construction of Target Populations: Implications for Politics and Policy." *American Political Science Review* 87: 334–47.

Schor, Elana, and Dan Glaister. 2008. "Superdelegates Switching Allegiance to Obama." *The Guardian*, February 22.

Schwartz, Mildred A. 1990. *The Party Network: The Robust Organization of Illinois Republicans.* Madison: University of Wisconsin Press.

———. 2011. "Continuity and Change in the Organization of Political Parties." *Canadian-American Public Policy* 78(Dec.): 1–88.

———. 2016. "Party Movements." *Politics: Oxford Research Encyclopedias.* Edited by William Thompson.

Sclar, Jason, Alexander Hertel-Fernandez, Theda Skocpol, and Vanessa Williamson. 2016. "Donor Consortia on the Left and Right: Comparing the Membership,

Activities, and Impact of the Democracy Alliance and the Koch Seminars." Working paper.

Shafer, Byron E., and William J.M. Claggett. 1995. *The Two Majorities: The Issue Content of Modern American Politics.* Baltimore: Johns Hopkins University Press.

Shapiro, Robert. 2018. "The New Economics of Jobs Is Bad News for Working-class Americans—and Maybe for Trump." Brookings, January 16.

Shea, Daniel M. 2017. "Our Addiction to Elections Is Killing American Democracy." *The Nation.*

Shea, Daniel M., and John C. Green. 1994. *The State of the Parties: The Changing Role of Contemporary American Parties.* Lanham, MD: Rowman & Littlefield.

————. 2006. *Fountain of Youth: Strategies and Tactics for Mobilizing America's Young Voters (Campaigning American Style).* Lanham, MD: Rowman & Littlefield.

Shear, Michael D., Maggie Haberman, and Michael S. Schmidt. 2016. "Critics See Stephen Bannon, Trump's Pick for Strategist, as Voice of Racism." *New York Times,* November 14. https://www.nytimes.com/2016/11/15/us/politics/donald -trump-presidency.html?_r = 0.

Shefter, Martin. 1994. *Political Parties and the State.* Princeton, NJ: Princeton University Press.

Shepard, Steven. 2017. "Political Parties Transformed by Racial, Religious Changes." http://www.politic.com.story/2017/09/06/political-parties-religion-race-242322.

Shor, Boris, and Nolan McCarty. 2011. "The Ideological Mapping of State Legislatures." *The American Political Science Review* 105: 530–51.

Sides, John. 2014. "The Political Ideology of the State of the Union Address (in 1 graph)." The Monkey Cage, *The Washington Post,* January 28, 2014. https://www .washingtonpost.com/news/monkey-cage/wp/2014/01/28/the-political-ideology-of -state-of-the-union-addresses-in-1-graph/?utm_term = .86dd95b7bb58.

Sides, John, and Michael Tesler. 2016. "How Political Science Helps Explain the Rise of Trump (Part 3): It's the Economy, Stupid." The Monkey Cage, *Washington Post,* March 4.

Sides, John, Mark Tesler, and Lynn Vavreck. 2018. *Identity Crisis: The 2016 Presidential Campaign and the Battle for the Meaning of America.* Princeton, NJ: Princeton University Press.

Sides, John, and Lynn Vavreck. 2013. *The Gamble: Choice and Change in the 2012 Presidential Election.* Princeton, NJ: Princeton University Press.

Siegel, Mark. 2017. "Nominating the President 2020 (Seriously): Part 1—The Democrats." *Huffington Post.* May 17. Accessed July 26, 2017. http://www.huffington post.com/mark-siegel/nominating-the-president_b_10010430.html.

Silver, Nate. 2016. "Pollsters Probably Didn't Talk to Enough White Voters without College Degrees." FiveThirtyEight.com, December 1. https://fivethirtyeight.com/ features/pollsters-probably-didnt-talk-to-enough-white-voters-without-college -degrees/.

————. 2017a. "The Real Story Of 2016." FiveThirtyEight.com, January 19. http:// fivethirtyeight.com/features/the-real-story-of-2016/.

————. 2017b. "The Media Has a Probability Problem." FiveThirtyEight.com, September 21. https://fivethirtyeight.com/features/the-media-has-a-probability-prob lem/.

Singer, Paul. 2016. "Trump's Donor History Proves Odd: Billionaire Has Said He Gave Money to Both Parties for Business Reasons." *Dayton Daily News* (Ohio): Z3.

Skinner, Richard M. 2005. "Do 527's Add Up to a Party? Thinking about the 'Shadows' of Politics." *The Forum* 3(3): Article 5.

———. 2006. "The Partisan Presidency." In *The State of the Parties: The Changing Role of Contemporary American Parties*, 5th ed., edited by John C. Green and Daniel J. Coffey, 331–42. Lanham, MD: Rowman & Littlefield.

Skinner, Richard, Seth Masket, and David Dulio. 2013. "527 Committees, Formal Parties, and Party Adaptation." *The Forum* 11(2): 137–56.

Skocpol, Theda. 2003. *Diminished Democracy: From Membership to Management in American Civic Life*. Norman: University of Oklahoma Press.

———. 2012. *Obama and America's Political Future*. Cambridge MA: Harvard University Press.

Skocpol, Theda, and Alexander Hertel-Fernandez. 2016. "The Koch Network and Republican Party Extremism." *Perspectives on Politics* 14: 681–99.

Skocpol, Theda, and Vanessa Williamson. 2013. *The Tea Party and the Remaking of Republican Conservatism*. New York: Oxford University Press.

Skowronek, Stephen. 1993. *The Politics Presidents Make: Leadership from John Adams to George Bush*. Cambridge, MA: Belknap Press.

Slapin, Jonathan B., and Sven-Oliver Proksch. 2008. "A Scaling Model for Estimating Time-Series Party Positions from Texts." *American Journal of Political Science* 52: 705–22.

Soffen, Kim, Ted Mellnik, Samuel Granados, and John Muyskens. 2016a. "In a Crucial Democratic Stronghold, Trump Surged. Clinton Didn't." *Washington Post*, November 11.

———. 2016b. "Two Swing States Show Why Clinton Lost." *Washington Post*, November 9.

SpeechNow.org v. Federal Election Commission. 2010. 599 F.3d 686 (C.A.D.C.)

Steen, Jennifer A. 2006. *Self-Financed Candidates in Congressional Elections*. Ann Arbor: University of Michigan Press.

Steger, Wayne P. 2013. "Two Paradigms of Presidential Nominations." *Presidential Studies Quarterly* 43(2): 377–87.

———. 2015. *A Citizen's Guide to Presidential Nominations: The Competition for Leadership*. New York: Routledge Press.

———. 2016. "Conditional Arbiters: The Limits of Political Party Influence in Presidential Nominations." *PS: Political Science & Politics* 49(4): 709–15.

———. Forthcoming. *Maelstrom of American Populism*. New York: Routledge Press.

Steinhauer, Jennifer, and Alexander Burns. 2016. "Paul Ryan Says He Is 'Not Ready' to Endorse Donald Trump." *The New York Times*. May 5. Accessed October 6, 2017. https://www.nytimes.com/2016/05/06/us/politics/paul-ryan-donald-trump.html?_r = 0.

Stimson, James A. 2004. *Tides of Consent: How Public Opinion Shapes American Politics*. New York: Cambridge University Press.

Stonecash, Jeffrey M. 2017. "The Puzzle of Class in Presidential Voting." *The Forum* 15(1), April: 29–49.

Stratmann, Thomas. 2005. "Some Talk: Money in Politics." *Public Choice* 124: 135–56.

Suls, Robert. 2016. "Educational Divide in Vote Preferences on Track to Be Wider Than in Recent Elections." Washington, DC: Pew Research Center. www.pew research.org/fact-tank/2016/09/15/educational-divide-in-vote.

Sykes, Charles J. 2011. *A Nation of Moochers: America's Addiction to Getting Something for Nothing.* New York: St. Martin's Press.

Tajfel, Henri, and John Turner. 1979. "An Integrative Theory of Intergroup Conflict." In *The Social Psychology of Intergroup Relations,* edited by W. G. Austin and S. Worchel. Monterey, CA: Brooks/Cole.

Tanenhaus, Sam. 2017. "The Tribunes of Discontent." *New York Review of Books,* November 23.

Tankersley, Jim. 2016. "How Trump Won: The Revenge of the Working Class." *Washington Post,* November 9.

Taub, Amanda. 2016. "The Rise of American Authoritarianism." *Vox,* March 1.

Teixeira, Ruy, and Joel Rogers. 2000. *America's Forgotten Majority: Why the White Working Class Still Matters.* New York: Basic Books.

Tesler, Michael. 2016. *Post-Racial or Most-Racial? Race and Politics in the Obama Era.* Chicago: University of Chicago Press.

Tesler, Michael, and David O. Sears. 2010. *Obama's Race: The 2008 Election and the Dream of a Post-Racial America.* Chicago: University of Chicago Press.

Tesler, Michael, and John Sides. 2016. "How Political Science Helps Explain the Rise of Trump: The Role of White Identity and Grievances." The Monkey Cage, *Washington Post,* March 3.

The Democratic Party. 2017. "Unity Reform Commission." Accessed July 26, 2017. https://democrats.org/page/unity-reform-commission.

Theodoridis, Alexander G. 2017. "Me, Myself and (I), (D), or (R)? Partisanship and Political Cognition through the Lens of Implicit Identity." *Journal of Politics* 79: 1253–67.

Thornburgh, Ron. 2004. "Canvassing Kansas." Kansas Secretary of State. (September). https://www.kssos.org/forms/communication/canvassing_kansas/sept04.pdf.

Tilly, Charles. 1998. *Durable Inequality.* Berkeley: University of California Press.

Tocqueville, Alexis de. 1966. *Democracy in America,* edited by J. P. Mayer. New York: Harper & Row.

Trump Campaign. 2017. Closing ad for "Argument for America." Accessed October 20.

Tulis, Jeffrey K. 1987. *The Rhetorical Presidency.* Princeton, NJ: Princeton University Press.

Urban Institute. 2017. "Nine Charts about Wealth Inequality in America (Updated)." Accessed October 10, 2017. https://apps.urban.org/features/wealth-inequality -charts/.

U.S. Department of Education. 1983. "A Nation at Risk." Accessed at https://www2 .ed.gov/pubs/NatAtRisk/risk.html.

VandeHei, Jim. 2016. "Bring On a Third Party Candidate." *Wall Street Journal,* April 26.

Vogel, Kenneth. 2014. *Big Money: 2.5 Billion Dollars, One Suspicious Vehicle, and a*

Pimp—On the Trail of the Ultra-Rich Hijacking American Politics. New York: Public Affairs.

Wagner, John. 2016. "Not Continuing to Run Would Be 'Outrageously Undemocratic,' Bernie Sanders Says." *Washington Post,* March 17.

Wagner, John, and Scott Clement. 2017. " 'It's Just Messed Up' ": Most Think Political Divisions as Bad as Vietnam Era, New Poll Shows." *Washington Post,* October 28.

Wagner-Pacifici, Robin, and Iddo Tavory. 2017. "Politics as a Vacation." *American Journal of Cultural Sociology* 5(3): 307–21.

Ward, Jon. 2016. "Trump's Victory Stunned Even GOP Digital Team." Yahoo News, November 9.

Warren, Elizabeth. 2016. "National Public Radio Interview." June 27.

Webster, Steven W., and Alan I. Abramowitz. 2017. "The Ideological Foundations of Affective Polarization in the U.S. Electorate." *American Politics Research* 45: 621–647.

Weigel, David. 2016. "Democratic Superdelegates: The Villains of a 'Rigged' System, According to Sanders's Supporters." *The Washington Post.* June 7. Accessed October 6, 2017. https://www.washingtonpost.com/politics/democratic-superdelegates -the-villains-of-a-rigged-system-according-to-sanders/2016/06/07/634f6df2-2cba -11e6-9b37-42985f6a265c_story.html/.

Wells, Chris, Katherine J. Cramer, Michael W. Wagner, German Alvarez, Lewis Friedland, Dhavan V. Shah, Leticia Bode, Stephanie Edgerly, Itai Gabay, and Charles Franklin. 2017. "When We Stop Talking Politics: The Maintenance and Closing of Conversation in Contentious Times." *Journal of Communication* 67: 131–157.

Whitby, Kenny J. 2014. *Strategic Decision Making in Presidential Nominations: When and Why Party Elites Decide to Support a Candidate.* Albany: State University of New York Press.

Wielhouwer, Peter W. 2003. "In Search of Lincoln's Perfect List: Targeting in Grassroots Campaigns." *American Politics Research* 31: 632–669.

Wilcox, Clyde. 1989. "Share the Wealth: Contributions by Congressional Incumbents to the Campaigns of Other Candidates." *American Politics Quarterly* 17: 389–408.

Wildavsky, Aaron. 1965. "The Goldwater Phenomenon: Purists, Politicians, and the Two-Party System." *Review of Politics* 27(July): 386–413.

Williams, Joan C. 2017. *White Working Class: Overcoming Class Cluelessness in America.* Boston: Harvard Business Review Press, 17–20.

Williamson, Vanessa, Theda Skocpol, and John Coggin. 2011. "The Tea Party and the Remaking of Republican Conservatism." *Perspectives on Politics* 9(March): 25–43.

Wilson, James Q. 1962. *The Amateur Democrat: Club Politics in Three Cities.* Chicago: University of Chicago Press.

———. 1974. 1995. *Political Organizations.* Princeton, NJ: Princeton University Press.

Wilson, Jim. 2003. "Final Rules on Coordinated and Independent Expenditures." *Federal Election Commission Record* 29(1): 14.

Wood, Thomas. 2017. "Racism Motivated Trump Voters More Than Authoritariansim." The Monkey Cage, *Washington Post,* April 17.

Wright, John R. 1989. "PAC Contributions, Lobbying, and Representation." *Journal of Politics* 51: 713–29.

————. 1990. "Contributions, Lobbying, and Committee Voting in the U.S. House of Representatives." *American Political Science Review* 84: 417–38.

Yates, Elizabeth A. 2017. " 'Staying Engaged': Tea Party Political Culture Paves the Way for the Trump Campaign." Paper presented at the annual meeting of the American Sociological Association, Montreal.

Young, Iris Marion. 2000. *Inclusion and Democracy*, Oxford Political Theory. Oxford; New York: Oxford University Press.

Ziblatt, Daniel. 2017. *Conservative Parties and the Birth of Democracy*. New York: Cambridge University Press.

Index

About the Contributors

Alan Abramowitz is the Alben W. Barkley Professor of Political Science at Emory University in Atlanta, Georgia. He is the author or co-author of six books and dozens of journal articles and contributions to edited volumes dealing with American elections and voting behavior. His newest book, *The Great Alignment: Race, Party Transformation and the Rise of Donald Trump*, was published in 2018 by Yale University Press.

Joseph Anthony is a PhD candidate in political science at the University of Missouri-St. Louis. Joseph studies political parties, and his dissertation examines how local party organizations in rural Missouri have changed over time. Anthony also studies elections administration and is the co-author of a book chapter on ranked choice voting in *Changing How America Votes* (Rowman & Littlefield 2018). Before beginning his PhD in 2014, he worked for 15 years with parties and interest groups as a political organizer.

Julia R. Azari is an associate professor of political science at Marquette University. She is the author of *Delivering the People's Message: The Changing Politics of the Presidential Mandate*. She blogs regularly at the Mischiefs of Faction on Vox.com and is a contributor at FiveThirtyEight.com. Her research interests include American political parties, presidential communication, and American political development.

Paul A. Beck is professor emeritus and academy professor of political science at The Ohio State University. He is co-coordinator of the Comparative National Election Project and has published widely on political parties and voting behavior, especially in the United States.

Edward G. Carmines is distinguished professor, Warner O. Chapman Professor of Political Science and Rudy Professor at Indiana University. He has published widely in major journals in the discipline including the *American Political Science Review, American Journal of Political Science,* and *Journal of Politics.* Additionally, he is the co-author of six books, including two that won best book awards from the American Political Science Association.

Tyler Chance is a PhD candidate in political science at the University of Missouri–St. Louis. His main area of study is American politics with an emphasis on religion and politics. Tyler is currently writing his dissertation on the influence of religious institutions and personal religiosity on racialized attitudes in Ferguson, Missouri, and the greater St. Louis area. He has been published in the *Washington Post*'s Monkey Cage, the *Journal of Race, Ethnicity, and Politics*' "Politics of Color" blog, and on the Active Learning Political Science website.

Daniel J. Coffey is an associate professor of political science at the University of Akron and a research fellow in the Ray C. Bliss Institute of Applied Politics. His research interests include political parties, state politics, and political psychology. He has published articles in *State Politics and Policy Quarterly, PS: Political Science & Politics, The Journal of Political Science Education,* and the *American Behavioral Scientist.*

David B. Cohen is a professor of political science and assistant director of the Ray C. Bliss Institute of Applied Politics at the University of Akron. His primary areas of research and teaching interest are the American presidency (particularly White House organization and staffing), Congress, and homeland security policy.

Diana Dwyre is professor of political science at California State University, Chico. She has coauthored two books, *Legislative Labyrinth: Congress and Campaign Finance Reform* (2000) and *Limits and Loopholes: The Quest for Money, Free Speech and Fair Elections* (2007), and published many journal articles and book chapters on U.S. political parties and campaign finance. She was an APSA Congressional Fellow (1998) and a Fulbright Distinguished Chair at the Australian National University (2010).

Michael J. Ensley is associate professor of political science, Kent State University. He received his PhD in political science from Duke University. His research has been published in journals such as the *American Journal of Political Science, American Politics Research, American Behavioral Scientist, Public Choice,* and *Legislative Studies Quarterly.*

John C. Green is distinguished professor of political science and director of the Ray C. Bliss Institute of Applied Politics at the University of Akron. His most recent publication is *The Faith Factor: How Religion Influences American Elections* (2007).

Richard Gunther is professor emeritus and academy professor of political science at The Ohio State University. He is co-coordinator of the Comparative National Election Project and has published widely on political parties and voting behavior, especially in southern Europe.

Jennifer A. Heerwig is an assistant professor of sociology at SUNY–Stony Brook. Her work in political sociology uses longitudinal methods to examine the role of individual donors in the American campaign finance system and the influence of money on American politics. Her work has appeared in journals such as the *American Journal of Sociology, Demography, Social Science Research,* and *Social Science Quarterly.*

Paul S. Herrnson is a professor of political science at the University of Connecticut. His research and teaching interests include political parties and elections; money and politics; and voting technology and election administration. Herrnson has published numerous articles and books, including *Congressional Elections: Campaigning at Home and in Washington; Voting Technology: The Not-So-Simple Act of Casting a Ballot;* and *Interest Groups Unleashed.*

Caitlin E. Jewitt is an assistant professor of political science at Virginia Tech. Her research focuses on presidential and congressional primary elections. Her forthcoming book, *The Primary Rules: Parties, Voters, and Presidential Nominations,* explores the balance of power between party elites and voters in the presidential nomination process, with a specific focus on the electoral rules of the system.

David C. Kimball is professor of political science at the University of Missouri–St. Louis. He is the coauthor of *Helping America Vote* (2012), *Lobbying and Policy Change* (2009), and *Why Americans Split Their Tickets* (2002), and the co-editor of *Controversies in Voting Behavior,* 5th ed. (2011). He has written several articles on voting behavior, election administration, public opinion, and interest group lobbying in the United States.

Robin Kolodny is professor of political science at Temple University. Professor Kolodny served as an American Political Science Association Congressional Fellow in 1995 when she worked in the office of Congresswoman

Nancy L. Johnson of Connecticut. In 1999, she received the Emerging Scholar Award from the Political Organizations and Parties Section of APSA. During 2008–2009, Professor Kolodny was a Fulbright Distinguished Scholar to the United Kingdom, affiliated with the Department of Politics and Contemporary European Studies at the University of Sussex and the Sussex European Institute (SEI). She has published widely on the topics of political parties, elections, and campaign finance, including her book *Pursuing Majorities: Congressional Campaign Committees in American Politics.*

Drew Kurlowski is an assistant professor of politics at Coastal Carolina University. His research interests focus on political parties and elections, with specific attention paid to election administration, party identification, and polarization.

Seth Masket is a professor of political science and director of the Center on American Politics at the University of Denver and the author of *The Inevitable Party: Why Attempts to Kill the Party System Fail and How They Weaken Democracy.* He teaches and researches on political parties, state legislatures, and campaigns and elections. He is a regular contributor to *Pacific Standard,* *Vox's* "Mischiefs of Faction," and FiveThirtyEight.com.

Erik C. Nisbet is associate professor of communication and political science at the Ohio State University. He is the principal investigator of recent election surveys in Britain (funded by the National Science Foundation), France, Iran, Russia, Turkey, and the United States and has published widely on comparative political communications, public opinion, and science policy.

Sam Rosenfeld is assistant professor of political science at Colgate University. He is the author of *The Polarizers: Postwar Architects of Our Partisan Era* (2018).

Daniel Schlozman is assistant professor of political science at Johns Hopkins University. He is the author of *When Movements Anchor Parties: Electoral Alignments in American History* (2015).

Mildred A. Schwartz is professor emerita in the department of sociology at the University of Illinois at Chicago and visiting scholar in the department of sociology at New York University. She specializes in the sociology of politics and organizational analysis. In 2018, she coauthored with Raymond Tatalovich *The Rise and Fall of Moral Conflicts in the United States and Canada.*

Daniel M. Shea is professor of government at Colby College. He has written widely on parties and elections, civility in politics, youth mobilization, and campaign management. He is also the lead author of *Living Democracy*, an introductory text now used in over 150 colleges and universities.

Douglas M. Spencer is professor of law and public policy at the University of Connecticut. His research emphasizes the importance of using empirical evidence to judge voting rights, campaign finance, and election administration cases in the courts. His work has been published in the *Columbia Law Review, California Law Review, Journal of Law & Courts,* the *Election Law Journal,* and other journals. In addition to work with the Lawyers' Committee for Civil Rights, he previously served as an election monitor in Thailand for the Asian Network for Free Elections, and a researcher for the Pew Center on the States' Military and Overseas Voting Reform Project. He teaches constitutional law and election law among other courses.

Wayne Steger is professor of political science and distinguished honors faculty at DePaul University. His research focuses on campaigns and electoral competition, presidential nominations and elections, and the American presidency. His books include *A Citizen's Guide to Presidential Nominations: The Competition for Leadership* and *Campaigns and Political Marketing.* His current work focuses on the sociocultural and economic forces that have contributed to the rise of populist sentiment in America.

Jeffrey M. Stonecash is Maxwell Professor, Emeritus, at Syracuse University. He is the author of *Polarization and the Politics of Personal Responsibility* (2015) and *Interpreting Congressional Elections: The Curious Case of the Incumbency Effect* (2019).

Eric C. Vorst earned his PhD in political science from the University of Missouri–St. Louis in 2017. His main research interests include social network analysis, political communication and behavior, the impact of incivility on the political process, and American political development. He was named American Political Science Association Member of the Month in April, 2017, for his ongoing analyses of social network engagement at political science conferences.

Michael W. Wagner is Louis A. Maier Faculty Development Fellow and associate professor in the school of journalism and mass communication at the University of Wisconsin, Madison. He has published in a wide range of journals across political science and mass communication, including *Journal of*

Communication, Human Communication Research, Annual Review of Political Science, Political Research Quarterly, and *Political Communication.*

Steven W. Webster holds a PhD in political science from Emory University. He studies the ways in which anger and other emotions shape patterns of political behavior and public opinion. His work has been published or is forthcoming in *Political Science Research & Methods, Political Behavior, Electoral Studies, American Politics Research, Advances in Political Psychology, American Behavioral Scientist,* and *Social Science Quarterly.*